T5-CVM-501

Nicholas Hobbs

GENERAL EDITOR

Principal Staff Members
Margaret H. Matheny, Linda Odom,
Wanda McNeil, Donald P. Bartlett,
and Jerry P. Black

HQ
773
I84
v.1

ISSUES IN THE CLASSIFICATION OF CHILDREN

VOLUME ONE

LIBRARY

MAY   2 1975

FAIRFIELD U

WITHDRAWN
FAIRFIELD UNIVERSITY
LIBRARY

 Jossey-Bass Publishers
San Francisco • Washington • London • 1975

ISSUES IN THE CLASSIFICATION OF CHILDREN, Volume One
A Sourcebook on Categories, Labels, and Their Consequences
Nicholas Hobbs, General Editor

Copyright © 1975 by: Jossey-Bass, Inc., Publishers
615 Montgomery Street
San Francisco, California 94111
&
Jossey-Bass Limited
3 Henrietta Street
London WC2E 8LU

Copyright under International, Pan American, and
Universal Copyright Conventions. All rights
reserved. No part of this book may be reproduced
in any form—except for brief quotation (not to
exceed 1,000 words) in a review or professional
work—without permission in writing from the publishers.

Library of Congress Catalogue Card Number LC 73-20966

International Standard Book Number ISBN 0-87589-244-2

Manufactured in the United States of America

JACKET DESIGN BY WILLI BAUM

FIRST EDITION

Code 7438

THE JOSSEY-BASS
BEHAVIORAL SCIENCE SERIES

140758

140758

PREFACE

Elliot L. Richardson, when Secretary of Health, Education, and Welfare, called for a systematic review of the classification and labeling of exceptional children, and these two volumes are the result of that request. He specified that the review was to include an assessment of the consequences that ensue from current policies and procedures. He expressed his concern in these words: "The inappropriate labeling of children as *delinquent, retarded, hyperkinetic, mentally ill, emotionally disturbed,* and other classifications has serious consequences for the child. Although experts in the various disciplines concerned with exceptional children have undertaken useful studies on appropriate diagnostic procedures and practices, there is lacking sufficient dissemination of their findings to professionals and the public and nationwide standardization and enforcement of appropriate diagnostic procedures."

In response to Secretary Richardson's promptings, ten federal agencies joined together to sponsor the Project on the Classification of Exceptional Children. The objectives of the project were (1) to increase public understanding of problems associated with the classification and labeling of children who are handicapped, disadvantaged, or delinquent; (2) to provide a rationale for public policy, along with practical suggestions for legislation and administrative regulations and guidelines bearing on classification and its consequences; and (3) to improve the professional practice of educators, psychologists, physicians, lawyers, social workers, and others responsible for the well-being of exceptional children.

Issues in the Classification of Children: A Sourcebook on Categories, Labels, and Their Consequences presents a systematic and reasonably comprehensive summary of current thinking about the classification of exceptional children and its many attendant problems. The information included here is intended to provide the foundation for public policy. To make this foundation as broad and strong as possible, ninety-three experts from diverse fields (educators, psychologists, psychiatrists, pediatricians, sociologists, public administrators, lawyers, and, to cap the list, parents) were invited to summarize existing knowledge in particular topical areas, in accordance with an overall plan designed to achieve comprehensive coverage and minimum overlap. The experts, working alone or in small task groups, prepared thirty-one papers covering six major topics: (1) theoretical issues in classification; (2) systems for classifying handicapped, disadvantaged, and delinquent children and youth; (3) institutional experiences that children have as a consequence of being classified; (4) classification and its consequences from the perspective of parents, minority-group members, and children themselves; (5) classification and the legal status of exceptional children; and (6) public-policy issues affecting exceptional children.

Issues in the Classification of Children is addressed primarily to professional people, to graduate and professional students in relevant disciplines, and to policy makers who need in-depth treatment of specific topics. The authors were asked to write for a literate audience and to avoid professional technicalities and jargon. While great pains have been taken in editing the book to eliminate overlap among chapters, to compress arguments, and to clear up obscurities, an overriding consideration has been the preservation of each author's thought and style. Each chapter is distinctive; yet they all fit together in a rational pattern laid out in advance.

Part One: Theoretical Issues. In the understanding of a complex practical problem, prior appreciation of relevant theory is often of great value. Three theoretical perspectives seem especially pertinent here. They bear upon classification as a science itself, with its own rational requirements; psychometric procedures, especially as they are used in classification; and the sociological consequences of classification as illuminated by labeling and social-control theory. These themes thread their way through the six chapters in this part.

Rue Cromwell, Roger Blashfield, and John Strauss (Chapter One) present a set of criteria for a logical classification system, proposing open-ended and multiaxial systems as alternatives to single-level ones. This chapter is solidly based on empirical work with emotionally disturbed children. It emphasizes linkages between etiology, diagnosis, treatment, prognosis, and outcomes. And it underscores the tremendous importance of developmental stages in infancy, childhood, and youth.

Leslie Phillips, Juris Draguns, and Donald Bartlett (Chapter Two) survey current conceptual approaches to the classification of behavior disorders in children. They argue for a classification system that is pragmatic, provisional, and explicitly open to change in response to experience; for narrowing the gulf between clinical classification and research results; for avoiding the pitfalls of "adultamorphism," manifested in the tendency to see in the disorders of children the replicas and predecessors of analogously named conditions in adults; for sensitivity in classification systems to particular stages of development; for a system embracing multidimensional diagnosis; and for situation-specific information as vital to understanding a child's behavior.

Morton Kramer (Chapter Three) brings his long experience as a biometrician to bear in a chapter that stresses the purposive nature of classification, that describes the role of classification in research and epidemiological studies and in the control of pathological conditions in large groups, and that recounts efforts to develop international classification systems for diseases of various kinds and especially for disorders of childhood.

Prudence Rains, John Kitsuse, Troy Duster, and Eliot Freidson (Chapter Four) discuss the issues involved in the sociology of deviance, where a labeling perspective prompts the question of how persons come to be defined and treated as deviants. They are especially concerned with "the behavior which is a *consequence* of the assignment of persons to deviant statuses," and how such assignment "systematizes and stabilizes forms of behavior among labeled individuals." This phenomenon, working in often indeterminate ways in the classification and treatment of children, is a major source of contemporary concern over the deleterious and defeating aspects of labeling.

William Rhodes and Mark Sagor (Chapter Five) survey the history of community reactions to such deviant behavior as delinquency, mental retardation, and mental illness. They see an increasingly humane attitude developing in the treatment of exceptionality, and they call for a yet greater understanding and acceptance of individuality among mainstream culture bearers.

Jane Mercer (Chapter Six) describes the impact of current school classification practices on children from minority groups. She proposes an assessment procedure which studies a child's behavior in relation to his own culture as well as to the mainstream Anglo-American culture. Mercer addresses an issue of great social consequence in a period of heightened attention to social justice and individual rights.

Part Two: Classification Systems. A dozen or more categories (categories such as mental retardation, emotional disturbance, and learning disability) have acquired, through some science and much tradition, legitimacy in the classification of exceptional children. Within these major categories, numerous subdimensions result from specific efforts to classify children for one purpose or another. Taken all together, the various systems and schemes for the classification of exceptional children fall considerably short of what current understandings permit. Serious problems are introduced by a lack of sophistication in taxonomy, by strong-running professional biases, by preoccupation with dominant symptoms to the neglect of important determinants of behavior, by transposing adult-appropriate schemes to children, and by the use of classification to legitimize social control of the individual. The nine chapters in this part by no means cover all the categories of exceptionality, but they embrace the major ones. They illuminate the complexity of classification and illustrate promising ways of improving systems and procedures.

Richard Blanton (Chapter Seven) treats the classification problem in mental retardation in historical perspective. He shows how changing conceptions of man, broad social movements, and emerging technologies influence conceptual schema involved in classification and labeling. This is an introductory piece of high heuristic value because the same exercise, carried out with other categories (such as emotional disturbance or blindness), would show that they too deal not with simple functional phenomena alone but with period-bound conventions and transient modes of thought as well.

John Filler, Cordelia Robinson, Roger Smith, Lisbeth Vincent-Smith, Diane Bricker, and William Bricker (Chapter Eight) emphasize the inadequacy of classification systems based on psychometric data, such as IQ, for supplying information which can be used by a teacher or a parent to help a child learn. They present an accumulation of evidence that disposition on the basis of IQ alone decreases opportunities for the child to acquire socially desirable behavior. The empirical analysis of behavior in a developmental model, such as that proposed by Jean Piaget, provides a structure for the classification of behavior (not of children) which can be used to design effective instructional programs. Utility in improving instruction is the central criterion advanced by these authors for any system for the classification of mental retardation.

Frances Connor, Richard Hoover, Kathryn Horton, Harry Sands, Leon Sternfeld, and Gloria Wolinsky (Chapter Nine) examine systems currently in use for labeling children as blind or visually handicapped, deaf or hearing-handicapped, and physically handicapped. The subsections of this chapter reveal an important emergent shift from structural to functional criteria for classification. Visual impairment, for example, is assessed not on the basis of visual acuity alone but also, and primarily, on the extent to which a child can use vision for reading and other purposeful activities. A functional assessment ties readily to treatment needs and procedures, a linkage often lacking in classical classification schemes.

Dane Prugh, Mary Engel, and William Morse (Chapter Ten) address the complex problem of classifying emotional disturbance in children. Adult-oriented classification systems have dominated thinking in this area for years. The authors break with this tradition and present a schema that is both responsive to the formal requirements of classification systems and sensitive to the problems of children: to developmental changes and to genetic and experiential variables. They introduce "environmental responsivity" as an index of the extent to which experience or treatment can be expected to change the child. Aware of the vocabulary biases of various professional groups, they seek a simple, functional language acceptable to the many persons on whom exceptional children depend.

Joseph Wepman, William Cruickshank, Cynthia Deutsch, Anne Morency, and Charles Strother (Chapter Eleven) attempt to untangle the web of attributions attached to the term *learning disabilities*. They find "an excess of syndromes, diagnostic categories, remedies, and nostrums to the point that to say a child has a learning disability is by itself frequently more misleading than helpful." They advance a rigorous and limiting requirement on the definition of "specific learning disability," which, if adopted, would substantially clarify a now highly confused and confusing picture.

Paul Dokecki, Barbara Strain, Joe Bernal, Carolyn Brown, and Mary Robinson (Chapter Twelve) discuss some of the ways in which society views children from poor families and minority-group families and propose new policies to replace current punitive and emergency-oriented relief measures. They advocate a guaranteed minimum income for families as a first essential step in addressing the handicapping conditions imposed by poverty and often associated with minority-group status.

Frank Orlando and Jerry Black (Chapter Thirteen) describe the destructive effects of the juvenile court system—originally planned as a system for counseling and rehabilitating troubled children—on the children it labels. They make several recommendations concerning definitions and procedures that would help protect the child from abuses that have become so common as to impeach the court itself.

Herbert Quay (Chapter Fourteen) points out that the term *delinquency* is a legal concept that does not supply guidelines for prevention and treatment. There is need for classification of adjudicated delinquents on the basis of psychological and sociological characteristics. Quay describes in some detail two systems of subgroup classification that have demonstrated relevance for intervention.

Oakley Ray and John Wilson (Chapter Fifteen), working at the growing edge of classification problems, inquire into ways of categorizing for constructive purposes young people who use and abuse drugs. Their tough-minded, pragmatic, and promising approach emphasizes, as no other system here reported does, the concept that the problem resides not alone in the individual but in the individual-in-society. Their analysis of a special classification problem, drug taking, is rich in instruction for classifiers of other problems, who, influenced by long tradition, tend to accept without question that the problem resides exclusively in the child.

Part Three: Institutions. This part puts in place the important observation that classification has consequences. It is not just that a child is labeled (which may or may not do him harm) but that classification often leads to a sequence of experiences, enduring often over long periods of time, that profoundly affect a child's development. For example, a child who "borrows" an automobile for a joy ride might, if apprehended, be classified as mentally retarded, emotionally disturbed, or delinquent on the basis of factors (such as the socioeconomic status of his family) that have little to do with either his abilities or his conduct. How he is classified, however, determines his admission to institutional experiences of widely divergent character, each with its own metaphorical requirements, its own demands upon the child, and its own prognosis for the future. If we are to understand classification and labeling in the lives of children and in the shaping of their futures, we must see the process whole and include the long-term consequences of being classified in one way or another.

Herbert Goldstein, Claudia Arkell, S. C. Ashcroft, Oliver Hurley, and Stephen Lilly (Chapter Sixteen) consider classification in the context of the public schools, the institution responsible for the education of all but a small percentage of exceptional children. This extraordinarily rich analysis of the problem defies succinct summary in the space here available. The authors, all people with long experience in the public schools, are concerned essentially with the relationship between classification and educational objectives, and to this end they discuss problems of children with physical, sensory, mental, and emotional handicaps.

Robert Edgerton, Richard Eyman, and Arthur Silverstein (Chapter Seventeen) review studies of the effects of institutionalization on children classified as retarded, recommending against a hasty closing of all institutions until conclusive research has been done. They point out the danger that normalization (the currently popular term) "may result in a trade of large institutions for small ones without any improvement in the quality of life. Worse still, there is the danger that bad large institutions will be replaced by small ones that are even worse."

Donald Cohen, Richard Granger, Sally Provence, and Albert Solnit (Chapter Eighteen) address the issue of how children proceed through and exit from the mental health service system. By organizing their chapter on the basis of developmental stages, they emphasize what other writers comment on in passing: that classification and treatment of children are highly dependent upon developmental stages, a concept acknowledged but often ignored by clinicians accustomed to dealing with adults. Further, they are sensitive to social contexts: "[One] cannot think of children without thinking of their parents and their community, and [one] cannot consider mental health services without an awareness of the social-political-cultural context in which human needs are manifested and out of which human services arise and are elaborated."

Robert Coates, Alden Miller, and Lloyd Ohlin (Chapter Nineteen) consider the relationship between labeling theory and correctional philosophy, the decision-making points in the juvenile justice system, and the competing interests which must be dealt with politically in destigmatizing juvenile corrections. Basing their observations on a study of the Massachusetts experiment in closing down most juvenile correctional facilities, they conclude: "The fragmentary evidence about the ultimate effect of reform measures on recidivism, while not showing conclusively beneficial effects, clearly suggests that reform to reduce the stigmatizing effects of thoughtless or malicious labeling probably will not increase recidivism, will surely help to humanize the way we treat our children, and may even ease the drain on the taxpayer's pocket." The authors discuss the formidable opposition engendered by efforts to reform the system.

Part Four: Special Perspectives. A point of special vantage for seeing what it means to be categorized, labeled, and provided (or not provided) some special service or placement is the view of the exceptional child himself and of his family or others seeking to get help for him. Another vantage point, useful in perceiving the classification problem whole, is the special perspective of members of a minority group. Such matters are treated in the four chapters in this part.

Kathryn Gorham, Charlotte Des Jardins, Ruth Page, Eugene Pettis, and Barbara Scheiber (Chapter Twenty), basing their observations on personal experience and the results of a survey of parents of handicapped children, describe the frustrating attempts of parents to find help for handicapped children and the emotional impact of the experience on the families. The system stands indicted as insufficiently responsive to the efforts even of well-educated, determined, and economically sufficient families; what happens to poor, uneducated, and distracted families is another matter altogether. These authors make an especially valuable contribution in their suggestions for redefining the relationship between the professional person and the parents of a handicapped child.

Samuel Guskin, Nettie Bartel, and Donald MacMillan (Chapter Twenty-One) address the issue of classification from the perspective of the labeled child. They demonstrate the need for caution in assuming that labeling inevitably has deleterious effects since the research is equivocal, and they point out that deemphasizing labeling could lead to even less effective connection between children and the services they need than obtains now.

Wendell Rivers, Donald Henderson, Reginald Jones, Joyce Ladner, and Robert Williams (Chapter Twenty-Two) present the problem of the child who is both black and handicapped or who is declared to be handicapped on the basis of procedures judged to be prejudicial. The classification process, often an essential first step toward services, is itself confounded by racism and poverty. Services are distributed unevenly, so that children disadvantaged by poverty and minority-group status become further disadvantaged. But, as the authors point out, the very term *disadvantaged* suggests a disparaging view of children not shared by the children themselves. Finally, the authors examine the complex problem of standardized ability testing with respect to opportunities for black children.

Edward De Avila and Barbara Havassy (Chapter Twenty-Three) explore the problems of testing Spanish-speaking children in Anglo-American schools. Dissatisfied with the inadequacies of standard intelligence-test procedures, they present an alternate assessment model based on the work of Piaget. After noting a number of advantages of a developmental model, the authors write: "Lack of congruence between the neo-Piagetian and standardized measures, which is generally due to poor performance on standardized measures, only points to problems associated with schools and curriculum. Children are not responsible for such circumstances and should not be penalized for them."

Part Five: Legal Aspects. The past two decades have seen a resurgence of concern for individual rights in general, with the courts playing a major role in delineation of these rights. The movement has had a profound effect on public perceptions of problems of the handicapped and the delinquent. While practical consequences may not yet be substantial, the redefinition of the problem is bound, in time, to make a difference in what happens to children.

Alan Abeson, Robert Burgdorf, Patrick Casey, Joseph Kunz, and Wanda McNeil (Chapter Twenty-Four) concern themselves with means of ensuring that a child identified as needing help gets the help he needs. The failure of schools, communities, and institutions to provide adequate service is a consequence, in part at least, of undifferentiated, group approaches to treatment. The individual child does not benefit because he does not fit a standard remedial pattern. To counter standardized intervention programs that ignore individual differences, the authors propose a formal written contract, drawn to the requirements of a particular child in a particular setting at a particular time, specifying the formal obligation of all parties responsible for providing help. The contract has the further virtue of providing a basis for assessing the effectiveness of efforts on behalf of exceptional children.

Robert Burt (Chapter Twenty-Five) examines the theoretical and pragmatic consequences of recent court decisions affecting the rights of retarded children. While the decisions have been widely acclaimed, Burt shows that they are not without flaw as guides for future efforts to achieve justice. "If courts do battle for the retarded, as they have done for blacks, it will be a significant victory ultimately if the retardate label does not carry an immediate implication of stigmatizing social isolation, if the state makes substantial effort to avoid such isolation for all the children whom it now casts away, and if many are thereby saved."

David Kirp, Peter Kuriloff, and William Buss (Chapter Twenty-Six) undertook to study firsthand, under the auspices of the project, the effects of court decisions and legislation affecting special education. They examined the aftermaths of landmark court decisions in Pennsylvania and the District of Columbia and the effects of special education legislation in California. While lawyers have been called the "new heroes of special education," the authors show that court decisions do not necessarily lead to social reform. Decisions may define the requirements of justice, but purposeful, organized, and tenacious effort is required to translate legal requirements into programmatic realities.

Part Six: Public-Policy Questions. The special needs of exceptional children often exceed what the normal family can provide. Principles of equity require the provision of special opportunities by the state. Thus, a rounded treatment of the problem of classification requires coverage of public policy.

William Buss, David Kirp, and Peter Kuriloff (Chapter Twenty-Seven), drawing on the court cases and legislation on which they report in Chapter Twenty-Six, examine the usefulness and limitations of various procedures for special classification and placement of children and suggest alternatives. The authors emphasize that different special-education decisions may require different procedures and that no single set of procedures is appropriate for all programs.

James Gallagher, Patria Forsythe, Daniel Ringelheim, and Frederick Weintraub (Chapter Twenty-Eight), in an original study undertaken for the project, provide "(1) a review of federal agency funding of categorical programs; (2) a review of congressional attitudes toward programs for the handicapped, as revealed in their speeches, floor statements on pending legislation, and questions during appropriations or authorization hearings; and (3) a survey of state special education leadership personnel on the potential impact of possible changes in categorization." This rich chapter provides new understandings of values and attitudes that underlie public-policy decisions, and it thus provides new guideposts for organizations and individuals who seek to shape public policy to serve exceptional children.

Jane Mercer and John Richardson (Chapter Twenty-Nine) present the results of an original investigation undertaken for the project, in which they trace the course of public interest and action in the area of mental retardation in California from 1864 to the present. They detect historical cycles of broad sweep, each with identifiable phases falling into predictable patterns. Further, they find that reform movements based on advanced conceptions of the nature of the problem inevitably carry with them the seeds of their undoing. "It would have been impossible for Goddard to foresee the educational-welfare cycle of the 1940s as he contemplated the 'menace' of the feebleminded in the 1920s. . . . [or] for the parents and school psychologists struggling for educational programs in the 1950s to foresee that the very success of their efforts would create a civil rights problem in the 1960s. Thus, it is impossible for us to foresee what new social problems may be generated in the next decade by current attempts to solve the social problem of mental retardation as it is defined in the current civil rights cycle."

John Meier (Chapter Thirty) presents a comprehensive and competent survey of the effectiveness of screening programs in detecting developmental difficulties. Current public policy places great confidence in the reliability and validity of screening programs; thus, a critical analysis of the state of the art and of what must be done to improve it is especially valuable.

Charles Lister, Michael Baker, and Raymond Milhous (Chapter Thirty-One) discuss the complicated problem of confidentiality of records of exceptional children. In an age inundated by information, with individuals tracked by computers of capacious memory and extensive network linkages, attention must be paid to ground rules to ensure fair play and to prevent inaccurate record keeping and unwarranted intrusion into the lives of individuals. The authors lay out specifications for fairness in the keeping of records on children and thereby contribute to the realization of a just society.

The final report of the Project on the Classification of Exceptional Children is published separately in a book entitled *The Futures of Children* (Jossey-Bass, 1975). The report attempts to convey the significance of classification and labeling in the lives of millions of children; it explores the function of classification in social control, a complex matter indeed; it presents a systematic summary of the state of the art of classification of handicapped, disadvantaged, and delinquent children and youth; it rejects the currently popular notion that classification can be abandoned and presents a comprehensive plan for linking services with the needs of individual children; it describes how formal efforts to help children can sometimes do damage by nurturing the very conditions that the efforts are designed to remedy; it addresses the important issues of classification and the legal status of exceptional children, and of due process and privacy in classification procedures; it treats the persistent problems of fragmentation and duplication of services and of children lost in the system; and, finally, it presents a series of recommendations to the Secretary and to others concerned with the well-being of exceptional children.

These recommendations, some forty in number, cover seven major areas: helping families help exceptional children, improving classification systems and reducing the harmful effects of categories and labels, improving educational and treat-

ment programs and reducing the harmful consequences of classification, coordinating services for exceptional children, establishing patterns of funding programs for exceptional children,
providing manpower and training, and increasing the amount of
research on child development and public policy. The need for
new knowledge is singled out as requiring early and sustained
attention since so many policy issues affecting exceptional children rest, at the present time, on a precarious knowledge base.

So many people have contributed significantly to the
project that attempts at individual acknowledgements run the
risk of important omission or inadvertent misstatement of the
significance of each person's work. But gratitude is deep and
acknowledgement of the help of others a source of pleasure.

Inappropriate classification of exceptional children was a
frequently stated concern of Secretary Richardson. Early in
1972, Edward Zigler, then director of the Office of Child Development, proposed the project, gained the Secretary's support
for it, and arranged the remarkable coalition of agencies that
sponsored the work. Martin Gula of the Office of Child Development served with skill and tack as project officer and chairman of the Interagency Task Force. The Office of Secretary
Caspar Weinberger has been responsive to our every need for
assistance. Vanderbilt University provided a congenial setting
for carrying out the project.

It would be hard to overstate the importance of the members of the National Advisory Committee, particularly in the
design stages of the project. Their wide-ranging competence and
general good sense made it possible for the staff to proceed with
confidence that the scope of the work was well conceived.
Members of the Interagency Task Force also provided helpful
guidance.

The task force groups whose work makes up these two
volumes were constituted on the advice of the National Advisory Committee and the Interagency Task Force. Members of
the project staff prepared general outlines for chapters, helped
organize task groups, aided the groups in their work, and edited
early drafts of their reports. The work of the principal staff
members was so important that it could best be recognized by
making them coeditors of these volumes. I am grateful for their
skill, wisdom, and patience in carrying out complex and exact-
ing assignments.

Margaret Matheny deserves special recognition for editorial management of superb quality. She worked closely with all the task groups and shepherded their manuscripts with tact and good judgment to completion and presentation. Dorothy Conway, editor at Jossey-Bass, has been extraordinarily helpful in bringing these chapters and the final report of the project into publishable form.

My deepest appreciation is reserved for the contributors to these volumes. They responded promptly and effectively to the challenge of the project, and they brought diverse views and talents to their tasks. A brighter future for exceptional children will be their sure reward.

Nashville   Nicholas Hobbs
September 1974

CONTENTS

VOLUME I

xxi

Contents

VOLUME II

Part Three: Institutions

CONTRIBUTORS

Contributors to both volumes are listed below.

Alan Abeson, Ed.D., *director, State-Federal Information Clearinghouse, The Council for Exceptional Children, Arlington, Virginia*

Claudia Arkell, M.Ed., *fellow, Department of Special Education, University of Maryland*

S. C. Ashcroft, Ed.D., *professor of special education, University of Maryland*

Michael A. Baker, Ph.D., *Department of Sociology, City University of New York, Brooklyn*

Nettie R. Bartel, Ph.D., *chairman, Department of Special Education, Temple University*

Donald P. Bartlett, Ph.D., *professor of psychology, State University of New York at Buffalo*

Joe J. Bernal, M.Ed., *executive director, Commission for Mexican American Affairs, San Antonio*

Jerry P. Black, J.D., *professor of law, Vanderbilt University*

Richard L. Blanton, Ph.D., *professor of psychology, Vanderbilt University*

Roger K. Blashfield, Ph.D., *professor of psychology, The Pennsylvania State University*

Diane D. Bricker, Ph.D., *professor of pediatrics, Mailman Center for Child Development, University of Miami*

William A. Bricker, Ph.D., *Kennedy Professor of Psychology, Mailman Center for Child Development, University of Miami*

Carolyn S. Brown, B.S., *coordinator of early childhood education program development, Metropolitan Nashville Public Schools*

Robert L. Burgdorf, Jr., J.D., *staff attorney, National Center for Law and the Handicapped, South Bend, Indiana*

Robert A. Burt, J.D., *professor of law, University of Michigan*

William G. Buss, LL.B., *professor of law, University of Iowa*

Patrick J. Casey, J.D., *attorney, National Center for Law and the Handicapped, South Bend, Indiana*

Robert B. Coates, Ph.D., *study director, Center for Criminal Justice, Harvard Law School*

Donald J. Cohen, M.D., *professor of pediatrics and psychiatry, Yale University School of Medicine and Child Study Center*

Frances P. Connor, Ed.D., *professor of special education, Teachers College, Columbia University*

Rue L. Cromwell, Ph.D., *head, Division of Psychology, University of Rochester School of Medicine*

William M. Cruickshank, Ph.D., *director of the Institute for the Study of Mental Retardation and Related Disabilities and professor of maternal and child health, education, and psychology, University of Michigan*

Edward A. De Avila, Ph.D., *director of research, Children's Bilingual Television, Oakland, California*

Charlotte Des Jardins, B.A., *coordinator, Coordinating Council for Handicapped Children, Chicago*

Contributors

Cynthia P. Deutsch, Ph.D., *professor of psychology, School of Education, and senior research scientist of the Institute for Developmental Studies, New York University*

Paul R. Dokecki, Ph.D., *professor of psychology and director of the Peabody Child Study Center, George Peabody College*

Juris G. Draguns, Ph.D., *professor of psychology, The Pennsylvania State University*

Troy Duster, Ph.D., *professor of sociology, University of California, Berkeley*

Robert B. Edgerton, Ph.D., *professor in residence, Neuropsychiatric Institute, Departments of Psychiatry and Anthropology, University of California, Los Angeles*

Mary Engel, Ph.D., *professor of psychology, City College, City University of New York*

Richard K. Eyman, Ph.D., *associate research psychologist, Neuropsychiatric Institute, University of California, Los Angeles, and Pacific State Hospital Research Group, Pomona, California*

John W. Filler, Jr., Ph.D., *research associate, Toddler Research and Intervention Project, John F. Kennedy Center for Research on Education and Human Development, George Peabody College*

Patria Forsythe, M.A., *confidential assistant to the Assistant Secretary for Education; executive secretary, National Advisory Committee on Education of the Deaf, Washington, D.C.*

Eliot Freidson, Ph.D., *professor of sociology, Washington Square College of Arts and Science, New York University*

James J. Gallagher, Ph.D., *director, Frank Porter Graham Child Development Center, University of North Carolina, Chapel Hill*

Herbert Goldstein, Ed.D., *professor and director of the Curriculum Research and Development Center in Mental Retardation, Yeshiva University*

Kathryn A. Gorham, M.A., *director of community relations, Montgomery County (Maryland) Association for Retarded Citizens; research associate, National Special Education Information Center; parent of handicapped child*

Richard H. Granger, M.D., *professor of clinical pediatrics, Yale University Child Study Center*

Samuel L. Guskin, Ph.D., *professor of special education, Indiana University*

Barbara E. Havassy, Ph.D., *senior test developer, Far West Laboratory for Educational Research, San Francisco*

Donald M. Henderson, Ph.D., *associate provost, University of Pittsburgh*

Richard Hoover, M.D., *chief of ophthalmology, Greater Baltimore Medical Center*

Kathryn Horton, M.S., *professor of hearing and speech, Vanderbilt University; chief of language development programs, Bill Wilkerson Hearing and Speech Center, Nashville*

Oliver L. Hurley, Ph.D., *professor of special education, University of Georgia*

Reginald L. Jones, Ph.D., *professor of education and ethnic studies, University of California, Berkeley*

David L. Kirp, J.D., *professor, Graduate School of Public Policy, University of California, Berkeley*

John I. Kitsuse, Ph.D., *professor of sociology, Northwestern University*

Morton Kramer, Sc.D., *chief, Biometry Branch, National Institute of Mental Health*

Joseph W. Kunz, Ed.D., *executive director, National Center for Law and the Handicapped, South Bend, Indiana*

Peter J. Kuriloff, Ed.D., *professor, Program in Psychological Services, Graduate School of Education, University of Pennsylvania*

Joyce A. Ladner, Ph.D., *professor of sociology, Howard University; associate fellow, Metropolitan Applied Research Center, New York City*

M. Stephen Lilly, Ed.D., *professor of special education, University of Minnesota, Duluth*

Charles Lister, J.D., *lawyer, Covington and Burling, Washington, D.C.*

Contributors

Donald L. MacMillan, Ed.D., *professor of education, University of California, Riverside*

Wanda McNeil, B.A., *research assistant, Project on Classification of Exceptional Children, Vanderbilt University*

John H. Meier, Ph.D., *director, John F. Kennedy Child Development Center, and professor of pediatrics and psychiatry, University of Colorado Medical Center*

Jane R. Mercer, Ph.D., *professor of sociology, University of California, Riverside*

Raymond L. Milhous, M.D., *chief, Department of Rehabilitation Medicine, College of Medicine, University of Vermont*

Alden D. Miller, Ph.D., *assistant director of research, Center for Criminal Justice, Harvard Law School*

Anne Morency, M.A., *associate director, Speech and Language Clinic, University of Chicago*

William C. Morse, Ph.D., *professor of educational psychology and psychology, University of Michigan*

Lloyd E. Ohlin, Ph.D., *professor of criminology, Center for Criminal Justice, Harvard Law School*

Frank A. Orlando, J.D., *circuit judge, Family Division, Seventeenth Judicial Circuit, Broward County, Florida*

Ruth Page, B.A., *parent of handicapped child, Arlington, Virginia*

Eugene Pettis, M.S.W., *program associate in social work, Institute for the Study of Mental Retardation and Related Disabilities, University of Michigan*

Leslie Phillips, Ph.D., *professor of psychology, Vanderbilt University*

Sally A. Provence, M.D., *professor of pediatrics, Yale University Child Study Center*

Dane G. Prugh, M.D., *professor of psychiatry and pediatrics, University of Colorado Medical Center*

Herbert C. Quay, Ph.D., *professor, Division of Educational Psychology, Temple University*

Prudence M. Rains, Ph.D., *professor of sociology, McGill University*

Oakley S. Ray, Ph.D., *professor of psychology, Vanderbilt University*

William C. Rhodes, Ph.D., *professor of psychology and program director in psychology for the Institute for the Study of Mental Retardation and Related Disabilities, University of Michigan*

John G. Richardson, Ph.D., *professor of sociology, University of Alaska*

Daniel Ringelheim, Ph.D., *deputy assistant commissioner of education for special education and pupil personnel services, New Jersey State Department of Education*

L. Wendell Rivers, Ph.D., *research professor and director of the Mental Health Specialists Program, University of Missouri, St. Louis*

Cordelia C. Robinson, Ph.D., *professor, University of Nebraska College of Nursing; director, Infant Stimulation Program, Meyer Children's Rehabilitation Institute, University of Nebraska Medical Center*

Mary Electa Robinson, M.A., *research sociologist, Office of Child Development*

Mark Sagor, M.A., *research assistant, Department of Psychology, University of Michigan*

Harry Sands, Ph.D., *director of program planning and evaluation, Epilepsy Foundation of America, Washington, D.C.*

Barbara Scheiber, B.A., *associate director, National Special Education Information Center; parent of handicapped child, Falls Church, Virginia*

Arthur B. Silverstein, Ph.D., *research specialist, Neuropsychiatric Institute, University of California, Los Angeles*

Roger A. Smith, Ph.D., *research associate, Parent Teaching Style Assessment Program, George Peabody College*

Albert J. Solnit, M.D., *director and professor of pediatrics and psychiatry, Yale University Child Study Center*

Contributors

Leon Sternfeld, M.D., Ph.D., *medical director, United Cerebral Palsy Associations, Inc., New York City*

Barbara A. Strain, M.A., *research associate, Peabody Infant Laboratory, John F. Kennedy Center for Research on Education and Human Development, George Peabody College*

John S. Strauss, M.D., *professor and director of clinical psychiatry research programs, University of Rochester School of Medicine*

Charles R. Strother, Ph.D., *professor of psychology, University of Washington*

Lisbeth J. Vincent-Smith, M.A., *research associate and director of parent training, Early Development Assistance Program, John F. Kennedy Center for Research on Education and Human Development, George Peabody College*

Frederick J. Weintraub, M.A., *assistant executive director for governmental relations, The Council for Exceptional Children, Arlington, Virginia*

Joseph M. Wepman, Ph.D., *professor of psychology and surgery and director of the Speech and Language Clinic and Research Laboratory, University of Chicago*

Robert L. Williams, Ph.D., *professor of psychology and director of the Black Studies Program, Washington University*

John T. Wilson, M.D., *professor of pediatrics and pharmacology, Vanderbilt University Medical Center*

Gloria F. Wolinsky, Ed.D., *professor of education, Hunter College*

ISSUES IN THE CLASSIFICATION OF CHILDREN

VOLUME ONE

A Sourcebook on Categories, Labels, and Their Consequences

ONE

〜〜〜〜〜〜〜〜〜〜〜〜〜〜〜〜〜

THEORETICAL ISSUES

〜〜〜〜〜〜〜〜〜〜〜〜〜〜〜〜〜

To understand a complex practical problem it helps to have an appreciation of relevant theory. Three theoretical perspectives are specially pertinent here. They have to do with classification as a science itself, with its own rational requirements; psycho-metric procedures, particularly as they are used in classification; and the sociological consequences of classification as illumi-nated by labeling and social-control theory. These themes thread their way through the six chapters in this part.

CHAPTER 1

CRITERIA FOR CLASSIFICATION SYSTEMS

Rue L. Cromwell, Roger K. Blashfield, John S. Strauss

This first chapter presents a set of criteria for a logical classification system, proposing open-ended and multiaxial systems as alternatives to single-level ones. Solidly based on empirical work with emotionally disturbed children, the chapter emphasizes linkages between etiology, diagnosis, treatment, prognosis, and outcomes. It underscores the tremendous importance of developmental stages in infancy, childhood, and youth.

CHAPTER 2

CLASSIFICATION OF BEHAVIOR DISORDERS

Leslie Phillips, Juris G. Draguns, Donald P. Bartlett

Phillips, Draguns, and Bartlett survey current conceptual approaches to the classification of behavior disorders in children. They argue for a system that is pragmatic, provisional and open to change in response to experience. They want to narrow the gulf between clinical classification and research results, and they want to avoid the tendency to see in the disorders of children the replicas or predecessors of analogously named conditions in adults. They urge that classification systems be sensitive to particular stages of development and that they embrace multidimensional diagnosis. Finally, they argue that situation-specific information is vital to understanding a child's behavior.

CHAPTER 3

DIAGNOSIS AND CLASSIFICATION IN EPIDEMIOLOGICAL AND HEALTH-SERVICES RESEARCH

Morton Kramer

This chapter stresses the purposes of classification and describes its role in research, epidemiological studies, and the control of pathological conditions in large groups. Bringing to bear his long experience as a biometrician, Kramer recounts efforts to develop international classification systems for diseases of all kinds—especially for disorders of childhood.

CHAPTER 4

THE LABELING APPROACH TO DEVIANCE

Prudence M. Rains, John I. Kitsuse,
Troy Duster, Eliot Freidson

This chapter tackles the issues involved in the sociology of deviance, asking how persons come to be defined and treated as deviants. The authors are especially concerned with behavior that is a *consequence* of assigning deviant status to individuals. They consider how such procedures systematize and stabilize certain forms of behavior among the labeled.

CHAPTER 5

COMMUNITY PERSPECTIVES

William C. Rhodes, Mark Sagor

Rhodes and Sagor survey the history of community reactions to such deviant behavior as delinquency, mental retardation, and mental illness. They see an increasingly humane attitude developing in the treatment of exceptional persons, and they call for an even greater understanding and acceptance of individual differences among mainstream culture-bearers.

CHAPTER 6

PSYCHOLOGICAL ASSESSMENT AND
THE RIGHTS OF CHILDREN

Jane R. Mercer

This last chapter in Part One describes the impact of current school classification practices on children from minority groups. Mercer proposes an assessment procedure that studies a child's behavior in relation to his own culture as well as to the mainstream Anglo-American culture.

3

1

CRITERIA FOR CLASSIFICATION SYSTEMS

Rue L. Cromwell, Roger K. Blashfield,
John S. Strauss

When the students of George Herbert Meade assembled their lecture notes to publish a book posthumously under his name (Meade, 1934), they included his references to the origin of language. According to Meade, three criteria are necessary for the origin of language: First, an observable response (referred to as a *symbol*) must be made by a sender. Second, the response must be repeatable in other situations. Thus, vocal sounds, the clenched fist, other movements, and also marks written on transportable materials may develop as they prove convenient to common sharing. Third, a receiver must respond in a con-sistent way to the sender's behavior. This receiver's response is designated as *the meaning of the symbol* (the meaning of the

4

sender's response). With these strikingly simple criteria, a significantly new position was taken in the understanding of language (see also Wittgenstein, 1953). The gulf of dualism between objective symbols and subjective meanings was modified.

A number of implications were apparent. From this position language, and indeed meaning, does not develop except in a social context. A symbol can be any kind of response at all, as long as it is reacted to. Before consistent meanings of external symbols can be privately held (Meichenbaum and Goodman, 1969), they must be initiated socially and affirmed externally to become a part of public language. Therefore, since a spoken word or a gesture or a written mark has no meaning unless it is responded to, the receiver—not the sender—ultimately controls meaning. An intended meaning by a sender has no viability unless the receiver responds accordingly. And, indeed, that recipient response is the meaning. A clenched fist would have no meaning of threat if it aroused a random response among observers. A word of love would lose its intended meaning if listeners responded with fear.

We are brought immediately to one of the issues in labeling and classification of children, on both a scientific and a nonscientific basis. The labels applied to children are symbols constructed by senders to serve given purposes. As time passes, as the group of listeners broadens, as the needs, intents, and subsequent responses of listeners change, the concepts (that is, the meanings of the labels) change. Labels that once had technical meanings take on additional meanings. Labels which could point to (and mean) help for a child may come to be used arbitrarily to discriminate or derogate. Much to the discontent of the original users of the labels, these changing reactions do indeed the meaning of the labels. In the final analysis, the meanings are the property of the community that uses the terms (see also Chapter Five in this volume) and not the exclusive property of the one who originally defines them. From time to time, therefore, we should take stock of labels and classifications and their meanings in order to determine what purposes and injustices they are serving.

Scientific Labels and Classes

When science developed as a means to extend knowledge, specific criteria were needed to prescribe how concepts should

be developed; that is, how labels and classes should be applied
to referents. These criteria tended to preserve the uniformity of
concepts and to reduce change over time. As these criteria came
to be applied, labels and their referents were often referred to as
scientific constructs. In general, the effect of these criteria was
to guide the establishment of meanings of given constructs and
to clarify the relations between constructs in a way that was
empirically based.

Philosophers of science still differ about the criteria they
would apply to scientific constructs; they generally agree, however, that such constructs must be clear and useful. That is, the
definition of a construct must lend itself to publicly observable
assessment (people must be able to determine whether and to
what extent the construct describes a given observable event);
and the construct must bear a relationship to another set of
events (to other constructs). For example, gravity proves itself a
clearly defined construct when people agree that a falling object
represents a gravitational event and that gravity can be defined
in terms of a mathematical formula of accelerated movements.
By the second criterion, gravity proves its worthiness when one
can predict when a falling object in a vacuum will hit the earth,
how movement will occur among planets, and when and where
a rocket ship will land on the moon. Malaria becomes established as a clear construct when people can empirically agree on
the symptoms and manifestations that constitute its definition.
It proves useful when it bears a relationship to swamps and
other environmental constructs, to mosquitoes, to blood plasma
levels, and, on the predictive side, to improvements with qui-
nine and other drugs.

How much, if any, *surplus meaning* (meanings or attributes that cannot be directly measured and perhaps are impossible to observe or measure) may be ascribed to scientific constructs? Can we say, for example, that a perceptually disordered
child has minimal brain damage when the deficiency in brain
structure and function is impossible to assess? Scientists and
philosophers of science give different answers as a function of
whether their emphasis is upon accomplished fact or upon conjecture for future exploration. Those who put strong emphasis
on the *language of fact* tend to eschew surplus meaning and to
rely solely on that which is clearly observable and measurable.
Their definitions are restricted to the operation of measurement, and their utility statements are restricted to empirical
correlations that are known for sure. Thus, perceptual disorders

in children would be defined in terms of the specific tests to identify and measure them. The status of a child on a test would be associated empirically with the effectiveness of one educational procedure over another, but not with a condition of the brain or a causal force in the environment which is impossible to measure or verify. In contrast, scientists who emphasize *the language of conjecture* believe that surplus meaning (hypothesized, nonvalidated, conjectured meaning) should be used to suggest new avenues of investigation. Such a scientist might prefer to ascribe minimal brain dysfunction to a perceptually disordered child because specific hypotheses concerning brain-behavior relationships may be suggested and pursued. Another "language-of-conjecture" scientist may reject the surplus meaning in terms of brain dysfunction but develop other surplus meaning in terms of early experience, genetics, social maturation, or other areas.

All scientists, for practical purposes, agree to an overt language of fact. Disagreement occurs as to whether the language of conjecture should be unexpressed, expressed in surplus meaning and connotation, or expressed separately. Science has not reached the point of formalizing two different language systems, one for fact and one for conjecture. Confusion often arises when the languages of fact and conjecture are intertwined through core and surplus meaning within the same concept.

Clearly, surplus meaning can become core meaning if the surplus meaning proves later to be correct. On the other hand, if it is not correct or amenable to eventual test, surplus meaning can block progress in advancing knowledge. Scholars who oppose surplus meaning argue that knowledge advances primarily through disconfirming accumulated surplus meanings. For example, movement of bodies in the solar system took on surplus meaning from the Ptolemaic conception that the earth is the center of the universe and the sun moves around it. This "rut" in thinking retarded consideration of the more advanced Copernican notion that the sun is the center of our immediate system of planets. On the other hand, the concepts of temperature and pressure took on surplus meaning when scientists began to discuss temperature and pressure on the moon through inferences that could not be validated. Now that we have had the direct experience with these phenomena on the moon, these surplus meanings have been found useful in advancing our progress in the understanding of outer space.

When we assume that infantile autism results from a biochemical abnormality, are we attaching surplus meaning which is useful? Time will tell. Clearly, the adoption of one type of surplus meaning tends to preclude valid hypotheses foreign to the surplus meaning. Open hypothesis building gives way to "ruts" in thinking.

When we define mental retardation in such a way as to allow surplus meaning that the child is different and must be treated differently, to what extent are we preventing a useful understanding of the social role of the retarded? (For additional discussion, see Chapter Four in this volume.)

A useful purpose of periodic examination of labels and classification procedures is to examine the degree to which surplus meanings are meeting their intended purpose. Often they are. Sometimes, however, labels and connotations persist even after they have been tested and proved invalid; these labels are often not in the interest of adequate prognosis and intervention. Still further, some surplus meanings of constructs lead by definition to untestable propositions, often referred to as *dualistic* (that is, they explain a universe of observable phenomena on the basis of a universe of unobservable and unmeasurable phenomena). Philosophers of science agree that such propositions have no value in science. Even so, they persist. People, even scientists, have not learned to discriminate and cull out these dualistic and untestable surplus meanings from the useful ones. Thus, for example, a condition of psychosexual development in infancy—which, by definition, cannot be assessed even at the time of infancy—does not lend itself as acceptable conjecture regarding the cause of a later perceptual reading disorder in children.

Diagnostic Labels and Classes

Diagnostic constructs may be viewed as specialized types of scientific constructs. Thus, they must meet the criteria discussed in the previous section. In addition, they have their own specialized characteristics. Their definitions are restricted to (A) historical-etiological and/or (B) currently assessable characteristics. Their usefulness in the clinical, educational, or social care of the individual is determined by the extent to which (C) given treatments or interventions, or, contrarily, no intervention at all, leads to (D) given levels of prognosis.

In other situations the usefulness of diagnosis is aimed at

prevention of a given condition in others in the society. Rather than the care or plight of the individual with the diagnosed problem, the object may be to lower the incidence of the disorder in the community or society. In such cases, two other classes of data may be identified: (E) the intervention carried out on other individuals in the society and (F) the outcome of this intervention. Thus, the traditional clinical, educational, and social approaches to the problem-ridden individual, family, or group may be diagnosed and understood in terms of ABCD relationships. The broader preventive approach may be understood in terms of ABEF relationships. (For discussion of the epidemiological importance of classification, see also Chapter Three in this volume.)

When examining data classes A and B in performing a diagnostic labeling, one must not ignore the *situational and cultural context* within which the A and B observations arise. Although context might be considered as a separate data class, it can perhaps more appropriately be considered a part of data classes A and B. In the examination, diagnosis, and treatment of a sore throat, it is important to observe what types of infections are going around the community. When a child is referred for treatment for stealing, it is important to know whether stealing is common in his subculture and peer group. When a preventive program is being planned for malaria, it is important to know the local mosquito and swamp situation as well as to know the current prevalence of malaria. A disregard of situational context represents a hazard in objective behavioral ratings and observations. If constructed inappropriately, rating scales may take behaviors out of context. Thus, it is usually important to construct rating scales to assess behavior as it deviates from the situational and cultural context where it occurs.

What is the role of etiology in diagnostic classification? We have noted that the definition of a diagnostic construct is based in class A, class B, or both. The clinical-utility criterion is based in class D, with or without class C. The utility criterion for prevention must be based on E and F (intervention-outcome relationships). Historically, much empirical evidence has supported the importance of class-A data. Therefore, etiology (necessary historical events) is often viewed as crucial to diagnosis. This, however, is an empirical issue to be judged from case to case. From a practical clinical point of view, the definitional data should depend on what leads to the most favorable treat-

ment-prognosis (or intervention-outcome) prediction. To remove a wart, to clear up a sore throat, to alleviate a deprived
social environment, or to eliminate a child's emotional disturbance may or may not depend upon understanding the etiology.
It does depend on some kind of observation which can predict
some kind of outcome.

In adult psychopathology, the premorbid adjustment of
the individual (class-A data) is often the strongest predictor of
an individual's possibility of discharge from the hospital after a
schizophrenic illness (Farina and Webb, 1956); diagnostically
relevant symptoms (class-B data) are considered less important
(Strauss and Carpenter, 1972). Similarly, in a study of A, B, C,
and D data in 491 emotionally disturbed children in various
treatment centers, Cromwell (1972) found a high number of
ACD relationships and very few BCD relationships. This striking
finding called into question the emphasis which psychologists
give to behavioral-test data as opposed to historical data.

One reason why current behavioral (symptom) data fall
behind historical-etiological data in usefulness is that symptom
data cannot readily be separated from the substrate of personality and competence dispositions that are present before, during, and after the disturbance. For example, Silverman (1964)
has shown that schizophrenic symptoms differ as a function of
an individual's cognitive style of scanning (his manner of taking
in information). One is left to speculate whether different disorders called *schizophrenia* are being expressed in different individuals or whether a single disorder is manifesting different
symptomatology as a function of different cognitive styles. Zigler and Levine (1973) have demonstrated that schizophrenic
patients of low social competence tend to manifest nonparanoid
symptoms, while schizophrenics of high social competence
show one of two different patterns: paranoid symptoms or
turning-against-self symptoms of depression. With these personality and competence variables clouding the picture, the difficulties in classifying symptoms are evident.

Whenever class-C data (treatment or intervention procedures) do not exist, class-D data alone determine the value of a
construct. For example, Down's syndrome (mongolism), a disorder that currently has no known cure, is defined in terms of
current manifestations of chromosomal and other physical characteristics. As a diagnosis, it is useful primarily in predicting the
level of retarded intellectual functioning when the child grows

up. Thus, it is a BD construct. When specific interventive or preventive procedures are discovered, it will become a BCD or even an ABCD construct, depending on the role of historical-etiological factors in determining the interventive procedure. If birth-control counseling for older women or some other preventive approach should prove effective in reducing the incidence of Down's syndrome, then the construct also should become BEF in nature.

Validity of Constructs

Diagnostic constructs that include C and D data (ACD, BCD, and ABCD) have clearly defined intervention procedures and prognostic statements. They are typically the most useful and valid diagnostic constructs. Diagnostic constructs that involve D without C (AD, BD, and ABD) have outcome predictions, positive or negative, independent of any known treatment for the condition. They are also valid diagnostic constructs but are useful only for prognoses. Still other constructs may be invalid diagnostic or valid nondiagnostic constructs. AC, BC, or ABC constructs are invalid diagnostic constructs because they refer to currently used intervention procedures that have no known effect on outcome. Constructs developed from AB alone or CD alone are valid nondiagnostic constructs, which may be important for scientific understanding. AB constructs would describe relationships between historical and current observations, such as the relation of child rearing to current behavior. CD constructs describe intervention procedures associated with positive or negative outcomes, independent of the kind of diagnosis presented.

The following examples (Cromwell, 1972) illustrate the constructs just described. Each example is an empirically and mathematically derived product of the four data classes.

A valid diagnostic construct with positive prognosis is the praise-potency pattern, an ABCD construct. A child displays stealing and delinquent behavior oriented toward peer approval (class B) and has an ample history of parents rewarding with praise and giving minimal punishment (class A). When placed in a treatment center, a child characterized by this pattern needs no individualized treatment for deviant behavior (class C). When he is reassessed two years later, his behavior has distinctly improved (class D).

A valid diagnostic construct with negative prognosis is the intrusive-sadistic syndrome, another ABCD construct. A child aggressively retaliates to frustration, bullies to get his own way, intrudes, pouts, and is sadistic to smaller children (class B). His parents report a history of giving more punishment than praise, removing him to another room when he cries, and not valuing his own self-care efforts (class A). Child workers in a treatment center tend to focus on his aggression and admit that they stay angry with him longer than with other children (class C). Rejected by peers and adult workers alike, he is even more delinquent and revengeful in behavior two years later (class D).

A diagnostic construct with prognostic but not clearly identified treatment significance is the punishment-anticipation pattern, an AD construct. In this pattern parents report that they promise, delay, and are inconsistent in carrying out punishment for misdeeds (class A). Independent of treatment, such children, not knowing when and if they will get punished, are found to be deteriorating in attention and in socially responsive behavior two years later (class D). In contrast, a contingent-punishment pattern (a pattern in which consistent punishment is emphasized by parents, is inflicted immediately after a misbehavior, and is clearly associated with the misbehavior, so that the child does not anticipate subsequent punishment on a later occasion) has no long-term effect on overall adjustment. Thus, the uncertain anticipation of punishment, rather than punishment itself, clearly appears to be the crucial factor associated with behavior deterioration.

An invalid diagnostic construct would be the nonverbal-management pattern. In this pattern, parents use a nonverbal rather than a verbal approach in discipline (class A), and child workers later on in the treatment center tend also to use a nonverbal approach (class C)—probably because the child has not learned to respond to a verbal approach. This correlation of practice between parent and child worker has no relation to either a positive or a negative outcome as measured two years later. In other words, while A and C are related, no evidence exists to indicate that this circumstance affects D (prognosis).

An example of a valid nondiagnostic construct (AB) is the indecision pattern. Children who focus heavily on their parents' punishment, show genuine sorrow, seek love, do not talk back, and try to amend their ways when punishment is imminent (class A) tend very early to develop difficulty in making decisions on their own (class B). That is, their behavior is oriented toward averting parental punishment submissively but not toward making autonomous decisions. Since no identified treatment or outcome is associated with this pattern, the valid relationship has scientific but not diagnostic significance at this point.

Another valid nondiagnostic construct concerns treatment effects (CD) which are independent of diagnosis. For example, the peer-group-opinion technique (class C), where a child is given feedback about what his peers in a treatment center think of his actions, leads to generally improved behavior two years later (class D), regardless of the behavioral pattern and background data. In other words, this feedback technique tends to be highly applicable without regard to diagnostic category of the child.

Interestingly, a laissez-faire treatment approach, where the behavior of a child in a treatment center tends to be largely ignored by center workers (class C), is associated with improved behavior two years later (class D). Thus, when children are given an opportunity to "get their own heads on straight," without the adult workers' intervention, positive effects are found.

A nondiagnostic treatment construct associated with negative outcome is the "distraction" approach. When distraction (class C) is used for sexual acting-out behavior (usually distraction given by nurses in a medical setting), the children were found to be worse in many ways after two years (class D).

Relation of Diagnosis to Clinical Method

Although the guidelines for proper diagnostic classification are important, the initial diagnostic phase is only the first step in a much longer process, the clinical method. Facing a problem for the first time, a scientist, physician, or educator usually must make certain observations (a diagnosis or classification, an initial labeling) as a basis for taking initial action. However, once these initial observations and interventive steps are taken, new observations are available as a consequence. These new observations afford a new set of alternative hypotheses, which provide a basis for the decision to continue, modify, or change interventive procedures. When subsequent action is taken, as based on the most supportable alternative hypothesis, additional new observations are available. This procedure (sometimes called the *clinical method*, as opposed to the experimental or the test-and-measurement method of science) is repeated continuously until intervention is no longer required.

The continuity between initial diagnosis and ongoing clinical method is important to understand. Diagnosis is often only an entree to intervention. It attempts to point to the initial best possible interventions and their associated prognoses. It does not delimit or preclude treating an individual in terms of his individual characteristics and problems. The notion that diagnostic classification is the sole determinant of intervention and prognosis is also fallacious. Subsequent clinical observations modulate and guide intervention and prognosis once the proper diagnosis is made. For example, a child may be diagnosed as school-phobic; with subsequent clinical observations, however, detailed understanding of approach and avoidance motivational structures will make the initial diagnosis less important. Although the goals of treatment may still involve removing the school phobia, other more subtle factors may determine the treatment approach.

The classification and labeling process cannot be discarded as unnecessary, but it should not be overvalued. Before interventive procedures are chosen, observations have to be made. Whether these observations are handled in overt, systematic ways or in covert, vague, or loose ways, a diagnostic classification on some level of adequacy has been made.

Hazards in Creating a Diagnostic System

While formal classifications and terminology are developed by scientists and practitioners to meet their particular purposes for understanding and intervention, they become a part of broader public usage. Sometimes this broader usage is beneficial (favorable political, social, or economic decisions are made). Sometimes the broader usage is not beneficial (discrimination or loss of freedom occurs). Thus, the role of the diagnostic labels must be evaluated on different levels. Certain terms may be adequate and valuable in treating an individual child and harmful in terms of social decisions made with the label. Or the exact reverse is possible.

Diagnostic systems should have clear definitions and a coherent logical structure. Perhaps the poorest method of developing a classification system with logical integrity is through a broadly represented professional committee. History has shown that the products of such committees represent a set of compromises reminiscent of platform statements from smoke-filled political caucus rooms. For example, the diagnostic definition of schizophrenia in the *Diagnostic and Statistical Manual for Mental Disorders* (American Psychiatric Association, 1968) represents the Freudian influence (reality relationships, object cathexis, regression, and withdrawal mechanisms), the Bleuler influence (concept formation and stream-of-thought disturbance), and the Sullivan social-interpersonal influence (emotional harmony with others). The manual's classification of childhood schizophrenia reflects the separate influences of Margaret Mahler, Leo Kanner, and Lauretta Bender. In Heber's *Manual on Terminology and Classification in Mental Retardation* (1959), the definition of mental retardation represents a compromise between the proponents of an intelligence definition and the proponents of a social-competence definition. Compromises among emotionally committed points of view usually do not allow the full ascendance of empirical findings and logical rules for organizing the findings. As a consequence, a research team, collecting and conceptualizing data over a period of time, represents an alternative more likely to develop a classification system of integrity.

In the labeling and classifying of children, additional considerations are necessary which do not occur in other nosological systems. Formal nosologies often found useful for mature species have been "single-order"; that is, a defining set of characteristics bears a static relationship to each category. The recent research by Cromwell (1972) on classification of emotionally disturbed children suggests that this approach is not advisable. A child's developmental level must be taken into account before the categories and their defining characteristics can be clearly identified. A particular behavior or cluster of behaviors may contribute to the diagnosis of emotional disturbance at one developmental level and may fall easily within the range of normality at another. For example, frequency of crying, amount of empathy, or the lack of use of moral judgment has vastly different implications at different age levels. A particular brain lesion at one age may have a different diagnostic meaning than at another age. A given perceptual shortcoming may have different treatment implications at different age levels. Not only will different categories have different defining characteristics at different levels, but also some categories may be legitimate and useful at some developmental levels but not at others.

All data classes constituting diagnostic constructs for children must be reviewed to determine whether they normatively differ at different age levels. If they do not differ, then first-order nosologies, as have proved useful with adults, might be developed; if they do, then developmental constructs must supersede the first-order classification constructs. For example, an analysis of the four classes of data described earlier yields more than one diagnostic category of "acting-out" emotional disturbance. One type of acting out has different prognoses at different developmental levels. If the child's general cognitive level is advanced, the prognosis is remarkably good. This advanced level may be observed in the relatively high levels of social empathy, superego development, mental age, tendency to approach complexity, and tendency to be product-oriented. The acting out tends to be directed toward peer attention. On the other hand, when cognitive development of this type of acting-out child is not advanced, the prognosis is poor. For another category of acting out (the intrusive-sadistic syndrome mentioned earlier), the cognitive and other developmental factors are irrelevant. Behavior and background factors identify the child regardless of his age level. The child tends to get worse even in treatment, and the long-term prognosis is generally unfavorable. In spite of these differences, the two categories of acting-out disturbance have many similar behavioral manifestations. Thus, the importance of cognitive developmental level in addition to nosology cannot be overemphasized.

Criteria for Structure of Classification

Classification systems tend to follow two basic patterns. The first pattern involves a typological structure; the second is based on a dimensional structure. To understand the difference between the two, a distinction must be made between *extensional* and *intensional* definitions of classificatory terms (Buck and Hull, 1966). An extensional definition defines the terms by enumerating the members of a *set*. If a classificatory term such as *runaway reaction of childhood* is defined as a set, then the definition simply consists of an enumeration of all children with this disorder (John S., Mary Q., Paula T., Henry U., and so on).

An intensional definition defines classificatory terms as concepts; that is, by describing the characteristics (symptoms) associated with the concept. The official intensional definition of *runaway reaction of childhood* is "Individuals with this disorder characteristically escape from threatening situations by running away from home for a day or more without permission. Typically, they are immature and timid, and feel rejected at home, inadequate, and friendless. They often steal furtively" (American Psychiatric Association, 1968, p. 50).

A dimensional classification system uses only intensional definitions; that is, the terms refer only to concepts. A typological classification requires both intensional and extensional definitions of the terms; that is, the diagnostic terms refer both to concepts and to sets. The term *schizophrenia* refers both to the properties which characterize schizophrenia and to the people who have it.

Criterion 1: reliability. When the diagnostic terms of a classification system are applied to patients, the terms must be used in a reproducible manner. The main focus of psychiatric reliability has been on interclinician agreement. A classification system in which there is more variance from one clinician to another than from one term to another is of no value.

Criterion 2: coverage. In a typological classification the criterion of coverage refers to the degree to which the classificatory terms "cover" or are directly applicable to the population of individuals being classified. If, for example, the diagnostic terms used to classify exceptional children describe patterns of behavior (syndromes) not frequently observed in everyday practice (by teachers, social workers, psychologists, and the like), the coverage of the classification is limited and therefore of little practical significance. In a dimensional classification system the criterion of coverage refers to the degree to which the dimensions being used in the classification account for or describe the important aspects of the child's behavior. Or, in statistical terms, coverage refers to the percentage of variance accounted for by the dimensional classificatory terms. If, for example, Eysenck's three dimensions of introversion-extroversion, psychotism, and neurotism were used with children, these dimensions might not adequately describe all the relevant aspects of a child's behavior which teachers or parents or social workers might need to know.

Blashfield (1972, 1973) has argued that reliability and

coverage together are both fundamentally necessary for a classification because together these criteria can be used to assess how well a classification system functions as nomenclature. The basic purpose of a classification is to form a dictionary which clinicians, social workers, and teachers can use as a common basis for communication among themselves. In order to form this basis of communication, the classification system must be reliable (the terms must be used in the same way by different persons), and the system must have coverage (it must describe the relevant domain of interest).

Although both coverage and reliability are important criteria for a classification, the two are inversely related. That is, if the classificatory terms maximally cover the scope of the elements being classified, these terms are likely to suffer in reliability; on the other hand, if the terms are quite reliable, they tend to be molecular and limited in scope. For example, as Blashfield (1972, 1973) has shown, the diagnostic terms in the *DSM-II* classification of schizophrenia have greater reliability when they are used with comparatively little coverage than when they are used with maximal coverage. Blashfield's findings put a new light on the often-noted lack of reliability of psychiatric classification. Very simply, measured reliability could be increased if cases were dropped which did not fit clearly into one category or another. A system that compels itself to classify every person with a mental disorder necessarily limits its own reliability.

In any case, the problem of the inverse relation between reliability and coverage is not insoluble. Good classifications can exist which are high on both of these criteria. In fact, procedures such as factor analysis (for dimensional classifications) and cluster analysis (for typological classifications) were statistically designed to create classifications which achieve maximally efficient compromises for these two criteria.

Criterion 3: logical consistency. The following list of potential guidelines should be considered under this criterion: (1) A system should be clearly designated as dimensional, typological, or a mixture of both. The dimensional and typological aspects should be clearly and separately defined. (2) If a classification is hierarchical (see Gregg, 1954), the basis of the hierarchical relationship should be clearly specified. For example, if *runaway reaction of childhood* and *childhood schizophrenia* fall at the same level, the reason for such an ordering should be explicit. (3) A hierarchical typological classification should specifically require either mutually exclusive sets or overlapping sets. A classification with overlapping sets can be logically consistent (Jardine and Sibson, 1971) but unfortunately is more complicated. (4) The diagnostic-decision rules for making identification should be stated clearly, precisely, and explicitly (Feighner and others, 1972). This criterion of logical consistency seems quite obviously desirable; yet it has been blatantly neglected by the authors of the *DSM-II* classification (Lorr, Klett, and McNair, 1963). Some of the social-political reasons for this neglect were cited earlier.

    Criterion 4: clinical utility. The decision concerning whether a classification system should be dimensional or typological in structure has some effect on the potential clinical usefulness of the system. The simplest way of making clinical decisions is to use a typological classification in an all-or-none fashion. For example, one might say that if a child is diagnosed (on the basis of class-A data or class-B data or both) as a childhood schizophrenic, the treatment of choice (class-C data) is drugs. If the child is mentally retarded, the treatment of choice might be to use institutionalization with token economy systems. However, as Lubin (1968) has pointed out, other ways of using historical (class-A) and current-symptom (class-B) data are more likely to yield relevant treatment predictions (class-D data). Regression equations or Bayesian prediction equations based upon dimensions are much more likely to yield clinically useful predictions, since these prediction systems are more sensitive to nuances in the data. In other words, typological classifications, when used in an all-or-none fashion, simply ignore a great deal of potentially useful data which dimensional classifications can easily utilize. Thus, there is reason to believe that a dimensional classification is more likely to yield clinically useful information than is a simple typological classification.

    However, a mixed classification may in fact yield the most clinical utility (Strauss, 1973). In this last approach, a typological system is used to classify patients. Once they are classified, then dimensions are used to make clinical predictions. In this sophisticated typological classification, the decision rules for making treatment, prognosis, or prevention statements will be different for each different typological category. For example, if a child were diagnosed with the term *childhood schizophrenia,* dimensions such as age, degree of social-interpersonal disturbance, and social class of the parents might be used in making an institutionalization decision. On the other hand, if the child were diagnosed as mentally retarded, perhaps the valid predictor dimensions for institutionalization would be intelligence, degree of danger to self, and parental empathy.

The emphasis on the clinical usefulness of a classification is not trivial. Recent studies of the effects of labeling have persuasively shown that labeling children may lead to self-fulfilling prophecies which are destructive to the child (Scheff, 1966; Becker, 1964). One of the more eloquent discussions of this position has been offered by a sociologist (Matza, 1969), who describes a labeling process which he calls *signification.* This process is initiated by the labeling of an individual as deviant. This label then leads other members of the individual's society to expect that individual to behave deviantly. These other persons then shape the individual's behavior to conform with their expectations of him.

The antilabeling movement in mental health has demonstrated that classification of individuals can involve a loss for the individuals classified. Labeling an individual as a member of a particular political party, labeling a young man as 1-A for the draft, labeling a person in a bar as a college professor, or labeling a child as mentally retarded—all such labels imply some loss. The loss is defensible only when the diagnosis or label has some gain which more than offsets the loss imposed by the labeling process. If a classification system for exceptional children cannot demonstrate a significant degree of gain, then the classification system should not be used.

Criterion 5: acceptability to users. A classification system must be attractive enough for professional people to use. A complex system of high utility may fail in acceptance because people have difficulty learning it or thinking about individuals in terms of it. Even professional people seem more comfortable with typologies than with continua or dimensions. For this reason a number of classification systems have failed to gain popular usage. For example, a child classified by the AAMD (Heber, 1959) dimensions (measured intelligence, social adaptation, motor-sensory impairment, and personal-social impairment) is described by numbers reflecting half-standard-deviation units from the populational mean. In spite of obvious aspects of utility, the system did not catch on. On the other hand, the labeling of retarded children as educable, trainable, and custodial (instead of 1, 2, and 3, or mild, moderate, and severe) did catch on and gained broad acceptance during the 1950s and 1960s. Apparently, then, dimensions are more acceptable if they are segmented and if the segments are labeled like typologies; moreover, the particular labels chosen are more acceptable if they give some hint of the treatment-prognosis relationship associated with them. We therefore recommend the use of *segmented labeled dimensions*. The choice of labels for the segments to imply treatment-prognosis relationship, however, should be at most short-lived, since with increasing knowledge these relationships, as well as the classification system itself, should change.

Toward an Improved Diagnostic System

A difficult chore in developing a classification system is to determine where the professional user is in his habits and thinking. An acceptable diagnostic system should have elements which are highly familiar, so that people can understand and immediately deal with them; or else the elements must be so different that people can view the system as a new undertaking. Rutter, who is working with the World Health Organization project (see Tarjan and others, 1972), has suggested a multiaxial approach which attempts to comply with some of these demands. With this system, a child would be diagnosed along each of three axes: syndromes, intelligence, and associated physical and psychosocial conditions. The use of this multiple approach is further supported by Cromwell's findings. A child may be classified with as many factor-based diagnostic labels (ABCD relationships) as are appropriate for him. Each can be time-bound and could be discarded once the intervention procedures were used to maximal advantage. More specifically, the multi-axial approach can employ both typological and dimensional systems.

Based on these considerations, a diagnostic model for exceptional children might have the following structure. The first section (section I) might contain two sets of typologies: (1) syndromes or types of problems (highly familiar concepts describing the problem to be dealt with); (2) personality diagnosis (basic patterns of coping and relating—patterns that are more enduring than the syndrome or problem and/or do not represent the problem being classified). The next section (section II) would contain dimensions important for treatment, prognosis, and prevention. Each dimension should be segmented and labeled to reflect the magnitude of dysfunction on it. The dimensions could be compared and correlated with the nominal variables of the typology section for adequacy and interrelationship, respectively. Examples of dimensions might be as follows: impairment in social relationships, impairment in school or work achievement, impairment in intelligence, impairment in social competence (for instance, dressing, feeding, finding directions), impairment in sensory-motor function, subjective distress, danger to self, danger to others or to property.

Section III could include narrative statements regarding context: (1) environmental norms for problem, (2) age norms for problem. Antecedent factors could then be stated (in section IV): (1) associated psychosocial-history factors, (2) associated physical-history factors. Finally, a glossary of terms would be important to include in the manual of classification.

No matter what model or structure of classification is proposed, a carefully planned nationwide or worldwide pretesting would be important. Program A of the Mental Health Unit of the World Health Organization represents a method for such an approach. The pretesting should evaluate the acceptability of the system for adoption by users as well as the effectiveness of the system for the child populations.

Recommendations

1. Any system of classification should be dated and subject to periodic review and modification, not only because of the advancements in scientific knowledge relative to the classification data but also because public usage and surplus meanings change the meanings of labels and terms as time passes.

2. The structure of classification systems should meet the criteria of reliability, coverage, logical consistency, utility, and acceptability to users.

3. If a classification system is to be diagnostic in nature, then each diagnostic category should be understood in terms of the classes of data which contribute to its definition (historical-etiological, presently assessable characteristics) and the classes of data which determine its utility (treatment, prognosis, prevention, outcome).

4. Diagnostic classification systems should have preventive as well as treatment value.

5. The behavior of children should be classified and understood in terms of the situational, cultural, and age context from which the behavior deviates.

6. The application of measurement theory to historical data (as compared to behavioral-test data) should receive much greater attention by psychologists in the future.

7. Classification systems should be evaluated to determine whether the inevitable losses to the individuals are affected by the gains. The indirect gains and losses should be evaluated as well as the direct ones.

8. The formulation of classification systems by broadly based professional committees should be avoided, since logical integrity tends to yield to theoretical allegiances. Small research teams with coherent conceptual frameworks, working within child centers and educational settings, are preferable alternatives.

9. Dimensional or mixed typological-dimensional classification systems are recommended as more sophisticated and potentially more useful than simple typology systems.

10. The use of segmented labeled dimensions is recommended in formulating classification systems.

11. Both open-ended and multiaxial systems represent alternatives in single-level nosologies. In an open-ended system, a given classification would not preclude others. Diagnoses would be multiple and of indefinite number. Any given one should be dropped when the associated treatment-outcome statement is no longer appropriate. Multiaxial systems would have a definite number of dimensions and/or typology levels on which the child is always classified.

12. A glossary of terms meeting philosophy-of-science criteria is mandatory for any manual of classification.

13. Classification systems of major impact and coverage should be pretested on a national or worldwide basis. User acceptability as well as effectiveness for the child population would be important components for the pretesting.

References

American Psychiatric Association, Committee on Nomenclature and Statistics. *Diagnostic and Statistical Manual of Mental Disorders (DSM-II)*. (2nd Ed.) Washington, D.C.: American Psychiatric Association, 1968.

Becker, H. S. *Outsiders: Studies in the Sociology of Deviance*. New York: Free Press, 1964.

Blashfield, R. K. "An Evaluation of the *DSM-II* Classification of Schizophrenia." Unpublished doctoral dissertation, Indiana University, 1972.

Blashfield, R. K. "An Evaluation of the *DSM-II* Classification of Schizophrenia as a Nomenclature." *Journal of Abnormal Psychology*, 1973, *82*, 377-381.

Buck, R., and Hull, D. "The Logical Structure of the Linnaean Hierarchy." *Systematic Zoology*, 1966, *15*, 97-111.

Cromwell, R. "Classification of Emotionally Disturbed Children." Paper presented at meeting of Southeastern Society for Multivariate Experimental Psychology, Atlanta, Ga., April 1972.

Farina, A., and Webb, W. W. "Premorbid Adjustment and Recovery." *Journal of Nervous and Mental Disease*, 1956, *124*, 612-613.

Feighner, J. P., and others. "Diagnostic Criteria for Use in Psychiatric Research." *Archives of General Psychiatry*, 1972, *26*, 57-63.

Gregg, J. R. *The Language of Taxonomy*. New York: Columbia University Press, 1954.

Heber, R. F. *A Manual on Terminology and Classification in Mental Retardation*. American Journal of Mental Deficiency, 1959. Monograph supplement.

Jardine, N., and Sibson, R. *Numerical Taxonomy*. London: Wiley, 1971.

Lorr, N., Klett, C. H., and McNair, B. *Syndromes of Psychosis*. London: Pergamon Press, 1963.

Lubin, A. "A Diagnostic Dialog with a Drug-Devised-Typology Devotee." In M. M. Katz, J. O. Cole, and W. E. Barton (Eds.), *The Role and Methodology of Classification in Psychiatry and Psychopathology*. Washington, D.C.: U.S. Government Printing Office, 1968.

Matza, D. *Becoming Deviant*. Englewood Cliffs, N.J.: Prentice-Hall, 1969.

Meade, G. H. *Mind, Self, and Society from the Standpoint of a Social Behaviorist*. Chicago: University of Chicago Press, 1934.

Meichenbaum, D., and Goodman, J. "Reflection-Impulsivity and Verbal Control of Motor Behavior." *Child Development*, 1969, *40*, 785-797.

Scheff, T. J. *Being Mentally Ill: A Sociological Theory*. Chicago: Aldine, 1966.

Silverman, J. "The Problem of Attention in Research and Theory in Schizophrenia." *Psychological Review*, 1964, *71*, 352-379.

Strauss, J. S. "Diagnostic Models and the Nature of Psychiatric Disorder." Unpublished manuscript, 1973.

Strauss, J. S., and Carpenter, W. T. "The Prediction of Outcome in Schizophrenia." *Archives of General Psychology*, 1972, *27*, 739-746.

Tarjan, G., and others. "Classification and Mental Retardation: Issues Arising in the Fifth WHO Seminar on Psychiatric Diagnosis, Classification, and Statistics." *American Journal of Psychiatry*, 1972, *128* (111). May supplement.

Wittgenstein, L. *Philosophical Investigation*. New York: Macmillan, 1953.

Zigler, E., and Levine, J. "Premorbid Adjustment and Nonparanoid Status in Schizophrenia: A Further Investigation." *Journal of Abnormal Psychology*, 1973, *82*, 189-199.

2

CLASSIFICATION OF BEHAVIOR DISORDERS

Leslie Phillips, Juris G. Draguns,
Donald P. Bartlett

During the past decade the classification of psychological disturbance has undergone increasingly intense scrutiny, and numerous proposals have emerged for revising, reformulating, or abolishing the present system. Broadly speaking, recent criticisms of diagnostic and classificatory schemes in psychopathology have been stimulated by three kinds of considerations. First, the diagnostic system in use has been attacked (see, for instance, Zigler and Phillips, 1961; Zubin, 1967) for its empirical inadequacy—above all, in relation to the criteria of reliability, validity, and utility. Second, the traditional diagnostic

We are grateful to Roger Blashfield, Jane Mercer, and J. R. Newbrough for their helpful comments on an earlier draft of this chapter.

system has proved inadequate, even irrelevant, for the new modes of clinical practice that have developed, particularly in the form of behavior modification, community mental health, and humanistically inspired variants of psychotherapy. Third, theoretical analyses have brought to light implicit assumptions and undesirable consequences that are embedded in the practice of designating some people "mentally ill."

At the same time, proponents of the traditional framework of psychiatric diagnosis (frequently equated with the medical model) defend the theoretical assumptions and the practical operations of the existing diagnostic system, as exemplified by the original and revised versions of the *Diagnostic and Statistical Manual* (American Psychiatric Association, 1952, 1968). The task of this chapter is to contrast the currently established diagnostic framework with the several proposals for its revision or replacement, first in reference to psychiatric diagnosis in general and then in connection with the special problems inherent in classifying and assessing psychologically disturbed children.

Traditional View: Maladaptation as Mental Illness

The traditional view of mental disorder is based on medical concepts of the nature of illness. Within this framework the individual who exhibits disturbed and aberrant behavior is sick; he is suffering from an illness that prevents his normal adjustment in society. Observable aberrations in behavior are assumed to be only symptomatic of an underlying pathological process; thus, the therapist, in attempting to cure a disorder, must proceed from surface observation to underlying causation. If the disorder is to be effectively counteracted, its etiology must become known; the underlying pathological process needs to be elucidated in recognition of the fact that symptoms constitute only the observable and peripheral aspects of disorder. Thus, symptoms are vital for diagnosis and description; they are trivial for treatment. The task undertaken by early investigators into the nature of psychopathology was to classify regularly occurring symptom patterns which they presumed would characterize different underlying disease processes, a strategy analogous to the conceptual framework within which physical illness has come to be understood.

The medical model can be applied in either a literal or a metaphorical sense. Those subscribing to the literal view assume that classifying the symptoms associated with specific disorders will lead to the discovery of their biological sources and cures. In this regard, Kraepelin's contribution is particularly noteworthy. Working from a hypothesis of biological causation, Kraepelin and his nineteenth-century contemporaries developed a classification of mental illness which still forms the basis for the dominant system in use today. The current edition of the *Diagnostic and Statistical Manual* (American Psychiatric Association, 1968) clearly demonstrates its Kraepelinian heritage, as indeed do most current textbooks of abnormal psychology (Cole, 1970; Coleman and Broen, 1972; London and Rosenhan, 1969; Suinn, 1970; Ullmann and Krasner, 1969) as well as those of clinical psychiatry (Arieti, 1959; Freedman and Kaplan, 1967; Mayer-Gross, Slater, and Roth, 1969). The clinicians and investigators who hold a metaphorical view of the medical model do not accept the postulate of a biological causation for mental disorder; rather, they view the manifest features of mental illness as expressions of deeply ingrained patterns of faulty habits culminating in anxiety and avoidance behavior, character distortions, or other forms of maladaptive behavior. Thus, from a psychoanalytic perspective, for example, symptoms are the expression of a clash among various incompatible processes within the personality that are ultimately traceable to crucial parent-child encounters in the first six years of the child's life.

   Some recent writers (Price, 1972; Sarason and Ganzer, 1968) are impressed with the distinctness of these two frameworks (the biological and the psychodynamic) for conceptualizing psychopathology. Ullmann and Krasner (1969), however, lump both of them together as variants of the medical model, and the Israeli psychiatrist Jaffe (1969) regards them as variants of a regression model—in contrast to the adaptation models predicated upon the processes of learning and interchange between the organism and its environment. It is true that the factors presumed to activate symptom expression in the psychodynamic view are strikingly different from those to which the advocates of the biological-medical view would subscribe, as are the conceptions of treatment and case management that stem from these two positions. Moreover, psychodynamic formulations show a low degree of correspondence to the categories of the Kraepelinian classificatory grid. The important feature shared in both instances is that covert processes are hypothesized to account for manifest symptomatology. What is observable about disturbance is indispensable for diagnosis but quite inadequate for treatment. The disturbance underlies its visible manifestations; it must be removed, over and above the elimination of symptoms. To a lesser extent, the two structural positions also converge in emphasizing that the disturbance is something separate from the individual's customary baseline of adaptation. To a Kraepelinian, mental illness is distinct from (Foulds, 1965), and in some extreme versions even unrelated to (Sjobring, 1958), the premorbid personality of the patient. To the Freudian, many variants of psychological disturbance are reducible to ego-alien disruptions—disruptions occurring within the individual yet experienced as something alien or uncontrollable.

How has the medical model fared? Seven or more decades of biological, biomedical, and genetic research have isolated remarkably few physical bases for recognized forms of psychopathology. It is clear that the syphilitic infection in general paresis attacks the central nervous system and thus produces disturbance in thought processes; that a biochemical imbalance is the source of phenylketonuria (PKU); and that there is a definite, mathematically expressible, genetic potential for the inheritance of Huntington's chorea. Yet the forms of psychiatric disorder that account for the bulk of the psychologically impaired or incapacitated populations remain without demonstrated biological etiology. The yield from medical and biological research on schizophrenia has been described as inconclusive (Kety, 1959), although opinions to the contrary continue to be articulately voiced, and research animated by organic hypotheses in schizophrenia is vigorously pursued (Osmond and Hoffer, 1968). Organic correlates have also been identified in affective disorders (Coppen, 1967; Whybrow and Mendels, 1969), but it continues to be moot whether these indices are necessary components of psychotic mood disturbance. The evidence for biological dysfunction in neurosis and personality disorder is, with few exceptions (for instance, Pitts and McClure, 1967; Shields and Slater, 1961), inconclusive, fragmentary, or negative. In general, apart from presenting symptoms that would enable the clinician objectively to diagnose a psychological disorder (Scott, 1958; Zubin, 1968), research has not succeeded in identifying any pathognomonic signs.

If the concept of psychological disorder as disease is to be taken seriously, specific variants of such disorder should be manifested in approximately the same form in different socio-economic and subcultural milieus at different times and in different cultures. A number of recent reviews (Draguns, 1973; Draguns and Phillips, 1972; Kiev, 1972; Pfeiffer, 1968; Petras and Curtis, 1968; Phillips, 1968a, 1968b), however, call this expectation into question. Although the evidence presented in these reviews cannot be considered conclusive, it seems to point to a greater plasticity of psychological disturbance in response to the pressures of place and time than the traditional medical concept of disease would accommodate. Put more concretely, individuals identically diagnosed in different countries, subcultures, or times have been found to differ perceptibly, and sometimes markedly, in their observable symptomatology (see, for example, Draguns and others, 1971; Fundia, Draguns, and Phillips, 1971; Lenz, 1968; Teja, Narang, and Aggarwal, 1971; Seifert, Draguns, and Caudill, 1971; Varga and Nyiro, 1968). The contributions of the diagnostician and the patient are not quite disentangled in these investigations. The former component points to the inadequacy of the diagnostic system in use, especially as it is applied in heterogeneous social settings; the latter brings up the possibility of more basic defects in any diagnostic scheme that proceeds from the notion of illness or disease.

Closely related to the preceding points are the empirical data on the frequency of utilization of diagnostic categories (Gardner, 1968). These data indicate that some of the diagnoses listed in the *Diagnostic and Statistical Manual* are being applied more and more infrequently. Conversely, new patterns of maladaptation have appeared that defy classification within the existing diagnostic grid.

Several criticisms also have been made of the formal characteristics of the traditional classification schema. Prominent among these criticisms is the arbitrary and random nature of the traditional categories. Some of these categories are based on a presumed psychodynamic etiology for a disorder; others reflect disapproval of a given behavior; others are listed in simple descriptive terms. Other problems with the present schema concern the inadequate fit between the individual's behavior and the category to which he is assigned. That is, many individuals fail to manifest a substantial proportion of the behavioral characteristics that define the category in which they are placed and, in addition, often demonstrate deviant behaviors that help to define other diagnostic headings. Consequently, a "typical" sociopath, conversion hysteric, paranoid schizophrenic, or other deviant is much harder to find than their textbook descriptions would suggest. Correspondingly, two members of a diagnostic category may demonstrate none of the same symptoms. Empirical studies (Nathan and others, 1969; Thorne and Nathan, 1969; Zigler and Phillips, 1961) agree that assignment to rather general categories (such as neurosis or psychosis) is subject to a lesser degree of diagnostic disagreement than is assignment to rather specific categories (such as passive-aggressive or inadequate personality).

The conventional diagnostic system is least ambiguous and most free from potential criticism as a descriptive schema, a taxonomy of mental disorders analogous to the work of Ray and Linnaeus in biology. In this sense, an individual's inclusion in a class guarantees only that he exhibits some aspect of the defining characteristics of that class. As has been noted (Wittenborn, Holzberg, and Simon, 1953; Caveny and others, 1955; Hunt, Wittson, and Hunt, 1953), the present diagnostic system has useful administrative and, to a lesser extent, preventive implications. Practical applications of this system include legal determination of insanity, declaration of incompetence, ward placement in psychiatric institutions, and screening for the armed services and other government agencies. The diagnostic system also serves as a base for compiling census information and statistical data, which, in turn, are utilized in many different kinds of social planning.

Restrictive Models

During the past century the historic trend has been toward expansion of the concept of mental illness. Originally coextensive with acute and florid psychoses, it first expanded to include neuroses, then engulfed personality disturbance, and finally came to include various specific problems of living, renamed as symptom states: drug abuse, alcoholism, homosexuality, and many others. Several recent writers (Bleuler, 1969; Weitbrecht, 1969; Zubin, 1968) have sought to counter this trend and to establish limits to the practical and conceptual use of the term *mental illness*. Specifically, they would restrict the term *illness* to two broad classes of disorder: (1) conditions for which the expectation of biological causation remains realistic (for instance, schizophrenia); (2) states that are subjectively experienced as extraneous and as alien to the patient's control (for instance, neurosis). Unfortunately, the first criterion rests on an appraisal of currently ambiguous evidence concerning biogenesis and hence is bound to lead to disagreements; and the second criterion admits of a rather broad transitional band where classical symptom neuroses blend into more inclusive and ego-syntonic patterns of living. These proposals do have the merit, however, of raising the fundamental question of what constitutes disease.

The same issue is tackled by a number of other writers, who have attempted to formulate a unitary concept of mental illness—that is, one disorder variously expressed in different individuals. Foulds (1965) restricts the term *illness* to states discontinuous from, and disruptive of, the individual's usual mode of adaptation. In his view, manifestations of *mental illness* (symptoms) are fleeting, uncontrollable, and extraneous to the usual behavior style of the individual. Menninger (1963) also emphasizes commonalities among psychopathological manifestations. Reducing qualitative differences in expression to quantitative degrees of disruption in the "vital balance" (an equilibrium between the individual's attainment of his essential goals and the environment's barriers to their realization), he places all forms of maladaptation on a five-rung continuum: heightened vigilance (anxiety, nervousness), rigidification (most neuroses), explosiveness (most character disorders), distortions (most psychoses), and, finally, death (suicide, voodoo death, lethal diseases on a psychophysiological basis). The scheme provides simplicity and order where complexity and disarray usually reign. As such, it has both intellectual and esthetic appeal. Nonetheless, Menninger's proposed scheme remains controversial. No adequate empirical basis for placing the principal variants of psychopathology on a single axis is provided. Further, many professionals remain skeptical of Menninger's postulate of the lethal outcome of psychopathology when allowed to run its full course. This notion, which represents Menninger's application of the contested Freudian concept of a death instinct, is difficult to reconcile with the occurrence of suicides in troubled but reasonably mature individuals; the postulate that they have traversed the depths of rebellion and withdrawal violates conventional professional judgment.

Adaptation Models

Views of psychopathology based on the concept of illness stress the uniquely deviant features of disorder; mental disorder, in these views, is qualitatively distinct from normality. There is, however, another way to view behavioral deviations, and that is as forms of coping behavior that fail to meet particular environmental demands. In this section we shall consider some of the adaptation models that have achieved a degree of prominence in the literature.

Derivatives of behavior-modification techniques. Many writers (Franks, 1969; Kanfer and Saslow, 1965; Ullmann and Krasner, 1965, 1969; Yates, 1970) have demonstrated the lack of functional fit between diagnostic categories, as currently constituted, and various behavior-modification techniques. The theory and the practice of behavior modification challenge the traditional view that the underlying structure has to be known before deficits or excesses of behavior can be corrected. In keeping with the Skinnerian antecedents of many of its techniques, behavior modification bypasses understanding in favor of control. Understanding, then, may not be necessary to bring about effective and therapeutic change (Arthur, 1968, 1969).

Fundamental to this view is the notion that the symptom is not merely the external, visible manifestation of a disorder; the symptom *is* the disorder (Ullmann and Krasner, 1965). The question, then, is not "What does this symptom signify? What underlies it?" Rather, the practitioner of behavior modification asks: "How did this symptom arise? What maintains it despite the frustrations and punishment that it often evokes?" Answering these questions requires a functional analysis of the antecedents and consequences of symptomatic behavior, including the fluctuations of its occurrence in response to various contingencies. Simply put, the scientist committed to behavior modification wants to know what the individual is doing and what he is not doing, as well as when and how. (For a model that describes all of a person's behavior in functional terms, see Kanfer and Saslow, 1965.)

The practical enterprise of behavior modification is remarkably parsimonious in its assumptions. Its basic notions are that behavior exists; that it is divisible into units (called *responses*); and that responses come to be called *symptoms* by qualified professional observers, by strategically placed and powerful persons whose decisions may affect the individual's life, by peers, or by the person exhibiting the symptom. In the behavior-modification scheme, the term *symptom* has no objective status; rather, it is a shorthand designation of a social judgment that a particular category of behavior needs to be eliminated, reshaped, or corrected (Ullmann and Krasner, 1969). The behavior modifier then must decide whether to accept that judgment and whether to modify the target behavior (the symptom). He may refuse to do so for ethical reasons, or he may dismiss a particular complaint as trivial and hence unworthy of application of the technology of behavior modification.

With their emphasis on specific behavioral manifestations, proponents of behavior modification have not provided a taxonomy of behavior to be modified, although they have formulated a number of explicit and elaborate schemes of pretreatment data collection and assessment (Goldfried and Kent, 1972; Kanfer and Saslow, 1965). These schemes are noncategorical and individual-centered; the person in question is to be described and not classified. Behavior modification has not quite succeeded, however, in eschewing classificatory entities; in at least two prominent texts written from the point of view of behavior modification (Ullmann and Krasner, 1969; Yates, 1970), the subject matter is divided into chapters corresponding to the traditional diagnostic units.

Social-competence model. This model is built upon two cornerstones: social competence and psychiatric symptomatology (Phillips, 1968a). Social competence refers to an individual's premorbid level of achievement in educational, occupational, and interpersonal spheres. Social-competence scores are based on generally available and concrete biographical indices, such as the years of schooling completed, jobs held and their skill and prestige level, and marital status. As to symptoms, they are recorded and then grouped in accordance with their interpersonal character, or role, and their channel of expression, or sphere. Specifically, there are three roles (turning against self, turning against others, and avoidance of others) and four spheres (thought, affect, somatization, and action). For each person, the dominant sphere and role is calculated on the basis of the relative number of symptoms that fall within each category. The rationale of this new approach to classification rests on the principle of continuity: clinically recognized disorder is thought to be not an extraneous affliction but a continuation of the accustomed pattern of adaptation by unrealistic and ineffective means. The person's accustomed level of functioning, indexed by social competence, determines his characteristic mode of symptom expression, classified according to role and sphere. This categorization of symptom expression was developed to increase the differentiating power of symptom data. There is wide agreement in the research literature that discrete symptoms are transient and fleeting (Foulds, 1965), that they are susceptible to reinforcement and extinction in the immediate social milieu (Ayllon and Michael, 1959), and that they contain little diagnostically useful information (Lacquaniti, 1967; Thorne and Nathan, 1969; Zigler and Phillips, 1960). Collapsed into a limited number of categories, symptoms are expected to become more useful for diagnostic purposes.

Research based on this scheme of classification has been carried out both in this country (Phillips, Broverman, and Zigler, 1966, 1968; Zigler and Phillips, 1960, 1962) and in intercultural investigations (Draguns and others, 1970, 1971; Fundia, Draguns, and Phillips, 1971; Nachshon and others, 1972; Schooler and Caudill, 1964). These studies have demonstrated a host of correlates of this classification system in the premorbid, process, outcome, and social-milieu characteristics of psychiatric disorder. While discrete symptoms show virtually no relationship with conventional diagnostic categories, role and sphere dominance show high correlations with diagnostic judgments arrived at independently (Phillips, Broverman, and Zigler, 1968).

Community mental health approach. The scope of professional practice in the field of psychopathology has expanded considerably during this century. Psychiatrists and clinical psychologists at first worked primarily with institutionalized patients but eventually widened their practice to include ambulatory and voluntary (although problem-ridden) clients. More recently, mental health professionals have further widened their professional investments, with the blessings and financial support of the federal government, to the community as a totality. New forms of services, based outside both the office and hospital settings, have brought professionals into contact with subtle and complex forms of maladaptation previously seen only infrequently. As the range of the services provided and the populations served have grown, the traditional mental illness model, whether used literally or metaphorically, is increasingly recognized as an inadequate and incomplete guide to the range of maladaptations found in the community. Intuitively, some degree of similarity may be accepted between the behavior of a person acutely ill with fever and that of an individual so distraught as to be confused about his immediate surroundings. But the analogy with the consequences of physical illness appears forced when we encounter a person burdened by a lifetime of poverty who has been rendered ineffective in his adaptive attempts by faulty, incomplete, or inappropriate social learning. In what sense can this individual be presumed to be mentally or otherwise ill? Questions of this sort have prompted a number of recent critics to question the relevance of the mental illness model for community mental health programs (Albee, 1969; Hersch, 1968, 1969; Phillips, 1967).

Proponents of newer conceptual orientations in the field of community mental health (Albee, 1969; Newbrough, 1973; Phillips, 1967) propose that the phenomenon of maladaptation cannot be described purely in intrapsychic terms; rather, they suggest that failures in human adaptation are inherently social in character and consequence. This orientation implies the need for a diagnostic interaction model, one that Newbrough (1973) has recently attempted to provide. Blending a sociology of deviance with a psychophysical model, this framework examines tolerance for behavioral deviance within the social milieu. Newbrough notes that labels are applied by members of the community in order to explain and justify the social distance maintained from individuals who exhibit aberrant behavior. At the same time, members of the community differ in their degree of tolerance for deviance.

The important feature of this proposed model is that it includes the observer and the social context in the task of symptom determination. A symptom is not something that occurs or is manifested; rather, it is a social datum that emerges upon the encounter of the observer and the observed. Newbrough (1973) contends that this act of social evaluation obeys the laws of psychophysics, a discipline concerned with the relationship between physical properties of stimuli and psychological attributes of responses. Traditionally, psychophysics was focused upon the investigation of sensory qualities, such as brightness, loudness, or roughness. In recent years, however, psychophysical principles have also been applied to complex social judgments (Ekman and Sjoberg, 1965), such as "conservatism" or "emotional distance." Closer to the concerns of this chapter, Stone and Skurdal (1968) have demonstrated that psychiatrists' judgments of the severity and nature of mental illness yield curves that are akin to those obtained in traditional sensory psychophysical experiments. Yet it is also known that the acts of symptom detection and appraisal are susceptible to halo effects, stereotyping, and other cognitive distortions (Cohen, 1970; Hammond, Hursch, and Todd, 1964). Newbrough (1973) has attempted to move from the documentation of these pitfalls of social judgment to the formulation of the implicit lawfulness of placing a person on the many axes of psychiatric appraisal. He has proposed that in the process of executing such judgments, psychiatrists act as evaluators of deviance, social distance, and community tolerance of the behavior that they are diagnosing. The labels applied represent the various points of intersection of these continua.

Another direction taken in writings in the field of community mental health has been to urge assessment of the adaptive adequacy, rather than the inadequacy, of problem-ridden individuals. Albee (1969) and Phillips (1967) have called for such a reversal in orientation; they propose that evaluation of an individual's existing pattern of skills, assets, and strengths is at least as important as enumeration of his symptoms and deficits. In accordance with this orientation, professional intervention should aim at more than symptom removal or therapy; it should be directed at the enhancement of the individual's level of interpersonal and social effectiveness. This concern with social effectiveness brings the community mental health model into contact with the social-competence model. The former developed in the context of innovative clinical activity; the latter was formulated on the basis of a developmental integration of clinical and experimental information on psychopathology. At this point the two models overlap; as yet they have not merged.

Antilabeling Critiques

A number of voices have been raised over the years, from an existentialist as well as a phenomenological point of view (Laing, 1967; Maslow, 1960; Rogers, 1951), against the practice and effects of diagnostic categorization. The specific terms of the arguments differ, but one general theme remains constant: diagnostic labeling is inherently dehumanizing and incompatible with psychotherapy and widens the human gulf between the diagnostician and the diagnosed. In short, a diagnostic label stands like a screen between the two participants to a therapeutic relationship, making their human interaction difficult and perhaps impossible. Laing goes further and calls attention to the diagnostician's power in molding the patient's behavior so that it comes to conform to that associated with a diagnostic stereotype. Thus, far from being an objective guide to the prediction of the patient's behavior, diagnosis acts as a self-fulfilling prophecy. People become what they are called: schizophrenic, sociopathic, or neurotic. Beyond propounding these views, Laing has looked to their consequences for practice and has gone on to found an "antihospital" in England. In this setting the roles of patients and staff are deliberately blurred in order to allow everybody the freedom to explore fully the perspectives and possibilities inherent in unfettered psychotic experience. In this way treatment gives way to encounter; unilateral intervention is replaced by mutual learning.

Perhaps the most outspoken as well as the best-known critic of the concept of mental illness is Szasz (1961, 1969). The brunt of his criticism has been directed at the conceptual fallacy of equating problems of living with illness or disease, a term that is properly reserved for functional or structural disorders of bodily systems. Szasz contends that the consequences of this misapplication are far from being purely academic or semantic. Rather, they are injurious to all parties involved in the transaction: the person labeled mentally ill, the psychiatrist involved in labeling, and the public at large. The putative patient is stripped of his civil rights, removed from his customary context, and subjected to involuntary "treatment." The psychiatrists—as well as members of other mental health professions—are sidetracked from the exercise of functions for which they are professionally trained and legitimately equipped: those of helping to disentangle their voluntary clients' problems of living. Instead, they become custodians, judges, and policemen—tasks for which they lack both expertise and social sanction. At the same time, the public is victimized as regular legal processes are subverted through the creation of a category of people (the mentally ill) protected from the consequences of their acts and immune from prosecution. Sarbin's (1967, 1969) argument is similar in that it emphasizes both the semantic fallacy inherent in the concept of mental illness and the real-life consequences of this faulty categorization.

The objections of these writers overlap with those of a number of sociologically oriented investigators who have undertaken to analyze conceptually, investigate empirically, and illustrate clinically the adverse effects of imposing the label *mental illness* upon some classes of social deviance (Goffman, 1961, 1963; Scheff, 1966; Spitzer and Denzin, 1968). Social rejection, loss of status, and coercive social control have been highlighted among the consequences of such labeling. Moreover, these writers contend that the behavior of individuals designated mentally ill is primarily traceable to the setting in which they are placed and to the social control to which they are subjected. These formulations have received some independent empirical support from studies of the chronic-patient syndrome, reviewed by Paul (1969); from investigations of the response of mental health personnel to a normal individual who assumes the role of patient (Caudill, 1958; Rosenhan, 1973); and from accounts of real-life consequences of faulty psychiatric diagnoses (Zutt, 1970). On a broader plane, these sociological formulations are consonant with demonstrations, in both experimental and educational settings, that subjects' responses are shaped to fit observers' expectations (Rosenthal, 1967; Rosenthal and Jacobson, 1968). In an even more general sense, the sociological demonstrations are in keeping with the basic themes of behavior-modification and community mental health critiques of traditional diagnostic practices; all of them emphasize that the symptom is a product of the constant interplay between the individual and his milieu rather than a direct manifestation of any underlying intrapsychic pathology.

If these arguments are taken seriously, the response to them should be the abolition of all classificatory and labeling activity. But is such a course of action practical? Apparently not, since numerous writers (see, for instance, Jaspers, 1963; Thorne, 1967; Leary, 1970) have attempted to provide alternative modes of classification proceeding from existentialist and humanist premises. Jaspers reconceptualizes the traditional diagnostic scheme on an existentialist base. Thorne constructs an extremely elaborate novel typology of states of living. Leary proposes to restructure the classifying effort as a collaborative enterprise involving the classifier and the classified. Specifically, the classified (or individuals subject to classification) would provide the classifier with information about patterns of behavior that are similar or different among their peers and within their milieu. This use of subject groups as informants parallels the methodology of cultural anthropologists in the field. The resulting set of diagnostic categories would be flexible, unique to any given time and situation, and always open to revision in accordance with changes in the social perceptions of the participants.

Maladaptation in Children

The classification of childhood disorders involves some unique problems beyond the issues already cited. The child is a growing organism that has not fulfilled all its promise or realized all its shortcomings. How does one distinguish between disorder and developmental lag? Miller (1968, p. 262) warns: "We need strict semantic safeguards before giving a name to a fluid process which changes not only with the growth of each child but with each cultural landmark which the child reaches. Moreover, at each stage we are obliged to be alert for the emergence of these maturational signs, which a study of genetics can alone provide." As Eisenberg (1969) recognizes, the traditional approach to the classification of childhood mental disorders has been largely derivative and imitative of the descriptive psychiatry of adulthood. Thus, terms such as *childhood schizophrenia, childhood neurosis,* and even *depressions of childhood* have become part of the vocabulary of psychiatry. At the same time, until very recently, those behavioral disturbances of childhood without precise analogues in adult psychopathology have been lumped together under the catch-all label *primary behavior disorders of childhood.* This state of affairs carries with it two questionable and potentially harmful implications: (1) that the child is a miniature adult (a view that ignores developmental considerations) and (2) that children's disorders are but the early stages of analogous adult conditions, with ominous prognostic implications. Thus, many clinicians may infer that a child labeled *schizophrenic* will inevitably grow into an adult schizophrenic and that a child neurotic will become an adult neurotic. Several investigators (Robins, 1972; Rutter and Lockyear, 1967; Rutter, Greenfeld, and Lockyear, 1967) call into question such automatic progressions. On the basis of their findings, prognosis for childhood disorders is far more favorable than prior clinical judgment and earlier follow-up evidence with the identically named adult counterparts would suggest. These data strongly suggest that the core syndromes of childhood and their adult prototypes are qualitatively distinct.

To an even greater extent than with adults, classification of psychopathology in children is based on externally judged social transgressions, or deficiencies in intellectual or social performance. According to Eiduson (1968), two classes of information are used in describing psychiatric patients: disorder data (a self-contained, intrapsychic set of symptoms, as exemplified by a phobia) and system data (a continuing social interplay of action and reaction, as in the case of a dropout). It is our impression, in the absence of actual comparative studies along these lines in children and adults, that in children's disorders system data predominate over disorder data. The range of specifically symptomatic states in children is rather narrowly circumscribed; the scope of socially problematic behavior is wide and growing. Thus, the perception of deviant child behavior occurs in a context of adult expectations for acceptable patterns of behavior. Often, the idiosyncratic and judgmental perspectives and sensitivities of those observers who identify the disorder is not accorded specific recognition. Across cultures, a disorder as extreme as childhood autism is rarely seen even in the most sophisticated and specialized treatment facilities of India (personal communication, Ellen V. Piers, Pennsylvania State University) and is sanctified in West Africa (Zempleni and Rabain, 1965). Closer to home, aberrant behavior is more likely to be labeled *juvenile delinquency* when manifested by a lower-class rather than a middle-class child.

The complaints that bring a child to the attention of the clinical professions may be specific or vague, widely or minimally shared among relevant adults, and present across a wide or narrow range of environmental contexts. Present diagnostic labels, however, do not reflect such variations in context, and the label applied often becomes descriptive of the whole child in all settings and under all conditions. Thus, a child who reacts aggressively to a specific stimulus is often designated an *aggressive child*. Proponents of behavior modification (Ferster, 1965; Kanfer and Saslow, 1965) have been particularly explicit in calling attention to the dangers inherent in the assignment of such globally pejorative labels, but as yet few steps have been taken toward a situation-specific classification system.

Childhood disorder interweaves with normal developmental sequences, as well as within a context of the perceptions and expectations of significant adults. The designation of certain behaviors as deviant involves, then, both normative and ipsative judgments, established in relation to the child's own baseline and assumed central tendencies of his peers. This model is similar to Newbrough's (1973) formulation of psychological disorder as both a psychophysical act and a social process.

Several classification systems of child psychopathology have recently been proposed (Ferster, 1965; Förster, 1968; Freud, 1965; Group for the Advancement of Psychiatry, 1966; Rutter, Greenfeld, and Lockyear, 1967; Rutter and Lockyear, 1967; Rutter and others, 1969). All these schemes are multidimensional and attempt to take into account developmental sequences as well as to categorize the child's resources and strengths in addition to pathological systems and deficiencies. For example, the scheme developed by the Group for Advancement of Psychiatry incorporates references to developmental stages, degree of stress, and appropriateness of individual response. The result is a continuum from psychologically healthy through reactive responses to neurotic and psychotic dysfunction. Psychophysiological disorder, brain damage, and mental retardation remain outside this continuum but are explicitly recognized as separate diagnostic categories. In contrast, the approach of Rutter and his associates is more empirically based; it proceeds from presently established syndromes rather than from rational considerations. Such categories as the hyperkinetic child are maintained, as is a listing of educational retardation, independent of its antecedents in intellectual development or in neurotic dysfunction. This system is noteworthy for the authors' insistence that the disorder—and not the child— should be diagnosed.

As a younger and somewhat less traditional field of inquiry, child psychopathology—in comparison with the more traditional fields—has made substantial use of factorial and typological techniques (Achenbach, 1966; Jenkins, 1966, 1969; Kobayashi, Mizushima, and Shinohara, 1967; Patterson, 1964; Peterson, 1961; Quay, 1964; Quay and Quay, 1965), especially in charting lines of coherence and differentiation in peripheral areas such as juvenile delinquency. The increased differentiation in this area of dysfunction shown in the revised *Diagnostic and Statistical Manual* (American Psychiatric Association, 1968) is to a large extent the consequence of this research.

To summarize, the field of child psychopathology is faced with three challenges in attempting to group, differentiate, and name the various disorders of childhood. First, it is involved in a gradual process of emancipation from the models of adult psychopathology, both in concepts and in terminology. This progression is not yet complete, and a child-centered system of classification is not fully developed or articulated. Second, the field of child psychopathology is gradually coming to grips with the plasticity of adaptive and maladaptive processes in children, and with their potential for an often thoroughgoing modification over brief spans of time. This consideration highlights the need for a classification of behaviors and not of personalities, of disorders and not of individuals. It rests on the recognition that, in children, a disorder is typically a temporary state. Third, there is movement toward greater degrees of incorporation of empirical data on childhood disorders and on normal progressions of development. The gulf is narrowing between multivariate and other research on children's disorders and the diagnostic practices in hospitals and clinics. At the same time, the gap between child psychopathology and developmental psychology is gradually being bridged.

Current Trends

Transcending the several theoretical positions presented earlier, there is a tendency toward what elsewhere (Draguns and Phillips, 1971) has been called "dereification" of diagnostic concepts and labels, implicit in the recognition of their conditional metaphorical nature (Price, 1972). On the most basic level, there is an increasingly shared awareness of the noncorrespondence between the objects of clinical experience (that is, the observable behavior of psychologically disturbed individuals) and the designations applied to them. This lack of correspondence is traceable in part to the features of the diagnostic system in use—features that can be corrected. In part, however, it is the consequence of the simplification and distortion inherent in fitting unique cases into general categories and, as such, is not subject to correction. But in spite of these problems, classificatory activities and concepts have not been rejected; rather, there is simply a greater self-consciousness in their use. The numerous conferences, symposia, and volumes recently devoted to diagnosis and classification (for example, Eron, 1966; Katz, Cole, and Barton, 1968; Mahrer, 1970; Price, 1972) bear testimony to

this trend. Underlying this burst of self-examination is the implicit recognition that classification is to be scrutinized, reformulated, streamlined, and revised, but not abandoned or dis-
mantled. For a variety of compelling practical and theoretical
reasons, the task of assessing and classifying individuals faced
with problems of adaptation is here to stay.

This concern with reevaluating psychiatric classification
has had tangible consequences. Most important, it has led to an
increased awareness of the functional clinical utility of specific
diagnostic labels and of the broader social consequences that
stem from the application of diagnostic designation. The following questions are increasingly asked: What role does the attribution of a diagnostic label have in the chain of clinical decisions
that affect the interventions and treatments of the individual so
labeled? What is the functional utility of diagnostic categorization in terms of differential treatment? Many critics of the
traditional diagnostic scheme (Arthur, 1968, 1969; Kanfer and
Saslow, 1965; Zigler and Phillips, 1961) have answered these
questions negatively; others (Kramer, 1968; Meehl, 1959;
Zubin, 1967) have defended the pragmatic usefulness of classifying individuals in diagnostic categories. However, there is a
broad consensus that the consequences of psychiatric diagnosis
do not end with the professional interventions instituted.
Rather, it is now widely recognized that a varying, if sizable,
proportion of surplus meaning accrues to terms originally devised as technical and neutral designations. "The word *hysteric*
is often more expressive of insult than of diagnosis. The same
can be said of *psychopathy,* and we are now witnessing something similar happening to the term *schizophrenia.* That is why
some psychiatrists are reluctant to diagnose, as though they
were dealing with emotionally overinvested labels. . . . The same
attitude comes into play in the eventual segregation of psychiatric patients from society; physically, this segregation is
brought about by walls and laws; socially, it is accomplished by
diagnostic attribution" (Lopez Ibor, 1968, p. 65).

Some writers (for instance, Sarbin, 1967, 1969) want to
abandon such emotionally charged labels. Others want merely
to redefine them or to recognize their technical and conditional
character (Ellis, 1967; Begelman, 1971). Perhaps a point on
which everybody would agree is the need for careful monitoring
of potential and actual misuses of diagnosis by professionals
(Zutt, 1970), the lay public (Torrey, 1972), and holders of

political power (*A.P.A. Monitor*, 1973; Szasz, 1971). To this end, sociological analyses (Schroder and Ehrlich, 1968) and descriptive accounts of the social effects of psychiatric attribution (Goffman, 1961; Zutt, 1970) need to be continued and extended.

Concomitant with the emphasis on the social consequences and functional utility of diagnostic attribution, greater attention is being paid to technical standards for diagnostic classification. This concern goes far beyond mere determination of the validity and reliability of diagnostic labels. Rather, the size of diagnostic units, their specificity, and their inclusiveness are at issue (Blashfield, 1972). Moreover, those concerned with psychiatric classifications now realize that their problems are shared by a number of other taxonomic disciplines, from botany and zoology to library science, and that revisions of psychiatric nosology can be informed by the experience of these other fields of inquiry.

All the foregoing trends argue for the flexibility of classificatory systems in psychopathology. It remains to spell out the recommendations arising from these trends on the national level, and especially in reference to children.

First, and most important, recent thinking and research on psychiatric diagnosis argue for a system that is pragmatic, provisional, and explicitly open to change in response to experience, modification of rationale or purpose, or discovery of its adverse consequences. More specifically, the development and adoption of a classificatory system should carry with it provisions for its study and use and for modifications resulting from any discoveries of previously unanticipated undesirable human outcomes. This proposal is but the application of Campbell's (1971) much broader conception of reforms as experiments.

Second, the internal adequacy of a classificatory system needs to be investigated—not only initially but continuously. Does the system incorporate the findings of empirical research (see Phillips and Draguns, 1971)? Admittedly, the gulf between research results and clinically used classification has never been as wide in the case of children as it continues to be with adults. In particular, *DSM-II* has taken into account the factorial research of Jenkins (1966, 1968). But this, in any case, is only a modest beginning, since the empirical study of classification has advanced considerably beyond the mere identification of clusters, factors, and types.

Third, a problem specific to the classification of children needs to be tackled. As already pointed out, a child is of necessity classified by a specially trained adult. Moreover, the development of descriptive psychiatry with adults antedates by far the efforts to group and label the psychological disorders of children. The clinical professions and their practitioners should therefore be on guard against what, for lack of a better term, we will call the pitfalls of "adultomorphism," the tendency to see in the disorders of children the replicas and predecessors of analogously named conditions in adults.

Fourth, psychiatric classification of children needs to be accomplished in relation to particular stages of development (Freud, 1965; Santostefano, 1971), with the implication that many problems of adaptation are stage-specific and often self-corrective. In the theoretical literature on psychopathological nosology, much attention has been focused on the issue of whether the objects of classification are people, their behaviors, or an interaction of the two. In the diagnostic labeling of children, it is important to keep in mind that the object of classification is a child's behavior at a particular stage of his growth. The issue is both an evaluative and a normative one. What should be expected of a child, and why? At what age level does the behavior in question typically or universally occur? What are the immediate and long-range consequences of a developmental lag in a particular dimension of behavior?

Fifth, the requirements of informative, flexible, and realistic diagnosis argue for a multidimensional diagnosis. A discrete one- or two-word label never conveys sufficient information about the child in question. Development progresses and lags unevenly; condensing descriptive data about a child in a unitary typological label runs the risk of maximizing surplus meaning; fostering stereotypes; and onesidedly concentrating on maladaptive aspects of functioning, to the exclusion of adaptive ones. Described along several axes, a child is less likely to be turned into a type, either clinically or socially. Pragmatically, information on the child's social competence is at least as important as is the catalog of his supposed or real defects.

Sixth, children's normal and pathological behavior being to a high degree situation-specific, information on the situational context of the child's behavior and its fluctuations is mandatory for its complete description. The absence of such information invites overgeneralization, a cognitive leap from some to all. Too much is known about the self-fulfilling effect of expectations (Rosenthal, 1967; Paul, 1969; Rosenhan, 1973; Rosenthal and Jacobson, 1968) to allow these dangers to go unchecked.

Seventh and last, several of the considerations presented imply that the issues in construing, classifying, and labeling deviant behavior in children transcend the boundaries of the mental health professions. Rather, how to group and name these behaviors is a matter of general social concern. Moreover, whereas child psychiatrists and child clinical psychologists recognize the provisional, conditional, flexible, and multidimensional character of the classificatory scheme, the public all too often regards nosological entities as substantive and immutable or, at least, difficult to change. Accordingly, there is an imperative need to close this information gap between professionals and the public at large, especially the members of the several professions whose decisions and activities crucially impinge upon the lives of children: teachers, social workers, policemen, judges, and public officials. In proposing this course of action, we are on guard against excessive simplification and optimism. Surely, it will take more than translating some of the innovative positions on diagnosis into nontechnical language to assure their acceptance. The view that child psychopathology is a matter of a finite number of mental illnesses is too deeply ingrained in the minds of the public at large to yield easily in response to novel information. Sarbin and Mancuso (1970) have recently demonstrated how little the traditional mental health campaigns have accomplished in several decades of attempts at changing public attitudes toward the "mentally ill." Yet, a start must be made. The progressive dereification of diagnostic labels is a long-range objective that cannot be attained without continuous interaction with the citizenry—or at least its interested, concerned, and responsive segments.

We recognize, then, that classification is an indispensable administrative and clinical activity, and we part company with those who sweepingly suggest the abolition of all efforts at categorizing people (Laing, 1967; Szasz, 1969). Instead, we advocate the development of a practical, flexible, empirically based classificatory system—a system that will maximize the efficiency of behavioral prediction at the least possible cost in human suffering.

References

Achenbach, T. M. "The Classification of Children's Psychiatric Symptoms: A Factor-Analytic Study." *Psychological Monographs*, 1966, *80*(7).

Albee, G. W. "Emerging Concepts of Mental Illness and Models of Treatment: The Psychological Points of View." *American Journal of Psychiatry*, 1969, *125*, 870-876.

American Psychiatric Association. *Diagnostic and Statistical Manual of Mental Disorders (DSM-I)*. Washington, D.C.: American Psychiatric Association, 1952.

American Psychiatric Association. *Diagnostic and Statistical Manual of Mental Disorders (DSM-II)*. (2nd Ed.) Washington, D.C.: American Psychiatric Association, 1968.

A.P.A. Monitor. "Council Expresses Concern for P.O.W.'s, Use of Therapy for Political Purposes." *A.P.A. Monitor*, 1973, 4(1), 1.

Arieti, S. (Ed.) *American Handbook of Psychiatry*. (2 vols.) New York: Basic Books, 1959.

Arthur, A. Z. "Is Diagnosis Really Necessary?" *Ontario Psychological Association Quarterly*, 1968, *21*, 12-16.

Arthur, A. Z. "Diagnostic Testing and New Alternatives." *Psychological Bulletin*, 1969, *72*, 183-192.

Ayllon, T., and Michael, J. "The Psychiatric Nurse as a Behavioral Engineer." *Journal of Experimental Analysis of Behavior*, 1959, *2*, 323-334.

Begelman, D. A. "Misnaming, Metaphors, the Medical Model, and Some Muddles." *Psychiatry*, 1971, *34*, 38-58.

Blashfield, R. K. "An Evaluation of the *DSM-II* Classification of Schizophrenia." Unpublished doctoral dissertation, Indiana University, 1972.

Bleuler, M. (Ed.) *Eugen Bleuler's Lehrbuch der Psychiatrie*. Heidelberg: Springer, 1969.

Campbell, D. T. "Research Methods for the Experimenting Society." Invited address, Eastern Psychological Association, New York, April 1971.

Caudill, W. A. *The Psychiatric Hospital as a Small Society*. Cambridge: Harvard University Press, 1958.

Caveny, E., and others. "Psychiatric Diagnosis, Its Nature and Function." *Journal of Nervous and Mental Disease*, 1955, *121*, 367-380.

Cohen, R. "Objektive Klassifikationsverfahren." *Bulletin der Schweizerischen Akademie der Medizinischen Wissenschaften*, 1970, *25*, 125-141.

Cole, L. E. *Understanding Abnormal Behavior*, Scranton, Pa.: Chandler, 1970.

Coleman, J. C., and Broen, W. E. *Abnormal Psychology and Modern Life*. (4th Ed.) Glenview, Ill.: Scott, Foresman, 1972.

Coppen, A. "The Biochemistry of Affective Disorders." *British Journal of Psychiatry*, 1967, *113*, 103-137.

Draguns, J. G. "Comparisons of Psychopathology Across Cultures: Issues, Findings, Directions." *Journal of Cross-Cultural Psychology*, 1973, *4*, 9-47.

Draguns, J. G., and Phillips, L. *Psychiatric Classification and Diagnosis: An Overview and Critique.* Morristown, N.J.: General Learning Press, 1971.

Draguns, J. G., and Phillips, L. *Culture and Psychopathology: The Quest for a Relationship.* Morristown, N.J.: General Learning Press, 1972.

Draguns, J. G., and others. "Social Competence and Psychiatric Symptomatology in Japan: A Cross-Cultural Extension of Earlier American Findings." *Journal of Abnormal Psychology*, 1970, *75*, 68-73.

Draguns, J. G., and others. "Symptomatology of Hospitalized Psychiatric Patients in Japan and in the United States: A Study of Cultural Differences." *Journal of Nervous and Mental Diseases*, 1971, *152*, 3-16.

Eiduson, B. T. "The Two Classes of Information in Psychiatry." *Archives of General Psychiatry*, 1968, *18*, 405-419.

Eisenberg, L. "Child Psychiatry: The Past Quarter Century." *American Journal of Orthopsychiatry*, 1969, *39*, 389-401.

Ekman, G., and Sjoberg, L. "Scaling." *Annual Review of Psychology*, 1965, *16*, 451-474.

Ellis, A. "Should Some People Be Labeled Mentally Ill?" *Journal of Consulting Psychology*, 1967, *31*, 435-446.

Eron, L. D. (Ed.) *Classification of Behavior Disorders.* Chicago: Aldine, 1966.

Ferster, C. B. "Classification of Behavior Pathology." In L. Krasner and L. P. Ullmann (Eds.), *Research in Behavior Pathology.* New York: Holt, 1965.

Förster, E. "Entwurf einer Systematik der psychogenen Storungen aus der Sicht der jugendpsychiatrischen Praxis." In E. Förster and K. H. Wewetzer (Eds.), *Systematik der psychogenen Storungen.* Berne: Huber, 1968.

Foulds, G. A. *Personality and Personal Illness.* London: Tavistock, 1965.

Franks, C. M. *Behavior Therapy: Appraisal and Status.* New York: McGraw-Hill, 1969.

Freedman, A. M., and Kaplan, H. I. (Eds.) *Comprehensive Textbook of Psychiatry.* Baltimore: Williams and Wilkins, 1967.

Freud, A. *Normality and Pathology in Childhood.* New York: International Universities Press, 1965.

Fundia, T. A. de, Draguns, J. G., and Phillips, L. "Culture and Psychiatric Symptomatology: A Comparison of Argentine and United States Patients." *Social Psychiatry*, 1971, *6*, 11-20.

Gardner, E. A. "The Role of the Classification System in Outpatient Psychiatry." In M. M. Katz, J. O. Cole, and W. E. Barton (Eds.),

The Role and Methodology of Classification in Psychiatry and Psychopathology. Washington, D.C.: U.S. Government Printing Office, 1968.

Goffman, E. *Asylums: Essays on the Social Situations of Mental Patients and Other Inmates.* New York: Anchor, 1961.

Goffman, E. *Stigma: Notes on the Management of Spoiled Identity.* Englewood Cliffs, N.J.: Prentice-Hall, 1963.

Goldfried, M. R., and Kent, R. N. "Traditional Versus Behavioral Personality Assessment: A Comparison of Methodological and Theoretical Assumptions." *Psychological Bulletin,* 1972, *77,* 409-420.

Group for the Advancement of Psychiatry. *Psychopathological Disorders in Childhood: Theoretical Considerations and a Proposed Classification.* G.A.P. Report No. 62. New York: Group for Advancement of Psychiatry, 1966.

Hammond, K. R., Hursch, C. J., and Todd, F. J. "Analyzing the Components of Clinical Inference." *Psychological Review,* 1964, *71,* 438-456.

Hersch, C. "The Discontent Explosion in Mental Health." *American Psychologist,* 1968, *23,* 497-506.

Hersch, C. "From Mental Health to Social Action: Clinical Psychology in Historical Perspective." *American Psychologist,* 1969, *24,* 909-916.

Hunt, W. A., Wittson, C. L., and Hunt, E. B. "A Theoretical and Practical Analysis of the Diagnostic Process." In P. Hoch and J. Zubin (Eds.), *Current Problems in Psychiatric Diagnosis.* New York: Grune and Stratton, 1953.

Jaffe, R. "Psychiatric Classification and Theories." *Israel Annals of Psychiatry and Related Disciplines,* 1969, *7,* 145-157.

Jaspers, K. *General Psychopathology.* Chicago: University of Chicago Press, 1963.

Jenkins, R. L. "Psychiatric Syndromes in Children and Their Relation to Family Background." *American Journal of Orthopsychiatry,* 1966, *36,* 450-457.

Jenkins, R. L. "The Varieties of Children's Behavioral Problems and Family Dynamics." *American Journal of Psychiatry,* 1968, *124,* 1440-1445.

Jenkins, R. L. "Classification of Behavior Problems in Children." *American Journal of Psychiatry,* 1969, *125,* 1032-1039.

Kanfer, F. H., and Saslow, G. "Behavioral Analysis: An Alternative to Diagnostic Classification." *Archives of General Psychiatry,* 1965, *12,* 848-853.

Katz, M. M., Cole, J. O., and Barton, W. E. (Eds.) *The Role and Methodology of Classification in Psychiatry and Psychopathology.* Washington, D.C.: U.S. Government Printing Office, 1968.

Kety, S. S. "Biochemical Theories of Schizophrenia." *Science,* 1959, *129,* 1528-1532, 1590-1596

Kiev, A. *Transcultural Psychiatry.* New York: Free Press, 1972.

Kobayashi, S., Mizushima, K., and Shinohara, M. "Clinical Groupings of Children Based on Symptoms and Behavior." *International Journal of Social Psychiatry*, 1967, *13*, 206-215.

Kramer, M. "Classification of Mental Disorders for Epidemiologic and Medical Care Purposes: Current Status, Problems, and Needs." In M. M. Katz, J. O. Cole, and W. E. Barton (Eds.), *The Role and Methodology of Classification in Psychiatry and Psychopathology.* Washington, D.C.: U.S. Government Printing Office, 1968.

Lacquaniti, A. "Un contributo al depistage clinico delle tendenze nevtotiche in ambiente di lavore." *Medicina di Lavore*, 1967, *58*, 3-15.

Laing, R. D. "The Study of Family and Social Contexts in Relation to the Origin of Schizophrenia." In J. Romano (Ed.), *Origins of Schizophrenia.* Amsterdam: Excerpta Medica, 1967.

Leary, T. "The Diagnosis of Behavior and the Diagnosis of Experience." In A. R. Mahrer (Ed.), *New Approaches to Personality Classification.* New York: Columbia University Press, 1970.

Lenz, H. "Vergleichende psychopathologische Forschung in historischer Sicht." In *Proceedings, Fourth World Congress of Psychiatry.* Vol. 1. Amsterdam: Excerpta Medica, 1968.

London, P., and Rosenhan, D. (Eds.) *Foundations of Abnormal Psychology.* New York: Holt, 1969.

Lopez Ibor, J. J. "Discurso de apertura." In *Proceedings, Fourth World Congress of Psychiatry.* Vol. 1. Amsterdam: Excerpta Medica, 1968.

Mahrer, A. R. (Ed.) *New Approaches to Personality Classification.* New York: Columbia University Press, 1970.

Maslow, A. "Resistance to Being Rubricized." In B. Kaplan and S. Wapner (Eds.), *Perspectives in Psychological Theory.* New York: International Universities Press, 1960.

Mayer-Gross, W., Slater, E., and Roth, M. *Clinical Psychiatry.* (3rd Ed.) Baltimore: Williams and Wilkins, 1969.

Meehl, P. "Some Ruminations on the Validation of Clinical Procedures." *Canadian Journal of Psychology*, 1959, *13*, 102-138.

Menninger, K. *The Vital Balance.* New York: Viking, 1963.

Miller, E. "The Problem of Classification in Child Psychiatry." In E. Miller (Ed.), *Foundations of Child Psychiatry.* Oxford: Pergamon, 1968.

Nachshon, I., and others. "Psychiatric Symptomatology as a Function of Acculturation: A Study of an Israeli Child Guidance Clinic Population." *International Journal of Social Psychiatry*, 1972, *7*, 109-118.

Nathan, P. E., and others. "Thirty-Two Observers and One Patient: A Study of Diagnostic Reliability." *Journal of Clinical Psychology*, 1969, *25*, 9-15.

Newbrough, J. R. "Concepts of Behavior Disorder." In S. E. Golann and C. Eisdorfer (Eds.), *Handbook of Community Psychology.* New York: Appleton-Century-Crofts, 1973.

Osmond, H., and Hoffer, A. "A Comprehensive Theory of Schizophrenia." *International Journal of Neuropsychiatry*, 1968, *2*, 302-309.

Patterson, G. R. "An Empirical Approach to the Classification of Disturbed Children." *Journal of Clinical Psychology*, 1964, *20*, 326-337.

Paul, G. L. "Chronic Mental Patient: Current Status, Future Directions." *Psychological Bulletin*, 1969, *71*, 81-94.

Peterson, D. R. "Behavior Problems of Middle Childhood." *Journal of Consulting Psychology*, 1961, *25*, 205-209.

Petras, J. W., and Curtis, J. E. "The Current Literature on Social Class and Mental Disease in America: Critique and Bibliography." *Behavioral Science*, 1968, *13*, 382-398.

Pfeiffer, W. *Transkulturelle Psychiatrie*. Stuttgart: Thieme, 1968.

Phillips, L. "The Competence Criterion for Mental Health Programs." *Community Mental Health Journal*, 1967, *3*, 73-76.

Phillips, L. *Human Adaptation and Its Failures*. New York: Academic Press, 1968a.

Phillips, L. "A Social View of Psychopathology." In P. London and D. Rosenhan (Eds.), *Foundations of Abnormal Psychology*. New York: Holt, 1968b.

Phillips, L., Broverman, I. K., and Zigler, E. "Social Competence and Psychiatric Diagnosis." *Journal of Abnormal Psychology*, 1966, *71*, 209-214.

Phillips, L., Broverman, I. K., and Zigler, E. "Sphere Dominance, Role Orientation, and Diagnosis." *Journal of Abnormal Psychology*, 1968, *73*, 306-312.

Phillips, L., and Draguns, J. G. "Classification of the Behavior Disorders." *Annual Review of Psychology*, 1971, *22*, 447-482.

Pitts, F. N., Jr., and McClure, I. N., Jr. "Lactate Metabolism in Anxiety Neurosis." *New England Journal of Medicine*, 1967, *277*, 1329-1336.

Price, R. H. *Abnormal Behavior: Perspectives in Conflict*. New York: Holt, 1972.

Quay, H. C. "Dimensions of Personality in Delinquent Boys as Inferred from the Factor Analysis of Case History Data." *Child Development*, 1964, *35*, 479-484.

Quay, H. C., and Quay, L. C. "Behavior Problems of Early Adolescence." *Child Development*, 1965, *36*, 215-220.

Robins, L. N. "Follow-Up Studies of Behavior Disorders in Children." In H. C. Quay and J. S. Werry (Eds.), *Psychopathological Disorders of Childhood*. New York: Wiley, 1972.

Rogers, C. R. *Client-Centered Therapy*. Boston: Houghton Mifflin, 1951.

Rosenhan, D. "On Being Sane in Insane Places." *Science*, 1973, *179*, 250-259.

Rosenthal, R. "Covert Communication in the Psychological Experiment." *Psychological Bulletin*, 1967, *67*, 356-367.

Rosenthal, R., and Jacobson, L. *Pygmalion in the Classroom: Teachers' Expectations and Pupils' Intellectual Development.* New York: Holt, 1968.

Rutter, M., Greenfeld, D., and Lockyear, L. "A Five to Fifteen Year Follow-Up Study of Infantile Psychosis. II: Social and Behavioral Outcome." *British Journal of Psychiatry,* 1967, *113,* 1183-1199.

Rutter, M., and Lockyear, L. "A Five to Fifteen Year Follow-Up Study of Infantile Psychosis. I: Description of Sample." *British Journal of Psychiatry,* 1967, *113,* 1169-1182.

Rutter, M., and others. "A Tri-Axial Classification of Mental Disorders in Childhood." *Journal of Child Psychology and Psychiatry,* 1969, *10,* 41-61.

Santostefano, S. "Beyond Nosology: Diagnosis from the Viewpoint of Development." In H. E. Rie (Ed.), *Perspectives in Child Psychopathology.* Chicago: Aldine, 1971.

Sarason, I. G., and Ganzer, V. J. "Concerning the Medical Model." *American Psychologist,* 1968, *23,* 507-510.

Sarbin, T. R. "On the Futility of the Proposition that Some People Be Labeled 'Mentally Ill.' " *Journal of Consulting Psychology,* 1967, *31,* 447-453.

Sarbin, T. R. "The Scientific Status of the Mental Illness Metaphor." In S. C. Plog and R. B. Edgerton (Eds.), *Changing Perspectives of Mental Illness.* New York: Holt, 1969.

Sarbin, T. R., and Mancuso, J. C. "Failure of a Moral Enterprise: Attitudes of the Public Toward Mental Illness." *Journal of Consulting and Clinical Psychology,* 1970, *35,* 159-173.

Scheff, T. J. *Being Mentally Ill: A Sociological Theory.* Chicago: Aldine, 1966.

Schooler, C., and Caudill, W. "Symptomatology in Japanese and American Schizophrenics." *Ethnology,* 1964, *3,* 172-177.

Schroder, D., and Ehrlich, D. "Rejection by Mental Health Professionals: A Possible Consequence of Not Seeking Appropriate Help for Emotional Disorders." *Journal of Health and Social Behavior,* 1968, *9,* 222-232.

Scott, W. A. "Research Definitions of Mental Health and Mental Illness." *Psychological Bulletin,* 1958, *55,* 29-45.

Seifert, J. A., Draguns, J. G., and Caudill, W. "Role Orientation, Sphere Dominance, and Social Competence as Bases of Psychiatric Diagnosis in Japan: A Replication and Extension of American Findings." *Journal of Abnormal Psychology,* 1971, *78,* 101-108.

Shields, J., and Slater, E. "Heredity and Psychological Abnormality." In H. J. Eysenck (Ed.), *Handbook of Abnormal Psychology.* New York: Basic Books, 1961.

Sjobring, H. *Struktur och Utveckling.* Lund: Gleerups, 1958.

Spitzer, S. P., and Denzin, N. K. *The Mental Patient: Studies in the Sociology of Deviance.* New York: McGraw-Hill, 1968.

Stone, L. A., and Skurdal, M. A. "Judged Prognosis for Functional Psycho-
    sis Disorder Classifications: A Prothetic Continuum." *Journal of
    Consulting and Clinical Psychology*, 1968, *32*, 469-472.
Suinn, R. M. *Fundamentals of Behavior Pathology.* New York: Wiley,
    1970.
Szasz, T. S. *The Myth of Mental Illness.* New York: Harper, 1961.
Szasz, T. S. "Psychiatric Classification as a Strategy of Social Constraint."
    In T. S. Szasz (Ed.), *Ideology and Insanity.* Garden City, N.Y.:
    Doubleday, 1969.
Szasz, T. S. *The Manufacture of Madness.* New York: Harper, 1971.
Teja, J. S., Narang, R. L., and Aggarwal, A. K. "Depression Across Cul-
    tures." *British Journal of Psychiatry*, 1971, *119*, 253-260.
Thorne, F. C. *Integrative Psychology.* Brandon, Vt.: Clinical Psychology
    Publishing Company, 1967.
Thorne, F. C., and Nathan, P. E. "The General Validity of Official Diag-
    nostic Classification." *Journal of Clinical Psychology*, 1969, *25*,
    375-383.
Torrey, E. F. *The Mind Game: Witchdoctors and Psychiatrists.* New York:
    Emerson Hall, 1972.
Ullmann, L. P., and Krasner, L. "Introduction." In L. P. Ullmann and L.
    Krasner (Eds.), *Case Studies in Behavior Modification.* New York:
    Holt, 1965.
Ullmann, L. P., and Krasner, L. *A Psychological Approach to Abnormal
    Behavior.* Englewood Cliffs, N.J.: Prentice-Hall, 1969.
Varga, E., and Nyiro, G. "A Study of Neurosis in Budapest: A Social-
    Psychiatric Analysis of Clinical Cases Occurring in a Period of 30
    Years." *Psychiatria et Neurologia*, 1968, *153*, 37-52.
Weitbrecht, H. J. *Grundriss der Psychiatrie.* Berlin: Springer, 1969.
Whybrow, P. C., and Mendels, J. "Toward a Biology of Depression: Some
    Suggestions from Neurophysiology." *American Journal of Psychia-
    try*, 1969, *125*, 1491-1500.
Wittenborn, J., Holzberg, J., and Simon, B. "Symptom Correlates for De-
    scriptive Diagnosis." *Genetic Psychology Monographs*, 1953, *47*,
    237-301.
Yates, A. *Behavior Therapy.* New York: Wiley, 1970.
Zempleni, A., and Rabain, J. "L'enfant Nit Ku Bon. Un tableau psycho-
    pathologique traditionnel chez les Wolof et Lebou du Sénégal."
    Psychopathologie Africaine, 1965, *1*, 329-441.
Zigler, E., and Phillips, L. "Social Effectiveness and Symptomatic Behav-
    iors." *Journal of Abnormal and Social Psychology*, 1960, *62*,
    231-238.
Zigler, E., and Phillips, L. "Psychiatric Diagnosis: A Critique." *Journal of
    Abnormal and Social Psychology*, 1961, *63*, 607-618.
Zigler, E., and Phillips, L. "Social Competence and the Process-Reactive
    Distinction in Psychopathology." *Journal of Abnormal and Social
    Psychology*, 1962, *64*, 215-222.

Zubin, J. "Classification of the Behavior Disorders." *Annual Review of Psychology*, 1967, *18*, 373-406.

Zubin, J. "Perspectives on the Conference." In M. M. Katz, J. O. Cole, and W. E. Barton (Eds.), *The Role and Methodology of Classification in Psychiatry and Psychopathology*. Washington, D.C.: U.S. Government Printing Office, 1968.

Zutt, J. *Freiheitsverlust und Freiheitsentziehung*. Berlin: Springer, 1970.

3

DIAGNOSIS AND
CLASSIFICATION IN
EPIDEMIOLOGICAL
AND
HEALTH-SERVICES
RESEARCH

Morton Kramer

This chapter concerns the fundamental role of classification in the design and implementation of epidemiological research and in the collection and analysis of statistics on health services and their activities. Although the concepts presented relate essentially to research and service activities in the fields of public health and health care, they are generally applicable to similar activities in other subdivisions of the many fields now included under the umbrella term *human services*.

The chapter has two major themes. The first is that classifications of many kinds of phenomena are essential in our efforts to acquire knowledge to prevent and control disease, disability, and social problems and to promote physical, mental, and social well-being. These include classifications of persons; populations of which they are members; environments—physical, biological, and social—in which they live, work, and play; diseases, injuries, disabilities, and social problems which affect them from conception to death; causes of death; psychological, attitudinal, and cultural factors that affect their behavior, role functioning, value systems, mate selection, and styles of life; political, educational, health, social, correctional, and related human-service agencies and institutions; and many other things.

The following quotation sets the background for the second theme: "The protection and promotion of the health and welfare of our citizens is considered to be one of the most important functions of the modern state. This function is the embodiment of a public policy based on political, economic, social, and ethical considerations" (Rosen, 1958, p. 17). This theme is that classifications of the various factors previously listed constitute an essential part of the armamentarium of the modern state in carrying out its health protection and promotion functions. They are basic to the processes used to produce data required by governmental and nongovernmental agencies, and the private sector of the human-service-delivery industry, for planning and administering programs that apply knowledge to prevent and control disease; to treat and rehabilitate affected persons; to remove physical, social, economic, attitudinal, and other barriers to optimum delivery and utilization of available services; and to evaluate the quality and effectiveness of programs and services designed to protect and promote the health of individual citizens and of the communities in which they live.

In addition, classification of persons is the essential process in determining their eligibility for various health and social benefits and services to which they may be entitled and in the evaluation of their claims for such benefits. Governmental agencies must classify applicants to determine their eligibility for benefits provided by federal, state, and local laws and their claims for such benefits; nongovernmental social agencies carry out similar procedures in relation to the services and benefits they provide; commercial health insurance companies apply their criteria to determine an applicant's eligibility for their

plans and to evaluate covered persons' claims for reimburse-
ment. In short, classification plays a vital role in society and
affects the lives of all of us.

Epidemiology

A discussion of basic notions and statistical indices used
in epidemiological research and of the uses of knowledge so
gained will demonstrate the need for the great variety of classifications mentioned above.

Definitions. For a long time the term *epidemiology* was
commonly associated with the study of explosive outbreaks of
communicable diseases. However, the techniques used in the
study of communicable diseases were found to be quite applicable to the study of noncommunicable diseases and their sequelae. As a result, the concept of epidemiology has broadened
over the years. Although there are many definitions of epidemiology, the following is perhaps most appropriate for this
chapter: "[Epidemiology is] a science concerned with the study
of factors that influence the occurrence and distribution of disease, defect, disability, or death in aggregations of individuals"
(Clark, 1953, p. 31).

Gordon (1950, pp. 20-21) has interpreted epidemiology
as medical ecology:

> Many kinds of evidence from the field, from clinical
> studies, and from accumulated laboratory investigations
> contribute to an interpretation of epidemiology as medical
> ecology, wherein disease and health are seen as no more
> than selected instances among the many results of the total
> interaction between man and his environment. Ecology is
> the biological discipline concerning the general phenomena
> of mutual relationships between living organisms and their
> reaction to animate and inanimate surroundings. That part
> of human ecology relating to health and disease is medical
> ecology, and as it concerns groups of communities of peo-
> ple, it is epidemiology. With disease and injury regarded as
> problems of ecology, their behavior qualitatively and quan-
> titatively is a matter dependent upon the kind of balance,
> the nature of the biological equilibrium, currently existing
> between a living organism and its environment, more partic-
> ularly between the agents of disease and the human host. In
> every sense this is a state of balance that varies from time to
> time and under a variety of circumstances.

This theme is amplified in other publications (Gordon, 1952, 1958; Gordon and others, 1952).

In effect, "epidemiology relates observed distributions of disorders to the environments in which people live—the physical, biological, and social environments" (Gruenberg, 1968, p. 76).

Method. Merrell and Reed (1949, p. 105) provide the following description of the essence of the epidemiological method:

> The study of the epidemiology of some thing or event—cancer, for example—involves a recognition of the event we are talking about, so that the population can be separated into those who have cancer and those who have not. Moreover, the study demands classification of the population on other axes to determine the important related factors that single out those particular people for attack. Are they different in inheritance, in nutrition, in occupation, etc., from the rest of the population?
>
> Considerable imagination is required in seeking out the pertinent variable to study. We may search along one axis of classification assiduously and neglect some other more relevant one, and thus the real relationship may elude us. . . . If we are able to separate our population with regard to the event whose epidemiology we are studying and if we are able to relate this classification to the factors which produce it, we will understand the epidemiology of the event.

The above paragraphs emphasize two important requirements for epidemiological research: (1) We must recognize the condition we are talking about, so that we can classify members of a population into those who have it and those who do not. (2) We must classify the population on a variety of axes, in order to determine why certain persons are singled out for attack. Epidemiological studies of some conditions (for example, mental disorders as a group or specific subtypes such as behavior disorders of children) are hampered seriously by the lack of case-finding techniques which permit separation of the members of a population into those who have the conditions and those who do not: "Since description of the distribution of any disease in a population obviously requires that the disease must be recognized when it occurs, the development of epidemiology must follow and be limited by that of clinical diagnosis and of the rather complex machinery required for the systematic collection of morbidity and mortality statistics" (Frost, 1941, p. 496).

Many of the conditions that are the concern of this project present difficult problems in clinical diagnosis. Much research is needed to solve them and to provide the knowledge for developing highly sensitive and specific diagnostic instruments and valid and reliable case-finding procedures (Wilson and Jungner, 1968, p. 21; Reid, 1960, p. 66).

Classification for a purpose. Development of appropriate classifications to elucidate various aspects of the phenomenon being studied also poses many difficult problems. A basic tenet is that the classification must be relevant to the purposes for which the data are being collected. The importance of this fundamental principle has been underscored by the World Health Organization (1967, p. vii):

> Classification is fundamental to the quantitative study of any phenomenon. It is recognized as the basis of all scientific generalization and is therefore an essential element in statistical methodology. Uniform definitions and uniform systems of classification are prerequisites in the advancement of scientific knowledge. In the study of illness and death, therefore, a standard classification of disease and injury for statistical purposes is essential.
>
> There are many approaches to the classification of disease. The anatomist, for example, may desire a classification based on the part of the body affected. The pathologist, on the other hand, is primarily interested in the nature of the disease process. The clinician must consider disease from these two angles, but needs further knowledge of etiology. In other words, there are many axes of classification, and the particular axis selected will be determined by the interests of the investigator. *A statistical classification of disease and injury will depend, therefore, upon the use to be made of the statistics to be compiled.* [Emphasis added.]

Existing classifications often are quite inadequate for specific problems, and new ones must be developed; but developing relevant classifications can pose difficult problems because of the complexity of the phenomena being investigated.

Gruenberg (1968, p. 83) emphasizes the many different classifications that are required to meet the needs of the epidemiologist. Classifications of populations are needed by "age, sex (some people think there are only two and that this is an exhaustive, exclusive classification), occupation, marital status, etc." Classifications of people are needed according to "experiences they have been exposed to, places of residence, places of occurrence of the disorder, places of work, membership in groups, societies, segments of society, etc."

Statistical ratios. "By contrast with clinical medicine, the unit of study in epidemiology is the group [including both the sick and the well], not the individual; deaths, or any other event, are studied only if information can be obtained, or inferred, about the group in which the events occurred. The clinician deals with *cases*. The epidemiologist deals with cases in their *population*. He may start with a population and seek out the cases in it; or start with cases and refer them back to a population, or what can be taken to represent a population. But always the epidemiologist ends up with some estimate of cases/ population. In consequence, he can sometimes ask questions which the clinician may also ask, and get better or different information in reply. Sometimes he can ask questions that cannot be asked in clinical work at all" (Morris, 1955, p. 395).

Epidemiological research uses a great variety of statistical methods. However, two basic ratios of cases to population that the epidemiologist uses in studies of disease require some elaboration—the incidence rate and the prevalence rate.

Incidence refers to the number of new cases of a disease occurring in a population during a specified interval of time. Thus, incidence determines the rate at which new cases of a disease occur in a group of individuals. "New" cases must be carefully defined—as, for example, the first or initial attack of a disease during an individual's lifetime. The rate is computed by taking the ratio of the number of "new" cases in the specified interval to the appropriate population group exposed to risk of attack. This rate may be made specific for a variety of factors— such as age, sex, marital status, and socioeconomic status—so as to describe the rates at which a disease develops in specified segments of the population. Such computations require classifications of the total population and of the disease (by age, sex, etc.). Thus, sex-specific rates may be used to determine whether women are more likely than men to develop a particular disease. Rates specific for geographic areas may be used to determine whether a disease occurs more frequently in Area A than Area B. Observed differences may suggest hypotheses that lead to discovery of etiological agents, whether these be biological, genetic, physical, chemical, psychological, or socioenvironmental. The testing of such hypotheses requires carefully designed, controlled studies to be carried out in the laboratory, clinic, or community—or some combination of these situations—depending on the specifications of the experimental design.

Prevalence refers to the total number of cases of a disease present in a population group during a specified interval of time—the number of cases existing at the start of an interval plus the new cases that have developed during the interval. "The length of the interval of observation must always be specified if a prevalence rate is to be correctly interpreted, for we may speak of the number of persons who are sick at any time during a given day, week, month, or other arbitrary interval" (Dorn, 1951, p. 273). The characteristics of individuals who are to be counted as a case (for example, all persons who have "active" disease within the interval of study) must also be carefully defined. The prevalence rate is computed by taking the ratio of the number of cases in the specified interval to the number of people in the appropriate population group for which the rate is being determined. In studies of chronic disease there are two commonly used prevalence rates: *point prevalence,* the number of cases of disease as of a given date, and *interval prevalence,* the number of cases present during a year (Dorn, 1951). These rates may also be made specific for such factors as age, sex, geographic area, and socioeconomic status.

A simple relationship exists between the incidence rate and the point-prevalence rate in a stationary population. As indicated, incidence measures the rate at which new cases are added to the population of sick persons. Determination of the site and composition of the population of sick persons requires that the incidence rate be related to the decrement rate (that is, the rate at which the disease is arrested or cured or at which affected individuals are removed from the population by death). Thus, the prevalence rate of a disease is a function of the incidence rate and the duration of the disease (Kramer, 1957; McMahon, Pugh, and Ipsen, 1960; Gruenberg, 1968). This relation is important to keep in mind when comparing prevalence rates of disease between populations over time. Differences can be due to differences in incidence or duration or both.

Uses of epidemiology. The epidemiological method can be used to acquire data which will answer a variety of questions about health and disease in populations, and related problems. Morris (1964, pp. 274 ff.) describes seven uses:

I. To study the history of the health of populations, and of the rise and fall of diseases and changes in their character. Useful projections into the future may be possible.

II. To diagnose the health of the community, and the condition of the people, to measure the present dimensions and distribution of ill health in terms of incidence, prevalence, and mortality; to define health problems for community action, and their relative importance and priority; to identify vulnerable groups needing special protection. Ways of life change, and with them community health and health problems; new indices of health and disease must therefore always be sought.

III. To study the working of health services with a view to their improvement. Operational research translates knowledge of community health in terms of needs and demands. The supply of services is described and how they are utilized; their success in reaching standards and in improving health ought to be appraised. All this has to be related to other social policies and to resources. Knowledge thus won may be applied in experiment, and in drawing up plans for the future. . . . The regular supply of information on health and health services is itself a key service needing as much scrutiny as any.

IV. To estimate from the group experience what are the individual risks and chances, on average, of disease, accident, and defect.

V. To complete the clinical picture of chronic disease, and describe its natural history: by including in proportion all kinds of patients wherever they present, and by following the course of remission and relapse, adjustment and disability; by detecting early subclinical disease and relating this to the clinical; by discovering precursor abnormalities during the pathogenesis. Longitudinal studies are necessary to learn about the mechanisms of progression through these various stages, each of which may offer opportunities for research into causes and for preventive action.

VI. To identify syndromes by describing the distribution, association, and dissociation of clinical phenomena in the population.

VII. To search for causes of health and disease by studying the incidence in different groups, defined in terms of their composition, their inheritance and experience, their

behavior and environment. To distinguish causes, describe
their patterns, and estimate the relative importance of different causes in multiple aetiology; to investigate the mode
of operation of the various causes. With knowledge of
causes comes the possibility of preventing the incidence of
disease. Postulated causes will often be tested in naturally
occurring experiments of opportunity, and sometimes by
planned experiments in removing them.

Morris (1964) provides specific examples of these uses in a variety of health and social fields; Shepherd and Cooper (1964) and
Gruenberg (1968) provide specific examples in the mental
health field.

Health Services

Scope of field. An increasingly important area of statistics deals with the health services and their activities. Such statistics describe various aspects of the health services of a nation,
state, city, county, or local area (World Health Organization,
Expert Committee on Health Statistics, 1969). Statistics may be
compiled, for instance, in the following areas:

1. Statistics on resources
   a. Buildings, equipment, and facilities
   b. Manpower
   c. Finances

2. Statistics on utilization of resources
   a. By service and purpose
      (1) Curative (e.g., hospital, inpatient and outpatient;
          nursing home)
      (2) Preventive (e.g., immunization and screening
          services)
      (3) Environmental (e.g., water treatment, sewage
          disposal, air pollution)
      (4) Supporting services: diagnostic (e.g., laboratory),
          therapeutic (e.g., pharmaceutical), ambulance
          services, plant maintenance, licensing of facilities
          and manpower
   b. For special populations
      (1) Family planning
      (2) Maternal and child health
      (3) Children

(4) The aged
(5) Crippled, blind, deaf, and other handicapped
(6) Industrial populations
(7) Migrant populations
(8) Selected populations
c. Services for special disease groups
(1) Cancer
(2) Mentally ill
(3) Tuberculosis
(4) Other diseases

Statistical indices. A variety of statistical indices are derived from basic data on the characteristics of the resources and the persons who use them. As with epidemiological data, many classifications of populations, resources, and the persons who use them are needed to compute these statistics. Of particular interest to this project are statistics on patterns of use of mental health services. These include first admission, readmission, resident patient, release, and mortality rates for patients admitted to a universe of mental health services (public and private mental hospitals, psychiatric services of general hospitals, community mental health centers, day-care or night-care centers) or to specific elements of this universe. The literature is replete with similar examples (see Kramer, 1969; Kramer, Pollack, and others, 1972; Taube and others, 1969-1973).

Uses of statistics. Generally speaking, the seven uses of epidemiological data described by Morris (1964) have their counterparts in health-care statistics. Thus, the statistics may be used (1) to study the historical changes in patterns of use of specific types of services, their staffing and financing, and to make projections for the future; (2) to assess the availability of specific types of services and the extent of their use, populations served, staffing, location, accessibility, costs, manpower, and quality, effectiveness, and efficiency of services rendered; (3) to study the working of health services with a view to their improvement; (4) to estimate whether and to what extent persons using specific types of services will reach specified stages of recovery or die; (5) to investigate the causes of institutionalization and noninstitutionalization (for example, factors that determine pathways to care, behaviors and attitudes of consumers and providers of services, availability of community supports, and socioeconomic factors).

In addition, the medical records of patients admitted to

various types of facilities may be used in clinical, laboratory, and field research to carry out such other uses of epidemiology as (6) to complete the clinical pictures, (7) to identify syndromes, and (8) to search for causes of health and disease.

Further elaboration and examples of specific uses may be found in various publications (see World Health Organization, 1963, 1971; Kramer, 1967; Kramer, Rosen, and Willis, 1973; Kramer and Taube, 1973; Kramer, Taube, and Redick, 1973; Rosen and others, 1968; Gruenberg, 1966; Pasamanick, Scarpitti, and Dinitz, 1967; Wilner and others, 1962). All such uses require classifications not only of the characteristics of patients, agents of disease, and the environments in which persons live, but also of the institutions that provide the services, the political structure in which they exist, and the populations they serve.

International Classification of Diseases (ICD)

The *ICD* is an essential instrument for the development of comparable mortality and morbidity data throughout the world. Its use internationally has played a key role in stimulating the production of such data and in the development of procedures for improving the reliability and comparability of national and international statistics on causes of death and morbidity.

History. The *ICD* had its origin in the International Classification of Causes of Death (also referred to as the Bertillon Classification), which was adopted by the International Statistical Institute in Paris in 1893 (World Health Organization, 1967). The actions that resulted in this classification started with a resolution of the International Statistical Congress in 1853. In this resolution William Farr, the first medical statistician of the Register General Office of England and Wales, and Marc d'Espine of Geneva were asked to prepare a uniform nomenclature of the causes of death applicable in all countries. The lists so developed were revised at four succeeding congresses. The final classification was prepared in 1891 by a committee under the chairmanship of Jacques Bertillon, chief of statistical activities of the city of Paris, and adopted by the International Statistical Congress at its meeting in Chicago in 1893.

The *ICD* has been revised eight times at approximately

ten-year intervals. The revisions incorporate changes in disease classification resulting from new discoveries; amend errors and inconsistencies; and attempt to meet the changing and expanding needs of health and social agencies, research workers, and consumers of health statistics for improved classifications of diseases. The sixth revision, in 1946, marked the beginning of a new era in international vital and health statistics (World Health Organization, 1948). This revision resulted in sweeping changes in the *International List of Causes of Death* and produced a single classification to serve the dual purposes of coding morbidity and mortality data. The eighth revision, in 1965, also incorporated major changes in the classification of many of the major disease categories (World Health Organization, 1967). Currently, activities are underway for the ninth revision. (For additional information on the history of the development of the *ICD,* see World Health Organization, 1967; U.S. Department of Health, Education, and Welfare, 1967. For details about the development of the classification of mental disorders, see American Psychiatric Association, 1968.)

Purposes and uses. The *ICD* is a statistical classification of diseases; complications of pregnancy, childbirth, and the puerperium; congenital abnormalities; causes of perinatal morbidity and mortality; accidents, poisonings, and violence; and symptoms and ill-defined conditions. The principal use of the *ICD* is in the classification of morbidity and mortality information for statistical purposes. It has also been adapted for use as a nomenclature of diseases and in indexing medical records. The basic purpose of such indexing is to facilitate retrieval of medical records for a variety of purposes (for example, for studies of management of patients with specific conditions).

The *ICD* differs from a nomenclature of diseases in that a statistical classification must be confined to a limited number of categories which will encompass the entire range of diseases and morbid conditions. A nomenclature of diseases is a list or a catalog of approved terms for describing and recording clinical and pathological observations. To serve its full function, it must be sufficiently extensive so that any pathological condition can be accurately recorded. As medical science advances, a nomenclature must expand to include new terms necessary to record new observations. The *Standard Nomenclature of Diseases and Operations* (Thompson and Hayden, 1961) is such a catalog of diseases. It attempts to include every clinically recognizable disease in a way that avoids repetition and overlapping. By means of a six-digit numerical system, every disease is assigned first to a topographical system of the body (the first three digits) and then to a specific etiological classification (the second three digits).

Organization. The *ICD* is eclectic in its arrangement and does not have a single organizational structure for codifying the diseases and conditions in each of its sections. It is organized into seventeen major categories as follows:

  I. Infective and Parasitic Diseases
  II. Neoplasms
  III. Endocrine, Nutritional, and Metabolic Diseases
  IV. Diseases of the Blood and Blood-Forming Organs
  V. Mental Disorders
  VI. Diseases of the Nervous System and Sense Organs
  VII. Diseases of the Circulatory System
  VIII. Diseases of the Respiratory System
  IX. Diseases of the Digestive System
  X. Diseases of the Genito-Urinary System
  XI. Complications of Pregnancy, Childbirth, and the Puerperium
  XII. Diseases of the Skin and Subcutaneous Tissue
  XIII. Diseases of the Musculoskeletal System and Connective Tissue
  XIV. Congenital Anomalies
  XV. Certain Causes of Perinatal Morbidity and Mortality
  XVI. Symptoms and Ill-Defined Conditions
  XVII. Accidents, Poisonings, and Violence
      EXVII. Alternative Classification of Accidents, Poisonings, and Violence (External Cause)
      NXVII. Alternative Classification of Accidents, Poisonings, and Violence (Nature of Injury)

Each major system is subdivided into a defined set of subcategories and is assigned three digits, ranging from 000 to 999. Each subcategory is further subdivided into additional categories designated by a fourth digit (.0 to .9) so as to provide greater detail within the three-digit categories. The axes of classification differ within each of the seventeen major three-digit categories: "Compromises have been made in the *International Classification* between cause, pathological condition, anatomical site, age, and circumstances of the onset of the disease. Experience has shown that it is impossible to maintain a consistent axis of classification for all diseases" (Moriyama, 1960, p. 468).

The following outline illustrates the organization of the classification of three major groups of disorders: Infective and Parasitic Diseases (partial numerical listing only), Neoplasms, and Mental Disorders.

I. Infective and Parasitic Diseases (000-136)
   A. Intestinal infectious diseases (000-009)
      1. First three digits (type of disease—some by name, some by type of organism)
      2. Fourth digit: specific subgroups of disease
   B. Tuberculosis (010-019)
      1. First three digits:
         010 silico tuberculosis
         011-017 organ system affected
         018 disseminated tuberculosis
         019 late effects of tuberculosis
      2. Fourth digit: greater specificity within given system
   C. Zoonotic bacterial diseases (020-027)
   D. Other bacterial diseases (030-039)
   E. Poliomyelitis (040-046)
   F. Viral diseases accompanied by exanthem (050-057)

II. Neoplasms (140-239)
   A. Malignant neoplasms (140-199): classified according to site, as follows:
      1. Buccal cavity and pharynx (140-149)
      2. Digestive organs and peritoneum (150-199)
      3. Fourth digit: greater specificity within stated sites
   B. Benign neoplasms (210-228): classified by site as for malignant neoplasms
   C. Neoplasms of unspecified nature (230-239): classified by site as for malignant neoplasms

V. Mental Disorders (290-315)
   A. Psychoses

    1. Organic (290-294)
    2. Functional (295-299)
 B. Neuroses (300)
 C. Personality disorders and certain other nonpsychot-
    ic mental disorders (301-304)
 D. Physical disorders of presumably psychogenic ori-
    gin (305)
 E. Special symptoms (306)
 F. Transient situational disturbances (307)
 G. Behavior disorders of childhood (308)
 H. Mental disorders not specified as psychotic, asso-
    ciated with physical conditions (309)
  I. Mental retardation (310-315)
    A fourth digit provides additional specificity for
    each of the above three-digit rubrics as follows: for
    organic disorders (290-294, 309): associated condi-
    tion (infection, trauma, intoxication, circulatory
    disturbance, metabolic disorders, neoplasm, and so
    on); for functional psychoses (295-299), neuroses
    (300), and personality disorders (301-304): sub-
    types; for physical disorders of presumably psycho-
    genic origin (305): organ system affected.

Application to morbidity and mortality data.[1] Before the classification can be applied to actual data, it is necessary to decide what purpose is to be served by the statistics. More specifically, are the statistics to deal with the count of persons who are sick or have died, or with the conditions that produced the illness or death? Both kinds of statistics are important attributes of morbidity and mortality and warrant study.

    Let us consider first the application of the statistical classification to the underlying cause of death. Since the early records of death usually contained only a single cause, a few simple rules sufficed to secure uniform selection of the cause of death. The usual mortality table, therefore, is based on individuals who have died, with a single cause assigned to each death. As an increasingly larger proportion of the certificates of death contained multiple causes, the problem of selection became more

[1] This section is taken from the introduction to the eighth revision of the *International Classification of Diseases, Adapted for Use in the United States* (U.S. Department of Health, Education, and Welfare, 1967).

important in securing comparable statistics. Over the years, various principles and rules were established for the selection of the primary cause of death. The list of rules became increasingly complex, and the Eighth Revision Conference directed that they be reviewed and simplified without changing the assignment for primary mortality tabulations.

The classification also can be applied to the coding of multiple diagnoses, permitting a count of all diseases and conditions reported on death certificates. These counts may be made independently or in meaningful combinations; for instance, a count of combinations representing disease complexes would give a more complete view of causes of death than would otherwise be obtained from primary mortality tabulations. Or, in preparing tabulations to show associations between diseases, one could look at combinations of diseases with high frequency or those that occur more frequently than would be expected on the basis of chance alone. Other statistical procedures may be used to identify meaningful multiple-cause groups. Such counts of diseases and conditions are useful; for many purposes, however, a count of deaths involving specific diseases would be more useful—specifically, for estimating the number of persons who died who had certain diseases, such as cancer, cardiovascular diseases, or tuberculosis. Although the same person may be counted more than once in such a tabulation, useful information relating to morbidity in the population can be obtained by this procedure (U.S. Department of Health, Education, and Welfare, 1965).

The classification is somewhat more difficult to apply to causes of illness and disability, since morbidity is far less definite than mortality and represents a dynamic rather than a static phenomenon. The occurrence of death is a definite event, and the number of such events can be counted. An illness, on the other hand, varies from a minor deviation from normal health, which does not interfere with the performance of regular duties or activities, to the chronic case which calls for bedside or custodial care for an indefinite period. Furthermore, an individual afflicted with a disease may experience only one period of illness during the interval of observation, or he may have repeated illnesses from the same disease. In addition, during the same period of illness, an individual may suffer from two or more distinct diseases. Thus, the basic problem as to what is to be counted becomes very complex. Obviously, then, the application of the classification to morbidity statistics cannot be laid down as precisely and relatively simply as in mortality. The application will vary, depending on the kind of morbidity experience to be studied and on the purposes to be served by the statistics.

Comparability of diagnostic data. Comparisons of mortality and morbidity rates within and among countries may be meaningless and, indeed, misleading unless the basic data from which these rates are derived are reliable, comparable, accurately recorded, and appropriately processed and analyzed. Development of comparable diagnostic data requires the resolution of many complex problems. For instance, in different countries different terms often are used to describe a specific condition. The index to the *International Classification of Diseases*—an exhaustive alphabetical index of diagnostic terms in use throughout the world—can be used to resolve problems of comparability resulting from differences in terminology (U.S. Department of Health, Education, and Welfare, 1968). This index assists a coder in assigning a specific term—even the imprecise and undesirable ones—to the appropriate categories of the classification. Another problem, less easily resolved, results from the phenomenon of observer variation; that is, the differences in diagnoses that result when different physicians use an identical diagnostic term to describe conditions with quite different symptomatic profiles, or when they use different terms to describe the same condition. This is a problem of particular concern in the making of psychiatric diagnoses—a process largely dependent on the characteristics of the psychiatrist and on his techniques for carrying out an interview and for interpreting the information so obtained (Katz, Cole, and Lowery, 1969). This procedure is influenced by the clinician's training, the importance he attaches to diagnosis, his theoretical orientation to the etiology and treatment of specific mental disorders, and his clinical experience. "Whatever the situation in general practice, psychiatric procedures must be much more vulnerable to observer differences, for in dealing with most psychiatric patients there is a lack of external criteria by which psychiatrists' observations and decisions can be validated; it is usually necessary to rely upon what can be learned about the patient by means of interviews only. Until something is known about how to make the gathering and recording of interview information accurate and reliable, psychiatric diagnosis cannot rest upon a firm foundation" (Shepherd and others, 1968, p. 14).

Resolution of the types of problems mentioned requires the development of a uniform nomenclature of diseases, standard definitions, and criteria for the use of specific diagnostic terms. More accurate diagnostic techniques and more precise usage of diagnostic terminology also are needed to provide more valid, reliable, and comparable basic data.

Recent Activities Related to Classification of Mental Disorders

In the past decade many promising efforts have been made to improve classifications of mental disorders; diagnostic practice; and the reliability, validity, and comparability of national and international statistics of these disorders. The following is a summary of the kinds of activities that have taken place.

Revision of ICD. Revision of the *ICD* is a continuous process. Extensive preparatory work for the next revision starts immediately following the approval of a given revision by the World Health Assembly. These activities include such things as the development of revision proposals by agencies at the national level that compile health and vital statistics; bipartite or multipartite meetings of interested countries to develop joint proposals; coordination of programs of the health agencies in different regions with the programs of the WHO Centers for Classification of Diseases in London and Caracas and expert committee meetings on various technical subjects related to specific classification problems. The U.S. National Committee on Vital and Health Statistics, the focal point for these activities in the United States, prepares the final revision proposals that the United States government transmits to the WHO. With respect to the eighth revision, the National Committee established several subcommittees (including an expert subcommittee on classification of mental disorders) to develop revision proposals for several sections of the *ICD* that needed extensive revision.

The WHO made special efforts to involve the international community of psychiatrists in developing the classification of mental disorders for the eighth revision (Kramer, 1968). To resolve some practical problems related to the classification of mental disorders for international purposes, the Mental Health Unit of the WHO designated an expert group to develop a glossary of operational definitions of terms included in the eighth revision (World Health Organization, in press). This glossary was developed with great care and extensive international consultation, and has been widely used on an experimental basis. Through its use, greater uniformity should be achieved in the use of psychiatric terminology and in the coding of diagnostic terms in preparation of national and international statistics on mental disorders.

Although the classification of mental disorders in the eighth revision was a considerable improvement over the earlier revision, various aspects of it still seemed unsatisfactory. Therefore, in 1965 the Mental Health Unit of the WHO embarked on an intensive program to acquire systematic data on variations in diagnostic practice and use of diagnostic terms among psychiatrists from a large number of countries representing different schools of psychiatric thought and practice (Lin, 1967). This program consisted of a series of annual seminars on psychiatric diagnosis, classification, and statistics. Each was held in a different part of the world and concentrated on a specific group of mental disorders. A nuclear group of leading experts, representing different schools of psychiatry and statistics, participated in all seminars, together with psychiatrists from the area where the seminar was held who were chosen as experts in the field of study for each particular seminar. The seminars included representatives from thirty-five different countries and from many different schools of thought, and also ensured a weighting of expertise in the subject of the seminar.

Prior to each seminar, participants were required to diagnose, code, and make certain ratings on case histories precirculated in two parts—the first part giving all basic information at the time of first assessment; the second part providing follow-up findings. During each seminar there were similar diagnostic exercises based on videotape recordings of interviews with patients. The discussion at each seminar centered around the statistical analysis of these studies for that seminar. By these means, considerable data were accumulated on the strengths and weaknesses of the classification of mental disorders in the eighth revision. The reports of these WHO seminars constituted the main basis for the development of revision proposals for the classification of mental disorders in the forthcoming ninth revision of the *ICD*. In addition, the working papers prepared for each seminar discussed particular aspects of classification and constitute a very valuable source of information on these aspects. The seminars stimulated the development of a number of national and international studies on psychiatric classification for the ninth revision.

One of the important recommendations of these seminars concerns the need for a multiaxial scheme for the classification of all mental disorders. Such a scheme has already been developed for mental disorders in childhood (Rutter, Lebovici, and others, 1969). It contains four axes: (1) the clinical psychiatric syndrome; (2) the individual's intellectual level of functioning, regardless of etiology; (3) associated physical and organic etiological factors; (4) psychosocial factors in the etiology of the disorders being classified. As a result of these efforts and a special study of the multiaxial classification for child psychiatric disorders (Rutter, Shaffer, and Shepherd, 1972), an extensive revision was proposed for child psychiatric disorders, an area in which the eighth revision was especially weak.

The WHO Eighth Seminar on the Standardization of Psychiatric Diagnosis, Classification, and Statistics used the recommendations of the prior seminars as the basis for its proposal for the section on mental disorders in the forthcoming ninth revision of the *ICD*. The interested reader is referred to the report of this seminar (World Health Organization, 1973a) for the details of this proposal.

Research and conferences. In addition to the intensive international activities related to the eighth and forthcoming ninth revision of the *ICD,* a variety of national activities have taken place related to the classification of mental disorders and mental retardation. The following is only a partial listing of these activities: work conference on problems in field studies in the mental disorders, February 1959 (Zubin, 1961); *Diagnostic and Statistical Manual of the American Psychiatric Association* (American Psychiatric Association, 1968); *A Manual on Terminology and Classification in Mental Retardation* (Heber, 1961; Grossman, 1973); conference on the role and methodology of classification in psychiatry and psychopathology, November 1965 (Katz, Cole, and Barton, 1968); monograph on psychopathological disorders in childhood, including a proposed classification (Group for the Advancement of Psychiatry, 1966).

Studies on variability and comparability. Two major studies have been carried out on the problems of eliminating the effects of observer variability and of obtaining comparable data on mental disorders in different countries. One of these studies, the U.S.-U.K. Diagnostic Project, was designed to determine whether reported differences in diagnostic distributions between patients admitted to American and English mental hospitals—particularly the predominance of schizophrenics in America and of manic-depressives in England—were genuine or simply a product of differences in diagnostic criteria (Kramer, Zubin, and others, 1969; Gurland and others, 1970, 1972; Cooper and others, 1972). The second major study, the WHO International Pilot Study of Schizophrenia, is an undertaking of that part of the WHO program on psychiatric epidemiology devoted to comparative research on specific mental disorders (Lin, 1967). One of the major purposes of this program is to determine whether comparable cases of mental disorders can be identified in various populations with markedly different political, social, and economic characteristics. Because of its importance as an international public health problem, schizophrenia was selected as the initial subject of study (Lin, 1969; Sartorius and others, 1972; World Health Organization, 1973b).

These studies underscore the fact that instruments can be developed for the collection of comparable and uniform data on mental disorders under varying social and cultural conditions for scientific purposes, and that psychiatrists and other staff can be trained to use these instruments. But of greater significance are the far-reaching implications of these studies for the whole field of mental health, particularly in relation to such fundamental issues as communication among mental health professionals within and between countries, the reporting and interpretation of research findings, clinical practice in mental health, and training of clinicians in assessment techniques. An excerpt from a report on the effects of differences in diagnostic practice of British and American psychiatrists on national statistics of mental disorders (Cooper and others, 1972, p. 130) highlights this point:

> The disparity between American and British diagnostic concepts raises another issue of much greater importance than the question of whose diagnoses are the more useful. Diagnoses are the most important of all our technical terms because they are the means by which we identify the subject matter of most of our research. They are the labels by which we identify the patients whose amine metabolism we were studying, or who received the new drug whose efficacy we were testing. If these crucial terms are used in widely differing ways by different groups of psychiatrists, communication between them will be gravely hindered. Indeed, the large differences between American and British diagnostic usage revealed here imply that rather different interpretations must now be placed by British

psychiatrists on much recent American research on schizophrenia, and by American psychiatrists on several British
studies of affective disorders. The significance to British
psychiatrists of, for example, Lidz's studies of the families
of schizophrenics (Lidz, Fleck, and Cornelison, 1965), and
the etiological theories derived from these, must be affected
by the suspicion that they themselves would not have regarded many of his cases as schizophrenics in the first place.
Similarly, American psychiatrists may well need to revise
their assessment of several British studies of depressions, on
the grounds that many of the patients involved were not in
fact suffering from depressive illnesses in the sense in which
they understand the term. If, subsequently, serious differences in diagnostic usage are found within different centers
in the United States, the situation will become even more
chaotic. Psychiatrists in New York will have to disregard, or
be misled by, the work of Winokur and his colleagues in St.
Louis on manic-depressive illness (Winokur, Clayton, and
Reich, 1969), and they in turn will have to do the same for
Kallmann's genetic studies (Kallmann, 1946), and so on.
This is, of course, speculative and perhaps unnecessarily
pessimistic, but it does serve to underline our dependence
on a reasonable uniformity of diagnostic usage in our interpretation of all research conducted outside the walls of our
own institutes. Much clinical and biological research can be
partly shielded from the consequences of discrepant diagnostic criteria by restricting the case material to subjects
with very typical symptoms, but in epidemiological work
this is impossible, and for this reason findings in large parts
of this field may have to be qualified by uncertainty about
the diagnostic criteria employed.

Community mental health programs. Many efforts have
been directed toward developing classifications of persons from
data on the census of population to provide distributions of persons specific for living arrangements, household and family
composition, and the role an individual occupies in a family.
Distributions of populations derived from such classifications
are becoming increasingly important as a result of the extensive
development of programs of community care for the mentally
ill and other disabled individuals. They are needed as denominators for various rates used in epidemiological research and in
studies of delivery of health and social services. In addition,
they serve to identify high-risk groups that may be in need of
various types of services.

Relevant references are the United States Census's distributions of persons by family characteristics (U.S. Department of Commerce, 1964); demographic profiles of the catchment areas defined for mental health centers (Redick, Goldsmith, and Unger, 1971); and the studies by Pollack, Redick, and Taube (1968) on the relationship of familial factors to admission to psychiatric facilities.

Clinical trials of psychotropic drugs. Clinical trials (see Hill, 1971) of psychotropic drugs require precise diagnostic criteria in experiments designed to test the efficacy of such drugs as chlorpromazine, imipramine, and lithium carbonate on various types of patients. The following references illustrate the uses of diagnosis for such purposes: Raskin and others (1970); Prien, Klett, and Caffey (1972); Raskin (1968); Fieve (1971). The results of these experiments have important implications for the use of more precise diagnostic techniques by psychiatrists, internists, general practitioners, and other physicians who use the various psychotropic drugs in their practices.

Computer programs for psychiatric diagnosis. Within the past few years several computer programs have been developed to produce psychiatric diagnoses by applying a logical decision-tree program, which simulates the way a clinician makes a diagnosis, to the analysis of patient's responses to questions in a standardized psychiatric interview. The advantage of such a procedure is that the computer applies a set of rules of diagnosis in a systematic and uniform way to the interview data for differential diagnostic purposes and thereby minimizes the errors in diagnosis caused by clinician bias. To date, these procedures have been used in research studies, where the systematic basic interview data can be collected in the necessary detail under controlled conditions (Spitzer and Endicott, 1968, 1969; Wing, 1970; World Health Organization, 1973c). Considerable work must still be done before such procedures can be adapted for use in ordinary clinical practice.

Computers are also being used to classify patients (to assign patients to a group) on the basis of their similarities with respect to multiple characteristics (such as symptoms, demography, family history of mental disorders) rather than on the basis of the diagnosis assigned to them by a clinician. The technique used is cluster analysis, a computer-aided method for sorting patients into natural groups (groups consisting of patients with a set of characteristics in common). In contrast to the clinical and decision-tree procedures, which assume the existence of diagnostic classes, cluster-analytic techniques assume that their number and nature are not known a priori. Once the natural groups have been produced, the characteristics of these clusters can be defined operationally and methods can be developed for assigning new patients to the appropriate cluster. However, the application of these techniques to psychiatric data is still in the embryonic stages (Bartko, Strauss, and Carpenter, 1971; Strauss, Bartko, and Carpenter, 1973).

Conclusions

The preceding sections have illustrated uses of diagnostic and classificatory procedures in epidemiological research and in the collection and analysis of statistics on morbidity, mortality, and the health services. Despite their fundamental importance in these activities, diagnosis and classification pose a dilemma to society. On the one hand, they are needed in research on health and related social problems and on matters relevant to the planning, administration, delivery, and evaluation of the delivery of health and related human services. On the other hand, these processes may result in an individual's acquiring a label that can, and often does, have a serious effect on his opportunities for education, housing, employment, and many other aspects of his role functioning in society (Rosen, 1968). He may have acquired the label and diagnoses in many different ways—for instance, by having been a subject in a research project, by seeking and obtaining treatment for some disease or disabling condition, by submitting to a procedure required by some human-service agency to determine eligibility for service, by having performed some act, or by virtue of some natural or acquired trait he may possess.

In short, there is great need for classifications in research on social pathology; but there are also the potential dangers and complications of their premature application and hardening in practice. This dilemma has been a source of continuing concern to scientists engaged in such research:

> If we can speak with tempered optimism of the development of prediction skills, at least as much can be said for progress in classification. That young sciences should be much concerned with classification is normal

enough; and the social sciences are no exception. In social
pathology, as elsewhere in human experience, the same patterns recur, and one of the marks of increased understanding is the ability to recognize these. The proliferation of
new categories, such as "maladjusted," "educationally subnormal," "mental defective," "psychopath" is evidence
both of increasing awareness of this recurrence of patterns
and of increasing ability to discriminate between them—in
short, of improved skill in classification. In spite of certain
dangers, both theoretical and practical, every refinement of
classification brings us one step nearer to reality, for no
classification can be finely enough graded to match the continuum of human qualities. Nature knows nothing of a
crude dichotomy between "adjustment" and "maladjustment," but only an infinite gradation of degrees of adaptation to the environment. . . .

While it is true that every refinement in classification means a closer approximation to the infinite variety of
reality, nevertheless increased complexity of classification
necessarily means also increased risks of error. If the world
is divided into those who are raving mad and those who are
sane, the number of cases in which the classification of a
particular individual is likely to be called in question will
not be very numerous. But if the mad are subdivided into
the schizophrenics (of various brands), manic-depressives,
senile psychotics, and so on, and if in addition to the whole
class of the demonstrably mad, we have "psychoneurotics,"
"psychopaths," "maladjusted," "intellectually or emotionally handicapped persons," the potential occasions of dispute are vastly multiplied.

Once again this would not matter so much if these
classifications were purely theoretical exercises. But once
again they are not. For refinements of classification tend to
become incorporated into social practice with a speed quite
disproportionate to the interest generally evoked by other
advances in the social sciences: complication is always dear
to administration. Hence we are constantly in the position
of giving statutory or administrative recognition to new
categories, and of providing new forms of specialized provision. The psychopath, the maladjusted, the educationally
retarded, the mental defective, and the normal delinquent,
each must have his appropriate place in an ever more complex system of treatment.

Premature hardening of these categories into rigid
administrative structures is, however, liable to produce
unfortunate practical consequences, in spite of the theoreti-

cal virtues of finer discriminations. Particularly where specialized institutions (as distinct from specialized treatment within the same institution) are provided, classifications which do not deserve all the respect that they receive may well defeat their own ends. For the greater the number of categories requiring to be separately dealt with, the more complicated becomes the process of matching demand and supply, and the greater in consequence is the risk that a shortage of facilities for one category will coincide with a surplus in the case of another [Wooten, 1959, pp. 325, 331-332].

There is no single way to resolve the complex problems associated with classifying persons for research, for data-collection purposes, and in relation to their needs for health, social, and other human services. Their resolution requires that citizens understand the fundamental role of diagnostic and classificatory procedures in research and in service-delivery activities, and the fundamental nature of their own role in providing accurate and reliable information required for these procedures. To accept this state of affairs, citizens must have trust and confidence in the integrity and competence of the scientists, administrators, caretakers, and others involved in the use of this information for scientific and service purposes. On the other side of the coin, scientists, officials, administrators, and caretakers involved in research, data-collection, analysis, and classification activities must conduct themselves in ways that gain and hold the public's trust and confidence. In addition, they must provide whatever humanitarian, legal, or other safeguards may be required to prevent the damaging consequences of premature application and hardening into administrative practice of labeling, diagnostic, and classification procedures still in the research and experimental stages; the misuse and inappropriate applications of established and accepted procedures; and the indiscriminate use of labels and diagnostic terms.

Governmental agencies have already made considerable progress in developing policies and procedures to protect the rights and welfare of human subjects who participate in research, development, demonstration, or other activities supported by federal funds (U.S. Department of Health, Education, and Welfare, 1971); and to protect the confidentiality of data supplied by individuals and corporate respondents in health and social surveys (U.S. Department of Health, Education, and Wel-

fare, 1973) and of data supplied to the Social Security Administration by its beneficiaries (Steinberg and Cooper, 1967). We
should review carefully the principles and procedures developed
by these agencies to determine the extent to which they may be
adapted to resolve the various problems addressed in this volume.

References

American Psychiatric Association, Committee on Nomenclature and Statis-
tics. *Diagnostic and Statistical Manual of Mental Disorders (DSM-
II).* (2nd Ed.) Washington, D.C.: American Psychiatric Association,
1968.
Bartko, J. J., Strauss, J. S., and Carpenter, W. T. J. "An Evaluation of
Taxometric Techniques for Psychiatric Data." *Classification Soci-
ety Bulletin,* 1971, *2*(3), 1-29.
Clark, E. G. "An Epidemiologic Approach to Preventive Medicine." In
H. R. Leavell and E. G. Clark (Eds.), *Textbook of Preventive Medi-
cine.* New York: McGraw-Hill, 1953.
Cooper, J. E., and others. *Psychiatric Diagnosis in New York and London.*
Institute of Psychiatry Maudsley Monographs, No. 20. London:
Oxford University Press, 1972.
Dorn, H. F. "Methods of Measuring Incidence and Prevalence of Disease."
American Journal of Public Health, 1951, *41,* 271-278.
Fieve, R. R. "Depression in the 1970's: Introductory Remarks." In R. R.
Fieve (Ed.), *Depression in the 1970's: Modern Theory and Re-
search.* International Congress Series No. 239. The Hague: Excerp-
ta Medica, 1971.
Frost, W. H. "Epidemiology." In *Public Health and Preventive Medicine.*
New York: Thomas Nelson and Sons, 1927. Reprinted in K. F.
Maxcy (Ed.), *Papers of Wade Hampton Frost: A Contribution to
Epidemiologic Method.* New York: Commonwealth Fund, 1941.
Gordon, J. E. "The New Epidemiology." In *Tomorrow's Horizon in Public
Health.* New York: Public Health Association of New York City,
1950.
Gordon, J. E. "The Twentieth Century, Yesterday, Today, and Tomor-
row." In F. H. Top (Ed.), *The History of American Epidemiology.*
St. Louis: C. V. Mosby, 1952.
Gordon, J. E. "Medical Ecology and the Public Health." *American Journal
of Medical Science,* 1958, *235,* 337-359.
Gordon, J. E., and others. "The Biological and Social Sciences in an Epi-
demiology of Mental Disorders." *American Journal of the Medical
Sciences,* 1952, *223,* 316-343.
Grossman, H. (Ed.) *A Manual on Terminology and Classification in Mental
Retardation.* (3rd Ed.) *American Journal of Mental Deficiency,*
1973. Monograph supplement.

Group for the Advancement of Psychiatry, Committee on Child Psychiatry. *Psychopathological Disorders in Childhood: Theoretical Considerations and a Proposed Classification.* New York: Group for the Advancement of Psychiatry, 1966.

Gruenberg, E. M. (Ed.) *Evaluating the Effectiveness of Community Mental Health Services.* New York: Milbank Memorial Fund, 1966.

Gruenberg, E. M. "Epidemiology and Medical Care Statistics." In M. M. Katz, J. O. Cole, and W. E. Barton (Eds.), *The Role and Methodology of Classification in Psychiatry and Psychopathology.* Washington, D.C.: U.S. Government Printing Office, 1968.

Gurland, B. J., and others. "Cross National Study of Diagnoses of Mental Disorders: Hospital Diagnoses and Hospital Patients in New York and London." *Comprehensive Psychiatry,* 1970, *11,* 18-25.

Gurland, B. J., and others. "The Mislabelling of Depressed Patients in New York State Hospitals." In J. Zubin and S. A. Freyhan (Eds.), *Disorders of Mood.* Baltimore: Johns Hopkins Press, 1972.

Heber, R. *A Manual of Terminology and Classification in Mental Retardation.* (2nd Ed.) *American Journal of Mental Deficiency,* 1961. Monograph supplement.

Hill, A. B. "Clinical Trials." In *Principles of Medical Statistics.* (9th Ed.) New York: Oxford University Press, 1971.

Kallmann, F. J. "A Genetic Theory of Schizophrenia: An Analysis of 691 Twin Index Families." *American Journal of Psychiatry,* 1946, *103,* 309-322.

Katz, M. M., Cole, J. O., and Barton, W. E. (Eds.) *The Role and Methodology of Classification in Psychiatry and Psychopathology.* Washington, D.C.: U.S. Government Printing Office, 1968.

Katz, M. M., Cole, J. O., and Lowery, H. A. "Studies of the Diagnostic Process: The Influence of Symptom Perception, Past Experience, and Ethnic Background on Diagnostic Decisions." *American Journal of Psychiatry,* 1969, *125,* 937-947.

Kramer, M. "A Discussion of the Concepts of Incidence and Prevalence as Related to Epidemiologic Studies of Mental Disorders." *American Journal of Public Health,* 1957, *47,* 826-840.

Kramer, M. "Epidemiology, Biostatistics, and Mental Health Planning." In *Psychiatric Epidemiology and Mental Health Planning.* Psychiatric Research Report No. 22. Washington, D.C.: American Psychiatric Association, 1967.

Kramer, M. "The History of the Efforts to Agree on an International Classification of Mental Disorders." In American Psychiatric Association, Committee on Nomenclature and Statistics, *Diagnostic and Statistical Manual of Mental Disorders (DSM-II).* (2nd Ed.) Washington, D.C.: American Psychiatric Association, 1968.

Kramer, M. *Applications of Mental Health Statistics.* Geneva: World Health Organization, 1969.

Kramer, M., Pollack, E. S., and others. *Mental Disorders/Suicide.* Vital and

84   Issues in the Classification of Children

Health Statistics Monographs, American Public Health Association. Cambridge, Mass.: Harvard University Press, 1972.

Kramer, M., Rosen, B. M., and Willis, E. M. "Definitions and Distributions of Mental Disorders in a Racist Society." In C. V. Willie, B. M. Kramer, and B. S. Brown (Eds.), *Racism and Mental Health: Essays.* Pittsburgh: University of Pittsburgh Press, 1973.

Kramer, M., and Taube, C. A. "The Role of a National Statistics Program in the Planning of Community Psychiatric Services." To be published in *Proceedings* of Second World Psychiatric Association-Deutsche Gesellschaft für Psychiatrie und Nervenheilkunde Symposium on Psychiatric Epidemiology (in press, 1973).

Kramer, M., Taube, C. A., and Redick, R. W. "Patterns of Use of Psychiatric Facilities by the Aged: Past, Present, and Future." In C. Eisdorfer and M. P. Lawton (Eds.), *The Psychology of Adult Development and Aging.* Washington, D.C.: American Psychological Association, 1973.

Kramer, M., Zubin, J., and others. "Cross National Study of Diagnoses of Mental Disorders." *American Journal of Psychiatry,* 1969, *125,* supplement.

Lidz, T., Fleck, S., and Cornelison, A. R. *Schizophrenia and the Family.* New York: International Universities Press, 1965.

Lin, T. "The Epidemiological Study of Mental Disorders." *WHO Chronicles,* 1967, *21,* 509-516.

Lin, T. "Reducing Variability in International Research." In F. Redlich (Ed.), *Social Psychiatry.* New York: Association for Research in Nervous and Mental Disease, 1969.

McMahon, B., Pugh, T., and Ipsen, J. *Epidemiologic Method.* Boston: Little, Brown, 1960.

Merrell, M., and Reed, L. J. "The Epidemiology of Health." In *Social Medicine, Its Derivation and Objectives.* New York: Commonwealth Fund, 1949.

Moriyama, I. M. "The Classification of Disease—A Fundamental Problem." *Journal of Chronic Diseases,* 1960, *11,* 462-470.

Morris, J. N. "Uses of Epidemiology." *British Medical Journal,* 1955, *2,* 395-401.

Morris, J. N. *Uses of Epidemiology.* (2nd Ed.) Baltimore: Williams and Wilkins, 1964.

Pasamanick, B., Scarpitti, F. R., and Dinitz, S. *Schizophrenics in the Community: Experimental Study in the Prevention of Hospitalization.* New York: Appleton-Century-Crofts, 1967.

Pollack, E. S., Redick, R. W., and Taube, C. A. "The Application of Census and Socioeconomic and Familial Data to the Study of Morbidity from Mental Disorders." *American Journal of Public Health,* 1968, *58,* 83-89.

Prien, R. F., Klett, C. J., and Caffey, E. M. *Comparison of Lithium Carbonate and Imipramine in the Prevention of Affective Episodes in*

Recurrent Affective Illness. Washington, D.C.: Veterans Administration, Department of Medicine and Surgery, 1972. (Mimeo.)

Raskin, A. "The Prediction of Antidepressant Drug Effects: Review and Critique." In D. H. Effron and others (Eds.), *Psychopharmacology: A Review of Progress, 1957-1967*. Washington, D.C.: U.S. Government Printing Office, 1968.

Raskin, A., and others. "Differential Response to Chlorpromazine, Imipramine, and Placebo." *Archives of General Psychiatry*, 1970, *23*, 164-173.

Redick, R. W., Goldsmith, H. F., and Unger, E. L. *1970 Census Data Used to Indicate Areas with Different Potentials for Mental Health and Related Problems*. Washington, D.C.: U.S. Government Printing Office, 1971.

Reid, D. D. *Epidemiological Methods in the Study of Mental Disorders*. Public Health Papers No. 2. Geneva: World Health Organization, 1960.

Rosen, B. M., and others. *Utilization of Psychiatric Facilities by Children: Current Status, Trends, Implications*. Washington, D.C.: U.S. Government Printing Office, 1968.

Rosen, G. *A History of Public Health*. New York: MD Publications, 1958.

Rosen, G. *Madness in Society: Chapters in the Historical Sociology of Mental Illness*. Chicago: University of Chicago Press, 1968.

Rutter, M., Lebovici, S., and others. "A Triaxial Classification of Mental Disorders in Childhood." *Journal of Child Psychology and Psychiatry*, 1969, *10*, 41-61.

Rutter, M., Shaffer, D., and Shepherd, M. "An Evaluation of the Proposal for a Multiaxial Classification of Child Psychiatric Disorders (the British study)." Report to the World Health Organization, Preliminary Communication. *Psychological Medicine*, 1972, *3*, 244-250.

Sartorius, N., and others. "WHO Pilot Study of Schizophrenia: Preliminary Communication." *Psychology and Medicine*, 1972, *2*, 422-425.

Shepherd, M., and Cooper, B. "Epidemiology and Mental Disorder—A Review." *Journal of Neurology, Neurosurgery, and Psychiatry*, 1964, *27*, 277-290.

Shepherd, M., and others. "An Experimental Approach to Psychiatric Diagnosis: An International Study." *Acta Psychiatrica Scandinavica*, 1968, *44*, Supplement 201.

Spitzer, R. L., and Endicott, J. "Diagno: A Computer Program for Psychiatric Diagnosis Utilizing the Differential Diagnostic Procedure." *Archives of General Psychiatry*, 1968, *18*, 746-756.

Spitzer, R. L., and Endicott, J. "Diagno II: Further Developments in a Computer Program for Psychiatric Diagnoses." *American Journal of Psychiatry*, 1969, *125*, 12-21.

Steinberg, J., and Cooper, H. R. "Social Security Statistical Data: Social Science Research and Confidentiality." *Social Security Bulletin*, Aug. 1967, pp. 1-14.

Strauss, J. S., Bartko, J. J., and Carpenter, W. T. "The Use of Clustering Techniques for the Classification of Psychiatric Patients." *British Journal of Psychiatry*, 1973 (in press).

Taube, C. A., and others. *Statistical Notes.* Biometry Branch, Office of Program Planning and Evaluation, National Institute of Mental Health, Health Services and Mental Health Administration. Washington, D.C.: U.S. Department of Health, Education, and Welfare, 1969-1973.

Thompson, M. T., and Hayden, A. C. (Eds.) *Standard Nomenclature of Diseases and Operations.* (5th Ed.) New York: McGraw-Hill, 1961.

U.S. Department of Commerce, Bureau of the Census. *U.S. Census of Population: 1960 Final Report PC(2)-4B. Persons by Family Characteristics.* Washington, D.C.: U.S. Government Printing Office, 1964.

U.S. Department of Health, Education, and Welfare. *Vital Statistics of the United States, 1955. Supplement: Mortality Data, Multiple Causes of Death.* Washington, D.C.: U.S. Government Printing Office, 1965.

U.S. Department of Health, Education, and Welfare. *Eighth Revision, International Classification of Diseases, Adapted for Use in the United States (ICDA).* Tabular list. Public Health Publication No. 1693. Vol. I. Washington, D.C.: U.S. Government Printing Office, 1967.

U.S. Department of Health, Education, and Welfare. *Eighth Revision, International Classification of Diseases, Adapted for Use in the United States (ICDA).* Alphabetical Index. Public Health Service Publication No. 1693. Vol. II. Washington, D.C.: U.S. Government Printing Office, 1968.

U.S. Department of Health, Education, and Welfare. *Institutional Guide to DHEW Policy on Protection of Human Subjects.* DHEW Publication No. (NIH) 72-102. Washington, D.C.: U.S. Government Printing Office, 1971.

U.S. Department of Health, Education, and Welfare. *Policy Statement— National Center for Health Statistics.* Washington, D.C.: U.S. Government Printing Office, 1973.

Wilner, D. M., and others. *The Housing Environment and Family Life: A Longitudinal Study of the Effects of Housing on Morbidity and Mental Health.* Baltimore: Johns Hopkins Press, 1962.

Wilson, J. M. G., and Jungner, G. *Principles and Practice of Screening for Disease.* Public Health Papers No. 34. Geneva: World Health Organization, 1968.

Wing, J. K. "A Standard Form of Psychiatric Present State Examination." In E. H. Hare and J. K. Wing (Eds.), *Psychiatric Epidemiology.* London: Oxford University Press, 1970.

Winokur, G., Clayton, P. J., and Reich, T. *Manic Depressive Illness.* St. Louis: C. V. Mosby, 1969.

Wooton, B., with Seal, V. G., and Chambers, R. *Social Science and Social Pathology.* New York: Macmillan, 1959.

World Health Organization. *Manual of the International Statistical Classification of Diseases, Injuries, and Causes of Death.* Sixth Revision of the International List of Diseases and Causes of Death, Adapted 1948. Vol. I. Geneva: World Health Organization, 1948.

World Health Organization, Expert Committee on Health Statistics. *Hospital Statistics and Other Matters.* Eighth Report. WHO Technical Report Series, No. 261. Geneva: World Health Organization, 1963.

World Health Organization. *Manual of the International Statistical Classification of Diseases, Injuries, and Causes of Death.* Geneva: World Health Organization, 1967.

World Health Organization, Expert Committee on Health Statistics. *Statistics of Health Services and of Their Activities.* Thirteenth report. WHO Technical Report Series No. 429. Geneva: World Health Organization, 1969.

World Health Organization, Expert Committee on Health Statistics. *Statistical Indicators for the Planning and Evaluation of Public Health Programmes.* Fourteenth Report. WHO Technical Report Series No. 472. Geneva: World Health Organization, 1971.

World Health Organization, Study Group on the Classification of Diseases, Ninth Revision of the ICD. *Proposed Revision of Chapter V, Mental Disorders.* Document ICD/WP/72.5. Geneva: World Health Organization, 1973a. (Mimeo.)

World Health Organization. *Report of the International Pilot Study of Schizophrenia.* Geneva: World Health Organization, 1973b.

World Health Organization. "Clinical Classifications by Computer." In *Report of the International Pilot Study of Schizophrenia.* Geneva: World Health Organization, 1973c.

World Health Organization. *Glossary of Mental Disorders.* Geneva: World Health Organization (in press).

Zubin, J. (Ed.) *Field Studies in the Mental Disorders.* New York: Grune and Stratton, 1961.

THE LABELING
APPROACH TO
DEVIANCE

Prudence M. Rains, John I. Kitsuse,
Troy Duster, Eliot Freidson

In this chapter we discuss some of the issues—theoretical, methodological, and empirical—involved in the "labeling" approach to the sociology of deviance (an approach also identified by the terms *interactionist, societal reaction,* and *social control*). While the labeling approach has raised these issues, it has not produced an explicitly formulated theory of deviance and therefore has been subjected to criticism by friendly as well as hostile commentators (Gibbs, 1966; Gove, 1970; Mankoff, 1971; Manning, 1973; Schur, 1971; Thio, 1973). It has, nevertheless, been productive in clarifying some of the underlying assumptions of more conventional views and in defining a distinctive perspective from which problems of deviance might be conceived and formulated.

In essence, the labeling perspective shifts the theoretical concern from the etiological question of deviant behavior (how persons come to act in ways that are different, disapproved of, abnormal) to the question of how deviants are controlled (how persons come to be defined and treated as deviant) and how the label *deviant* systematizes and stabilizes forms of behavior among labeled individuals (Lemert, 1967). "Deviant behavior" as such, however, reappears in a new context. A distinction is made between behavior which may be the occasion for the imputation of deviance (the traditional conception of deviant behavior) and the behavior *which is a consequence* of the assignment of persons to deviant statuses (the labeling perspective). From this new perspective, the investigation of deviant behavior is directed to the limitations imposed by deviant statuses on the access of deviants to the "rights of citizenship" routinely accorded to nondeviants. Thus, specifically *deviant* behavior is theoretically linked to the processes of social control. As a result of this shift in emphasis, the relationship between deviance and social control is reformulated. The conventional idea that deviance leads to social control is held open, so that we may investigate whether and how social-control activities generate deviance (Lemert, 1967) by selecting the forms of behavior and the types of persons who make up officially defined populations of deviants.

Social Process of Classification

The labeling perspective on deviance raises a number of implications for the classification of exceptional children. The perspective suggests, first of all, that the designation *exceptional child* should be considered a social status rather than a complex of biological, psychological, cultural, and social characteristics shared by a population of individuals. That is, the labeling perspective directs attention to the prevailing *conceptions* of the various categories of exceptional children—conceptions ranging from the most common everyday notions to the most sophisticated and scientifically grounded ideas. Conceiving of the problem of exceptional children in this way leads us to ask how the category came into being: What are the historical, cultural, social, political, and legal processes that produced the various categories of exceptional children? This line of investigation is exemplified in deviance research by Sutherland's (1950) analysis of the development of sexual psychopath laws; by various studies of drug-control legislation (Lindesmith, 1947; Becker, 1963; Duster, 1970); by Gusfield's (1963) study of the prohibition movement; by Chambliss's (1964) historical study of vagrancy laws; and by Platt's (1969) analysis of the juvenile court movement.

Historically, it appears that the development of the categories of exceptional children—unlike those of sexual psychopath, vagrant, and drug addict—was grounded in an ideology of help and service rather than punishment. But more detail than that is necessary for understanding their character. For example, in what institutional areas was the "problem" or "condition" said to exist—the family, the school, the correctional institutions, the medical facilities? What groups were involved in defining and describing the nature of the problem? Which other groups were solicited to support and sponsor these category-defining activities? And how were the various interests of these groups reflected in the developing "official" conception of the social category, the criteria by which members of the category are to be identified, the programs that would make those criteria operational, and the treatment to be applied to populations produced by such operations?

These questions lead us to the view that any consideration of the classification of exceptional children should begin with a question that examines the assumptions contained in the category itself: What is an "exceptional child" and who says so? Answers to such a question lead to a further question: What makes this category of child exceptional to those who define it as such, and why this child and not others? The answer to *this* question is likely to be considered obvious, but some cases are more obvious than others. Surely, the blind are more "exceptional" than the left-handed, and the mentally retarded are more exceptional than the child with a speech impediment. But is the bilingual child more exceptional than the black child, or are the children of migrants more exceptional than those from the upper-middle class? It is just as sensible to ask why blind, mentally retarded, or culturally deprived children should be considered exceptional as to ask about left-handed, upper-middle-class, or gifted children. Clearly, the children considered "exceptional" are the children who create "social problems" for institutions responsible for their welfare. Thus, categories of exceptional children are expressions of values that may vary with time and place. This conception of social problems—a conception that contains assertions about the existence of certain "social conditions" considered undesirable, harmful, or otherwise detrimental to the individuals in question and to the welfare of society—provides the basis, then, for identifying populations of children as exceptional (Kitsuse and Spector, 1973).

But what is a "social problem" and who says so? The question reflects the distinctive emphasis of the labeling perspective on deviance: "Social groups create deviance by making the rules whose infraction constitutes deviance, and by applying those rules to particular people and labeling them as outsiders" (Becker, 1963, p. 9). The political character of the deviant-defining process is clearly underlined in this statement, as is the view that the quality of deviance does not reside in the acts defined but in the application of socially generated rules. This view contains the general proposition that—given any status category and given a set of criteria, implicit or explicit, to identify members of that category—it is a matter of political authority (in the general sense) whether and how a population of that category will be produced. The relationship between the presumed criteria on which a population is being differentiated and the application of those criteria in the process of identification and differentiation of populations is considered problematic.

We do not mean to imply that the social processes producing populations of deviants should be investigated in an effort to make the process more "efficient"—that is, so that the criteria of classification will be more systematically and rigorously applied. Rather, the processes should be investigated in an effort to understand how individuals, quite heterogeneous with respect to the stated criteria of classification, come to be differentiated as members of the same population. From this perspective, then, a study of individuals who are classified, categorized, and differentiated in a common population is not likely by itself to yield an understanding of "the problem" or a basis for assessing the relative values of programs of remediation and treatment. Quite literally, it is the process of differentiation that has created and defined "the problem" and assigned it to those identified as "having" it. Whatever characteristics such individuals may or may not have had in common prior to their classification, it is their involvement in the classification process that has generated the characteristics they all share—their social fate as members of a status category. Thus, just as it has been said that law is the formal cause of crime, so can it be said that classification is the formal cause of mental retardation, speech impediments, and school phobias.

Uses of Classification in Social Agencies

As indicated, the social and political contexts in which a condition is defined as a problem are of fundamental interest in the examination of the status-differentiation process. Of particular interest are the claims advanced by various groups as to the nature of the problem, the terms in which the range and intensity of that problem are documented, the proposed methods for identifying the problem population, and the rationale of treatment programs for the classified populations. Sociologists of labeling have examined a range of such issues—among them, the relation between politics and the definition of deviant categories, the application of "objective criteria" in differentiating populations, the manipulation of classification criteria to expand and contract target populations, and the effects of bureaucratic considerations on the restriction of service to particular segments of the classified population.

According to the labeling perspective, the agencies authorized to classify and treat populations of deviants should be closely examined before the deviant populations themselves are examined. This argument, based on a critique of the uses of official statistics (Kitsuse and Cicourel, 1963), interprets classification schemes (and the statistics they produce) with reference to the organizational practices in which they are applied rather than the logic that presumably provides their rationale. The general argument is that, whatever their original sources (psychiatric, educational, medical, legal), classification systems are in fact used to fit the purposes and needs of those who employ them organizationally. (Chapters in Part III of this book discuss the uses of classification in various organizational settings.)

In mental institutions, particularly in public institutions that house a wide variety of persons, the effective and practical distinctions useful for the organization of staff activities are grounded not in psychiatric theory but in more practical considerations: whether or not patients are ambulatory, can feed themselves, remain continent, and so forth. In such settings personnel who must deal with patients daily are likely to view medical diagnoses as formal classifications and to treat such diagnoses perfunctorily as they go about organizing treatment activities. In settings more constrained to employ a given set of categories (for example, in legal settings), the categories in use will be adaptations of the scheme to the problems at hand and thus will reflect organizational practices for dealing with persons rather than the realities presumably described in the categories.

Sudnow (1965), in his study of a public defender's office, notes that the defenders gradually adapted a set of legal categories to their own routine conceptions of the "normal" crimes for that area. Another example is provided in a study (Brand, 1973) of an inner-city school heavily populated by a wide variety of recent immigrants. In that setting teachers used the services of a regularly visiting speech therapist as one of a number of strategies for dealing in a practical, ad hoc way with the systematic classroom problems posed by children whose difficulties could not be understood. Since it was not clear whether the children had learning difficulties, emotional problems, or merely problems in understanding English, the speech therapy classes were converted *in practice* from a specialized service to a general organizational resource for dealing with the teachers' more immediate problems.

These examples given may be extreme, but they are not exotic. Schools, like mental hospitals and courts of law, have a large and varied clientele, and thus face numerous practical problems in organizing limited resources. They have, therefore, good organizational reasons for putting specialized facilities to a variety of uses, many of which may not have been envisioned in the setting up of those facilities. They have to make do, and the practical schemes for categorizing and dealing with their clientele will almost inevitably take precedence over logical and more theoretically coherent schemes. In such circumstances, the labeling perspective directs attention to the fact that persons who are officially processed on the basis of formal criteria of classification (for instance, mental retardates, senile, criminally insane) may be actually treated and managed on quite practical grounds of concrete organizational convenience and exigency.

The labeling perspective also regards the distinction between deviant and conventional acts or persons as intrinsically ambiguous and arbitrary. The distinction is not "given," so to speak, by reality. Instead, salient and socially meaningful differences among persons (and acts) are a product of our ways of looking, our schemes for seeing and dealing with people. Thus, people are *made* different—that is, socially differentiated—by the process of being seen and treated as different in a system of social practices that crystallizes distinctions between deviant and conventional behavior and persons. For example, the legal definition of blindness is clear-cut, but it includes poorly sighted persons as well as persons who are totally impaired visually. The legal definition therefore serves to crystallize blindness as both a social status and an experience of self for those persons who might not otherwise have defined themselves as blind. Similarly, the differentiation of juvenile delinquents is made possible by a variety of special standards for children—including unspecified offenses such as "incorrigibility," "malicious mischief," "obscene language"—to which adults are not held. In this sense, the labeling view underlines the inevitable arbitrariness of the distinctions produced by the deviant-defining process, leading in turn to the view that any *classification* scheme is inevitably arbitrary, since it organizes and enforces distinctions that are intrinsically ambiguous in reality.

Although this notion of intrinsic ambiguity may seem merely a nice philosophical point, the view that the deviant-producing process is differentially selective is more sharply focused. This theme emphasizes the fact that the persons designated and treated as deviants are in no sense a random sample of all persons who presumably might be qualified by the criteria that social agencies purport to apply for identifying and treating populations. The activities of agencies that produce populations of deviants often are organized by considerations and concerns that may be quite independent of the acts, characteristics, or qualities of persons so identified. Professional ideologies concerning those who are "sick" and "need help," the particular population that an agency takes to be its "clientele," and the patterns of interagency referrals that produce new clients may lead to a highly selected and biased sample of "deviants."

One variant of the differential-selection theme from the labeling perspective focuses on the ways that persons become enmeshed in the net cast by the official agencies of social control. Studies pursuing this line of investigation (see, for instance, Goffman, 1959, pp. 123-124) document the contingencies that account for the presence of persons in the client populations of one or another social-control agency. Most frequently, according to these studies, people are admitted to these agencies not because the specific acts imputed to them make them appropriate for a specific form of social control but as the result of arbitrary processes and practices. Scheff (1966), for example, in his study of the legal procedures for the commitment of the mentally ill, focuses on the question: To what extent is entry to the status of mental patients independent of the behavior or the "condition" of the patient? His data indicate a most tenuous relationship between the psychiatric criteria that presumably are applied to document the existence of mental illness and the behavior of the persons alleged to manifest that illness. Similarly, Sudnow's (1965) study of the processing of cases in a criminal court provides data that show the problematic relationship between the acts with which defendants are charged and the legally defined acts on which they are prosecuted and adjudicated.

A number of other studies point out that social-control agencies do not acquire or handle their clients merely or even necessarily on the basis of behavior, but on the basis of matters essentially unrelated to it. In their study of a police agency, for example, Skolnick and Woodworth (1967) observed that 40 percent of the statutory rape complaints came from the family-support division by way of applications for aid to dependent children. Information about rape typically was revealed in conjunction with complaints about poverty-related problems of pregnancy rather than with charges of statutory rape as a legally defined or even a socially defined violation. Similarly, studies of legal commitment of the mentally ill suggest that the proceedings do not examine the validity of the complaints by legal or psychiatric standards in deciding the question of commitment.

Scott's (1969) study of social agencies established to "help" their clients illustrates another facet of the differential-selection process. In contrast to the agencies of social control, which select persons for attention and treatment without regard to the fact of offense, the helping agencies often ignore or reject those who are qualified. Scott argues, for instance, that the massively funded and numerous agencies for the blind systematically service children and young adults, who account for a very small proportion of the total blind population, and systematically underservice the aged blind, who constitute a very large proportion of that population. Administrators and personnel of such agencies, like other production-oriented organizations, tend to be attentive to the segment of their client population that is most likely to show a payoff for rehabilitative programs. This form of differential selection has been called "creaming" the client population—selecting that segment of the population most amenable to yielding results that will redound to the credit of the helping organization. One interpretation of this phenomenon is that it tends to differentiate those who are least different, while simultaneously reinstituting the same differences one notch lower for those who have already suffered from these differences. To illustrate, workshops for mentally retarded young adults that reward their workers on the basis of their productivity or capabilities for learning may benefit the most capable mental retardates; but they do so at the expense of the less capable, who are being classified according to the same system of values that assigned them their primary status as mental retardates. The creaming of the mental retardate population simply grades those most disadvantaged in such a system one notch lower; thus, the social agencies impose the double disadvantage of classifying mental retardates vis-à-vis the "normal" population as well as identifying them as the least capable among the retardates.

Scott has made much of the differences in orientation of services for the blind as administered and staffed by the blind themselves, as compared to those run by "blindness" workers. In the former, the orientation is practical and technical and focuses on maximizing remnant sight; in the latter, the orientation is psychological and focuses on getting the person to accept his blindness. A similar conflict between the deaf and professionals who work with the deaf concerns the use of sign language as a supplement to the oral approach. The deaf favor the inclusion of "signing," which of course reduces the usual advantage of hearing on the part of the professionals who work with the deaf.

These observations on the helping agencies suggest that the presuppositions underlying their activities should be reexamined—particularly the assumption that the professionals know everything that is relevant about their clients (the problems they must cope with, the stigma they suffer, the realities they must accommodate). It is likely that disadvantaged persons, even mental retardates and children, are a great deal more capable of appreciating their own situation than has been acknowledged by the professionals.

Effect on the Classified

The term *self-fulfilling prophecy* is commonly used to indicate the formidable effects of labels on the organization of treatment accorded deviants by "normal" members of society, and in turn on the self-conceptions and behaviors of individuals on whom those labels are imposed. The consequences of labels for the treatment accorded those labeled have been more systematically investigated than the self-definitional effects. Goffman (1961) and Rosenhan (1973), for instance, have shown that a person's presence in a mental institution serves as an interpretive scheme for his conduct in the eyes of others. The argument here is not so much that persistent treatment of a person as mentally ill necessarily makes that person mentally ill, but rather that treatment may allocate identities which are real for those around the person and must therefore be taken into account by the deviant, even when those identities appear murky, elusive, and difficult to confront. In an experimental study by Schwartz and Skolnick (1962), for example, subjects were presented with various legal dossiers of the criminal records of fictitious persons. When such dossiers were presented to prospective employers as part of the application for employment, those with records of conviction and imprisonment were most frequently rejected.

When an agency designates persons as *deviant*, then, is the agency thereby producing deviants rather than simply identifying them? To what extent does the self-fulfilling prophecy operate in these classification processes? The relationship between definition and conduct with regard to deviance has been most systematically formulated by Lemert (1951). His analysis of "secondary deviation" is widely regarded as the central concept in the labeling approach to deviance. The concept has, however, been the subject of commentary and criticism but relatively little systematic empirical research. Lemert's own work on stutterers (1967) provides a model for such an investigation. As Lemert shows, the reactions encountered by persons with speech impediments in various institutional contexts form the bases for their conceptions of themselves as stutterers. In a more focused "institutional approach to the study of self,"

Goffman (1959) demonstrates that the treatment of patients in mental hospitals provides the framework for their construction of the "mental patient" self-image. Rains's (1971) study of the processes shaping the self-conceptions of unwed pregnant girls in maternity homes provides further documentation of the internalization by inmates of the institutional definitions of their condition. Similarly, Spradley (1970) has investigated the self-conceptions that "drunks" develop as a result of the punitive "revolving-door" treatment to which they are subjected by the law-enforcement and adjudication process. More recently, Zimbardo (1973) has shown that persons randomly assigned to roles as inmates and guards in a simulation of a prison assume the behaviors, attitudes, and self-conceptions of their respective roles.

The labeling view of the relation between the societal reaction toward "deviants" and the self-definitional effects has been criticized as excessively deterministic (Manning, 1973). Such criticism is based on an uncharitably simplistic reformulation, not on a close interpretation. Lemert's formulation (1951), for example, allows for individual variations with regard to the actions taken by those who invoke and apply the label as well as the reactions of the putative deviant to the label imposed upon him. In the present state of theoretical development, the issue is not a matter of deciding the deterministic effects of labels but rather of investigating variations in the *systematic articulation* of the labeling of populations and the treatment accorded them. For example, we might expect that labeling and treatment will have different effects in informal peer groups than in formally organized bureaucratic settings. Likewise, we might expect the relation between treatment and self-conception to vary along dimensions such as the degree to which the setting constitutes a "total institution" (Goffman, 1961), the existence of counterdefinitions and groups supporting them, organizational schisms among personnel that undermine the systematic effects of the treatment, and the like. (The perspective of the labeled child is considered in Chapter Twenty-One.)

Conclusions

The labeling perspective in the study of deviance is one among several possible analytic angles of inquiry. As such, it has the virtues and drawbacks of any perspective: it organizes and emphasizes certain elements in the phenomenal field, and by so doing deemphasizes or ignores other elements. And like any perspective, it is in continual danger of being reified by those who employ it conceptually, simplified by those who use it practically in empirical investigation, and vulgarized into a tautology by those who reduce a point of view to a definition.

We have tried to show that this perspective can produce a different level of insight into the study of deviance and a fuller understanding of the larger issues of control. Specifically, the labeling perspective inclines the observer to be more attentive to the social organization of status differentiation and status categorization and to be more sensitive to the effects of these matters on those who occupy organizationally processed social statuses—the effects on their self-conceptions, competencies, wills, potentialities, and activities. A particularly global, unique, and skilled observer with the traditional etiological approach to deviance might well be sensitive to these matters listed above, but the labeling approach *systematically* sensitizes any observer who uses it to be skeptical about reifying deviant-status categories. It is this compelling attention to the process of social organization of categorizing "deviants" that makes for the doubts and inquiries about the use of such institutionalized labels as *mental retardate* or *underachiever* or *behavior problem*.

The assumption that is built into helping agencies and institutions is that persons so categorized need a kind of help that is based less upon tapping the potential variety of competencies and interests and desires of those so categorized, and more upon the prevailing conventional wisdom of the "normals" as practical actors in these agencies. Since a skeptical or critical attitude is a near prerequisite to fruitful empirical investigation, if this were the only value of applying the labeling approach to the study of various classifications of exceptional children, it would be a contribution of considerable significance.

References

Becker, H. S. *Outsiders: Studies in the Sociology of Deviance.* New York: Free Press, 1963.

Brand, J. "Teaching in an Inner City School." Unpublished master's thesis, McGill University, 1973.

Chambliss, W. J. "A Sociological Analysis of the Law of Vagrancy." *Social Problems*, Summer 1964, *12*, 66-77.

Duster, T. S. *The Legislation of Morality.* New York: Free Press, 1970.

Gibbs, J. P. "Conceptions of Deviant Behavior: The Old and the New." *Pacific Sociological Review*, Spring 1966, *9*, 9-14.

Goffman, E. "The Moral Career of the Mental Patient." *Psychiatry*, May 1959, *22*, 123-142.

Goffman, E. *Asylums*. New York: Anchor Books, 1961.

Gove, W. R. "Societal Reaction as an Explanation of Mental Illness: An Evaluation." *American Sociological Review*, Oct. 1970, *35*, 873-884.

Gusfield, J. *Symbolic Crusade*. Urbana: University of Illinois Press, 1963.

Kitsuse, J. I., and Cicourel, A. V. "A Note on the Uses of Official Statistics." *Social Problems*, Fall 1963, *11*, 131-139.

Kitsuse, J. I., and Spector, M. "Toward a Sociology of Social Problems: Social Conditions, Value Judgments, and Social Problems." *Social Problems*, Spring 1973, *20*, 407-419.

Lemert, E. M. *Social Pathology*. New York: McGraw-Hill, 1951.

Lemert, E. M. *Human Deviance, Social Problems, and Social Control*. Englewood Cliffs, N.J.: Prentice-Hall, 1967.

Lindesmith, A. R. *Opiate Addiction*. Bloomington, Ind.: Principia Press, 1947.

Mankoff, M. "Societal Reaction and Career Deviance: A Critical Analysis." *Sociological Quarterly*, Spring 1971, *12*, 204-218.

Manning, P. K. "Survey Essay: On Deviance." *Contemporary Sociology*, March 1973, *2*, 123-138.

Platt, A. M. *The Child Savers: The Invention of Delinquency*. Chicago: University of Chicago Press, 1969.

Rains, P. M. *Becoming an Unwed Mother*. Chicago: Aldine Press, 1971.

Rosenhan, D. L. "On Being Sane in Insane Places." *Science*, Jan. 1973, *179*, 1-9.

Scheff, T. J. *Being Mentally Ill*. Chicago: Aldine Press, 1966.

Schur, E. M. *Labeling Deviant Behavior: Its Sociological Implications*. Englewood Cliffs, N.J.: Prentice-Hall, 1971.

Schwartz, R. D., and Skolnick, J. K. "Two Studies of Legal Stigma." *Social Problems*, Fall 1962, *10*, 133-142.

Scott, R. *The Making of Blind Men*. New York: Russell Sage, 1969.

Skolnick, J. K., and Woodworth, J. R. "Bureaucracy, Information, and Social Control: A Study of a Morals Detail." In D. J. Bordua (Ed.), *The Police*. New York: Wiley, 1967.

Spradley, J. P. *You Owe Yourself a Drunk*. Boston: Little, Brown, 1970.

Sudnow, D. "Normal Crimes: Sociological Features of the Penal Code in a Public Defender's Office." *Social Problems*, Winter 1965, *12*, 255-276.

Sutherland, E. H. "The Diffusion of Sexual Psychopath Laws." *American Journal of Sociology*, Sept. 1950, *56*, 142-148.

Thio, A. "Class Bias in the Sociology of Deviance." *American Sociologist*, February 1973, *8*, 1-12.

Zimbardo, P. "A Pirandellian Prison." *New York Times Magazine*, April 8, 1973, pp. 38-60.

5

COMMUNITY PERSPECTIVES

William C. Rhodes, Mark Sagor

Classification systems, as they now exist in caretaking agencies in our society, perform the twin functions of social and psychic control for the dominant culture bearers, who determine inclusion and exclusion from the social mainstream. Ours is not the only society that has chosen particular classification systems as the basis for inclusion and extrusion of its members. This collective process is part of any society (Benedict, 1934; Rhodes,

We acknowledge our indebtedness to the work of several others, both groups and individuals. The idea of viewing deviance from "the other side" is consonant with some social-deviance theorists (see, for instance, Becker, 1963). Much of the historical data is taken from a series of reviews of individual service-delivery systems authored by Lee Atkinson, Margaret Fraser, Ed Hoffman, Barry Moore, Daniel Pekarsky, and Christopher Unger. While acknowledging this debt, we personally assume all responsibility for our interpretations and for the implications drawn in this chapter. The committee that directed our work consisted of Peter Mattis (deceased), University of Michigan; Philip Mann, University of Indiana; and Richard Esparaza, University of Michigan.

1972). Our society, however, has been able to carry the trait and style preferences further than most past societies because our caretaking agencies have benefited from advanced technology for detecting, fixing, and separating even the slightest nuances of departures from chosen types. As receptacles for eliminating psychological threats, negative categories and caretaking agencies provide the technical equivalent of the scapegoating rituals which have been a part of any society in any period of time. Because the image ideal becomes more sharply drawn and constricted as cultures evolve over time (Benedict, 1934, p. 72), and because of the extensive range of contradicting impulses, desires, and behavioral tendencies in any human being, the dominant culture bearers are in a constant bind and need to ward off these recurrent internal threats to their narrow image ideal. Also, because daily existence is filled with real external threats (natural disasters, wars, disease, social conflict), the integrity of the psychic self-image is constantly bombarded and almost overwhelmed with anxieties which have to be extruded. Thus, the classification systems can provide the social emptying pots into which to project and extrude all manner of psychological threat.

This is not to imply that there may be no differences in people to begin with. Some individuals are born with or develop decided differences. The central issue is what society does with these differences, real or imagined. In crystallizing restricted life-style and character-trait biases, our society has created a predicament for itself—the deviance predicament. The predicament lies in the tight, narrow borders that the dominant culture bearers have drawn around themselves, so that large numbers of their members have been relegated to the other side of the wall. The roots of this predicament go back to European culture at the end of the Middle Ages, when madness came upon the stage in a particular role. Madness had certainly existed before that time; but it now took on a new social interpretation and moved into the obsessive, threat-absorbent spaces formerly occupied by leprosy. "Madness was perceived through a condemnation of idleness and in a social immanence guaranteed by the community of labor. This community acquired an ethical power of segregation, which permitted it to eject, as into another world, all forms of social uselessness. It was in this *other world*, encircled by the sacred powers of labor, that madness would assume the status we now attribute to it. If there is [in this notion of madness] something which refers elsewhere and to *other things*, it is no longer because the madman comes from the world of the irrational and bears its stigmata; rather, it is because he crosses the frontiers of bourgeois order of his own accord, and alienates himself outside the sacred limits of its ethic" (Foucault, 1973, p. 58).

The bourgeois notion of madness and other forms of deviance was sustained and animated by a moral perception. Poverty, it was held, is not caused by scarcity of commodities, or by unemployment, but by the weakening of discipline and the relaxation of morals. The edict of 1657 is full of similar moral denunciations and strange threats: "The libertinage of beggars has risen to excess because of an unfortunate tolerance of crimes of all sorts, which attracts the curse of God upon the state were they to remain unpunished" (quoted in Foucault, 1973, p. 59). This deviance ethos has a very familiar ring. One of the knottiest problems in the deviance predicament of our modern society is that the scientific terminology of our classification systems and the scientific "treatment" of our caretaking agencies completely obscure the moral maledictions and proscriptions underlying them. One way to begin to uncover these roots is to examine their growth and development in the historical context of our nation. (For a discussion of the historical development of classification, see Chapter Seven in this book.)

We do not argue that this conceptual framework is a truer, or even a more accurate, representation than that of the professional classifiers. We merely present it as an alternative view, a view that is perhaps necessary to temper and augment professional dogma. It tries to adopt a frame of reference arising out of the dynamic events of community life rather than out of the theoretical constructions of professionals and scientists. It may seem strange and alien to professional readers who are used to approaching the problem by tracing the origins and evolution of their own classification and intervention theories. This latter approach would produce only a house history, one written from inside. It would end up being every bit as partisan as this particular version might appear to the professionals; after all, professionals do have a vested interest in classification.

Our current national classification systems for children emerged from a nation subjected to constant floods of change: heavy influxes of alien groups; major social philosophies which dominated public thinking in different periods; and strong, charismatic leaders who became spokesmen for such philosophies. Notice, for instance, the sense of alarm of the dominant Protestant-American population of the United States in response to the influx of aliens into this country during the late nineteenth and early twentieth centuries: "Instead of assimilating at once with customs of the country of their adoption, our foreign population are too much in the habit of retaining their national usages, of associating too exclusively with each other, and living in groups together. These practices serve no good purposes, and tend merely to alienate those among whom they have chosen to reside. It would be a part of wisdom to abandon at once all usages and associations which mark them as foreigners, and to become in feeling and custom, as well as in privileges and rights, citizens of the United States" (from the Boston *American*; quoted in Handlin, 1959, p. 185). Somewhat later, a psychologist sounded a similar alarm in response to another group of "aliens"—the mentally retarded and the mentally ill: "There are two million people in the United States who, because of their weak minds or their diseased minds, are making our country a dangerous place to live in. The two million is increasing both by heredity and by training. We are breeding defectives. We are making criminals" (Goddard, 1921, p. iv).

In the community model suggested here, alarm becomes distilled into public residual labels, collective images which act as common signals for defense. Once such labels are fixed in the public repository, they may function autonomously, like alarm systems gone awry—constantly alerting, constantly warning, constantly stirring response. Even after the events which brought them into existence have passed, they can go on existing in the living repository of collective life as though past events were current threats to the integrity of the whole. They provide exponential power to any other threats which may be occurring in the here and now.

Another part of this threat potential seems particularly pertinent to our own experience. That is, the alarm directed toward alien custom carriers such as immigrant groups, and toward certain human conditions such as poverty and dependency, is also directed toward the residential spaces where the "foreign populations carry out their alien usages and practices, associating with each other and living in groups together" (Handlin, 1959, p. 185). Thus, certain spaces of the city take on the threatening quality of their "foreign" residents, and become

Community Perspectives 105

provocative and fearful to those who reside in the larger masses of space surrounding them. In 1893, the *New York Times* said of the Jewish community in the Lower East Side: "This neighborhood, peopled almost entirely by the people who claim to have been driven from Poland and Russia, is the eyesore of New York and perhaps the filthiest place in the western continent. It is impossible for a Christian to live there because he will be driven out, either by blows or the dirt and the stench—They cannot be lifted up to a higher plane because they do not want to be" (quoted in Bernard, 1973, p. 19). In the Massachusetts senate documents of 1847 it is recorded that the Irish are displacing "the honest and respectable laborers of the state; and— from their manner of living—work for much less per day—being satisfied with food to support their minimal existence alone— while [native American workers] not only labor for the body but for the mind, the soul, and the state" (quoted in Handlin, 1959, p. 185).

Various protective barriers can come to be erected between alien territories and alienated populations. References to "the other side of the tracks" or "the undesirable side" of the river or the expressway indicate certain physical barriers. Protective real estate practices in the surrounding areas are still another type of barrier. Still another way of putting distance between these territories and the territories surrounding them is through the use of public mediating structures: police and corrections, social services, mental health, and education. All these structures, as they focus on child clientele, are closely associated with historical shorthand alarm signals, concentrated in such terms as *incorrigible and dissolute, dependent and neglected, diseased minds,* or *weak minds.* These emotionally laden terms are distilled symbols which stand for a permeating ethos of protective anxiety. The distilled symbols are probably less disturbing phenomenologically than the fantasied experiences of direct contact with the areas and individual presence for which they stand. In a sense, the symbols might be said to be a way of cooling and diluting the fear of what they stand for. They might be conceived of as second-order symbols for feared direct experiential exposure to the alien area, its population, and its phenomenologically threatening individuals.

Still more distant, and perhaps less disconcerting to the main-line culture bearer, are the scientific and professional language labels of the mediating systems of care giving. These labels transfer the immediate threat to an even more removed language level, a third-order level. Instead of *incorrigible* and *dissolute,* the child is called a *delinquent*—a term coined by the Chicago Child Savers (Platt, 1969). Instead of Goddard's *diseased minds* or *weak minds,* the phenomenological language becomes *emotionally disturbed* or *mentally retarded.* These encapsulating terms somehow keep the threatening behaviors, conditions, and ethnic areas from arousing full-scale fear. However, the shorthand label does seem to stand for a much more inclusive referent. It seems to mean an alien area, an alien population, an alien way of life, a set of human conditions, an array of foreign behaviors. These alien components can be conjured up by the labels, even though the links between the current professional terms and the original phenomenological referents may have been lost in the passage of historical time out of which they have evolved.

Recently, however, the lost connections between current professional labels and past threat-recoil cycles associated with defense against alien infusions have been uncovered—by researchers in the areas of mental illness (Szasz, 1961, 1970), mental retardation (Mercer, 1973), criminality (Menninger, 1968), and delinquency (Platt, 1969). The views of Ivan Illich (1971) on the processing of children into social classes and of Christopher Jencks (1972) on the myth of equality production by schools are other examples of such uncovering.

Historical Background: Threat

American society after the Civil War was "predominantly one of small farms, small businesses, and small towns, in which both the hopelessly poor and the overwhelmingly rich were limited in number" (Goldman, 1952, p. 4). However, the war and rapid industrialization weakened this traditional social order. It was a time of swift and well-publicized rags-to-riches stories. There were also railroad scandals, bank scandals, and the Credit Mobilier affair involving the vice-president of the United States. Members of the old aristocracy, with their stern Protestant morality, felt threatened by the new concentrations of wealth, the dishonest practices, and the anonymous urban centers.

The 1860s witnessed the rise of the urban "boss" politician and "machine" politics. "Steadily, ineluctably, such politics went to extremes. The plundering became so bold and systematic that it amounted to a regular graft of a million dollars a month. The contempt for honesty reached the point where, in an election that worried [Boss] Tweed, the machine dutifully delivered a majority 8 percent greater than the total number of registered voters" (Goldman, 1952, p. 12). The "boss" represented the immigrants in the urban centers. His lieutenants met the newcomer at the dock. Later they might find him a job, loan him a few dollars, or get him out of trouble with the police. This method of political organization and control threatened traditional notions of American democracy.

During the 1870s the transition from the conditions of an agrarian society to an urban society created more tension and threat for the established social order. There were industrial and economic depressions of a magnitude unknown to a previously agricultural economy. The small businesses which could not survive the Depression were being absorbed and consolidated in monopolies like Standard Oil. In 1877, the United States had its first nationwide strike. Twenty-five people were killed in the streets of Pittsburgh in a strike-related incident. The frustration of the time was expressed by Henry George in *Progress and Poverty*: "We add knowledge to knowledge, and utilize invention after invention. . . . Yet it becomes no easier for the masses of our people to make a living. On the contrary, it is becoming harder . . . the gulf between the employed and the employer is growing wider; social contrasts are becoming sharper; as liveried carriages appear, so do barefooted children" (quoted in Goldman, 1952, p. 27).

During the next decade, the millions of immigrants who arrived from southern and eastern Europe found that America was no longer in a generous "give-us-your-poor" mood. These immigrants were generally impoverished and untrained in industrial skills. They were predominantly Catholic or Jewish. Their customs, appearance, and religion aroused many concerns. The national speech developed ethnic slurs: "wop" and "dago" for the Italian, "bohunk" for the Hungarian, "grease-ball" for the Greek, and "kike" for the Jew. The American Protective Association organized around anti-Catholic sentiments, and anti-semitism spread widely. In the immigrant slums the European doctrine of socialism had many supporters. In addition, the anarchist movement was quite strong until a bomb went off during an 1886 demonstration, indelibly associating anarchism with horror in the public mind.

The deviance predicament of that era was expressed in terms of Social Darwinism. Social Darwinism viewed society as an organism evolving slowly and evenly according to the dictates of nature. The best parts of society will survive and the worst will perish, leaving an improved society if man can resist the temptation to rig the process. "The dominant groups in America had simply done what dominant groups usually do. They had, quite unconsciously, picked from among available theories the ones that best protected their position and had impressed these ideas on the national mind as truth" (Goldman, 1952, p. 66). The Protestant doctrine of predetermination was used to justify the economic inequalities that were emerging as the companion to a mass industrial society. According to the famous New York preacher Henry Ward Beecher, "God has intended the great to be great and the little to be little." The very rich, following this doctrine, were identified as the most virtuous and efficient and the very poor as intemperate and extravagant. In other words, poverty was looked upon as a sin and a moral deficiency.

Between the threat of collectivization from the left and the rationale of indifference on the right stood a group interested in reform. This group included many people who were negatively affected by the power and status redistributions of the period: professionals, clergymen, farmers, women, and members of the preindustrial aristocracy. The clergy's reform motivation can readily be applied to other elements of the progressive or reform movement. Their social criticism was not due "solely to their disinterested perception of social problems and their earnest desire to improve the world, but also to the fact that as men who were in their own way suffering from the incidence of the status revolution they were able to understand and sympathize with the problems of other disinherited groups" (Hofstadter, 1955, p. 152).

Institutional Responses to Threat

School systems. Between 1852 and 1918 all of the United States enacted compulsory-school-attendance legislation. As the stability of American society became more tenuous (for reasons interpreted in the previous section), the tendency toward rigid enforcement increased. The poverty, brutality, and violence of the immigrants' tenement life contributed to a profound sense of threat. The enforcement of compulsory-education laws was supported by those who wanted to get the immigrant children off the street, by those who wanted to "Americanize" these strangers, and by those with humanitarian interests. In any case, this legislation transformed the school "from a relatively minor societal institution, catering largely to the middle class, to one which was not only *available* to all segments of the society, but which was legally empowered to *compel* all children to attend" (Hoffman, 1972, pp. 11-12).

In 1898 the educational commission of the city of Chicago evaluated the ailing Chicago school system at the request of the mayor and city council. This study (called the Harpur report), with its recommendations for the establishment of special "ungraded" classes and "parental" schools for children who could not be handled in the regular classes, influenced the policies of many urban school systems in the United States. "Public education did not take much interest in such special schools or classes until compulsory-attendance laws came into being. These laws forced all children of given ages into school. This brought to the attention of educators a group of children who for various reasons had previously been eliminated at an early age; they had not, therefore, caused the schools any trouble" (Heck, 1940, p. 21).

The language used to describe behaviorally variant children during the period when special classes were started reflects an orientation toward the threatening aspects of variance. Later, as the intensity of the perceived threat diminished, the vocabulary of behavioral variance would reflect etiological or explanatory concepts of deviance. But at that time the public image of deviance—exposed by threat, entangled with xenophobia, and expressed in administrative procedures—was closely associated with the image of the stranger, the outsider who threatened the established social order. The harsh language and defensive practices of that time are illustrated in a source quoted by the Harpur report, which related compulsory-attendance laws to the need for special classes: "The Compulsory Attendance Act has for its purpose the reformation of these vicious children. They cannot be received or continued in the regularly organized schools; they were admitted into these schools; they were reproved; they were punished for misconduct; they have been suspended from further attendance in their classes; their parents cannot or will not control them; teachers and committees fail to correct their evil tendencies and vicious conduct. What shall be done with them? The Compulsory Attendance Act commands that they shall be placed in schools; if not in regular schools then in other schools to be provided for them" (quoted in Hoffman, 1972, p. 14).

Other sections of the Harpur report emphasize the need to get these children off the streets: "There are also a large number of children who are constantly dropping out of our schools because of insubordination to discipline and want of cooperation between the parents and the teachers, and they are becoming vagrants upon the streets and a menace to good society. The welfare of the city demands that such children be put under restraint. . . . I therefore call attention again to the necessity of the establishment of a parental school for the benefit of such children" (quoted in Hoffman, 1972, p. 14).

In 1871 New Haven started the first ungraded school for mischievous and disruptive children. In 1879 the New Haven superintendent of schools stated: "The ungraded schools are an indispensable appendage to our graded system. They provide for a class of children, who, for any cause, must necessarily be irregular in their attendance, beyond certain limits. Unreasonably disobedient and insubordinate youths, who are a detriment to the good order and instruction of the school, are separated from it and placed here where they can be controlled and taught, without disturbing others. Truants, also, are placed in these schools for special discipline. The grade schools, relieved of these three classes, great burdens to the teachers, move on with greater ease and rapidity, while both pupils and teachers perform their duties with pleasure, satisfaction, and profit that would be impossible in the presence of disturbers of good order" (quoted in Hoffman, 1972, p. 17).

During the 1890s several major cities instituted special programs for "backward" children in the public schools. (For a more detailed summary of special education, see Chapter Sixteen in this book.) At the same time, special programs (called *steamer classes*) were being set up for non-English-speaking children. At that time, as at the present, the special classes were criticized for being a "dumping ground" for all children who could not be handled in the regular classes. H. A. Miller described the situation of the Cleveland schools in 1916: "At the present time such cases are often handled in a most unsatisfactory manner. The non-English-speaking child cannot keep up with his companions in the regular grades. For this reason he is sent to a special class, but if there is not a steamer class available, the pupil is all too frequently assigned to the backward class. This is not because the backward class is the right place for him, but rather because it furnishes an easy means of disposing of a pupil who, through no fault of his own, is an unsatisfactory member of a regular grade" (quoted in Hoffman, 1972, p. 18). It was also reported that backward children were assigned to steamer classes. The supervisor of primary schools in New Haven noted that "incorrigible boys, defective children, and children who speak no English" were placed together in special classes (Connecticut Special Education Association, 1936).

Public alarm over the behavior of "incorrigible" children was matched by public fears about the genetic "inferiority" of backward children. Even while Social Darwinism was being repudiated by social theorists, it was regaining an audience in the scientific guise of eugenics. In 1877 Richard Dugdale published his study of *The Jukes,* which was interpreted as supporting the view that poverty and immorality are determined primarily by biological inheritance. By the turn of the century the eugenics movement took organized form and "grew with such great rapidity that by 1915 it had reached the dimension of a fad" (Hofstadter, 1966, p. 161). Eugenists believed that the retarded were a menace to society because they threatened to populate the country with more criminals, dependents, imbeciles, and deviates. In 1907 the fears embodied in the movement were translated into the first sterilization law in the United States. By 1915 twelve states had similar laws.

Henry Goddard, recently saluted as a pioneer in special education (Irvine, 1971), helped sound the eugenic alarm in educational circles. In *The Kallikak Family* (1912) and *Feeblemindedness* (1916), Goddard advanced the theory that society's ills, social problems, and deviants were derived in large part from the genetic stock of the mentally deficient. He recommended mandatory sterilization for the mentally deficient. The threat posed by the backward child was further articulated by Paul Hanus (1913), a Harvard education professor, in a report to the New York City Commission on School Inquiry: "The means of discovering defective children and segregating them and caring for them, so far as they are segregated, are at present inadequate and defective; and . . . the danger of allowing such children to grow up at large is a very grave one. Such persons not only become a burden to society themselves, but propagate their kind in large numbers by marriage or illegitimate unions with each other or normal individuals. Whatever it costs, the city cannot safely perpetuate the inadequate measures of discovering and caring for its mentally defective children, and run the further risk of allowing the present progressive increase of mental defectives to continue unchecked" (quoted in Hoffman, 1972, p. 21).

Religious institutions. The alien inflowing populations were not only foreign; they represented doctrinal differences. Theological influences shaped the sense of threat experienced by the dominant American culture and also influenced the response to this threat. In contrast to the traditional Catholic views, Protestant theology advanced the view that salvation is by the grace of God alone and that its attainment is therefore totally independent of good works (Coughlin, 1965, pp. 19-20; Kohs, 1966, p. 139). What one does in this world, then, in no way influences his ultimate fate; for the love of God is a freely given gift, and He cannot be cajoled or bribed by the good works of aspiring human beings. Those who have attained grace, however, can be easily recognized. They are those who thrive in this world, who attain to positions of wealth and power through the efficient use of their time and energy, through their willingness to control distracting impulses and to delay gratification in the service of productivity, and through their thriftiness and ambition. The poor are not among God's loved ones, for they have failed to thrive in the world (Miller, 1961, p. 42). This kind of attitude toward the poor "dominated the thirteen colonies in North America and dictated the pattern of social services which emerged in the new nation. Poverty and dependency were looked upon as disgraceful, almost a crime; repressive measures were adopted; and provisions for relief were kept to an extreme minimum in the firm conviction that relief in any amount constituted an encouragement to moral turpitude" (Miller, 1961, p. 63).

Nineteenth-century immigration brought to this country masses of people who did not identify with a Protestant denomination, were not imbued with the Protestant ethic, and lived in separate communities governed by their own traditional customs and ideals. The dominant Protestant population viewed with alarm the intrusion of alien culture bearers who resisted assimilation, and tried to force the immigrants to take on American ways. It is in this connection that large-scale developments in social welfare took place in the late nineteenth century.

The initial response of organized Protestantism to the rise of the large immigrant class living in urban slums, however, was to place the greatest possible physical and spiritual distance between itself and the poor. "The city was the hothouse of every cancerous growth . . . yet Protestant Christianity, bound by doctrine and tradition to spiritual regeneration alone, did not adopt a satisfactory program of social ethics until late in the century. By rigidly separating body and spirit and denying religious value to the former, Protestant thought necessarily ignored the problem of human welfare in the great cities. . . . Until the mid-eighties the urban poor scarcely figured in Protestant missionary tactics. . . . As the working class crowded into the industrial quarters, the old parochial churches sought congenial sites on the great avenues uptown" (Abell, 1962, pp. 1-2, 6).

When the Protestant population did begin to intervene for the social welfare of the poor, its intervention took the form of "missionary" work. The child savers, for example, who came from the dominant Protestant culture, aimed their interventions directly at the children of a largely Catholic immigrant group. Children who were removed from cities, in order to be exposed to the tonic qualities of rural life, often ended up in Protestant homes, where they were repeatedly exhorted to make something of themselves through hard work, impulse control, and moral education. For Catholics concerned with the survival of Catholicism in this country, the paternalistic concepts of social work represented a threat. Their response to the child-saving movement was to seek additional ways to provide their own services for Catholic children. They developed their own school system, their own orphanages, their own social services. Jewish immigrants had somewhat similar experiences and reacted in somewhat similar ways. Both the Jewish and Catholic "newcomers" perceived themselves as involved in a critical struggle to resist the inroads of public institutions which were claiming their children and thus undermining their distinctive way of life. There has been an uneasy dialogue ever since between the governmental institutions which have become public monopolies and the counterreactive nonsecular systems which grew up as alternatives.

Correctional institutions. Before 1900 most American penologists accepted the concept of a criminal class and of biological determinism. In light of the research presented at that time, correctional officials believed that "a large proportion of the unfortunate children that go to make up the great army of criminals are not born right" (Platt, 1969, p. 23). However, although correctional workers used the language of Darwinism to stress the need for dealing with the crime problem, they worked through their national representatives to discredit the tenets of Darwinism. Correctional workers favored a more optimistic "nurture" theory because it helped to justify their work. Acceptance of the pessimistic "nature" model advocated by Darwinists meant acceptance of the role of keeper of the genetically inferior criminal class. This role was clearly unacceptable to the growing professional group of correctional administrators and social servants.

The development of therapeutic strategies in prisons and reformatories grew out of the self-image of correctional workers and the domination of physicians in criminological research. Physicians "furnished the official rhetoric of penal reform. Admittedly the criminal was 'pathological' and 'diseased,' but medical science offered the possibility of miraculous cures. Although there was a popular belief in the existence of a 'criminal class' separated from the rest of mankind by a 'vague boundary line,' there was no good reason why this class could not be identified, diagnosed, segregated, changed, and controlled" (Platt, 1969, p. 24). By the late 1890s hereditary theories of crime no longer dominated the thinking of correctional administrators. Sociological studies of crime, which emphasized the influence of social and economic circumstances on criminal behavior, were emerging.

The sociological research coincided with the general public feeling about cities: that cities were degrading, violent, and chaotic. The city was the nadir of industrial life. Programs were developed to remove children from the slums, "even if only once a week, into the radiance of better lives. . . . It is only by leading the child out of sin and debauchery, in which it has lived, into the circle of life that is a repudiation of things that it sees in its daily life, that it can be influenced" (Beverly Warner, 1893; quoted in Platt, 1969, p. 25).

The "new" penology, like the new "parental" classes in the public schools, attempted to compensate for the supposedly inadequate home environments of delinquent children. Reformatories should, according to this theory, approximate "healthy" family environments as closely as possible. Within this context of reform the child-saver movement developed. The child savers affirmed the values of home life, paternal authority, and rural life—values that were declining in society at large. In so doing, they called attention to new categories of deviance and helped launch an institutional system to counter the misbehavior. Children were removed from the adult criminal-law process and placed in the jurisdiction of a new tribunal, the juvenile court. Because juvenile proceedings were defined as civil actions, constitutional safeguards were not applicable. Statutory definitions of delinquency included such vague violations as "vicious or immoral behavior," "incorrigibility," and "truancy." "The juvenile court movement went far beyond a concern for special treatment of adolescent offenders. It brought within the ambit of governmental control a set of youthful activities that had been previously ignored or dealt with on an informal basis. It was not by accident that the behavior selected for penalizing by the child savers—sexual license, drinking, roaming the streets, begging, frequenting dance halls and movies, fighting, and being seen in public late at night—was most directly relevant to the children of lower-class migrant and immigrant families" (Platt, 1969, p. 29).

The practice of intervening in the lives of children without trial or due process, the concept that case workers need not be regulated in their right and duty to treat in the same way that the right to punish was regulated, and the strategies of indeterminate sentencings and preventive detention represent institutional embodiments of the public image of the child as a *dependent*. "The child savers were prohibitionists, in a general sense, who believed that adolescents needed protection from even their own inclinations" (Platt, 1969, p. 34). (For further treatment of juvenile delinquency and the correctional system, see Chapters Thirteen and Nineteen in this book.)

Mental health asylums. Eighteenth-century America devoted little energy to preparations for reform of offending or offensive citizens, whether poor, criminal, or insane. As a matter of fact, there was little discrimination among these various conditions of life. "Occasionally, in the course of the colonial period, some assemblies passed laws for a special group like the insane. But again it was dependency, and not any trait unique to the disease, that concerned them. From this perspective, insanity was really no different from any other disability. Its victim, unable to support himself, took his place as one among the needy. The lunatic came to public attention not as someone afflicted with delusions or fears, but as someone suffering from poverty" (Rothman, 1971, p. 4). Generally, relief was provided for the poor in their own homes or in the homes of other townspeople. At the same time, the incorporation of dependent strangers was actively discouraged. No special provisions beyond this effort had to be made, because towns were relatively small, and both the hopelessly poor and the overwhelmingly rich were limited in number (Goldman, 1952, p. 4).

However, the profound social and political disruptions of nineteenth-century America ushered in a radical change in the perception and treatment of the poor, the criminal, and the insane. From now on, they would be banished to special walled exiles, separated from the open community and its daily life. They had to be guarded. "The response in the Jacksonian period to the deviant and dependent was first and foremost a vigorous attempt to promote the stability of the society at a moment when traditional ideas and practices appeared outmoded, constricted, and ineffective. The almshouse and the orphan asylum, the penitentiary, the reformatory, and the insane asylum, all represent an effort to insure the cohesion of the community in new and changing circumstances" (Rothman, 1971, p. xviii).

Within a period of fifty years, beginning in the nineteenth century, the penitentiary was discovered and spread across the face of the states, and by 1860 twenty-eight of the thirty-three states had asylums for the insane. This development was coincidental with sudden rapid growth of the colonies and antedated only slightly the development of compulsory education and correctional programs for youth. In addition, the sense of threat associated with the large masses of immigrant children crowded in the slums of urban areas led to specialized confinement environments for such children. This was the period of the birth of orphanages, institutions for the retarded, refuges for delinquents, and special schools for all types of deviance. "There is no lot, as we all know, so hopeless and helpless as that of a destitute orphan; its career of sin and illness, when neglected, is almost certain" (Cincinnati Orphan Asylum, 1848, p. 3). Another asylum for destitute children announced as its goal the removal of children from "abodes of raggedness and want," where, "mingled with the cries of helpless need, the sounds of blasphemy assail your ears; and from example of father and of mother, the mouth of lisping childhood is taught to curse and revile" (quoted in Rothman, 1971, p. 170). Moral treatment was very much a part of these facilities. The harsh discipline and stern regimentation of those walled-in communities was seen as an antidote to, and reformation of, lives lived in the urban lower class. However, with the advent of the immigrant flood into the cities, these institutions had to abandon "moral treatment" and resort to custodial warehousing.

The discovery of confinement as an antidote to the intolerable anxieties of that fast-moving, unstable period created a new breed of defenders of the public good, the professional caretakers. The houses of confinement were seen, in their initiation, as moral utopias, safe from the vices and corruptions of urban society. At the same time, the most contaminated spirits in the community were walled in. The confinees were seen as token proxies, who could be subjected to this uncontaminated social test tube, exposed to moral exhortation and intervention, and turned into the perfect, rational, value-cleansed citizens which their captors prized in their American image ideal.

As early as 1844, thirteen of the leading medical superintendents in the new asylums across the nation had organized the first mental health professional organization. It was the Association of Medical Superintendents of American Institutions for the Insane, which later became the American Psychiatric Association. The professionals, following upon the defensive walling-out process introduced by antebellum society, took possession of the pariah populations banished to the other side of the community walls.

By the mid-1800s, the walling-out solution was concentrated primarily upon foreign settlers. "Inmates in this period were typically lower class, foreign-born, and the children of foreign-born—a group that local officials and citizens found convenient to incarcerate. Like other caretaker institutions, the refuge began as an attempt to eliminate delinquency and ended up as a practical method for getting rid of delinquents" (Rothman, 1971, p. 261).

One of the new breed of caretakers diagnosed the situation of these inmates as follows: "It may be supposed that much of poverty has a common origin with insanity—both of them represent internal mental character or physical condition as well as external circumstances" (Jarvis [1855], 1971, p. 55). He further argued that native-born insane should be placed in a

separate institution for state paupers rather than in the same
facilities as foreign-born because of "the wide differences between them and the mass of our people" (p. 149).

According to Rothman (1971), only 43 percent of the
poor insane who were native-born Americans ended up in a
state institution, whereas almost every one of the insane among
foreigners did. In Taunton, near Worcester, almost half of the
inmates in its first ten years, beginning in 1854, were immigrants, most of them Irish. Sixty-seven percent of the patients
at Ohio's Longview Asylum were immigrants. In the state
asylum in Wisconsin, there were 60 percent immigrants in 1872.

Thus, the dream wrapped up in the asylum as utopia collapsed when America became inundated with foreigners. At this
point the dream of middle-class American homogeneity could
be preserved only by reversion to radical custodial authoritar-
ianism within the confinement walls. Hopes for reform gave
way to the organized chaos of custodial caretaking. The exhor-
tations of Dorothea Dix and Samuel Howe had faded into the
background. It was as though the excitement over threatened
personal and social dissolution abated with the custodial
entombment of large masses of foreign-born paupers. There was
a long period of quiescence in which the twin specters of insanity and poverty seem to have gone underground. It was not until
the beginning of the twentieth century, when the Progressive
Era signaled a rise in reform movements in politics, economic
legislation, and social welfare, that the concern with irrational
man flamed up again.

In the first decade of the twentieth century many organizations devoted to preventive medicine came into being (Fraser,
1973). These included the National Tuberculosis Association
(1904), the American Social Hygiene Association (1909), and
the National Committee for Mental Hygiene (1909). The origins
of the mental hygiene movement were linked to the same forces
which fostered the development of other such organizations—
specifically, scientific and technological development, progressive social thought, and bureaucratized services. Clifford Beers
wrote *A Mind That Found Itself* (1908) and described his recovery within the bedlam of the mental hospital, thus awakening
the public belief in cure. Beers recommended the formation of a
national society to press for reforms in the prevention and treatment of mental illness. Many professionals reacted favorably,
including William James and Adolf Meyer, who recommended

the term *mental hygiene* for the new movement. The National Committee for Mental Hygiene was formed in 1909. In 1912 a donation of $50,000 was made to this committee to study existing facilities and recommend new ones (Ridenour, 1961). Professionals then began to exert the tremendous influence on mental health services that they command today. Their influence can be seen in the literature since that time. We begin to see the disappearance of such menacing classifications as *weak minds, diseased minds,* and *evil and pernicious children* and in their place such "scientific" terms as *mental deficiency, emotional disturbance,* and *delinquency.*

In the field of mental health, the mood of the country and the guiding paradigm of the new progressives—illness of the social institutions—became a perfect foil for the medically oriented theories of such figures as Adolf Meyer, Sigmund Freud, and William Goddard. Not only social illness but mental illness too became the great explanatory metaphor for the menacing conditions of life. All sorts of infectious diseases seemed on the way to extinction through the marvelous technology of medicine and public health. The illness paradigm, therefore, captured the imagination and hopes of the society. The great confinement and moral treatment had not solved the threats of collective life. Here, however, was a new tool, a new guiding principle by which we might tame the irrational and intractable parts of our own nature and the social institutions spawned by this nature. Early diagnosis, prevention, treatment, cure—all these terms brought a new sense of objectivity to the fearfulness of one's personal relationship to the unpredictability of social forces outside and irrational forces within.

The social progressive's ideal of prevention found a sympathetic resonance in the theory of psychosexual development. Despite the negative ambiance of sex, childhood became a focal point for action. Now one knew where to begin. William Healy, a psychodynamically oriented psychiatrist, founded the first juvenile psychopathic institute in Chicago in 1909. The child savers had already established the first juvenile court in Chicago in 1899. Social immorality became transmuted into psychic illness, and the concept of juvenile delinquency merged both public models of human problems into one big social solution. A national conference on the prevention of juvenile delinquency, jointly sponsored by the Commonwealth Fund and the National Committee for Mental Hygiene, was held in 1921. Its principal action recommendation was a five-year demonstration of child-guidance clinics. The famous Healy and Bronner report (1926), which was produced out of that demonstration, led to the vast child-guidance movement and the rapid proliferation of clinics throughout the United States. The clinic or "center" had supplanted the asylum as the institutional defense against the menacing presence of irrationality without and within. We no longer needed to wall out this infectious menace. We now had the tools for threat reduction through individual treatment within the open community. We could now segregate through scientific labels, and isolate through programs of intervention. The populations at risk were still the destitute, the powerless, and the culturally different. The preferred image was still that of the successful, hard-working, gratification-delaying, stable, middle-class Anglo-Saxon culture bearer living quietly behind the doors of his own home, on his own property, in a peaceful neighborhood. Now, however, with the advent of social sciences and the technologies of social services, there was an objectively validated rationale for one's character-trait and life-style preferences. There were indices of pathology determining who was and who was not socially and emotionally adapted. It was not a matter of arbitrary personal prejudice or social power. It was now a matter of science—the new national church; and thus the whole social institution of mental health came into being. The partnership between bourgeois order and medicine, formed around the threat of irrationality at the time of the Reformation and the disappearance of the scourge of leprosy, moved away from the religious ambiance of "moral treatment" into the aura of "public health." The powerful empirical antibodies of medical diagnosis and medical treatment would now be applied to social ills through the foreign invasions of disorganized community members. Medical treatment provided further protection to the contamination of individual by individual through the psychological distance of the subject-object split of modern science. Psychological mechanisms of displacement and projection were legitimized by this separation between the excitor and reactor. No longer did sane and insane share sin in common. The disease was within the excitor, not a mutual bond between excitor and reactor. The disease was communicable, but modern asepsis was more powerful than stone walls for protection against this type of transmission. No longer did the dominant culture bearer have to look into the mirror of irra-

tionality and say, "We have seen the enemy and they are us."
Now the threat to collective orderliness lay without.

Classification

A fairly clear connection can be argued to exist between
"scientific" classification systems and overwrought public
images of the threat of strangeness and divergence, as described
in the preceding section. The phenomenological interpretation
of such strangeness or divergence can be the deciding factor in
the kind of effect that divergence will have upon society. It is
not argued that differences are not real but that their collective
interpretation creates the negative or positive impact of such
differences upon the community psyche. Much of modern-day
concern with individual differences within the professions can
be interpreted as a product of the exigencies of our own history.

Many years ago Ruth Benedict (1934, p. 60) pointed out
that individual minority differences do exist in all cultures but
that the meaning of those differences can be radically opposite
in two separate cultures: "It does not matter what kind of
'abnormality' we choose for illustration, those which indicate
extreme instability or those which are much more in the nature
of character traits like sadism or delusions of grandeur or of per-
secution, there are well-described cultures in which these abnormals function at ease and with honor, and apparently without
danger or difficulty to the society." She gives numerous examples of cultures in which even the most extreme types of
minority behavioral differences are incorporated as important
and venerated characteristics for the society. Her general thesis,
like the thesis of this chapter, is cultural relativity: "Normality,
. . . within a very wide range, is culturally defined. It is primarily a term for the socially elaborated segment of human behavior
in any culture; and abnormality [is] a term for that segment
that the particular civilization does not use. The very eyes with
which we see the problem are conditioned by the long-tradition-
al habits of our society" (Benedict, 1934, p. 73). This chapter
makes something of the same argument as it looks at significant
labels of abnormality which exist in our society.

However, this chapter goes further and states that much
of what we do in public caretaking is a self-protective response
to a sense of intense threat, released at another period in his-

tory, by groups and the living settings they generated, which controverted the traditional habits of our society. The response was threat recoil and massive institutional efforts to assimilate such alien culture bearers into the dominant cultural type that was considered the mainstream.

A sense of disquiet over this prejudicial response and a sense of decency and fair play resulted in "scientizing" the recoil and in developing more "objective" categorical niches for unacceptable groups, habitats, and behaviors. The result of this humanistic effort, however, was to create more difficult problems for ourselves. Classificatory terms such as *weak minds, diseased minds, incorrigible, dissolute, sin and debauchery, sexual license, evil tendencies, vicious conduct,* and *menacing to society* had more direct threat referents when considered in terms of the prevailing codes of conduct of that time.

Over time, the awareness of fear and outrage generated by these alien inputs has faded into the background, and the original affective language describing this fear and outrage is also lost in the haze of history. In its place in the foreground of consciousness of the collective body remain only the third-order symbols or classifications. The professions themselves—as they go about their task of early identification, differential diagnosis, treatment, and cure—do not consider the possibility that their diagnostic categories themselves may mask the threat and hostility expressed by the dominant culture bearers toward behavioral types and ways of life discarded in the past.

Although there is no scientific agreement about the meaning of the diagnostic terms in use today (Scott, 1958; Mercer, 1973; Zigler, 1966; Tappan, 1960), if we look closely at the application of these terms to individuals in our society, we can observe a very interesting phenomenon. We find that these terms are bestowed, with disproportionate frequency, upon the same types of groups, behaviors, and behavior settings which aroused the original alarm in the main-line culture bearers. The proportion of individuals from alien, minority cultural groups, residing in "undesirable" areas of the city, who are assigned special classifications and processed into special institutional programs is not random. Such selection does not fit the laws of chance. And, significantly, such classifications and assignments shift over time from one ethnic group to another as groups gradually shuck divergent characteristics, become indistinguishable from the main-line culture bearers, and move out of the tabooed behavior settings.

Renaissance of Caring

Every classification carries with it a particular view of the situation or condition that invites the label. It carries a notion of the source of the problem, what the outcome of intervention should be, and what the intermediary should cause to happen. Intervention is value oriented and value directed. Without implicit or explicit values, interventions would not be undertaken. When there is general consensus about values, there is general acceptance of established classifications and interventions. Consequently, until recently our fixed classifications and intervention processes associated with teaching, therapy, counseling, and testing were rarely questioned. Teachers, therapists, counselors, and testers were considered necessary fixtures in a society which had maintained a consensus with respect to the right relationship between the individual and the society.

In the current period of rapidly shifting values, however, this consensus is dissolving. There is no social consensus about the right relationship between men and between man and society. Hence, there is no longer an agreement about human labeling or intervention structures. The whole area of human caretaking is under careful scrutiny and reexamination by many diverse segments of society. Many of the social and institutional arrangements for care giving and care receiving are being sharply questioned. Specifically, a new awareness seems to be developing that the caring experience is a necessary ingredient in the preservation of community life. Many groups of individuals, formerly uninvolved in the functions of care-giving institutions, are suddenly aware of the part they play in the process. Such groups are taking stances vis-à-vis these institutions and are examining what they do and whom they serve. Many of these groups are opening up previously closed conceptions of the place of caretaking institutions, from public schools to mental hospitals, in public life.

The care-giving and care-receiving metaphors themselves —*retardation, mental illness* and *disturbance, delinquency* and *criminality*—are coming into question (Szasz, 1970; Scott, 1958; Mercer, 1970; Menninger, 1968; Kvaraceus and Miller, 1959). Essentially, the critics agree, when any of the above conditions is attributed to individual members of the community, some degree of psychological projection, scapegoating, or arbitrary labeling is involved. These critics frequently examine the function that such assignments serve for society and present sound arguments and documentation that human caring is either absent or distorted in the assignment process. The technical processes and instruments by which these metaphors are assigned are being successfully challenged, and legal decisions are being handed down against them. Such litigation and the resulting decisions indicate a willingness to use the legal process to review and renew the care-giving and caretaking process. (See Chapters Twenty-Five and Twenty-Six in this book.) At the same time, a general revolt is taking place among the labeled groups against public stereotypes of themselves. Individuals and groups boxed into such narrow niches as *homosexual, criminal,* or *addict* are beginning to liberate themselves from these all-embracing social incantations. They are counterattacking both the metaphors being imposed upon them and the barriers to social participation which these metaphors erect. They not only challenge public authority to impose such barriers, but they are angry at their own previous acceptance of these barriers as natural and justified. They are angry at their previous self-rejection and are beginning to care for themselves.

The social dominance of care givers over care receivers also is being challenged. Specifically, the *investiture* procedure (that is, singling out candidates for labeling and then moving these candidates through a set of institutional decision-making structures and critical junctures to the exclusion niche), whereby an individual receives an official care-receiving title, role, and function in society, is being demonstrated to be frequently arbitrary and capricious (Mercer, 1970). This questioning of the investiture procedure expresses a new level of caring, a new willingness to act upon one's concern for fellow members who become victims of such caretaking investiture.

Still another important movement gives evidence of this new consciousness of caring: the qualifications of credentialized caretakers themselves are being questioned. For example, mental health workers at the Lincoln Mental Health Center have challenged the authority of the administration and professional staff; similarly, parents in inner-city neighborhoods such as the Oceanhill-Brownsville area have revolted against the professional authority of the school system. This challenge of the professional intervener is occurring on two grounds. The challengers argue that these professionals are too removed from the life and culture of the intervenee to be able to care about, understand, and deal with his crushing problems; they also question the legitimacy of the special expertness of these professionals. Teaching, psychotherapy, and counseling, the argument goes, are talents widely shared in the population. One does not require a special credentializing process and elite schooling to be effective in such interventions. Furthermore, this challenge to the unique authority of the professional intervener is tied to a broader examination of the use and abuse of care giving, caretaking, and care receiving.

There is also a growing concern about the size of our caretaking institutions and about their political and economic importance in this country. Ralph Nader's investigation of the National Institute of Mental Health (Chu and others, 1972), the questions being raised by the poor and the minority groups, the social critics such as Thomas Szasz (1970), Frantz Fanon (1968), John Holt (1964), and Ivan Illich (1971)—all demonstrate the new probing into the economics and politics of care. Behind such powerful reexamination is a strong concern for the real meaning of care, a desire to strengthen the sentiment of caring, and an attempt to disentangle it from some of the overlay of power and economics, so that it might be made clearer and free of some of its contaminants.

Critics also are questioning the legitimacy and power of educational institutions, correctional institutions, mental health institutions, and welfare institutions to regulate, control, or intervene in behavior. The care receivers themselves are raising questions about their mandated interactions with these institutions. Moreover, some of the professional and scientific groups aligned with these institutions, and increasingly large segments of the general populace, are also joining forces with the compulsory care receivers. The events at Attica prison, repeated in less dramatic fashion all across the nation, are an example of this trend. The various forms of student unrest in public schools and universities are another example. The wide questioning of and searching for an alternative to mental institutions is still a third example. In general, the criticism is against the way in which these facilities deal with their resident populations, against the quality of relationships, against the lack of compassion and relevance. Two recent experiments raise even more serious concerns. One is a Stanford University experiment in replicating a prison atmosphere and the simulation of inmate and custodial roles (Zimbardo, 1973). The simulation had to be halted after a few days because of the violent changes taking place in the feelings, attitudes, and behaviors of the role players. The other is a study (Rosenhan, 1973) in which eight subjects successfully feigned symptoms of schizophrenia, hoodwinking doctors at all twelve hospitals they visited in a five-state area. Diagnosed as schizophrenic, the pseudopatients were admitted as inpatients. They were not released until an average of nineteen days had passed, even though everyone had dropped the phony symptoms upon admittance.

These attacks on institutions from many quarters suggest that our major caretaking solutions are being declared irrelevant and inhuman. Providing care for deviant populations is no longer sufficient reason for being in today's society. New measures have to be found; new care-relating structures have to be created.

Along with the self-caring reaction of individually labeled groups such as homosexuals or prisoners, we are also witnessing a significant growing community sense among the underclass groups who now see themselves as the major recruiting pools from which the individual care-receiving categories are drawn. Their strengthening sense of community grows from their developing conviction that their own self-denigration of their underclass status, such as poor or black or Chicano or Indian, makes them particularly susceptible to the social contagion of such roles as mentally ill, alcoholic, addict, prostitute, or pimp. They are declaring to their fellow members that self-denigration makes it easy for main-line culture bearers to assign them such roles. Therefore, they argue, they must counteract self-denigration and foster self-respect and self-caring by emphasizing the exact antithesis of the public image assigned by society. (See Chapter Twenty-Two of this book.)

Finally, the many specific examinations of care-giving philosophies, attitudes, and structures in society have led to a rethinking of the melting-pot homogeneity assumption. Critics are asserting that this conventional belief system is based on a myth; that the real motif of this country has always been ethno-cultural pluralism; that the melting-pot assumption militates against group and individual rights and differences and sustains a fantasy of an ideal type, an inherent cultural normality, a single standard of behavior to which all can and should adhere. Furthermore, these critics point out, our care-giving efforts at treatment, remediation, education, and rehabilitation are aimed largely toward achieving in all members of the society some attainment of this vaguely hypothesized healthy, happy, normal individual.

The strength of the above-mentioned efforts indicates that the caring dynamic has become a deep force in the social order today, and promises to gain strength and power as it advances. No matter where one looks in the society today, there is evidence of this new awareness of conscious caring. It has led to a total examination of the right relationships between men and between men and community; in the process the whole fabric of our caring apparatus and assumptions is under scrutiny. Any thought about future labeling and interventions must take this force into account.

References

Abell, A. I. *The Urban Impact on American Protestantism, 1865-1900.* London: Archon, 1962.

Becker, H. S. *Outsiders: Studies in the Sociology of Deviance.* New York: Free Press, 1963.

Beers, C. W. *A Mind That Found Itself.* Garden City, N.Y.: Doubleday, 1953. Originally published 1908.

Benedict, R. *Patterns of Culture.* Boston: Houghton Mifflin, 1934.

Bernard, J. *The Children You Gave Us: A History of 150 Years of Service to Children.* New York: Jewish Child Care Association, 1973.

Chu, F. D., and others. *The Mental Health Complex: Part I: Community Mental Health Centers.* Washington, D.C.: Center for the Study of Responsive Law, 1972.

Cincinnati Orphan Asylum. *Annual Report for 1848.* Cincinnati: Asylum, 1848.

Connecticut Special Education Association. *Development and Progress of Special Classes for Mentally Deficient Children in Connecticut.* New Haven, Conn.: Columbia Printing Company, 1936.

Coughlin, B. J. *Church and State in Social Welfare.* New York: Columbia University Press, 1965.

Dugdale, R. *The Jukes.* New York: Putnam, 1877.

Fanon, F. *The Wretched of the Earth.* Trans. Constance Farrington. New York: Grove Press, 1968.

Foucault, M. *Madness and Civilization: A History of Insanity in the Age of Reason.* New York: Random House, 1973.

Fraser, M. *Treatment of Deviance by the Mental Health System.* Ann Arbor, Mich.: Institute for the Study of Mental Retardation and Related Disabilities, 1973.

Goddard, H. H. *The Kallikak Family.* New York: Macmillan, 1912.

Goddard, H. H. *Feeblemindedness.* New York: Macmillan, 1916.

Goddard, H. H. *Juvenile Delinquency.* New York: Dodd, Mead, 1921.

Goldman, E. F. *Rendezvous with Destiny.* New York: Knopf, 1952.

Handlin, O. *Boston's Immigrants.* Cambridge, Mass.: Belknap Press, 1959.

Hanus, P. H. *School Efficiency: A Constructive Study.* Yonkers, N.Y.: World Book Company, 1913.

Healy, W., and Bronner, A. *Delinquents and Criminals, Their Making and Unmaking, Studies in Two American Cities.* Montclair, N.J.: Patterson Smith, 1926.

Heck, A. O. *The Education of Exceptional Children.* New York: McGraw-Hill, 1940.

Hoffman, E. *The Treatment of Deviance by the Education System.* Ann Arbor, Mich.: Institute for the Study of Mental Retardation and Related Disabilities, 1972.

Hofstadter, R. *The Age of Reform.* New York: Knopf, 1955.

Hofstadter, R. *Social Darwinism in American Thought.* Boston: Beacon Press, 1966.

Holt, J. *How Children Fail.* New York: Dell, 1964.

Illich, I. *Deschooling Society.* New York: Harper, 1971.

Irvine, P. "Pioneers in Special Education: Henry Herbert Goddard." *Journal of Special Education,* 1971, *5*, 210.

Jarvis, E. *Insanity and Idiocy in Massachusetts: Report of the Commission on Lunacy.* Cambridge, Mass.: Harvard University Press, 1971. Originally published 1855.

Jencks, C. *Inequality.* New York: Basic Books, 1972.

Kohs, S. C. *The Roots of Social Work.* New York: Association Press, 1966.

Kvaraceus, W. C., and Miller, W. *Delinquent Behavior: Culture and the Individual.* Washington, D.C.: National Education Association, 1959.

Menninger, K. *The Crime of Punishment.* New York: Viking, 1968.

Mercer, J. "Sociological Perspectives on Mild Mental Retardation." In H. Haywood (Ed.), *Social-Cultural Aspects of Retardation.* New York: Appleton-Century-Crofts, 1970.

Mercer, J. *Labeling the Mentally Retarded.* Berkeley: University of California Press, 1973.

Miller, H. M. *Compassion and Community.* New York: Association Press, 1961.

Platt, A. M. *The Child Savers: The Invention of Delinquency.* Chicago: University of Chicago Press, 1969.

Rhodes, W. C. "Regulation of Community Behavior: Dynamics and Structure." In S. E. Golann and C. Eisdorfer (Eds.), *Handbook of Community Mental Health.* New York: Appleton-Century-Crofts, 1972.

Ridenour, N. A. *Mental Health in the United States: A Fifty-Year History.* Cambridge, Mass.: Harvard University Press, 1961.

Rosenhan, D. L. "On Being Sane in Insane Places." *Science,* 1973, *169,* 250-258.

Rothman, D. J. *The Discovery of the Asylum.* Boston: Little, Brown, 1971.

Scott, W. A. "Research Definitions of Mental Health and Mental Illness." *Psychological Bulletin*, 1958, *55*, 29-45.
Szasz, T. *The Myth of Mental Illness*. New York: Harper, 1961.
Szasz, T. *The Manufacture of Madness: A Comparative Study of the Inquisition and the Mental Health Movement*. New York: Harper, 1970.
Tappan, P. *Crime, Justice, and Corrections*. New York: McGraw-Hill, 1960.
Zigler, E. "Mental Retardation: Current Issues and Approaches." In L. W. Hoffman and M. L. Hoffman (Eds.), *Review of Child Development Research*. New York: Russell Sage Foundation, 1966.
Zimbardo, P. G. "A Pirandellian Prison." *New York Times Magazine*, April 8, 1973, pp. 38-60.

6

PSYCHOLOGICAL ASSESSMENT AND THE RIGHTS OF CHILDREN

Jane R. Mercer

Classification systems based on standardized tests have systematically labeled a disproportionately large number of persons from minority groups as intellectually *subnormal* and a disproportionately small number as *gifted*. As a result of this practice, a disproportionately large number of minority children are assigned to educational programs that limit upward mobility, such as classes for the mentally retarded, the slow learner, and

Data in this chapter were collected under the auspices of the following grants: Public Health Service Grant R01 MH20646-01 from the National Institute of Mental Health, Department of Health, Education, the "basic" student. These differentials have been widely publicized in California. Lawyers representing black and Mexican-American clients have successfully argued in court that present assessment procedures violate the rights of minority children (*Larry P. v. Wilson Riles*, 1972; *Diana v. State Board of Education*, 1970).

The classification of exceptional children did *not* become an issue because psychologists, educators, and medical practitioners were dissatisfied with the present system. This fact has great importance. It signifies that the *central issues are conceptual and ethical rather than technical and empirical. Basic assumptions are being challenged.* Because psychologists, educators, and clinicians have neither examined the assumptions underlying traditional practices nor adequately monitored the social implications of institutionalizing procedures based on these assumptions, the standardized testing movement is now being challenged. Those who have been labeled as deviant because of their low test scores are rejecting the labels and attacking the labelers. They are protesting the taken-for-granted value frame within which psychologists, educators, and test makers have been operating.

During the past twelve years, a group of social scientists at Pacific State Hospital, Pomona, California, have been studying mental retardation in Riverside, California (population 130,000). The study began as a basic research epidemiology operating from a traditional clinical perspective, but it eventually also became a study of the processes by which an American community sorts and labels persons as mentally retarded. This movement from a clinical perspective to a more relativistic

and Welfare, and Public Health Service General Research Support Grant 1-S01-FR-05632-02, from the Department of Health, Education, and Welfare, Socio-Behavioral Study Center in Mental Retardation, Pacific State Hospital, Pomona, California; Public Health Service Grant PH43-67-756; McAteer Grant M8-14A and M9-14 from the California State Department of Education, Office of Compensatory Education. The opinions and conclusions stated by the author are not to be construed as officially reflecting the policy of the funding agencies. Portions of the material in this chapter were presented at the Kennedy International Symposium on Human Rights, Retardation, and Research, Washington, D.C., October 16, 1971; the First Annual Study Conference in School Psychology, Temple University, June 1972; and the Tenth Annual Conference in Civil and Human Rights of Educators and Students, National Education Association, February 1972.

social-system perspective occurred primarily as a consequence of our working back and forth between empirical data and theoretical constructs. We concluded that present assessment procedures violate certain basic rights of children and that a system of pluralistic, multicultural assessment—a system that considers both adaptive behavior and sociocultural background in assessing the meaning of scores on standardized measures—is needed. In order to explain clearly the rationale behind the pluralistic assessment procedures which we are proposing, it is necessary to review briefly the conceptual models and design used in our earlier study.

Social-System Perspective: Labeling Process

Two contrasting conceptual perspectives were used in the Riverside epidemiology—a clinical perspective and a social-system perspective. The social-system perspective treated mental retardation as an achieved social status and a social role which some individuals play in some social systems. This aspect of the study focused on the labeling process and the characteristics of persons who achieve the status of mental retardate in various social systems in the community, especially the public school.

We contacted 241 organizations in the community and asked each organization to give us information on each mentally retarded person being served by that group. Because we were studying the labeling process, we did not impose one standard definition but asked each organization to use whatever definition was customarily used by its staff. When we identified those persons nominated by more than one organization, we found that 1493 nominations produced 812 individuals. When we studied the number of persons jointly nominated by various types of organizations, the public schools clearly held the commanding position. They not only had labeled more persons as mentally retarded than any other organization but they shared their labels more widely throughout the community. We then studied each type of formal organization to see what standards they were using in screening for mental retardation. We found that 46 percent of the persons nominated by the public schools had IQs above 70, and 62 percent had no reported physical disabilities. All other agencies, except law enforcement, were labeling persons with more deficiencies. For example, only 12 percent of those nominated by the Department of Mental Hygiene had IQs above 70, and only 11 percent were without physical disabilities. We concluded that the public school system is the primary labeler in the community. The schools label the most persons as mentally retarded, share the most labels with other organizations, and label the most persons with IQs above 70 and with no physical disabilities. Any public policy directed at modifying labeling practices in the community must include modification of public school labeling practices. Any major change in the labeling policies of this single system would have a significant impact on labeling processes in the community as a whole.

We next studied the characteristics of the 812 persons holding the status of mental retardate in one or more organizations in Riverside at the time of our census. We found that 72 percent of the persons on the register were five through twenty years of age, 7 percent were under five years of age, and 21 percent were over twenty. School-age children were "overlabeled" and preschool children and adults were "underlabeled" compared to their percentage in the general population of the community. Before children get to school, only those with the greatest number of physical disabilities and the lowest IQs are identified. After graduation from school, only the most intellectually and physically subnormal adults continue to be labeled.

We classified every person on the case register into ten groups according to the median value of the housing on the block on which he lived. We found that persons in the lowest socioeconomic categories were greatly overrepresented on the register and those from higher statuses were underrepresented. When we studied ethnic groups, we found 300 percent more Mexican-Americans and 50 percent more blacks than their proportion in the general population but only 60 percent as many Anglo-Americans (Caucasians whose primary language is English) as would be expected. Because most Mexican-Americans and blacks in Riverside come from lower socioeconomic backgrounds, ethnic group and socioeconomic status are correlated. When we held socioeconomic status constant, Anglos were still underrepresented and Mexican-Americans were still overrepresented in the case register but blacks appeared in their proper proportion.

Ethnic disproportions were especially marked among public school nominees. There were four and a half times more

Mexican-American children and twice as many black children labeled retarded as would be expected from their proportion in the population and only half as many Anglo children. When we compared Riverside school data with data from other school districts in California, we found that this overrepresentation of Mexican-American and black children in classes for the educable mentally retarded was statewide and not just a local pattern.

Clinical Perspective: Field Survey

A second phase of our study was conducted from a clinical perspective, the perspective commonly adopted by persons in the fields of medicine, psychology, social work, and education. Within the clinical perspective two definitions of "normal" tend to be used simultaneously and interchangeably: the pathological model and the statistical model. The pathological model, developed in medicine, defines diseases or handicaps by the biological symptoms which characterize them. A person is categorized as "abnormal" when pathological symptoms are present and "normal" when there is an absence of pathological signs. The statistical model defines abnormality according to the extent to which an individual varies from the average of the population on a particular trait. Ordinarily, if an individual is more than two standard deviations above or below the mean for the population on which a measure was standardized, he is regarded as "abnormal." The clinical perspective regards mental retardation as a pathology which is an attribute of the individual. His symptomatology may exist as an entity regardless of whether it has been identified and labeled by significant others in his social milieu. The trained diagnostician with his clinical measures believes that he can detect abnormalities not apparent to lay persons. The clinical perspective treats cultural differences as irrelevant to mental retardation, which is regarded as a biological condition.

Definitions. The definition of mental retardation operationalized in the clinical phase of our study was that of the American Association on Mental Deficiency: "Mental retardation refers to subaverage general intellectual functioning which originates during the developmental period and is associated with impairment in adaptive behavior" (Heber, 1961). This is a two-dimensional definition. Before a person may be diagnosed as mentally retarded, he must be subnormal in both intellectual

performance and adaptive behavior. Evidence of organic dysfunction or biological anomalies is not required. In the same
document "subnormal" is defined as performance on a standard
measure of intellectual functioning that is greater than one standard deviation below the population mean, approximately the
lowest 16 percent of the population (Heber, 1961).[1] Educational practice generally places the dividing line somewhat
lower. The highest intelligence-test score for placement in a
class for the educable mentally retarded ranges between 75 and
79, depending upon local usage. This cut-off point includes approximately the lowest 9 percent of the population. The test
designers suggest a cut-off point that more closely conforms
with traditional definitions, an IQ below 70, approximately 3
percent of the population (Wechsler, 1958; Terman and Merrill,
1960). In the clinical epidemiology, all three cut-offs were used
and the results compared.

Operations. Intellectual adequacy was measured in the
clinical epidemiology by using standardized measures of intelligence, primarily the Stanford-Binet LM and the Kuhlmann-
Binet. We conceptualized adaptive behavior as an individual's
ability to play ever more complex roles in a progressively widening circle of social systems. Because there are no generally accepted measures of adaptive behavior, we developed a series of
twenty-eight age-graded scales for this purpose, drawing heavily
on the work of Doll and Gesell, especially for the younger years
(Doll, 1965; Gesell, 1948a, 1948b, 1956). Questions were answered by a respondent related to the person being evaluated
(Mercer, 1973a).

Sample. The research design called for a first-stage screening of a large sample of the population of the community using
the adaptive behavior scales and then a second-stage testing of a

---

[1]The field work for this study was conducted in 1963. At that
time, the American Association on Mental Deficiency definition of mental
retardation was "subaverage intellectual functioning" defined as "performance on a measure of general intellectual functioning that is greater than
one standard deviation below the population mean" (Heber, 1961). In
1973 the definition was revised to read as follows: "Mental retardation
refers to significantly subaverage general intellectual functioning existing
concurrently with deficits in adaptive behavior, and manifested during the
developmental period . . . significantly subaverage refers to performance
which is two or more standard deviations from the mean or average of the
test" (Grossman, 1973, p. 11).

subsample using standardized intelligence tests. We called these samples the screened sample and the tested subsample, respectively.

The screened sample was a stratified area probability sample of 3198 housing units in the city of Riverside, California, selected so that all geographic areas and socioeconomic levels in the city were represented in their proper proportion. The forty-six interviewers were college educated, and thirty-six were teachers. Spanish-speaking interviewers were assigned to all households with Spanish surnames. Black interviewers were assigned to interview in housing located in predominantly non-white neighborhoods. Anglo interviewers were randomly assigned the remainder of the households. In each household one adult member, usually the mother, served as respondent and provided information about all other members of the household to whom she was related. Interviews were completed in 2661 of the 2923 occupied housing units, an overall response rate of 90.7 percent. In all, 6907 persons under fifty years of age were screened.

For individual intelligence testing, 483 persons were selected on the basis of a disproportionate random sampling frame. Tests were completed on 423 persons for an overall response rate of 87.6 percent. Intelligence-test scores were also secured from other sources for an additional 241 persons, making a total of 664 scores available. Each person in the tested subsample was assigned a weight according to the number of persons he represented in the larger, screened sample.

Typology of mental retardation. A simplified version of our working typology of mental retardation is shown in Table 1. The American Association on Mental Deficiency definition contains two primary symptoms—subnormality in intellectual performance and subnormality in adaptive behavior. Combinations of these two dimensions produce four major types of per-

Table 1

Typology of Mental Retardation

	Intellectual Performance	Adaptive Behavior
Clinically Retarded	Subnormal	Subnormal
Quasi-Retarded	Subnormal	Normal
Behaviorally Maladjusted	Normal	Subnormal
Normals	Normal	Normal

sons: the clinically retarded, the quasi-retarded, the behaviorally maladjusted, and the normals. The clinically retarded are those who are subnormal in both IQ and adaptive behavior. The quasi-retarded are those who are subnormal in IQ but normal in adaptive behavior. The behaviorally maladjusted are those who have normal IQs but are subnormal in adaptive behavior, while the normals are those who pass both dimensions.

Findings and Conclusions

Conclusion 1: Cut-off level for subnormality should be lowest 3 percent (IQ below 70). The behavioral characteristics of the adults in our sample who failed the traditional criterion, the lowest 3 percent, were compared to adults who failed only the educational or the AAMD criteria. We found that a majority of the adults who were failing at the 9 percent or the 16 percent criterion were, in fact, filling the usual complement of social roles for persons of their age and sex: 83.6 percent had completed eight grades or more in school, 82.6 percent had held a job, 64.9 percent had a semiskilled or higher occupation, 80.2 percent were financially independent or housewives, almost 100 percent were able to do their own shopping and to travel alone. Differences between their performance and that of persons failing the traditional criterion differed at the .001 level of significance on twenty-one out of twenty-six of the comparisons made. Most adults in the borderline category were managing their own affairs and did not appear to require supervision, control, and care for their own welfare. Their role performance appeared neither subnormal nor particularly unusual.

We compared the findings from our field survey with the actual labeling practices of clinicians in the community and found much higher rates from the field survey than from actual labeling practices when the 16 percent or the 9 percent cut-off was used. The greatest correspondence between field survey rates and rates of labeling occurred when the traditional 3 percent cut-off was used.

We concluded that the 3 percent cut-off—that is, IQ below 70 and adaptive behavior in the lowest 3 percent of the population—is the criterion most likely to identify those in need of special assistance and supervision and least likely to stigmatize as mentally retarded persons who would be filling a normal complement of social roles as adults. Persons scoring in the so-called "borderline" category should be regarded as low normals rather than as clinically retarded.

Conclusion 2: Both IQ and adaptive behavior should be evaluated in making diagnoses. We compared the social-role performance of the quasi-retarded (those who failed only the IQ test) with the clinically retarded (those who failed both the IQ test and the adaptive behavior scales). The clinically retarded school-age children had more difficulties with school learning, were more frequently behind the school grade expected for their age, had repeated more grades, and were more likely to be enrolled in special education classes; the quasi-retardates, in spite of low intelligence-test scores, avoided falling behind age mates or being placed in special programs. We found that 80 percent of the quasi-retarded adults had graduated from high school; they all read books, magazines, and newspapers; all had held jobs; 65 percent had white-collar positions; 19 percent had skilled or semiskilled positions while 15.7 percent were unskilled laborers. All of them were able to work without supervision, participated in sports, traveled alone, went to the store by themselves, and participated in informal visiting with coworkers, friends, and neighbors. In other words, their social-role performance tended to be indistinguishable from that of other adults in the community.

Assessment of adaptive behavior is important in evaluating persons from ethnic minorities and lower socioeconomic levels, backgrounds that do not conform to the modal social and cultural pattern of the community. Many of them may fail intelligence tests mainly because they have not had the opportunity to learn the cognitive skills and to acquire the knowledge needed to pass such tests. Yet they demonstrate by their ability to cope with problems in other areas of life that they are not comprehensively incompetent.

We concluded that clinicians should develop a systematic method for evaluating adaptive behavior as well as intelligence in making clinical assessments of ability and should operationalize the two-dimensional screening procedure advocated by the AAMD many years ago.

Conclusion 3: Sociocultural factors should be systematically taken into account in interpreting clinical scores. The IQ tests now being used by psychologists are, to a large extent, Anglocentric. They tend to measure the extent to which an individual's background is similar to that of the modal cultural configuration of American society. Because a significant amount of the variance in intelligence-test scores is related to sociocultural characteristics, we concluded that sociocultural factors must be taken into account in interpreting the meaning of any individual score.

Specifically, we studied two different samples of persons to determine the amount of variance in intelligence-test scores which could be accounted for by sociocultural factors. The first group were the 100 Chicanos, 47 blacks, and 556 Anglos from seven months through fifty years of age for whom IQs were secured in the field survey or in the agency survey and for whom we also had information on the sociocultural characteristics of their families. Eighteen sociocultural characteristics were dichotomized so that one category corresponded to the modal sociocultural configuration of the community and the other category was nonmodal. IQ was used as the dependent variable in a stepwise multiple regression in which the sociocultural characteristics were used as independent variables. The multiple correlation coefficient for this large heterogeneous sample was .50 ($p < .001$), indicating that 25 percent of the variance in the IQs of the 703 culturally and ethnically heterogeneous individuals in this group could be accounted for by sociocultural differences.

In a similar analysis we studied 1513 elementary school children in the Riverside public schools. For this analysis we used thirteen sociocultural characteristics of the families as independent variables and Full Scale WISC IQ as the dependent variable. The 598 Chicanos and 339 black children in the sample included the total school population of the three segregated minority elementary schools which then existed in the district. The 576 Anglo children were randomly selected from eleven predominantly white elementary schools in the district. The multiple correlation coefficient was .57, indicating that 32 percent of the variance in the IQs of this socioculturally heterogeneous group of elementary school children could be accounted for by differences in family background factors; 68 percent of the variance was residual (unaccounted for).

Conclusion 4: Psychological assessment procedures must not deny civil rights. We believe, on the basis of our findings, that psychological assessment procedures have become a civil-rights issue because they tend to deny minority children an opportunity to be fully educated, without stigmatizing labels, in culturally relevant learning environments.

Rights of Minority Group Children

We believe that present assessment and educational practices violate at least five rights of children from minority groups: (1) their right to be evaluated within a culturally appropriate normative framework; (2) their right to be assessed as multidimensional, many-faceted human beings; (3) their right to be fully educated; (4) their right to be free of stigmatizing labels; and (5) their right to cultural identity and respect.

Evaluation within a culturally appropriate normative framework. In our studies we found that ethnic disproportions were very marked, both among those labeled as mentally retarded by community agencies and among those screened as having the "symptoms" of mental retardation in the field survey. Ethnic disproportions were especially marked in those social agencies, such as the public schools, that rely on "intelligence" tests to make a "diagnosis" of mental retardation. Our analysis of the labeling process in the schools indicated that these disproportions first occur at that stage in the process when an intelligence test is administered (Mercer, 1971a, 1971c). Rates of labeling were negatively correlated with the extent to which the sociocultural characteristics of the family conform to the Anglo-American mode. Scores on "intelligence" tests were positively correlated with the anglicization of the family. We concluded that sociocultural differences are so marked and are so highly correlated with test scores, both within and between racial/ethnic groups, that the usual practice of making a diagnosis of biological potential by comparing scores for persons from different sociocultural settings within the same normative framework is not justified and should be abandoned. The reasons for these difficulties are clear when we examine the history of psychological assessment and the nature of the traditional statistical model of "normal."

Binet and Simon developed their original test of "intelligence" to identify those French children who would not benefit from the regular school program and should be placed in special schools (Binet and Simon, 1905). Items for the test were selected from those aspects of French culture which, Binet and Simon believed, all French children would have had an opportunity to learn. When the testing movement spread to the United States, subsequent test makers followed the general practice established by Binet. Consequently, the content of

American intelligence tests has been drawn from the Anglo-American cultural tradition, and the criterion for testing the validity of these measures has been their ability to predict performance in an Anglocentric public school system.

Another characteristic of present assessment procedures which reinforces and legitimates a monocultural value system is the fact that all "standardized" assessment procedures are based on a statistical definition of "normal" which uses a *single* normative framework for interpreting the scores of all children. This single norm is used to arrange individuals along a continuum based on their relative location in the distribution of others who have been measured on the characteristics being studied. Persons more than two standard deviations above or below the mean are usually classified as "abnormals" while those within two standard deviations of the mean are in the "normal" range. The statistical model differs in significant respects from the medical-pathological and social-system models for defining "normal" (Mercer, 1972b, 1973a).

The traditional statistical model, based on a single "normal" curve and interpreted from a clinical perspective, has five characteristics which have implications for children's rights:

1. The clinical perspective assumes that there is *one* normal curve and that this single distribution can be used to classify the behavior of all children, irrespective of their cultural background.

2. The statistical model generates its own abnormals. If there is any variability in the population measured, some persons will be at the top and others at the bottom of the distribution. By definition, a statistical model will always classify approximately 3 percent of its norming population as abnormally high and 3 percent as abnormally low.

3. The type of behavior which will be regarded as "normal" or "abnormal" depends upon the typical behavior of persons in the population on which the norms were established. Because all but the simplest behavior is learned in a sociocultural setting, the characteristics of "normal" and "abnormal" behavior will vary with the culture of the persons on whom the norms are based and are not absolute in any sense. Before any inferences can be made about differences in the learning potential of two groups on the basis of their relative performance on a test of learned behavior, they must be from the same cultural population. They must have had equal exposure to the knowl-

edge and skills covered in the test; they must have been equally
motivated to learn those skills; and they must be equally familiar with and comfortable in the test situation. Children from
different cultural heritages in American society are not identical
in these respects. The average scores of children from different
heritages whom we tested on so-called intelligence and achievement tests were statistically different ($p < .001$). This finding
has been reported in virtually every similar study (Mercer and
Smith, 1972). Children from different cultural heritages do not
meet the assumptions of the inferential model on which diagnostic conclusions are based. We cannot assume that they are
from the same population. Thus, behavioral norms established
on one sociocultural group cannot be generalized beyond that
cultural group (Mercer and Brown, 1973).

4. Including non-Anglo children in the norming sample in
proportion to their number in the total population does *not*
solve the issue of sociocultural differences. The statistical model
assumes that the behavioral characteristics being measured are
normally distributed. If this is not the case, a statistically defined "normal" is misleading. In a skewed distribution, the
mean moves in the direction of the skew. In a bimodal or tri-
modal distribution, the mean does not adequately represent the
behavior of any of the subgroups making up the distribution.
When two or more cultural groups are included in a norming
population, as happens in the standardization of many tests, the
largest subgroup has the greatest influence in establishing the
behavioral norms. Cultural groups which differ systematically in
their language, values, or behavioral style from the majority
group will be defined as "abnormal" (Mercer, 1972b).

5. Establishing separate norms for an entire racial/ethnic
group or developing culture-specific tests for each racial/ethnic
group does not solve the problem. Important sociocultural differences exist not only between but within racial/ethnic groups.
In the sample of black and Mexican-American children mentioned earlier, we were able to identify five levels of sociocultural modality, ranging from a group completely assimilated
into the Anglo-American culture to a group having little contact
with modern industrial America (Mercer, 1972a). Such cultural
heterogeneity must somehow be recognized in psychological assessment.

The problems mentioned above have been clearly documented by numerous investigators (Eells and others, 1951;

Darcy, 1963). Unfortunately, the implications of cultural biases in the content and norming of tests when used in the assessment of non-Anglo children have never been fully appreciated. Findings confirming cultural bias have had very little impact on the training of psychologists or the practice of psychological testing as it has been institutionalized in the public schools during recent decades. We found little evidence that clinicians were taking cultural factors into account in interpreting standardized test scores. We believe that each child has a right to be evaluated within a culturally appropriate normative framework. Children should not be classified as "abnormals" primarily because they have been socialized into a non-Anglo cultural tradition.

Assessment as a multidimensional human being. Although official definitions of mental retardation require "that an individual manifest deficiencies in both adaptive behavior and intellectual functioning" (Grossman, 1973), we found that most community agencies, especially the public schools, were relying mainly on measures of "intelligence" in "diagnosing" mental retardation. Ninety-nine percent of the labeled retardates nominated by the public schools had been given an intelligence test, but only 13 percent had received a medical diagnosis. The only measure of "adaptability" was implicit. If a child's behavior violated the norms of the teacher and he was referred for psychological evaluation, he was judged to be maladapted (Mercer, 1971b). No community agency systematically assessed the child's ability to perform complex nonacademic tasks in his home, neighborhood, and community. Assessment procedures were unidimensional. They focused only on the narrow band of behavior sampled in the psychometric situation.

As mentioned earlier, the field survey used a series of scales to measure adaptive behavior. We found that a multidimensional assessment was particularly important in understanding the human potential of persons from non-Anglo backgrounds. We estimated that 60 percent of the Mexican-American and 90 percent of the black adults who scored below 70 on tests of "intelligence" were performing adequately in their occupational, parental, and community roles. When we interviewed the mothers of children labeled *mentally retarded* by the schools, we found that many were "situationally" retarded. They were "retarded" for the six hours they were in school but were regarded as "normals" by their family and friends. Some were carrying a heavy load of responsibility in the home. Others

were known in their neighborhoods for their mechanical aptitude and their ability to figure things out (Mercer, 1971a).

Our studies convinced us that a child has a right to be
assessed as a multifaceted person playing roles in many social
systems. A child who is succeeding in nonacademic roles is *not*
comprehensively retarded even though he may score as "subnormal" on a standardized test of intelligence. In our study we
classified those who failed the intelligence test but had normal
adaptive behavior as the quasi-retarded. We believe that a systematic multidimensional assessment of a child's adaptive
behavior in nonschool settings would provide information on
his competencies. This in turn would assist the school in understanding and appreciating him as a human being and would
provide useful information for planning an educational program. Such a program could build on his assets and accomplish-
ments rather than classifying him by his deficits. Measuring
adaptive behavior would help to shift psychological assessment
from a "deficit" to an "asset" model.

Full Education. A few children (we estimated less than 1
percent of the population) have suffered biological damage and
have a very low ceiling on their learning ability (Mercer, 1973b).
Such children need special education programs geared to their
needs. Other children (we estimated as many as 75 percent of
those in public school programs for educable mental retardates)
perform poorly on tests of intelligence but are not comprehensively retarded. Many are in the borderline category—IQ scores
70 to 84. They will escape the retarded label when they leave
the purview of the school and begin to function as adults. Some
are quasi-retardates who have school-specific problems but are
performing adequately in other social systems. Others are from
non-Anglo families. They are having difficulty coping with the
Anglocentric style and program of the school. Such children
cannot be educated to the limit of their potential in classes
designed for the mentally retarded. They need supplemental
help (such as tutorial assistance, training in English as a second
language, speech therapy, or remedial reading) to remain in the
regular educational programs. Given prompt assistance early in
their educational career, many of them would eventually be
able to progress without special help. Placed in a special education class for the mentally retarded, they will never be fully
educated.

One of the most persistent complaints we heard from

parents of children inappropriately placed in classes for the mentally retarded was their concern about the limited and repetitious nature of the educational program. For example, one black mother in our study said, "Bill is being retarded in special education. . . . We have to make Bill go to school because the class does not offer a challenge to him. What they do is repetitious—the same thing over and over. . . . He does not like school."

Freedom from stigmatizing labels. There are children whose physical anomalies and behavioral deficits are so visible that they deviate from the normative expectations of every social system in which they participate. When such children are formally labeled as mentally retarded and placed in special programs, they do not acquire a new stigma. There is convergence between social-system definitions and clinical definitions of abnormality (Mercer, 1973a, chap. 15). However, many of the children in special programs have no physical anomalies. Sixty-seven percent of the children in special classes in our labeling study were not viewed as subnormal by other social systems. This disparity was especially marked for minority children. Forty-eight percent of the children labeled mentally retarded in only one social system were Anglo-American, 36.5 percent were Mexican-American, and 11.9 percent were black. Conversely, the ethnic proportion for those labeled mentally retarded in all the social systems in which they participated approximated the ethnic proportions in the general population. Approximately 78 percent were Anglo-American, 13 percent were Mexican-American, and 5 percent were black. More minority children were burdened with school-specific stigmatizing labels.

As early as 1905, Binet expressed his concern with stigmatization. "It will never be to one's credit to have attended a special school. We should at the least spare from this mark those who do not deserve it. Mistakes are excusable, especially at the beginning. But if they become too gross, they could injure the name of these new institutions" (Binet and Simon, 1905). We are no longer at the "beginning" in psychological assessment. "Mistakes" are no longer excusable. We believe that children have a right to be free of stigmatizing labels. Such labels, we concluded, result primarily from a failure to take adaptive behavior into account in clinical assessment and from the practice of classifying persons who score between one and two standard deviations below the mean on intelligence tests as "borderline retardates." We have recommended a return to the traditional cut-off level proposed by Wechsler and Terman. They suggest that only those who score more than two standard deviations below the mean should be regarded as subnormal—the lowest 3 percent of the population, IQ below 70 (Wechsler, 1958; Terman and Merrill, 1960). The revised edition of the American Association on Mental Deficiency *Manual for Classification in Mental Retardation* has eliminated the "borderline" category. It defines "significantly subaverage" functioning as "performance which is two or more standard deviations from the mean" (Grossman, 1973). Some states are redefining standards for placement in special classes. For example, the 1971 California Legislature lowered the general cut-off level for placement to two or more standard deviations below the mean while allowing psychologists some discretionary power in placing persons with IQs above 70 (California State Legislature, 1971). Such tightening of standards will free many children from stigmatizing labels.

Ethnic identity and respect. Achievement and intelligence tests are designed to predict a child's probability of "success" in American public schools, which are culture bearers for the Anglo-American tradition. The curriculum and teaching style in the public schools reflect the language, literature, values, and history of the white, Anglo-Saxon, Protestant segment of American society, whose cultural domination was established during the colonial period and has been maintained ever since. Traditionally, the public schools have been a mechanism for the Americanization of non-Anglo migrants to the United States. The standard curriculum includes training in the English language and the study of English literature, Anglo-American history, and Anglo-American political and social systems. All instruction is in standard English; speaking a language other than English has been consistently discouraged. For example, 32 percent of the 5800 schools surveyed recently in five southwestern states (United States Commission on Civil Rights, 1972) discourage the use of Spanish in classrooms. Children from Spanish-speaking homes are expected to learn English with no special assistance from the schools. In 1970 there were only 131 bilingual programs in American public schools to serve the entire Spanish-speaking population.

When some parents protested to us in interviews that present psychological assessment procedures are "a conspiracy to keep minorities down" and are "most unfair," they were expressing their feeling that, somehow, their cultural tradition and way of life are being systematically devalued by the schools. When institutionalized processes, such as intelligence testing, have the objective consequence of assigning a disproportionate number of persons from non-Anglo cultural groups to educational programs and tracks which have low ceilings and provide limited access to higher education and upward mobility, those practices serve the latent function of perpetuating the superordinate position of Anglo-Americans and the subordinate position of non-Anglos in American society. The implicit assumption that the only criterion for "normal" is meeting Anglo-American cultural expectations devalues the performance of children who have knowledge of a non-Anglo cultural tradition or language and simultaneously tends to denigrate such cultural traditions. This practice leads to educational models that interpret cultural differences as deficits and perceive culturally different children as "empty vessels" (Wax and others, 1964) who are "culturally deprived" (Reissman, 1962). Finally, standardized testing provides a mechanism for blaming the child and his family when the educational program of the school fails (Mercer, in press). The total effect legitimates the monocultural, Anglocentric program of the school and denigrates other cultural traditions and the bicultural child.

In our interviews with non-Anglo parents, we found some who accept the "Americanization" process. They want their children to assimilate completely into Anglo-American society and to relinquish all other linguistic and cultural ties. At the opposite pole were a few cultural separatists who do not want their children to participate in or adopt an Anglo-American life style. The third group, probably the majority, want their children to be bicultural. They want their children to be able to speak standard English, to secure good jobs, and to share in the benefits and resources available to persons who participate in modern, industrial American society. However, they also want their children to be literate in their own native language and to perpetuate its cultural traditions. In the past, public policy has supported only Anglo conformity. Present classification systems and measurement procedures implement that monocultural value frame.

We believe that psychological assessment and public educational policy should recognize the integrity and value of different cultural traditions. At the very least, cultural differences should not appear as "deficits" in the standardized test situation. Preferably, bilingualism and biculturality should be valued and encouraged. Persons who speak more than one language and can participate in more than one cultural tradition have a much richer experiential world than persons who know only one language and one tradition. If multiculturalism were valued, children from minority and majority cultural traditions would be encouraged to become multicultural. Public schools would be developed to foster multiculturality.

A truly multicultural psychological assessment system would evaluate each child's performance in terms of multiple cultural traditions. The child who understands more than one language and is informed about the history, values, institutions, and customs of more than one cultural tradition would be evaluated more highly than the child who is familiar with only one cultural tradition and language.

We recognize that development of a multicultural, pluralistic approach to assessment will not, alone, have any impact on public education unless other aspects of the educational system and the larger social structure also change in the direction of multiculturality. Thus, we view our efforts as simply a small beginning in what we hope may become a more general movement. The system of multicultural assessment which we are developing has a relatively modest goal: to develop a system that presents a more comprehensive view of the child's performance (taking into account both academic and nonacademic social systems) and that considers a child's socialization setting when interpreting the meaning of a particular set of scores in planning his educational program. Such changes would bring greater congruence between clinical definitions and social-system definitions of abnormality and would help to move assessment from a "deficit" to an "asset" model. It would be an initial step toward greater cultural pluralism in public education.

Policy Implications

The same minority differentials which we found in our study were found and have been widely publicized in California as a result of the annual ethnic survey of the public schools conducted since 1965 by the State Board of Education. Evidence indicates that such disproportions are a national pattern. Concern is mounting. In June of 1970, the San Francisco Board of Education discontinued the use of group mental-ability tests and recommended a moratorium on the use of individual tests of intelligence with black children unless specifically requested by the parents of the children (San Francisco Board of Education, 1970). Other cities have taken similar action. In October 1970, the Bay Area Association of Black Psychologists proposed a moratorium on the use of group and individual tests of intelligence and group tests of scholastic ability in the assessment of black children throughout the state of California. The Association of Psychologists of *La Raza* has petitioned the American Psychological Association and various governmental agencies to remedy inequalities in job placement and educational opportunities resulting from the misinterpretation of intelligence tests given to persons of Mexican-American heritage. They charge that standardized tests are being misused in the placement of Mexican-American children in classes for the mentally retarded.

The California Legislature recently dropped group mental-abilities tests from the list of tests required under the state-mandated testing program. In both the 1972 and 1973 California Legislatures Assemblyman Willie Brown introduced a bill (Assembly Bill 483) that "prohibits school districts from administering to pupils in the district any test which measures or attempts to measure the scholastic aptitude of pupils" (California State Legislature, 1972). This bill was passed by an overwhelming majority in both the House and the Senate but was twice vetoed by the governor.

In 1971 the California Legislature amended the education code to provide a legal framework for pluralistic assessment. Following are some of the salient provisions of that bill:

> The legislature . . . declares . . . that pupils should not be assigned to special classes . . . for the mentally retarded if they can be served in regular classes.
> Before any minor is admitted to a special education program for mentally retarded minors . . . the minor shall be given verbal or nonverbal individual intelligence tests in the primary home language in which the minor is most fluent and has the best speaking ability and capacity to understand. . . .
> No minor shall be placed in a special education class

for the mentally retarded if he scores higher than two standard deviations below the norm. . . .

No minor may be placed in a special education program for the mentally retarded unless a complete psychological examination by a credentialed school psychologist
investigating such factors as developmental history, cultural
background, and school achievement substantiates the retarded intellectual development indicated by the individual
test scores. This examination shall include estimates of
adaptive behavior. . . . Such adaptability testing shall include but is not limited to a visit, with the consent of the
parent or guardian, to the minor's home by the school
psychologist or a person designated by the chief administrator of the district [California State Legislature, 1971].

This legislation provides a legal framework for imple-
menting a system of multicultural pluralistic assessment in the
public schools. We are currently involved in developing a method for operationalizing the concepts contained in this legislation. We have tested a representative sample of 2100 California
public school children, five through eleven years of age (700
Anglo-American, 700 Afro-American, and 700 Mexican-American children), and have interviewed their mothers. From these
data, we are developing a series of measures and an interpretive
framework which we hope will provide a system that will recognize the cultural identity of each child, locate him within a
culturally relevant framework, describe him as a multidimensional person playing roles in many social systems, and ultimately lead to the development of educational programs that
will enable him to function in a pluralistic society.

Multicultural pluralistic assessment includes identification
of the socialization milieu in which the child is being reared,
evaluation of the child's general academic readiness in relation
to the general public school population and to his own sociocultural milieu, assessment of the child's adaptive behavior in
nonacademic activities, an inventory of the child's health history, and screening for physical impairments. Information on
the socialization milieu, the child's adaptive behavior, and the
child's health history are secured in a structured interview with
the mother or principal caretaker. Information on the child's
general academic readiness and screening for physical impairments is secured during an assessment session with the child. We
will briefly describe each of these measures.

Socialization milieu. No child can be understood and properly educated in a vacuum. Pluralistic assessment procedures begin with an analysis of the socialization milieu in which a child is being reared, so that his performance can be interpreted in relationship to his socialization setting. Information about each child's socialization milieu will be used to establish multiple normative frameworks for interpreting performance. Four measures will be included in the socialization profile for each child: (1) *Sociocultural Modality*—a measure of family characteristics that predict readiness for academic work in the public schools: occupational level of head of household, educational level of head of household, urbanization of parents, residential mobility, family size, family structure, language usage, participation in formal organizations, cultural values (Mercer, 1972b; Mercer and Brown, 1973). (2) *Opportunity Structure*—a measure of the number and variety of social roles that a child has available in his environment. Children from geographically or socially isolated settings have less opportunity to learn a wide variety of social roles. This lack of opportunity is consistently reflected in lower performance of poor and/or rural children in academic settings which assume a broad experiential world. (3) *Role Permissiveness*—a measure of the number and variety of roles a child is permitted to play. Some families are highly permissive and allow children to attempt a wide variety of roles with little adult supervision; other families are more restrictive and closely supervise every aspect of a child's life. These differences reflect the cultural tradition of the family and are an important dimension in understanding a child's behavior. (4) *Family Involvement in Socialization*—a measure of the extent to which the child's principal caretaker has a comprehensive knowledge of the child's current activities and his life history. A child being reared by foster parents or distant relatives may find himself in a socialization setting in which the significant socialization agents know very little about him. This situation will be reflected in his performance.

General academic readiness: Cognitive skills. In the usual public school situation, the teacher is the first person to note that a child is having academic difficulty and is the person most likely to refer the child for assessment. At this juncture, the school psychologist is likely to administer one of the standardized individual tests of intelligence. If the child scores low on this test, the school psychologist can predict, with a high level of accuracy, that the child will have difficulty succeeding in the regular public school program without supplemental assistance. We believe that one of the primary problems with present assessment procedures occurs at this point—the confusion of symptom identification with diagnosis and prognosis.

A "symptom" is a sign that indicates the existence of something else. A low score on a measure of cognitive skills is a "sign" indicating that the child will need special assistance if he is to be fully educated. Like most symptoms, a low score on a standard test is only a sign. It is not self-explanatory. Just as a fever is a symptom that may result from many different biological causes, so a low score on a standardized test is a symptom that may result from many different causes. Once the symptom has been identified, the diagnostic task is to determine the cause of the symptom in each specific case. In our community study, we found that clinicians typically assumed that the cause of the symptom of a low score on the standard norms for an intelligence test was almost always "mental retardation." They confused symptom identification with "diagnosis" or symptom interpretation. This confusion results from the assumption that intelligence tests are measuring the child's "raw resources" (educational inputs) while achievement tests are measuring his "learning" (educational outputs).

We have argued elsewhere that this distinction between intelligence tests and achievement tests is not warranted, either by differences in their cultural component or their statistical relationship to each other (Mercer and Brown, 1973; Mercer, in press). Both are designed to predict public school performance, both measure learning, and both can be used as signs of a child's academic readiness for the American public school program, as compared to the academic readiness of his age peers. The tests are essentially interchangeable. Either test score can be used as a sign to identify a child who is likely to have academic problems. Neither can be used to diagnose the cause of the problem.

There are many physical, sociocultural, emotional, and motivational reasons why a child may have a low score on either an intelligence or an achievement test. The task of the diagnostician is to determine which factors are operating in a particular case; that is, which factors are causing the depressed score. When the cause of the symptom has been *diagnosed*, then the clinician can make a *prognosis*, a prediction of the probable future course of the "condition." When treatments have been developed for a particular condition, then two prognoses may be possible—the prognosis without intervention and the prognosis with intervention.

In our study of labeling the mentally retarded in the community, we found clinicians treating the symptom (the low intelligence-test score) as if it were a diagnosis (mental retardation) and recommending a single treatment (special education in classes for the mentally retarded). In the public schools the low test score was almost universally interpreted as a symptom of low biological potential, and no alternative diagnoses were explored. Consequently, the prognoses (predictions) based on these diagnoses were inaccurate. Most persons diagnosed as mentally retarded in school were no longer regarded as mentally retarded when they left school. The interventions based on such diagnoses were also inadequate, because persons who scored low on the standard test were all treated as if the cause of their symptom was mental retardation. The situation was not unlike a medical doctor's giving all his patients the same treatment for a fever without bothering to diagnose whether the fever was caused by an infected appendix, infected tonsils, rheumatic fever, measles, or some other malady. A pluralistic diagnosis would have revealed many different causes producing the symptom in different children, each cause requiring a different treatment.

We are using the Wechsler Intelligence Scale for Children (WISC) as the basic measure of the child's general academic readiness (Wechsler, 1973 revision, in press).[2] In our earlier studies we found that children's scores on some subtests of the WISC were more highly correlated with the characteristics of their socialization milieu than others. Sociocultural characteristics could account for between 5 percent and 38 percent of the variance in children's scores on different subtests (Mercer and Brown, 1973). When subtests are grouped according to the extent to which they are correlated with sociocultural factors, it will be possible to compare the score of an individual child *with the scores of other children from a similar socialization milieu,* as well as comparing his performance with the general popula-

[2]We thank James H. Ricks, Alexander Wesman, Jerome E. Doppelt, and Alan Kaufman of the Psychological Corporation for providing us with the test materials used in standardizing the 1973 revision of the WISC, so that we could include the latest version of that test in our System of Multicultural Pluralistic Assessment (SOMPA).

tion norms. By comparing the child's performance on the sociocultural norms with his performance on the standard norms, the
psychologist can diagnose the extent to which the child's performance reflects sociocultural differences. This information
can be used to plan the child's educational program. Prognosis
and treatment will vary according to the relationship between
the two sets of scores.

Multidimensional performance. Traditional assessment
procedures evaluate whether the child is meeting the expectations of one social system—the school. If he is referred by his
teacher for psychological assessment, we know that he has
somehow been identified as a "problem" and is not meeting
educational norms. Standardized achievement tests and intelligence tests are formal assessments of competence in terms of
the norms of the school. There is a high correlation among all
these assessment procedures because they all represent the expectations of a single social system which is the culture bearer
for the dominant society. To secure a multidimensional view of
the child, we need an assessment in terms of the norms of social
systems other than those represented by the clinician, psychologist, teacher, and school.

In assessing a child's adaptive behavior, we wish to secure
information about his social-role performance in the family,
neighborhood, and community *as perceived by significant
others in those social systems.* We are developing a set of questions which assess his ability to perform successfully in those
nonacademic social roles considered appropriate for his age and
sex in his sociocultural setting. The construct of adaptive behavior includes both the development of skill in interpersonal
relations and the emerging ability to play ever more complex
roles in an expanding range of social systems. The sociological
concept of the social role is the unifying focus. Items for the
inventory were collected from a wide variety of sources. The
most fruitful source was in-depth interviews with the mothers
of Anglo-American, Mexican-American, and black elementary
school children. In these interviews the mothers described, in
detail, their children's activities in the family, neighborhood,
and community.

Health history and impairment screening. The public
school does not have sufficient resources for a complete medical
examination for each child referred for psychological evaluation. However, there is no reason why the school cannot secure

from the mother relevant information about each child's health history and conduct a preliminary screening for possible physical impairments in vision, hearing, manual dexterity, and so forth. Such information, if systematized into a usable form, could assist the school in identifying those high-risk children who should receive a complete physical examination. We believe that such screening should become a standard part of every assessment, and we are norming a set of procedures for this purpose. The health history consists of a structured set of questions answered by the child's mother or principal caretaker. Questions are stated in nontechnical, nonmedical terms. The inventory covers four major areas: prenatal and postnatal complications; serious, acute illnesses; chronic conditions; and major operations and injuries. The impairment screening includes a measure of visual-motor skills (Bender, 1946) and a series of tasks measuring fine- and gross-motor coordination.

Advantages of Multicultural Pluralistic Assessment

Pluralistic assessment, using multiple measures and multiple normative frameworks, will make it possible for a psychologist to interpret the meaning of a child's performance so that the best educational program can be planned for each child. We will be working through the details of the interpretive scheme as our analysis proceeds. These procedures, we believe, will recognize each child's right to be evaluated within a culturally appropriate normative framework, his right to be treated as a multidimensional person playing roles in many social systems, his right to be fully educated, his right to be free of stigmatizing labels, and his right to cultural identity and integrity.

By developing multiple normative frameworks to describe children from different sociocultural settings, pluralistic assessment will recognize the child's right to be evaluated within an appropriate sociocultural framework. Assessing a child's performance in relation to that of other children from similar backgrounds will free evaluation from the single normal curve, adjust definitions of "normal-abnormal" for differences in sociocultural background, and take into account sociocultural differences within ethnic/racial groups.

An adaptive behavior inventory, to describe performance in nonacademic settings, will provide information on a child's social-role performance as perceived by others in his own sociocultural setting. This assessment will identify those children whose problems are school-specific. It will provide information on each child as a whole person who demonstrates his abilities in a variety of different roles in varied social systems. This information can be used to identify each child's competencies and can serve to move evaluation from a deficit to an asset model.

By clearly differentiating symptom identification from diagnosis and prognosis, pluralistic assessment will make it possible to locate those children who are having difficulty in the public schools primarily because the culture of their homes differs from the culture of the school. Such children can be fully educated only when cultural differences are recognized and appropriate programs are developed to foster biculturality.

Pluralistic assessment procedures will reduce stigmatization by bringing greater convergence between psychological definitions of "abnormal" and the perceptions of persons in other social systems. Only those children in the lowest 3 percent of the population on the general population norms and on the socioculturally relevant norms for measures of cognitive skills and adaptive behavior would be regarded as mentally retarded.

By explicitly recognizing that children come from a variety of sociocultural backgrounds and providing a mechanism so that no child is penalized by the public school assessment process because he is from a non-Anglo background, pluralistic assessment will tend to move the school from a monocultural to a multicultural perspective and can lead to greater multicultural programming in the public schools.

References

Bender, L. *The Bender Gestalt Test for Young Children.* New York: American Orthopsychiatric Association, 1946.

Binet, A., and Simon, T. "Sur la nécessité d'établir un diagnostic scientifique des états inférieurs de l'intelligence." *L'Année Psychologique*, 1905, *11*, 1-28.

California State Legislature. Senate Bill 33. Approved by governor, May 18, 1971.

California State Legislature. Assembly Bill 483. Regular session. Introduced by Assemblyman Brown, February 18, 1972.

Darcy, N. T. "Bilingualism and the Measurement of Intelligence: Review of a Decade of Research." *Journal of Genetic Psychology*, 1963, *103*, 259-282.

Diana v. State Board of Education. NOC-70-37, U.S. District Court, Northern District of California (1970).

Doll, E. A. *Vineland Social Maturity Scale, Condensed: Manual of Direction.* (Rev. Ed.) Minneapolis: American Guidance Service, 1965.

Eells, K., and others. *Intelligence and Cultural Differences.* Chicago: University of Chicago Press, 1951.

Gesell, A. L. *The First Five Years of Life.* New York: Harper, 1948a.

Gesell, A. L. *Studies in Child Development.* New York: Harper, 1948b.

Gesell, A. L. *Youth: The Years from Ten to Sixteen.* New York: Harper, 1956.

Grossman, H. J. (Ed.) *A Manual on Terminology and Classification in Mental Retardation.* (3rd Ed.) *American Journal of Mental Deficiency.* Special Publication Series No. 2, 1973.

Heber, R. F. (Ed.) *A Manual on Terminology and Classification in Mental Retardation. American Journal of Mental Deficiency,* 1961. Monograph supplement.

Larry P. v. Wilson Riles. NOC-71-2270 RFP, U.S. District Court, Northern District of California (June 21, 1972).

Mercer, J. R. "Institutionalized Anglocentrism: Labeling Mental Retardates in the Public Schools." In P. Orleans and W. R. Eliss (Eds.), *Race, Change, and Urban Society.* Vol. V. Los Angeles: Sage Publications, 1971a.

Mercer, J. R. "The Meaning of Mental Retardation." In R. Koch and J. Dobson (Eds.), *The Mentally Retarded Child and His Family: A Multidisciplinary Handbook.* New York: Brunner/Mazel, 1971b.

Mercer, J. R. "Sociocultural Factors in Labeling Mental Retardates." *Peabody Journal of Education,* 1971c, *48,* 188-203.

Mercer, J. R. "IQ: The Lethal Label." *Psychology Today,* 1972a, *6,* 44-47, 95-97.

Mercer, J. R. "Who Is Normal? Two Perspectives on Mild Mental Retardation." In E. G. Jaco (Ed.), *Patients, Physicians, and Illness.* (Rev. Ed.) New York: Free Press, 1972b.

Mercer, J. R. *Labeling the Mentally Retarded.* Berkeley: University of California Press, 1973a.

Mercer, J. R. "The Myth of 3 Percent Prevalence." In G. Tarjan, R. Eyman, and C. E. Meyers (Eds.), *Sociobehavioral Studies in Mental Retardation: Papers in Honor of Harvey L. Dingman.* Washington, D.C.: American Association on Mental Deficiency, 1973b.

Mercer, J. R. "Latent Functions of Intelligence Testing in Public Schools." In L. P. Miller (Ed.), *The Testing of Black Students.* Englewood Cliffs, N.J.: Prentice-Hall, in press.

Mercer, J. R., and Brown, W. C. "Racial Differences in IQ: Fact or Artifact?" In C. Senva (Ed.), *The Fallacy of IQ.* New York: Third Press, 1973.

Mercer, J. R., and Smith, J. M. "Subtest Estimates of the WISC Full Scale IQ's for Children." In U.S. Department of Health, Education, and Welfare, Public Health Service, *Vital and Health Statistics.* Series

2, No. 47. Washington, D.C.: U.S. Government Printing Office, 1972.

Reissman, F. *The Culturally Deprived Child.* New York: Harper, 1962.

San Francisco Board of Education. Minutes of Special Meeting, June 16, 190.

Terman, L. M., and Merrill, M. A. *Stanford Binet Intelligence Scale.* Boston: Houghton Mifflin, 1960.

United States Commission on Civil Rights. *The Excluded Student: Educational Practices Affecting Mexican-Americans in the Southwest.* Report III. Washington, D.C.: U.S. Government Printing Office, 1972.

Wax, M. L., and others. *Formal Education in an American Indian Community.* Atlanta: Emory University Press, 1964.

Wechsler, D. *The Measurement and Appraisal of Adult Intelligence.* (4th Ed.) Baltimore: Williams and Wilkins, 1958.

Wechsler, D. *Wechsler Intelligence Scale for Children.* 1973 revision. New York: Psychological Corporation, in press.

TWO

CLASSIFICATION SYSTEMS

A dozen or more categories—such as mental retardation, emotional disturbance, and learning disability—have acquired legitimacy, through some science and much tradition, in the classification of exceptional children. Within these major categories, numerous subdimensions result from specific efforts to classify children for one purpose or another. Taken all together, the various systems and schemes for the classification of exceptional children fall considerably short of what current understandings permit. Serious problems are caused by a lack of sophistication in taxonomy, by strong professional biases, by preoccupation with dominant symptoms to the neglect of important determinants, and by the use of classification to legitimize social control of the individual. The nine chapters in this part illuminate the complexity of classification and illustrate promising ways of improving systems and procedures.

CHAPTER 7

HISTORICAL PERSPECTIVES ON CLASSIFICATION OF MENTAL RETARDATION
Richard L. Blanton

This chapter shows how changing conceptions of man, broad social movements, and emerging technologies influence the conceptual schemes of classification and labeling. Blanton's piece has high heuristic value because a similar historical perspective, applied to other categories (such as emotional disturbance or blindness), would show that they too deal not only with simple functional phenomena but also with conventions of the times and transient ways of thinking.

CHAPTER 8

MENTAL RETARDATION
John W. Filler, Jr., Cordelia C. Robinson, Roger A. Smith, Lisbeth J. Vincent-Smith, Diane D. Bricker, William A. Bricker

This chapter emphasizes the inadequacy of classification systems based on psychometric data, such as IQ, for supplying information that can be used by a teacher or a parent to help a child learn. The authors present evidence that disposition of children on the basis of IQ alone decreases opportunities for them to acquire socially desirable behavior. The empirical analysis of behavior in a developmental model, such as that proposed by Jean Piaget, provides a structure for the classification of behavior (not of children) that can be used to design effective instructional programs. Utility in improving instruction is the authors' central criterion for any system for the classification of mental retardation.

CHAPTER 9

PHYSICAL AND SENSORY HANDICAPS
Frances P. Connor, Richard Hoover, Kathryn Horton, Harry Sands, Leon Sternfeld, Gloria F. Wolinsky

The authors examine current systems for labeling children as blind or visually handicapped, deaf or hearing-handicapped, and physically handicapped. This chapter reveals the emergence of an important shift from structural to functional criteria for classification. Visual impairment, for example, is assessed not on the basis of visual acuity alone but primarily on how well a child can use vision for reading and other activities. A functional assessment ties in readily with treatment needs and procedures, a connection often lacking in traditional classification schemes.

CHAPTER 10

EMOTIONAL DISTURBANCE IN CHILDREN

Dane G. Prugh, Mary Engel, William C. Morse

Prugh, Engel, and Morse address the complex problem of classifying emotional disturbance in children. Adult-oriented classification systems have dominated thinking in this area for years. The authors break with this tradition and present a schema that is both responsive to the formal requirements of classification systems and sensitive to the problems of children. It is responsive to developmental changes and to genetic and experiential variables. They introduce "environment responsivity" as an index of the extent to which experience or treatment can be expected to change the child. Aware of the vocabulary biases of various professional groups, they seek a simple, functional language acceptable to the many persons exceptional children depend on.

CHAPTER 11

LEARNING DISABILITIES

Joseph M. Wepman, William M. Cruickshank,
Cynthia P. Deutsch, Anne Morency, Charles R. Strother

Chapter Eleven attempts to untangle the web of attributions attached to the term *learning disabilities*. The authors find such an excess of syndromes, diagnostic categories, remedies, and nostrums that to say a child has a learning disability is by itself frequently more misleading than helpful. They propose a rigorous and limiting requirement on the definition of "specific learning disability," which, if adopted, would substantially clarify a now highly confused and confusing picture.

161

CHAPTER 12

LOW-INCOME AND MINORITY GROUPS

Paul R. Dokecki, Barbara A. Strain, Joe J. Bernal,
Carolyn S. Brown, Mary Electa Robinson

Discussing the ways society views children from poor and minority-group families, this chapter proposes new policies to replace current punitive and emergency-oriented relief measures. It advocates a guaranteed minimum income for families as an essential first step in addressing the handicapping conditions imposed by poverty and often associated with minority-group status.

CHAPTER 13

THE JUVENILE COURT

Frank A. Orlando, Jerry P. Black

Orlando and Black describe the destructive effects of the juvenile court system—originally planned as a system for counseling and rehabilitating troubled children—that derive from labels. They make several recommendations concerning definitions and procedures that would help protect the child from abuses that have become so common that they question the credibility of the court itself.

CHAPTER 14

CLASSIFICATION IN THE TREATMENT OF DELINQUENCY AND ANTISOCIAL BEHAVIOR

Herbert C. Quay

Quay points out that the term delinquency is a legal concept that does not supply guidelines for prevention and treatment. There is need for classification of adjudicated delinquents on the basis of psychological and sociological characteristics. Quay details two systems of subgroup classification that have demonstrated relevance for intervention.

162

CHAPTER 15

DRUG-TAKING BEHAVIOR

Oakley S. Ray, John T. Wilson

Ray and Wilson, working at the expanding frontier of classification problems, inquire into ways of categorizing—for constructive purposes—young people who use and abuse drugs. Their tough-minded, pragmatic, and promising approach emphasizes the concept that the problem resides not only in the individual but in the individual-in-society. Their analysis of a special classification problem, drug-taking, is rich in instruction for classifiers of other problems, who, influenced by long tradition, tend to accept without question that the problem resides exclusively in the individual child.

7

HISTORICAL PERSPECTIVES ON CLASSIFICATION OF MENTAL RETARDATION

Richard L. Blanton

Since the classification of exceptional children has been a matter of professional concern for public officials, physicians, and educators, there are three types of problems—legal, medical, and educational—to which classification is a practical response. This paper will consider primarily the implications of classification for education, touching on legal and medical issues only as these relate to social and educational problems. It will deal primarily with the area of mental retardation, since it is in this area that social and educational problems have been most difficult.

Classification of Mental Retardation

The first clear definition of mental retardation was given by J. E. D. Esquirol, the great psychiatrist. "Idiocy," he stated, "is not a disease, but a condition in which the intellectual faculties are never manifested, or have never been developed sufficiently to enable the idiot to acquire such amount of knowledge as persons of his own age and placed in similar circumstances with himself are capable of receiving" (Esquirol, 1845, p. 446). Esquirol grouped the retarded into two classes, *idiots* and *imbeciles,* on the basis of speech development. The use of the criterion of speech development as a rule of thumb for classifying the retarded persisted throughout the nineteenth century. In 1830, in company with a young physician named Edward Seguin, Esquirol opened a private school for "idiots."

After the revolution of 1848, Seguin came to America, where his work with the retarded received wide attention. His book *Idiocy and Its Treatment by the Physiological Method* (1866) formed the basis for training programs in institutions for the retarded in this country. In 1876, with six of his followers, Seguin founded the American Association for the Study of the Feebleminded. In Seguin's view, mental retardation, except for cases of brain damage, is caused by sensory isolation or deprivation; the brain, then, is simply dormant and can be aroused by powerful stimuli, especially motor and tactual ones. From such a beginning, training in movement in response to tactual, visual, and auditory signals, discrimination training, classification, association of objects, and logical operations could be developed in sequential fashion. Seguin's methods were widely used until the turn of the century, when they gradually ceased to be used, although they continued to be basic in education of the deaf. In 1912, Maria Montessori's book on the Montessori method, detailing methods which she developed from Seguin's work, was published. Recent interest in cultural deprivation and the lack of early stimulation has revived interest in the Seguin-Montessori methods.

Seguin followed the French school of sensationism,

which held that atrophy of the brain, like atrophy of muscle, is often a result of disuse. Stimulation was thought to produce electrical excitement in the nervous system, which in turn resulted in vascular dilation and increased blood flow and finally in adequate nutrition and growth and development. He classified idiots, accordingly, on the basis of the centrality of the anomaly of the nervous system. Profound idiots, in his view, had disturbances of the central brain systems; superficial idiots had disturbances of the more peripheral systems. This theory was opposed by that of nativism, which stressed the influence of heredity and held neurological damage to be irreversible. Pinel, at the beginning of the nineteenth century, and Binet at its end were leading proponents of nativism.

These two points of view have determined the philosophy of education and rehabilitation in the field of mental retardation for almost two hundred years. Sensationism had its beginnings in the philosophy of Locke. Condillac offered the most popular French version, and Rousseau developed a theory of pedagogy based on it. From 1789, beginning with Pereire's methods for the "sensory" training of the deaf and the adaptation of these methods for the retarded by Itard and Seguin, until 1889, when Binet began his work on mental processes, sensationism was widely held. During this time, there was general optimism about the prospects for rehabilitation of the retarded.

The development of scientific neurology during the two decades after 1850, principally the work of Charcot, led to a detailed system of classification of brain pathology and to examination methods for assessing the integrity of the nervous system. Medical classification of the mentally retarded developed rapidly, and by 1900 the principal forms of brain pathology were reasonably well described.

The development of medical science, with classifications based on brain pathology, did much to dampen the optimism of the sensationists. The change in viewpoint during the last half of the nineteenth century becomes clear when one compares the classification proposed by Duncan and Millard in 1866 with that offered by Ireland in 1898.

Duncan and Millard divided the retarded into two major classes, congenital and noncongenital. The congenital cases were classified functionally into (1) profound idiots; (2) those able to stand and walk; (3) those able to use hands for easy mechanical work and to feed themselves; (4) feebleminded cases who require supervision for their own protection and that of others. Noncongenitals were divided into those with disease or injury to the brain after birth, those with epilepsy, hydrocephalics, and those debased during early youth from vice. The congenitals could not usually be so classified. Diagnostic judgments were made primarily for the purposes of training and for guidance of the courts rather than for medical purposes.

By the end of the century, considerable evidence had developed with regard to hereditary defects. Theories such as Morel's (1857) and Lombroso's (1876) had been proposed to account for them. Down (1866) offered a careful description of monogolian idiocy and interpreted it in terms of evolutionary concepts, Darwinism being an advanced scientific position at the time. He proposed that the condition, characterized by Mongoloid facial features, was an atavism, a throwback to the more primitive evolutionary status which he presumed to be occupied by the Mongoloid races.

By 1898, Ireland was able to offer a more elaborate schema exclusively along etiological lines: (1) genetous (*sic*), (2) microcephalic, (3) eclampsic, (4) epileptic, (5) hydrocephalic, (6) paralytic, (7) cretinism, (8) traumatic, (9) inflammatory, and (10) idiocy by deprivation. It should be noted that genetic defects are placed first in the list. The tenth category was not meant to include cases of "cultural deprivation" in the modern sense, but was for cases of deaf-blindness, such as Helen Keller and Laura Bridgman, and for children isolated from social contacts, such as the Savage of Aveyron and Kaspar Hauser.

Binet, while taking a nativist position, was nevertheless convinced of the importance of training the feebleminded in practical social skills. He was very skeptical of Seguin's work, calling it "empirical" and misdirected, arguing that time devoted to "sensory" training would be better devoted to teaching the retarded to read street signs and simple instructions (Binet and Simon, 1914). Convinced that basic cognitive and intellectual abilities could not be improved by training, he nevertheless insisted that the needs of society for maximal education of its members should be met.

While the development of the biological sciences permitted the differentiation of the retarded on an etiological basis, the primary social need was for functional classifications which could be used for educational and legal decisions. This need became ever more pressing as the last quarter of the nineteenth century passed (G. E. Johnson, 1894). The reasons for this should be discussed, since they have significance for the present situation.

Manufacturing and commercial development led to exponential growth of urban areas in England, the European continent, and on the eastern seaboard and in the upper Midwest of the United States. The natural growth rate in America was supplemented by substantial influxes of immigrants from Europe, beginning with the great immigration of impoverished Irish in the decade 1850-1860. Social and economic conditions were especially stressful for the less competent. Problems of physical and mental health were increasingly visible, and the increased problems in the maintenance of public order brought the incompetent much more frequently to the attention of the courts, with consequent increase in the numbers shown in population statistics.

The problem of classification of children for educational purposes began to trouble the courts in the various states during the 1880s. That similar problems were developing in Europe can be discerned from several sources. The history of the problem in England is especially instructive.

After the Compulsory Education Act of 1876, it gradually became apparent that there were substantial numbers of children who could not be satisfactorily taught in the public schools, although they were not sufficiently defective to be certified as idiots or imbeciles requiring institutional care under the Idiots Act of 1886. A departmental committee of the English board of education was appointed in 1896 to consider the question, and reported two years later that approximately 1 percent of the elementary school population were intermediate between certifiable imbeciles and those considered ordinary dullards. It was observed that these children could benefit considerably from special attention and instruction, but could not benefit from ordinary instruction. The committee recommended special classes, which were authorized by law in 1899 with the passage of the Defective and Epileptic Children (Education) Act. Mentally defective children were defined as those who "not being imbecile, and not being merely dull and backward, are defective—that is to say, by reason of mental (or physical) defect are incapable of receiving proper benefit from the instruction in the ordinary public elementary schools but are not incapable, by reason of such defect, of receiving benefit from instruction in such special classes and schools as are in this act mentioned" (quoted in Tredgold, 1937). Local education authorities were not compelled to establish such facilities by the 1899 act, but a supplementary act passed in 1914 obligated them to do so.

In 1904 an English royal commission was appointed to study means of dealing with problems of the feebleminded, and undertook the most careful survey of prevalence which had been performed up to that time. Nine areas in England, two in Wales, one in Scotland, and four in Ireland were studied by hired visitors, who visited all public institutions, rooming houses, or lodgings of any sort where abnormal persons might be housed. All persons on relief, all ministers, physicians, officers of the law, charity organizations, and similar agencies were contacted for reports. While prevalence rates varied considerably between areas, an estimate could be made of an overall rate of 4.03 per 1000 of the population.

The 1904 royal commission was able also to accumulate considerable information on the educational problems of the mentally retarded. Its work was expressed in the Mental Deficiency Act of 1913, which applied the term *feebleminded* to persons with the mildest grade of mental deficiency—persons requiring supervision for their own protection. "Feebleminded" children were those requiring supervision who also had "disability of mind of such nature and extent as to make them incapable of receiving education at school" as provided in the Education Acts. The Education Act of 1921 created another legal definition of mental defect, based on educational but not social incapacity, which was restricted to persons between the ages of seven and sixteen years. The purpose was to enable the schools to assign children to special educational facilities. The effect was to provide for a time-limited definition of feeblemindedness, applicable for legal purposes only to a specific age group. The Act of 1913 had specified that the condition was a permanent one. Tredgold (1937) points out that the educational defect was not permanent in many cases, since, depending on the district, up to 20 percent of the children who had been placed in special classes were later returned to the regular schools. Since such recovery from "real" mental deficiency was assumed to be impossible, the defect was assumed to be due to social factors, and the Act of 1921 thus provided for a definition limited to the period of compulsory education.

The interrelationships between the biological, social, and educational definitions of mental retardation were matters of study and debate throughout the first half of the twentieth century. Tredgold, in the first edition of his text, attempted to establish a biological definition, "incomplete cerebral development," to which social and legal concepts could be related (Tredgold, 1908, p. 2). In the sixth edition (Tredgold, 1937), he recognized that social and educational criteria were fundamental and had to be established and used. At the same time, he held that the "scientific reality" of mental deficiency is biological. On the one hand, educational and social incompetence occur in persons without apparent brain pathology; on the other, cases of brain disease occur without apparent educational and social incompetence (pp. 1-11). These issues became, in effect, the twentieth-century grounds for the nativism-sensationism controversy. While medical science progressed steadily, uncovering many new genetic, metabolic, and anatomical mechanisms underlying mental deficiency, the disputes regarding educational and social implications continued. At the center of these disputes was the mental testing movement.

The Mental Testing Movement

The problems of educational retardation came to the attention of psychologists during the 1890s, and the approaches to the classification issue changed rapidly as a result.

The first intellectual functions to be measured in the retarded were those of memory. Jacobs (1887) tested normal children, and Galton (1887) made estimates of the memory span of retarded children at North London School and at Earlswood Asylum in England. Apparently Galton selected only the retarded children regarded as most competent and made no attempt to obtain a statistical distribution, although Jacobs tested normal children at all age levels from eight to nineteen. Bourdon in Paris reported similar data on normal children in 1894. In general, results showed that feebleminded children fell far below normals in memory span, but that there were exceptional cases who had better span than the averages for normals.

Alfred Binet began publishing his work on mental tests in 1895, evaluating testing methods. He also described several tests thought to reflect more complex processes, such as reasoning and judgment. He felt that tests, rather than providing an absolute measure of ability, should rate persons with respect to each other (Binet, 1898). In 1900 he published a study of reaction time, perception, immediate memory, and several other tasks in two groups of children who differed greatly in ability as judged by their teachers (Binet, 1900a). In 1904 Binet and a colleague, Theophile Simon, began to collect materials and develop new tasks that might succeed in classifying children by level of intellectual development. The first Binet-Simon scales were published in 1905; the authors revised them in 1908 to include the mental-age concept, with tasks so classified (Binet and Simon, 1905, 1908). Concurrently, De Sanctis (1906) reported the development of some short performance tests in Italy.

In 1910 H. H. Goddard, director of the training school at Vineland, New Jersey, after giving the Binet test to four hundred children at Vineland, reported his results. Using teacher ratings, with discrepancies resolved by discussion, he found an "amazing correspondence" between his classification by the tests and those resulting from extended evaluation by teachers. The population of children studied ranged in mental age from one to twelve years. He proposed that children of mental age less than two be classified as *idiots*; those from three to seven, *imbeciles*; and those with a mental age of eight to twelve, *morons*. Children with a mental age above twelve would be classified as normal (Goddard, 1910).

In 1910, papers on the Binet intelligence scale appeared by a number of psychologists in America, England, Belgium, Germany, and Italy; and the number of investigations and reports grew annually. It has been said that no development in the history of psychology has had so much impact on so many problems, workers, and fields in such a short period of time. An annotated bibliography prepared in 1914 listed 254 titles in four languages (Kohs, 1914).

The test received considerable criticism as well as praise. Decroly and Degand (1907, 1910) presented data on groups of Belgian children of different socioeconomic ranking from those on which Binet had standardized his scale, and obtained somewhat different results. Treves and Saffiotti (1910-1911), after testing more than six hundred children of diverse social classes from the elementary schools of Milan, found very substantial differences in the performance of children of the same chrono-logical age but different social status. Their attempts to regroup the tests to reflect the socioeconomic variable produced such a spread of results that they argued against the concept of mental age and in favor of much looser groupings. No one, they argued, could interpret statistical results without taking into account cultural and racial factors. Therefore, since comparisons of vari-ous ages, classes, and races were impossible from one standardi-zation alone, special population norms would have to be devel-oped. In addition, they rejected the theory of "pure intelli-gence" proposed by Binet. Instead, they argued, "Intelligence develops under the influence of the milieu. . . . Furthermore, all the responses to the tests reveal the influence of the school instruction. . . . The intelligence, as the supreme expression of the total personality, demonstrates in the last analysis the ca-pacity of the individual to adapt himself to social life" (Treves and Saffiotti, 1910, p. 339). The cultural anthropologists—Boas, Thomas, Lowie and others—soon entered the lists on the side of the cultural relativism of Saffiotti and Decroly.

None of these cautions, however, could stem the rush to use the test in the schools. Goddard published a revision of the tests in English in 1911; Kuhlmann (1911a) offered supple-mentary materials for the lower age levels, where Binet's tasks tended to overestimate ability. Terman published a tentative revision in 1912. Ayres (1911) presented a critical evaluation, arguing that the tests relied too much on verbal fluency, were really scholastic rather than general, and should not be assumed to measure native ability. Kuhlmann (1911b) replied at length, concluding that Ayres lacked sufficient clinical experience with the tests to be a valid judge. And so it went for decades.

These issues were never settled effectively, perhaps be-cause the application of mathematical and statistical methods to arithmetical scores gave a specious scientific validity to infer-ences which were often dubious and inadequate for the making of practical judgments in single cases. The "scientific reality" of test scores now supplemented the "scientific reality" of brain disease as a basis for the definition of feeblemindedness. The term *mental retardation,* which came to be the preferred term for general use, reflects this concern with psychoeducational development and its quantitative measurement.

Schreuder, in Germany, is credited by Young (1924) with being the first to apply Quetelet's binomial expansion curve and

Gauss's error curve to the analysis of Binet results. However, the English workers (especially Galton's students, Pearson and Burt) were very active in correlational analysis of test data in the first decade of the century. By the time Binet's test emerged as a presumably definitive technique, the methods for statistical evaluation and analysis were already well developed. In the United States, the basic approaches had been well developed by Cattell. Thorndike, Terman, Kelly, and Otis were all active in the first two decades in statistical theory and application.

Both the biological and educational definitions of mental retardation were now scientific, but the practical consequences of the mental test definition were probably more substantial. A technological innovation that will provide scientific grounds for making difficult socially relevant decisions is a very significant thing. The great saving in public funds which ensues from excluding the unfit child from the regular classroom, the economic value added to the potential earning power of a dull child effectively trained, and the enhanced feeling of effectiveness which results from success in teaching and learning are indisputably valid goals. The mental testing movement went determinedly forward toward such goals, consoled by the hope and faith that classification errors were usually a product of inexact use of the instruments and not of their application to inappropriate cases. But the problem of valid application, the determination of appropriate cases, and the reliable identification of inappropriate ones were matters of continual discussion and remonstrance. Wallin (1911) offered a practical guide for making such determinations and continued throughout the next two decades to try to persuade psychologists to develop uniform standards, not only for administration but for making clinical estimates of the validity of single test records, in part and in whole.

In general, one can agree with Young (1924) that the argument has been between quality and quantity. The French, according to Young, had tended to study individual cases with a view to understanding total adjustment. The English and Americans, in the main, had been prone to express generalizations in statistical terms, averages, measures of dispersion, and correlations. "Following the statistical lead, a number of studies have been made on immigrant children, negroes, college students, and elementary and high school populations for the determinations of averages, dispersions, and correlations. While these studies have usually been used only to show general trends, segregation of pupils has been resorted to on the basis of group test" (Young, 1924, p. 42).

Scientific and technical information is used by persons who have been given responsibility for making practical decisions. Especially where such decisions concern other persons, they are made in a context of recognized and unrecognized values, precedents, persuasive communications, and public policies—a domain, in short, of social value and attitude. A practical decision, therefore, is never exclusively scientific, no matter what the information on which it is based; and scientific information, no matter how accurate or erroneous, is always applied in the interest of practical human goals.

But a difficulty arises here which is usually not recognized by scientists: Where value conflicts exist, scientific information may not be equally relevant for all values in competition. It may, in fact, lend support to an attitude, value, or belief which later events prove to be false or inimical to the general welfare. To see how this process operates, we should examine the history of one social movement to which the evidence from intelligence tests was very useful. We will consider, briefly, the history of the eugenics movement in Europe and America in the period 1880-1930, the intellectual thrust of which has been called Social Darwinism.

The Eugenics Movement

Darwin's evolution hypothesis was developed to account for the variation through time and habitat of plant and animal populations. It was quickly applied to human social organizations by Herbert Spencer (1876). To Spencer, a society is an organism subject to the same principles of natural selection as plants and animals. Since its survival depends upon adequate adaptation to change, it will be damaged by the preservation of unfit members. The growth of cities had brought the attention of the country to increasing numbers of the poor. Spencer's theory of social selection precluded state aid for the poor: "The whole effort of nature is to get rid of such, to clear the world of them and make room for better" (Spencer, 1865, p. 414).

America after the Civil War was rapidly expanding, fiercely competitive, and highly oriented toward achievement. Spencer's philosophy found a ready audience among the very wealthy, who saw themselves as living proof of its principles. Andrew Carnegie was one of Spencer's main supporters, and Chauncey Depew, J. J. Hill, and John D. Rockefeller publicly subscribed to his principles. Intellectual leadership for the philosophy was assumed by William Graham Sumner, professor of social science at Yale, who set forward the principles in a number of magazine articles. Without inequalities, Sumner insisted, society cannot operate and evolve; one of the necessary inequalities is that of wealth, which makes possible the accumulation of capital and the occurrence of economic progress. In Sumner's view, the principles of social evolution negate the traditional American values of equality and natural rights; and he was highly skeptical of the democratic ideal, interpreting the federal structure as an attempt by an essentially elite group of founding fathers to limit a rampant and dogmatic democratic tradition (Hofstadter, 1944).

Since Darwinism assumed the inheritance of characteristics acquired through adaptation (although the mechanism was not identified until Mendel's work appeared), a progressive society, Sumner concluded, must not preserve the unfit. Naturally operating social forces, according to the theory, should have the effect of limiting the reproduction of the unfit and facilitating that of the naturally superior; but, in fact, the poor seemed to be reproducing much more prolifically than the rich. A system of social forces to correct this imbalance was obviously desirable. The eugenics movement in England and the United States was begun in the hope that such a remedy could be found.

The first and greatest eugenist was Sir Francis Galton (1869), who collected an impressive set of pedigrees of famous men to prove that human abilities, whether intellectual, artistic, or athletic, are inherited. He developed methods for measuring abilities and for statistically analyzing the data obtained. Among other phenomena, he discovered the law of regression, expressing the relationship between abilities of parents and offspring in terms of what was called the *regression* (correlation) *coefficient*. His student Karl Pearson carried on the work with considerable ingenuity, developing what has come to be called *biometrics*, including most of the basic methods of modern statistical analysis.

Criminal anthropology. Meanwhile, on the continent another hereditarian movement was under way. B. A. Morel (1857) purported to show that criminality, insanity, epilepsy, feeblemindedness, and alcoholism are all products of hereditary taint and that moral degeneracy is manifested in certain physical deformations in successive generations—with alcoholism in one generation followed by criminality in the next, and insanity and finally idiocy through succeeding ones. Cesare Lombroso (1876), a professor of legal medicine at Turin, relied principally on physical anthropology and provided extensive measurements of the skulls, brains, and body conformation of criminals. Lombroso claimed that most criminals are atavisms, throwbacks to primitive ancestors, since their cephalic indices often were like those of negroid or Mongoloid races rather than European ones. The strongly hereditarian features of the theory were very attractive to the English and American eugenists. Galton was given a number of photographs of prisoners by the authorities, and attempted, by means of successive photographing of the faces on the same negative, to determine whether there were consistent criminal features. He subsequently employed the same techniques in studying feebleminded and delinquent children. Results were inconclusive.

The method of establishing validity of measurements of population differences had been used by Darwin in experiments on the growth of plants. Galton was familiar with the general concepts but did not, for some reason, apply them to the data of criminal anthropology. The generalizations of Morel and Lombroso, although unsupported by comparative measurements on noncriminal populations, were widely accepted in England and America and continued to be used in police work throughout the continent. The Nazis in the 1930s adapted these notions to the racial-psychology concept and published volumes of work on the degeneracy of races. They included photographs and quantitative analyses to lend scientific validity to their propaganda materials.

British eugenics movement. As mentioned, the eugenics movement began in England as an organized expression of the belief that the "defective classes" are victims of heredity and pass on defective traits to their offspring. Medical specialists encountered instances of mental deficiency and insanity in successive generations of the same family. Superintendents of hospitals for the insane and schools for the feebleminded, both in England and America, frequently reported accumulations of such data and made public speeches on the subject.

Galton spent the last decade of his life in the development of a eugenics movement which, according to Haller (1968), was for him "an emotional equivalent for religion." The Eugenics Education Society was organized in 1907 with many distinguished scientists and literary figures as active members. With the rediscovery of Gregor Mendel's papers on the inheritance of traits in plants, a theory with some scientific standing was available. Galton had endowed the National Eugenics Laboratory in 1904, and two years later Karl Pearson became its director.

American eugenics movement. In 1903 the American Breeders' Association was formed by agricultural and biological workers with the avowed goal of improving the breeding of animals. In 1906 it established a committee on eugenics to "investigate and report on heredity in the human race." Membership on the committee was held by such notables as David Starr Jordan (president of Stanford), Alexander Graham Bell, and Luther Burbank. One of its members, Charles B. Davenport, became the prophet of the eugenics movement and secured the support of the Carnegie Foundation for a research institute. In 1910, Davenport established the Eugenics Record Office at Cold Spring Harbor, where he carried on work previously begun in genetics. Davenport succeeded in broadening the committee structure of the American Breeders' Association to include groups on deaf-mutism, feeblemindedness, insanity, mental traits, criminality, and epilepsy. Significantly, a committee on immigration—headed by Prescott Hall, a leader of the Immigration Restriction League—was established.

Mendelian theory provided enthusiasts like Davenport with a rationale for attributing biological and behavioral deviations to heredity. A handbook called *The Trait Book* listed as hereditary traits not only eye color and feeblemindedness but such temperament and personality characteristics as lack of adventuresomeness and interest in reading. A rationale was provided for compiling family trees, and this activity became an important enterprise in the institutions for the retarded.

Goddard was especially active in this work. His book *Feeblemindedness* (1914) documented the thesis that crime, pauperism, prostitution, and alcoholism are largely due to heredity, with mental retardation being the principal factor in such socially repugnant conditions. In addition to these social deviations, Goddard identified as genetic taints all discoverable instances of tuberculosis, stroke or apoplexy, cancer, epilepsy, goiter, and speech defects among the ancestors of his cases.

One of Goddard's early discoveries was a girl called Debo-
rah Kallikak, who was quickly discerned as worthy of an entire
book in herself. Elizabeth Kite, one of Goddard's colleagues,
assembled the family tree of the Kallikaks. She found that Martin Kallikak, a Revolutionary War soldier, had had two lines of
descendants. From a liaison with a feebleminded girl, he had a
son (generally called "Old Horror") who had 480 descendants.
Of these descendants 143 were feebleminded, 46 were normal,
and the rest were of doubtful or unknown ability. This group
contained 26 illegitimate children, 24 alcoholics, 33 sexually
immoral persons, and 3 criminals. In contrast, the descendants
from Kallikak's union with a Quaker wife included a series of
highly respected professional persons.

Goddard's book *The Kallikak Family* (1912) became a
classic, a companion study to Richard Dugdale's study of the
Jukes family (1877). Dugdale, an inspector of prisons for New
York State, discovered in one of the jails of rural Ulster County
six relatives all being held at the same time. He traced the
family and found in six generations (numbering 709 persons) 18
brothel keepers, 128 prostitutes, 200 welfare cases, and 76
criminals. Dugdale estimated that the Jukes family had cost the
public a total of $1,308,000 in welfare, penal, medical, and
legal services. A. H. Estabrook (1916) restudied Dugdale's notes
and traced down a total of 2111 Jukes, of whom more than half
were said to be feebleminded and 171 criminals.

The eugenists published many such studies in the first
three decades of the century. Most accepted Goddard's thesis
that feeblemindedness is a simple Mendelian recessive; they
could conclude, therefore, that all the offspring of matings
between two such persons would be feebleminded. The erroneous belief that mentally retarded women are highly prolific
was also accepted. No attempt was made to study the population in general, but selected cases were presented as proof of the
generalization. The proof was evidently acceptable, to legis-
lators at least: by 1930 thirty states had passed sterilization
laws, and thirty-nine states regulated marriage among the feebleminded, insane, and epileptic. All these laws, however, were
inconsistently enforced.

The evidence was less acceptable to a number of professionals with extensive clinical experience. These workers (Healy,
1915; Bronner, 1917; Wallin, 1917) strongly criticized the
hereditarian view of delinquency and feeblemindedness. Wallin's

work is especially notable for its cautiousness in drawing general rules and its careful citation of disconfirming instances to rules discovered by others. Healy, on the basis of considerable work with delinquents, recognized mental defect as a factor in delinquency but argued that the use of the twelve-year level to define feeblemindedness often caused persons to be labeled as retarded who were socially and economically competent and law-abiding. Moreover, other factors in the selective use of intelligence data soon appeared. Hollingworth (1922) studied the special classes for subnormal children in the public schools of New York City and found more than two boys for every girl. She concluded that defective males were less tolerated in the home, school, or community than girls. Tredgold (1937) noted the same phenomenon and noted also that the incidence of mild "curable" cases of feeblemindedness was considerably greater in the cities, whereas severe idiocy and imbecility had higher rates in rural areas.

In 1922 Wallin reviewed his experience of more than a decade of work with several thousand cases in evaluation and classification of the retarded. He arrived at the following conclusions (see Wallin, 1922a, 1922b): (1) Many persons with mental age in the eight- to twelve-year range are self-maintaining, effective members of society. (2) The eugenists are probably mistaken in their claims that mental deficiency is hereditary, since not more than 8 percent of the children referred to the clinic had siblings who were referred at any time. (3) Claims that the feebleminded are criminal or vicious are untrue (of nearly 2000 cases seen for reasons of delinquency, only about 6 percent could be diagnosed as feebleminded and only 11 percent as borderline). (4) Mental deficiency has different implications for the sexes, higher levels of behavioral and intellectual competence being expected for males, whereas retarded females are often maintained in dependent status in the home.

The most disturbing body of information, however, came from the extensive studies of intelligence in the United States army during World War I. These studies, directed by Yerkes and reported by him in 1921, were no less than estimates of the intelligence of the entire nation. Yerkes and a committee of distinguished psychologists compiled two group tests, the Army Alpha (for literates) and the Army Beta (for illiterates), and acquired data on 81,000 native-born whites, 12,000 foreign-born whites, and 23,000 native-born blacks. According to these data, 47 percent of the white inhabitants of the country and 89 percent of the Negroes had mental ages of twelve years or less. As indicated, the twelve-year level had been set by Goddard as the upper limit of mental deficiency in 1910, and workers with the schools and courts had been classifying persons at this level as mentally defective for almost a decade.

The data from the army testing had profound implications for the issue of classifying ability by mental tests. Goddard immediately claimed that his term *moron* was not meant to apply to all persons with mentality eight to twelve, but only to the group of feebleminded with mentality eight to twelve. "The term *moron* is improperly used when it is applied to any person who is not feebleminded, no matter what his mentality" (Goddard, 1921, p. 49). He argued that patterns of extreme scatter on the tests would indicate "psychopathic" conditions and provide a basis for classification. This was an explicit argument that the criteria should be qualitative rather than quantitative. Porteus and Doll had already begun to work on the problem of social competence, which was to result in the Vineland Social Maturity Scale (Doll, 1953)—an attempt to shift the emphasis away from cognitive, memory, and reasoning factors toward those factors of social competence with which society is principally concerned.

The eugenists, however, were not dissuaded from their beliefs by the army test data. To them it implied that the intelligence of the nation as a whole was much too low and that radical action was needed to preserve the nation's future. The army data contained hundreds of scores on persons of varying nationalities. Carl Brigham, Carl Brown, and Mark May, working with E. G. Boring, developed methods of analysis of the data to show their implications for national policy. The results were published by Brigham (1923) in what appeared to be an impressive argument for the selective restriction of immigration.

The foreign-born who had taken the tests were compared by nationality. The English and Scotch scored highest, followed by the Dutch and Germans, these four groups being higher than the native-born whites. The Scandinavians followed; then came the Irish, Austrians, Turks, Greeks, Russians, Italians, and last the Polish, who were slightly higher than the American Negroes. Somewhat specious reasoning was used to argue that neither English language as a native tongue, social milieu, nor adaptation to the situation of the examination could account for the differences. That argument, which clearly reveals the implicit assumptions of the eugenics position, is worth recounting here. Garth (1921) had insisted that differences between races should be disregarded unless the groups had had the same educational and environmental opportunities. But Brigham argued that educational and environmental status are products of intellectual ability rather than causes of it: "To select individuals who have fallen behind in the struggle to adjust themselves to the civilization their race has built as typical of that race is an error, for their position itself shows that they are, for the most part, individuals with an inferior hereditary endowment" (Brigham, 1923, p. 194).

Using the division of races proposed by Grant (1916), Brigham analyzed the data for Nordic (British Isles, Scandinavian, German), Alpine (Austrian, Polish, Russian), and Mediterranean (Italian, Greek, Turkish) peoples, comparing these with the native white and Negro populations. He then made a strong plea for restriction of immigration: "According to all evidence available, American intelligence is declining and will proceed with an accelerating rate as the racial admixture becomes more extensive. The decline of American intelligence will be more than the decline of the intelligence of European national groups, owing to the presence here of the Negro. . . . Immigration should not only be restrictive, but highly selective" (Brigham, 1923, p. 210).

These arguments found a ready audience in the United States Congress, which began debates regarding the restriction of immigration. It was soon observed that the order of ability in the army data was approximately the same as that of the proportions of the nationalities in the population generally. Hence, if immigration were restricted to a constant fraction of the nationality in question in the American population, the numerical superiority of Nordics in future immigration could be ensured. Several acts of Congress finally culminated in the national quotas policy of 1929, which governed immigration thenceforward.

In 1932, however, H. J. Muller dealt a death blow to old-style eugenics by stating his conviction that what has been called the "dysgenics of the superior" is an economic matter and the overbreeding of the poor a matter of ignorance. Muller, who had won the Nobel Prize for his work in genetics, argued that there are no "pure races" but only populations with variable gene frequencies. "There is no basis," he stated, "for the conclusion that socially lower classes, or technically less advanced races, really have a genetically inferior intellectual equipment, since the differences between their averages are accounted for fully by the known effects of environment. . . . In a society having such glaring inequalities of environment as ours, our tests are of little account in the determination of individual genetic differences in intelligence" (Muller, 1934, pp. 141-142).

The Nature-Nurture Problem

Meanwhile, the study of the nature-nurture problem had begun in earnest. Two major developments in psychology were placing the weight of theoretical opinion on the side of growth and development variables rather than genetic ones. J. B. Watson's *Behaviorism* (1919) argued that conditioning and learning, rather than genetics, account for human achievement, and Sigmund Freud's psychoanalytic theory placed principal emphasis on early social learning, especially within the family, as a source of most differences in personality.

Twin studies. The study of the nature-nurture problem was active throughout the 1920s and 1930s, the most impressive review being that of Barbara Burks (1927). In general, her findings suggested that about 83 percent of ability is determined by genetic factors, with 17 percent accounted for by differences of environment. The 83 percent figure was based on some rather unsatisfactory studies of twins reared apart and together. Since the correlation of foster parent and child intelligence was .42, the 17 percent figure is the square of that correlation, representing the proportion of the variance accounted for by the correlation. However, the correlation between parents and children is only about .56, making the variance due to parental heredity about 30 percent. The remaining 50 percent of the variance was assigned by Burks to the ancestral stock of the child, this allocation being justified by the twin data, although some portion of it, as yet uncertain in extent, must be accounted for by differences in environmental influences outside the home. Burks' findings were in general confirmed by Leahy (1935). Both the Burks and Leahy studies suffer from restriction of range on the environmental variable, most foster parents being those who for social and financial reasons are both willing and qualified to adopt children. This homogeneity would tend to allocate most of the variance to the genetic factor.

In contrast, Muller (1934) pointed out that IQ differences between identical twins reared in greatly different social classes are fifteen to twenty points, suggesting a far greater effect of environment on intellectual ability than had been believed.

The most impressive body of work following that of Burks was carried out in England by Sir Cyril Burt (1955, 1958, 1966; Burt and Howard, 1956, 1957). Burt based his conclusions on an impressive body of sophisticated mathematical methods derived from Fisher's (1939) models for genetic analysis in plant and animal breeding. He cited two lines of evidence: (1) Studies of the abilities of children in orphanages (Burt, 1914-1931) show that the variability of IQ is as great in such populations as in random samples of children from the general population, indicating that "identical" environments do not reduce the variance in behavior due to ability differences. (2) Studies of identical twins reared apart (Burt 1955, 1958, 1966) provide estimates of the variance attributable to heredity. In his twin studies Burt analyzed data on a group test and on the London revision of the Terman-Binet for identical twins reared apart as well as for identical twins reared together, fraternal twins reared together, and siblings reared together and apart. Data on educational and physical characteristics were also analyzed.

Impressive as Burt's credentials may be, his tables of correlations show a number of puzzling features. To illustrate this point, Table 1 shows the correlations between pairs of twins reared apart. Even a novice in statistics will note at once that identical correlations, .771 and .843, are given for studies based on varying numbers of subjects. The probability of obtaining such results to the third decimal place based on samples which

Table 1

Correlations Between Identical Twins Reared Apart
(from Burt's Twin Studies)

	1955 (N = 21)	1958 (N = 30)	1966 (N = 53)
Group test	.771	.771	.771
Binet	.843	.843	.863

differ even partially is exceedingly remote, so much so as to raise extreme doubt or outright disbelief.

Various hypotheses could be offered to account for these figures, the simplest being that Burt did not recompute the correlations to include the new cases for the group tests in any instances and for the Binet did not do so in the first two. An inspection of the table shows this to be a likely explanation; but the last figure, .863, could be a typographical error, implying no recomputations at all. On the other hand, Burt offers surprisingly high figures for reliability, considering that the tests were administered by several examiners, some of whom were contacted by mail. One would have to conclude that while Burt's argument is impressive, his data seem to be flawed.

Dobzhansky (1967) criticized such classical theories as that of Fisher (from whom Burt derived his method) on the grounds that human cells carry thousands of mixed genes for which the individual is heterozygous, a much larger number than had been thought possible. For characteristics determined by joint action of several genes, like intelligence, such heterozygosity would make the phenotypic variation an inextricable intermingling of environmental and genetic features. To generalize about a population from the behavioral characteristics of those who happen to be identical twins requires many unwarranted assumptions about the way such characteristics are expressed. "The heritability [of abilities]," said Dobzhansky, "is fairly low, and parent-offspring similarities in behavioral traits may well be due more to the cultural than the biological inheritance" (pp. 47-48). Layzer (1974) rejects Fisher's genetic theory on the ground that its assumption of zero correlation between genotype and environment cannot be met for any human data and is actually false for animal populations where experiments permit it to be measured. When this assumption fails, no quantitative inferences about heritability can be drawn from measured phenotypic variances and covariances. To base social and educational policy on the presumed covariance in genetic characteristics of parents and children is therefore quite unwarranted, since we cannot determine what that covariance is or how it is expressed behaviorally.

Racial comparisons. Peterson and Lanier (1929) found Negro-white differences to be greatest in language and speed factors but found no clear differences of accuracy in performance. Some populations showed differences in favor of Negroes.

It was therefore necessary to show whether such differences were due to a favorable selection from the Negro population or to environment. Garth (1933) showed in a study of Indian children that differences in percentage of Indian blood were unrelated to intelligence scores. The most important of these interracial studies, however, was an extensive series of careful investigations of rural and urban whites and Negroes performed by Klineberg. His studies showed "quite definitely that the superiority of the northern over the southern Negroes and the approximation to the scores of the whites are due to factors in the environment and not to selective migration" (Klineberg, 1935, p. 62). He was able to show that the performance of Negro as well as white urban children on intelligence tests was directly related to the length of residence in the city.

Most of the studies of the nature-nurture problem have suggested that personality and temperament variables are more subject to the influence of environmental differences than are the abilities measured by intelligence tests. We would conclude, however, that no adequate studies have been done of the nature-nurture problem.

Special Education and Training of Teachers

Training materials showed continued improvement over the decades, both in soundness of scholarship and research and in recommendations for practice. Beginning as reviews of published literature by workers with little depth of field experience (Schiedman, 1926) or as tracts which attempted to establish particular racial viewpoints (for example, Ellis, 1928), text materials came gradually to consist principally of research-established findings and generalizations based on extensive clinical work. In this regard, the text by Baker (1944) can be taken as an index of the maturity of the field of special education. Since World War II, the standards of research and problem analysis have continually progressed. However, empirical studies of the nature and scope of actual classification operations rely principally on statistical data provided by school systems. Careful studies by workers functioning with relative independence of the system being studied are badly needed. While it was established by Whipple (1916) that group tests should never be used for the assignment of children to special ungraded classes, informal classification operations are carried out by teachers on the basis of such information and enter into classroom practices in several ways. What in the first decades of the century began as classification for the purpose of remedial training is now often seen as labeling which determines teacher expectancies and educational outcomes (Rosenthal and Jacobson, 1968).

Before 1950 the educational problems of the retarded child were regarded as primarily those related to low achievement (Baker, 1927). The assumption that special classrooms were necessary, with resulting segregation of the retarded, was widely held during the first half of the century, and was supported by the *Forty-Ninth Yearbook* of the National Society for the Study of Education (1950). Criticism of segregation practices had already emerged, however. A panel at the twenty-second annual meeting of the International Council for Exceptional Children in 1945 debated the issues and concluded that some segregation might be necessary in the early years, since the special needs of the retarded child could not easily be met from the beginning in the usual classroom (Robb, 1946). However, the resulting social isolation and discrimination were seen as serious problems in the later school years, and it was generally felt that educable retardates should be returned to the normal school environment as soon as possible.

G. O. Johnson (1950) studied the social adjustment of mentally handicapped children in the normal classroom and found serious problems. The handicapped children were rarely chosen as friends, apparently because of their aggressive behavior as well as more frequent lying and stealing. This behavior pattern appeared to result from the retarded child's frustration after frequent failures at academic tasks. While the study implied that special classes were needed, Johnson was convinced that not enough basic information was available to determine what sorts of programs were best for these children. Johnson and Kirk (1950) concluded that mentally handicapped children were, in fact, segregated when placed in regular grades, but confessed that the desirability of special classes was not thereby proved, since data regarding the later social consequences of special class segregation were lacking. Blatt (1960) studied the characteristics, achievement, and social adjustment of mentally handicapped children in special classes as compared to those in regular grades. He found that academic achievement was comparable for the two but that the handicapped children in the special classrooms appeared to have better social maturity and emotional adjustment—possibly because the teacher in the special classroom showed greater acceptance of the handicapped child.

The significance of the teacher as a variable in the achievement of the mentally handicapped child was pointed out in an extensive study by Thurstone (1959). She found that children in regular classes did better academically than those in special classes, but she also found a significant difference between teachers. By 1960 research studies were showing generally superior achievement for students in the regular classroom environment but better social adjustment for those in the "sheltered" special classroom environment (G. O. Johnson, 1962).

Dunn (1968) presented convincing arguments against special classrooms, citing the effects of classification and labeling on the attitudes and expectancies of teachers and the impact of labeling and special class placement on self-concept and adjustment to peers. During the 1950-1970 period, results of studies of the comparative effects of special as opposed to regular class placement showed more and more evidence in favor of the latter. Whether this finding represents changes in effectiveness of educational methods, in social processes in the educational system, or in educational and social philosophy of educators and researchers is unclear. Wallin (1955), observing the trend at the end of a half century of active work on behalf of the special education of the moderately retarded, complained that educators were turning back the clock to the period when such children received no education at all. He predicted that the effects would be negative and serious.

In our opinion, this reversal of attitude toward segregation of exceptional children is related to the intense struggle regarding racial segregation which began in the middle 1950s. The judgment that segregated education is intrinsically inferior and, most important, the observation of instances in which special classrooms became filled with black children were the principal factors. The latter phenomenon could be, and frequently was, seen as a disguised method of perpetuating racial segregation. The decline of the special classroom is probably, therefore, a complex social phenomenon intimately related to a conflict between the social values of achievement and equality of opportunity.

Perspectives

A major incentive to the classification of exceptional children has been the need of a rapidly expanding public education system for solutions to important practical problems. The guiding values under which the schools developed were *achievement* and *equality of opportunity*. Throughout the first half of the twentieth century, discrepancies between ideal opportunity structures in the society and those actually obtaining in practice became more and more apparent. The origins of these discrepancies became the central matter of heated political debates, in which conservatives gave priority to the value of achievement and liberals to the value of equality of opportunity. The school system has had a basic institutional function in this value conflict: by evaluating and accrediting achievement, it selectively determines opportunities. The practice of classification appears to bias this process in two ways: (1) it may rely on criteria not generally sanctioned by the society (psychological tests), and (2) it places the child in an achievement situation, the special classroom, which for various reasons precludes his entry into the mainstream of educational and vocational opportunity. There is no doubt that these presumed biases operate more invidiously in some communities than in others. They are undoubtedly more destructive at some age levels than at others. But there is no doubt also that the problems raised are the greatest challenge to public education since its beginnings.

For research workers in fields related to education, the history of the problem contains several lessons. The dispute regarding the use of normative and statistical data to make probabilistic generalizations about individual cases has been with us from the beginning of the mental testing movement and is still unsettled. At its core is the ethical issue of making crucial decisions about persons on the basis of probabilities without clear knowledge of the costs of decision errors for the person and for the society. Another lesson is to be found in the intensely political aspects of the problems of values, the ways in which one side or the other of the value contest may use scientific information for political goals. Scientists are, as individuals, part of the political and social process; as individuals, they use research findings and interpret data in relation to their own preferred social and political goals and values. The scientific community badly needs to devise means to study and evaluate the political significance of research findings. The history of the eugenics movement reveals that politically significant scientific information may lead to widespread organizational and institutional activity, elicit substantial financial resources, and pervert the search for truth in potentially disastrous ways. The scientific community has its first value in its commitment to the quest for truth; if this value is not to be compromised, we must devise some sort of judicial system for overseeing political issues in the use of scientific data and the allocation of financial resources to research.

References

Ayres, L. P. "The Binet-Simon Test for Measuring Intelligence: Some Criticisms and Suggestions." *Psychological Clinic,* 1911, *5,* 187-196.

Baker, H. J. *Characteristic Differences in Bright and Dull Pupils.* Bloomington, Ind.: Public School Publishing, 1927.

Baker, H. J. *Introduction to Exceptional Children.* New York: Macmillan, 1944.

Binet, A. "La mésure en psychologie individuelle." *Revue Philosophique,* 1898, *46*(2), 113-123.

Binet, A. "Attention et adaptation." *L'Année Psychologique,* 1900a, *6,* 248-404.

Binet, A. *L'étude experimentelle de l'intelligence.* Paris: Schleicher Freres, 1900b.

Binet, A., and Simon, T. "Sur la nécessité d'établir un diagnostic scientifique des états inférieurs de l'intelligence." *L'Année Psychologique,* 1905, *11,* 163-190.

Binet, A., and Simon, T. "Le développement de l'intelligence chez les enfants." *L'Année Psychologique,* 1908, *14,* 1-94.

Binet, A., and Simon, T. *Mentally Defective Children.* Trans. W. B. Drummond. New York: Longmans, Green, 1914.

Binet, A., and Simon, T. *A Method of Measuring the Development of the Intelligence of Young Children.* Trans. Clara H. Town. Chicago: Chicago Medical Book, 1915.

Blatt, B. "Some Persistently Recurring Assumptions Concerning the Mentally Subnormal." *Training School Bulletin,* 1960, *57,* 48-59.

Bourdon, B. "Influence de l'age sur la mémoire immédiate." *Revue Philosophique,* 1894, *34,* 148-167.

Brigham, C. C. *A Study of American Intelligence.* Princeton, N.J.: Princeton University Press, 1923.

Bronner, A. *The Psychology of Special Abilities and Disabilities.* Boston: Little, Brown, 1917.

Burks, B. S. "A Summary of Literature on the Determiners of the IQ and the EQ." *National Society for the Study of Education Yearbook*, 1927, pp. 248-350.

Burt, C. *Annual Reports of the Psychologist to the London County Council.* London: London County Council, 1914-1931.

Burt, C. "Evidence for the Concept of Intelligence." *British Journal of Educational Psychology*, 1955, *25*, 158-177.

Burt, C. "The Inheritance of Mental Ability." *American Psychologist*, 1958, *13*, 1-15.

Burt, C. "The Genetic Determination of Differences in Intelligence." *British Journal of Psychology*, 1966, *57*, 137-155.

Burt, C., and Howard, M. "The Multifactorial Theory of Inheritance and Its Applicability to Intelligence." *British Journal of Statistical Psychology*, 1956, *9*, 95-131.

Burt, C., and Howard, M. "Heredity and Intelligence: A Reply to Criticism." *British Journal of Statistical Psychology*, 1957, *10*, 33-63.

Decroly, M. O., and Degand, J. "Les tests de Binet et Simon pour la mésure de l'intelligence: Contribution critique." *Archives de Psychologie*, 1907, *6*, 27-130.

Decroly, M. O., and Degand, J. "La mésure de l'intelligence des infants normaux d'après les tests de mm. Binet et Simon." *Archives de Psychologie*, 1910, *9*, 81-108.

De Sanctis, S. "Types et degrés d'insufficence mentale." *L'Année Psychologique*, 1906, *12*, 70-83.

Dobzhansky, T. "Of Flies and Men." *American Psychologist*, 1967, *22*, 41-48.

Doll, E. A. *The Measurement of Social Competence.* Minneapolis: Educational Test Bureau, 1953.

Down, J. L. H. "Observations on the Ethnic Classification of Idiots." *London Hospital Clinical Lectures Reports*, 1866, *3*, 229-262.

Dugdale, R. L. *The Jukes: A Study of Crime, Pauperism, Disease, and Heredity.* New York: Putnam, 1877.

Duncan, P. M., and Millard, W. *Manual for the Classification, Training, and Education of the Feebleminded, Imbecile, and Idiotic.* London: Churchill, 1866.

Dunn, L. M. "Special Education for the Mildly Retarded: Is Much of It Justifiable?" *Exceptional Children*, 1968, *35*, 5-22.

Ellis, R. S. *The Psychology of Individual Differences.* New York: Appleton, 1928.

Esquirol, J. E. D. *Mental Maladies.* Trans. E. K. Hunt. Philadelphia: Lea and Blanchard, 1845. Originally published [*Maladies mentales*] 1838.

Estabrook, A. H. *The Jukes in 1915.* Washington, D.C.: Carnegie Institution, 1916.

Fisher, R. A. *The Genetical Theory of Natural Selection.* Oxford: Clarendon Press, 1939.

Galton, F. *Hereditary Genius: An Inquiry into Its Laws and Consequences.* London: Macmillan, 1869.

Galton, F. "Supplementary Notes on 'Prehension' in Idiots." *Mind,* 1887, *12,* 79-82.

Garth, T. R. "White, Indian, and Negro Work Curves." *Journal of Applied Psychology,* 1921, *5,* 14-25.

Garth, T. R. "The Intelligence and Achievement of Mixed-Blood Indians." *Journal of Social Psychology,* 1933, *4,* 134-137.

Goddard, H. H. "Four Hundred Feebleminded Children Classified by the Binet Method." *Journal of Psycho-Asthenics,* 1910, *15,* 17-30.

Goddard, H. H. *The Kallikak Family: A Study in the Heredity of Feeble-mindedness.* New York: Macmillan, 1912.

Goddard, H. H. *Feeblemindedness.* New York: Macmillan, 1914.

Goddard, H. H. "The Subnormal Mind Versus the Abnormal." *Journal of Abnormal Social Psychology,* 1921, *16,* 47-54.

Grant, M. *The Passing of the Great Race.* New York: Scribner's, 1916.

Haller, M. H. "Social Science and Genetics, a Historical Perspective." In D. C. Glass (Ed.), *Genetics.* New York: Russell Sage Foundation, 1968.

Healy, W. *The Individual Delinquent.* Boston: Little, Brown, 1915.

Hofstadter, R. *Social Darwinism in American Thought.* New York: Braziller, 1944.

Hollingworth, L. S. "Differential Action upon the Sexes of Forces Which Tend to Segregate the Feebleminded." *Journal of Abnormal Social Psychology,* 1922, *17,* 35-57.

Ireland, W. W. *The Mental Affections of Children: Idiocy, Imbecility, and Insanity.* London: J. Churchill, 1898.

Jacobs, J. "Experiments on 'Prehension.' " *Mind,* 1887, *12,* 75-79.

Johnson, G. E. "Contribution to the Psychology and Pedagogy of Feebleminded Children." *Pediatric Seminar,* 1894, *3,* 246-301.

Johnson, G. O. "A Study of the Social Position of Mentally Handicapped Children in the Regular Grades." *American Journal of Mental Deficiency,* 1950, *55,* 60-90.

Johnson, G. O. "The Mentally Handicapped—A Paradox." *Exceptional Children,* 1962, *29,* 62-69.

Johnson, G. O., and Kirk, S. "Are Mentally Handicapped Children Segregated in the Regular Grades?" *Exceptional Children,* 1950, *17,* 65-89.

Klineberg, O. *Negro Intelligence and Selective Integration.* New York: Columbia University Press, 1935.

Kohs, S. C. "The Binet-Simon Measuring Scale for Intelligence: An Annotated Bibliography." *Journal of Educational Psychology,* 1914, *5,* 215-224, 279-290, 335-346.

Kuhlmann, F. "Binet and Simon's System for Measuring the Intelligence of Children." *Journal of Psycho-Asthenics,* 1911a, *15,* 79-92.

Kuhlmann, F. "A Reply to Dr. L. P. Ayres' Criticism of the Binet and Simon System for Measuring the Intelligence of Children." *Journal of Psycho-Asthenics*, 1911b, *16*, 58-67.

Layzer, D. "Heritability of IQ Scores: Science or Numerology?" *Science*, 1974, *183*, 1259-1266.

Leahy, A. M. "Nature-Nurture and Intelligence." *Genetic and Psychological Monographs*, 1935, *17*, 235-308.

Lombroso, C. *L'Uomo delinquent in rapporto Antropologia Giurisprudenza, e alle Discipline Carcerie*. Torino: Hoepli, 1876.

Montessori, M. *The Montessori Method: Scientific Pedagogy as Applied to the Children in the 'Children's Houses.'* Trans. Anne E. George. New York: Frederick A. Stokes, 1912.

Morel, B. A. *Traité des dégénérescences physiques, intellectuelles et morales de l'espèce humaine et des causes qui produisent ces variétés maladives*. Paris: Balliere, 1857.

Muller, H. J. "The Dominance of Economics over Eugenics." In C. B. Davenport (Ed.), *A Decade of Progress in Eugenics: The Third International Congress of Eugenics*. Baltimore: Williams and Wilkins, 1934.

National Society for Study of Education. *Forty-Ninth Yearbook*, 1950.

Peterson, J., and Lanier, L. "Studies in the Comparative Abilities of Whites and Negroes." *Mental Measurement Monographs*, 1929, series 5.

Robb, I. M. "Segregation vs. Nonsegregation of Exceptional Children: Report of a Panel Discussion at the 22nd Annual Meeting of the International Council for Exceptional Children." *Exceptional Children*, 1946, *12*, 235-240.

Rosenthal, R., and Jacobson, L. *Pygmalion in the Classroom: Teacher Expectations and Pupil's Intellectual Development*. New York: Holt, 1968.

Schiedman, G. *The Psychology of Exceptional Children*. New York: Appleton, 1926.

Seguin, E. *Idiocy and Its Treatment by the Physiological Method*. New York: Brandow, 1866.

Spencer, H. *Social Statics*. New York: Appleton, 1865.

Spencer, H. *Principles of Sociology*. London: Williams and Norgate, 1876.

Thurstone, T. G. *An Evaluation of Educating Mentally Handicapped Children in Special Classes and in Regular Classes*. Chapel Hill: School of Education, University of North Carolina, 1959.

Tredgold, A. F. *Mental Deficiency*. London: Bailliere, Tindall, and Cox, 1908.

Tredgold, A. F. *Mental Deficiency*. (6th Ed.) Baltimore: William Wood and Co., 1937.

Treves, Z., and Saffiotti, F. U. *La scala intelligenza di Binet e Simon. Espositione critica*. Parts I and II. Milan: Civelli, 1910-1911.

Wallin, J. E. W. "A Practical Guide for the Administration of the Binet-

Simon Scale for Measuring Intelligence." *Psychological Clinic*, 1911, *2*, 121-132.

Wallin, J. E. W. *Problems of Subnormality*. New York: World Book Co., 1917.

Wallin, J. E. W. "An Investigation of the Sex, Relationship, Marriage, Delinquency, and Truancy of Children Assigned to Special Public School Classes." *Journal of Abnormal Social Psychology*, 1922a, *17*, 19-34.

Wallin, J. E. W. "A Study of the Industrial Record of Children Assigned to Public School Classes for Mental Defectives and Legislation in the Interest of Defectives." *Journal of Abnormal Social Psychology*, 1922b, *17*, 120-130.

Wallin, J. E. W. *Education of Mentally Handicapped Children*. New York: Harper, 1955.

Watson, J. B. *Behaviorism*. Philadelphia: Lippincott, 1919.

Whipple, G. M. "Use of Mental Tests in the Schools." *National Society for the Study of Education Yearbook*, 1916, pp. 149-160.

Yerkes, R. M. (Ed.) "Psychological Examining in the United States Army." *National Academy of Science Memoirs*, 1921.

Young, K. "The History of Mental Testing." *Pediatric Seminar*, 1924, *31*, 1-47.

8

MENTAL RETARDATION

John W. Filler, Jr., Cordelia C. Robinson,
Roger A. Smith, Lisbeth J. Vincent-Smith,
Diane D. Bricker, William A. Bricker

During the last decade parents and professionals alike have voiced concern about the ethics of diagnostic labeling and classification—particularly in the field of mental retardation. Specifically, critics have questioned the ultimate effect upon the child of both diagnosis (determining "mental retardation") and

The preparation of this chapter was supported in part by NICHD Grants No. HD00973 and HD07073 and the Joseph P. Kennedy, Jr., Foundation. Portions of this paper are based on information presented in articles prepared by H. C. Haywood (1971 and in press).

194

classification (determining the degree of severity), the adequacy of the criteria used for diagnosis and classification, and the practical utility of standardized measures of intelligence. In this chapter we limit our discussion of the reliability and validity of particular measurement instruments and devote more effort to a general examination of what can happen to people labeled *mentally retarded* according to the requirements of various classification schemes. In addition, we discuss alternative procedures which, if refined, could contribute directly to the education of retarded children.

Intelligence and Retardation

"It is in connection with intelligence and the tests which measure it that some of the most violent polemics in psychology and in all the behavioral sciences have raged. These polemics have concerned the nature of man's intellectual capacities, how they should be measured, how mutable they are, and what the implication of the decisions on these issues should be for educating and improving the race" (Hunt, 1961, p. 3). Recognizing that attempts to resolve such issues in a single chapter would be a foolhardy endeavor, we turn instead to a discussion of what we perceive to be several currently held conceptions of intelligence.

Since the beginning of the testing movement, which is generally traced to Galton's (1883) study of individual differences in performance on sensory and motor tasks, intelligence has often been defined in terms of scores on tests. Admittedly, the specific items included in tests of intelligence have undergone considerable revision; the current psychometric definition of intelligence, however, reflects the predominant view—namely, that obtained scores constitute observable representations of a unitary and physically unobservable entity. From this perspective, intelligence is viewed as a hypothetical construct, the form and level of which is determined by the interaction of a number of directly observable antecedent genetic and environmental factors. Intelligence, the latent unobservable variable, is inferred from a sample of behavior obtained under highly structured conditions and takes the manifest or observable form of correct and incorrect responses to a number of items graded in difficulty according to the number of individuals of a given age who pass them.

Since Terman's 1916 revision of the original Binet-Simon scale, performance on intelligence tests has been expressed in terms of an IQ score. While current versions of the most popular tests of intelligence have maintained this practice, the value of the IQ score is no longer determined by the ratio expression: [mental age (performance)/chronological age] x 100. Since latent intelligence is assumed to be normally distributed in the general population, tests of intelligence have been constructed such that the obtained scores will distribute themselves according to the Gaussian function or normal curve (Haywood, in press). Hence, the latest revisions of the Stanford-Binet and the Wechsler series employ standard scores which allow an individual IQ score to be expressed in terms of its deviation in standard units from the mean or average of the theoretical distribution of all IQ scores.

A diagnosis of retardation requires that an IQ score be more than two standard deviations below the mean of the particular test employed. The 1973 revision of the *Manual on Terminology and Classification in Mental Retardation,* published by the American Association on Mental Deficiency (Grossman, 1973), lists four classifications of retardation based on measured intelligence (see Table 1).

According to the normal curve, only 2.27 percent of the general population would be expected to achieve scores greater than two standard deviations below the mean. Likewise, 2.27 percent of the population of IQ scores would be expected to achieve scores greater than two standard deviations above the mean. According to recent estimates (for example, Haywood, in press), however, the actual distribution of IQ scores does not seem to conform to the theoretical expectancies. Generally, a significantly larger number of individuals than would be pre-

Table 1

Classifications of Retardation by American Association on Mental Deficiency

Level of Retardation	*Standard Deviation Range*	*IQ Range by Test*	
		Binet	*Wechsler*
Mild	−2.01 - −3.00	68-52	69-55
Moderate	−3.01 - −4.00	51-36	54-40
Severe	−4.01 - −5.00	35-20	39-25
Profound	below −5.01	19 and below	24 and below

dicted from the normal curve obtain IQ scores greater than two standard deviations below the mean. This discrepancy between actual estimates and theoretical expectancies seems to increase as IQ scores decrease. Haywood (in press) gives a plausible explanation for the observed discrepancies:

> The theoretical distribution rests partially on the assumption that the level of general intelligence attained by any individual is genetically determined. There is a growing body of evidence that this is not wholly true; that is, experiences encountered by any individual after birth, and indeed up to adulthood, appear to play a large part in determining his ultimate intellectual growth, especially when one considers intelligence to be represented by a single global score. Variables which appear to influence intellectual growth and the expression of intelligence include ethnicity, social class, chronological age, race, relative cultural advantage-disadvantage, nutrition, education, general health, and specific child-rearing practices. One obvious fact that renders the empirical distribution asymmetrical is that there are many accidents that result in brain damage, hence lower intellectual functioning, but none that are known to result in higher intellectual functioning.

In opposition to the tendency to conceptualize intelligence as a hypothetical construct, the behaviorist argues that intelligence is essentially descriptive rather than causal. That is, an intelligence test merely provides an opportunity to observe a highly restricted sample of behavior, which is summarized as a numerical score. Since only behavior is observable, it is behavior which is more or less "intelligent." According to Skinner (1953), hypothetical-construct notions of intelligence transform adjectives to nouns and then attribute excess meaning to their functional significance. "Intelligent behavior" becomes "behavior which shows intelligence" and, finally, "behavior which is the effect of intelligence." Describing the use of hypothetical constructs as essentially antiscientific, Skinner (1953) and Bijou (1963) insist that the search for causative factors must center upon apparent antecedent conditions which can be related functionally to the topographies of essential forms of behavior, such as language and comprehension. Individual variations in competency across people are said to result directly from diversity in organismic and environmental factors rather than from deficiencies in mediating processes. From the behavioristic frame-

work, retardation is denoted by the detection of limited reper-
toires of behavior which result from atypical variations in a number of historical factors conceived as independent variables and
assumed to underlie all development. As Bijou (1963, p. 101) has
stated, "a retarded individual is one who has a limited repertory of
behavior evolving from interactions of the individual with his
environmental contacts which constitute his history."

A third view of the nature of intelligence has been provided by a number of sociologists (Becker, 1963; Farber, 1968;
Mercer, 1965, 1970) within the context of discussions concerning the status of deviancy and how it is achieved. According to
this view, social organizations develop procedures to sort people
who will fit the system from those who will not. In modern
societies with great technological knowledge, this sorting is
often done on the basis of intellectual ability indexed by performance on standardized tests, constructed according to the
prescriptions of the predominant social system. These tests
place a premium upon skills necessary for academic or school
performance and provide one means by which the social structure selects certain individuals for certain roles. From the social-
system perspective, then, intelligence is not something that is
necessarily within the individual but rather is an expression of
societal demands and expectations.

Mercer (1971, p. 191) defines mental retardation "as an
achieved social status which some persons hold in some social
systems." Thus, a child can be labeled *mentally retarded* by
several different sources: the family, the neighbors (community), the school, the psychometrist (Farber, 1968). As Mercer
(1970) has indicated, a child who is labeled *mentally retarded* in
school may not be considered retarded at home. That is, in one
situation (the school) the child does not fit the preexisting social organization, while in another (the family) he does. This is
especially true for members of minority groups whose native
cultures and mores may differ somewhat from those of the
society in which they currently function. Mercer's investigations
in California school systems clearly indicate that there are grossly disproportionate numbers of Mexican-American and black
children in special education classes.

Classification Systems

Three classification systems in mental retardation are currently used in the United States: the U.S. Department of

Health, Education, and Welfare's (1967) *International Classifi-cation of Diseases, Adapted for Use in the United States,* eighth edition *(ICDA-8)*; the American Psychiatric Association's (1968) *Diagnostic and Statistical Manual of Mental Disorders,* second edition *(DSM-II)*; and the American Association on Mental Deficiency's (AAMD) fifth revision of the *Manual on Terminology and Classification in Mental Retardation* (Heber, 1959, 1961), which has recently been replaced by a sixth revision (Grossman, 1973). *ICDA-8* and *DSM-II* are adaptations of the World Health Organization's (1968) *International Classification of Diseases,* which is currently undergoing revision. (For detailed reviews of these three systems, see Gelof, 1963; Spitzer and Wilson, 1968a, 1968b; Wilson and Spitzer, 1968, 1969.)

In the 1961 AAMD *Manual on Terminology and Classification in Mental Retardation,* mental retardation is defined as "subaverage general intellectual functioning which originated during the developmental period [prior to age sixteen] and is associated with impairment in adaptive behavior" (Heber, 1961, p. 3). The principal indicator of retardation here is measured intelligence (Brison, 1967). "Subaverage general intellectual functioning" refers to a score greater than *one* standard deviation below the mean on a standardized instrument. "Adaptive behavior" refers "primarily to the effectiveness of the individual in adapting to the social demands of his environment" and is reflected in maturation, learning, and social adjustment.

Three systems of classification are provided in this 1961 edition. The first reflects "an attempt to develop a scheme which is consistent with the concepts of modern medicine." Eight major etiological categories—ranging from "Diseases Due to Infection" to "Diseases Due to Uncertain (or Presumed Psychological) Cause with the Functional Reaction Alone Manifest"—are included. Also included is a Supplementary Term Listing. In the second major section of the manual, behavior is classified according to measured intelligence and according to adaptive behavior. Five degrees of severity of retardation are distinguished: borderline retardation (defined as an obtained score between one and two standard deviations below the mean), followed by mild, moderate, severe, and profound re-tardation. Adaptive behavior is categorized according to four levels, "scaled from mild (but apparent and significant) negative deviation from population norms in adaptive behaviors at Level I to complete lack of adaptation at Level IV." The actual forms of behavior to be observed to determine the level of functioning differ according to the age of the individual. For children from birth to five years of age, self-help, motor development, and communication skills are emphasized; individuals six to twenty-one years of age are judged mainly in terms of academic skills, while social and vocational skills are emphasized for adults. Since scales based upon normative data were notably lacking at the time, especially for older children and adults, classification according to adaptive behavior was often a matter of clinical judgment concerning the age appropriateness of the behavior exhibited. Nevertheless, the insistence upon the determination of deficit in adaptive behavior or social competence as necessary for the diagnosis of mental retardation represents a significant departure from earlier classification systems, which relied only upon measured intelligence (Gelof, 1963).

In the sixth revision of the AAMD's manual (Grossman, 1973), many aspects of Heber's (1961) manual have been retained, including the multidimensional requirement for the diagnosis of retardation and the view that retardation is not an irreversible disease. However, significant changes have occurred in the classification system.

First, the definition of mental retardation has been changed: "Mental retardation refers to significantly subaverage general intellectual functioning existing concurrently with deficits in adaptive behavior, and manifested during the developmental period [extended here to age eighteen]" (Grossman, 1973, p. 5). The phrase "significantly subaverage" refers to the establishment of two standard deviations below the mean as the upper limit for the classification of mental retardation according to measured intelligence. The category of borderline mental retardation is no longer included. If this change were accepted by school systems, which tend to rely heavily upon measures of intelligence, it could have a significant effect upon the number of students assigned to special education classes for the educable mentally retarded.

Second, the major categories of the medical classification scheme have been changed to conform to those of the *ICDA-8* and *DSM-II* systems. In essence, the number of major medical categories has been expanded from eight to ten (coded 0 through IX), and the specific disorders within each major classification have been reorganized. Additionally, the numerical coding system has been changed to conform to the one employed by the *ICDA-8* system.

Third, although the adaptive behavior levels (I through IV) have been maintained, Level I has been set at two standard deviations below the population mean rather than one standard deviation as in the Heber (1961) manual. However, this change is hardly worth noting because even now no suitable norms exist which would allow for the determination of negative deviation. Since the recently published AAMD Adaptive Behavior Scales (Nihira and others, 1969) include only institutionalized populations in the standardization samples, their unqualified use is not recommended. Unfortunately, clinical opinion remains the major factor in the determination of levels of adaptive behavior.

Finally, the glossary of terms has been revised. Phrases such as *labor induced,* which have no special meaning within the context of mental retardation, have been dropped; and terms such as *positive reinforcement, shaping,* and *contingency management,* which have considerable importance to educational programming, have been added.

Grossman's (1973) revision of the AAMD classification system is similar to the *ICDA-8* and *DSM-II* systems in that all three insist upon similar multiple criteria for the diagnosis of retardation and employ the same terminology to describe the different degrees of severity. However, two major differences exist. First, *ICDA-8* and *DSM-II* include the category of borderline mental retardation. Second, *ICDA-8* and *DSM-II* combine indices of measured intelligence and adaptive behavior into a single composite score, whereas the AAMD system encourages separate recording. Thus, "the intelligence score has two different meanings in the two systems. Under AAMD it reflects only the patient's measured intelligence; under *DSM-II* [and *ICDA-8*] it presumably reflects his general level of functioning" (Wilson and Spitzer, 1969, p. 430).

In spite of the admonitions contained in each of the classification manuals concerning the importance of augmenting results from IQ tests with "clinical judgment," IQ scores will probably continue to be used as the foremost criteria for differential classification. Even those diagnosticians who fully recognize the limitations imposed upon intelligence tests by a number of error factors (errors of administration or test construction) would place more weight on these test results than those obtained from interviews or rating scales of generally lower reliability (Adams, 1973).

Purpose of Classification Systems

"A classification system is designed primarily to furnish statistical data about groups of cases. The principal use of such a system will be to furnish classificatory data on incidence, prevalence, characteristics, and concomitant information. Providing a classification system makes possible increased precision in communication, in research work, and in administrative and program planning. The use of a medical classification system which offers descriptive symptoms of clinical conditions is of diagnostic value to physicians and adds new dimensions not found in other classification systems of diseases" (Grossman, 1973, pp. 6-7). Classification systems in mental retardation provide an objectively specifiable way of delimiting populations of individuals who for various reasons are likely to encounter difficulty in acquiring the skills necessary for successful community living. The provision of ways to identify and categorize people is, perhaps, absolutely necessary from the perspective of those responsible for distributing funds for special programs. In addition, scientific efforts to provide explanations of human development assume, as a prerequisite, adequate systems of description. For these reasons, we agree with Haywood (1971) that assigning individuals to categories is "not inherently evil." The "evil" lies in the insistence upon the validity of these classifications and the failure to recognize that they constitute little more than convenient groupings.

However, we must question the utility of classification systems which rely upon a *prediction* of academic success as the *criterion* for assigning large numbers of people to gross categories. First, prediction is not really the outcome we desire; second, academic achievement is a relatively poor measure of success in life (McClelland, 1973). As Haywood (1971) points out, "Outside the prediction of academic achievement, intelligence tests probably should not be used at all, especially for the prediction of social adjustment and ultimate success in living in communities." In addition, the categories of mild, moderate, severe, and profound imply that individuals within a particular category will exhibit highly similar forms of behavior. Given the pervasiveness of individual differences, variation within categories is probably much greater than has been assumed. Finally, categorization and subsequent labeling often proceed on the basis of an enumeration of the qualities an individual does not possess. Thus, the absence of behavior defines the nature of the label applied. In this regard, Haywood (1969, p. 379) has commented, "At the very least, a retarded individual should be diagnosed on the basis of behavior which he does demonstrate, not on the basis of characteristics which we are unable to find."

For the above reasons, we question the value of classification systems as presently constituted. The ultimate goal of such systems should be to contribute directly to the optimal adjustment of the individual. Obviously, the medical diagnosis of clinical syndromes is a necessary and desirable aspect of those classification systems in mental retardation which we described earlier. Many medical syndromes associated with retardation (such as phenylketonuria and hypothyroidism) are treatable. However, behavioral classifications (measured intelligence and adaptive behavior) as presently assessed do not specify educational treatment and disposition. To classify a child and attach a label cannot be justified unless the child demonstrably benefits from the process. In the next three sections of this chapter, we shall attempt to evaluate the efficacy of such systems from this perspective by examining what may happen to individuals diagnosed as "retarded."

Residential Placement

More than 200,000 individuals diagnosed as mentally retarded, about 30 percent of whom are children (fifteen years of age or younger), are residents of public institutions. Approximately 82 percent of these residents have obtained IQ scores below 50. Most of these institutionalized individuals have been classified as severely or profoundly retarded (Baumeister, 1970; Butterfield, 1969)—often on the basis of unknown etiological factors (Baumeister, 1970). Although these statistics represent less than 5 percent of the estimated prevalence of retardation, the institution continues to be a primary source of "treatment" for individuals classified at the lower end of the continuum of measured intelligence.

Extensive accounts of historical changes in the patterns of residential care for individuals diagnosed as mentally retarded have been provided from a sociological perspective in a number of recent reviews (for example, Baumeister, 1970; White and Wolfensberger, 1969; Wolfensberger, 1969, 1970, 1972; Kugel and Wolfensberger, 1969; see also this book, Chapter Seventeen). According to Wolfensberger (1969), the first American institutions, founded approximately 120 years ago, attempted to provide concentrated training in those social and academic skills necessary for adequate functioning in society. These residential facilities were typically small, were located in the center of communities, and served only individuals considered "curable." By 1880, however, as Baumeister (1970) points out, enthusiasm for the original educational goals had diminished, since these early institutions had failed to achieve those goals. Consequently, the educational model was replaced by a "pity model," in which deviants were looked upon as individuals to be protected from society (Wolfensberger, 1969). This shift in the concept of deviancy had tremendous ramifications. The new institutions that were founded were located great distances from communities, enlarged to accommodate more residents, and turned from an emphasis on educational activities to more custodial patterns of treatment.

The "pity model," however, was short-lived. By the turn of the century it had been replaced by the view that retarded persons constitute a "menace" to society and that society should be protected from the deviant. This view, held by proponents of the eugenics movement in this country (Baumeister, 1970; Wolfensberger, 1969), was manifested in the various attempts, between 1880 and 1925, to establish legislation with respect to preventive marriage, sterilization, and segregation. Although the recommendations stemming from the eugenics movement were not generally effective, segregation of retarded individuals from society remained as the primary solution to the problem of retardation (Baumeister, 1970). Institutions continued to increase in number and size while maintaining the structures of custodial care and segregation. Even today, "many of our institutions . . . operate in the spirit of 1925, when inexpensive segregation of the scarcely human retardate was seen as the only feasible alternative to combat a social menace" (Wolfensberger, 1969, p. 129).

Numerous studies have been made of the effects of institutionalization. One approach has been to compare institutionalized and noninstitutionalized groups of mentally retarded individuals. For example, Stedman and Eichorn (1964) compared two groups of Down's syndrome children—one group living at home, a matched group living in an institution. Their results indicated that the home-reared children were superior on physical, social, and mental indices of development. In a similar study Centerwall and Centerwall (1960) report results consistent with those obtained by Stedman and Eichorn. Other investigators have attempted to assess the relationship between length of residential placement and social and intellectual development. For example, Cutts and Lane (1947) compared groups of residents matched on chronological age and full-scale IQ who differed in length of institutionalization; short-term residents proved superior on verbal IQ measures. Moreover, institutionalization at an early age apparently results in greater loss in IQ points over time than institutionalization during adolescence or adulthood (Butterfield, 1967). Individuals from extremely disadvantaged home situations may actually show gains on IQ measures after institutionalization. While sex of the institutionalized individual does not seem to affect gains or losses on IQ measures, different diagnostic categories show differential losses and gains in IQ scores. Since noninstitutionalized control groups have generally not been utilized in this type of study, changes in IQ scores cannot necessarily be attributed directly to the institution per se.

A few investigators have employed noninstitutional comparison groups. Two of these, Lyle (1960) and Kirk (1958), actually manipulated the environment of the noninstitutional group. Lyle (1960) removed his subjects (sixteen children who scored between 25 and 50 on standardized IQ tests) from an institution ward and placed them in a homelike setting with housemothers. Although no formal education program was conducted, the housemothers were encouraged to talk and play with the children. After twelve months these children obtained higher scores on measures of speech and sound production, word naming, and verbal intelligence than children of similar ages (four and a half to ten and a half) and IQ scores who remained in the institution. Kirk (1958) selected two groups of subjects: a group of institutionalized children and a group of retarded children who lived in the community. The children ranged in IQ scores from 40 to 80 and in chronological ages from three to six. Half of each group of children participated in a six-hour-a-day nursery school program. These children showed greater gains on measures of social maturity and intelligence than counterpart control children who did not receive nursery school experiences. These two studies suggest the advantages of homelike environments and close interaction between staff and children for the development of retarded individuals. Such investigations serve to document the belief that the institution is probably not the optimal environment for the continued development of people diagnosed as mentally retarded.

Other investigators studying the effects of institutionalization have collected systematic follow-up data on individuals released from institutions. In reviewing longitudinal outcome studies before 1960, Heber and Dever (1970) conclude that the results are difficult if not impossible to interpret because of differences in sampling procedures, the definition of adequate "adjustment," age of admission, length of institutionalization before release, and outcome information. However, two more recent studies cited by Heber and Dever (1970) have been more informative. Windle (1962) studied groups of residents who were discharged from an institution but for various reasons failed to remain in the community. He found that 60 percent of the residents placed on home leave or on vocational leave were reinstitutionalized within a two-year period. Most of the individuals on home leave had returned to the institution because of an inadequate support system or "antisocial" behavior. Most of the individuals on vocational leave had returned to the institution because of inadequate "interpersonal" relations or poor work performance. Edgerton (1967) reported follow-up information on residents who had been released from an institution and had remained in the community. Most of these former residents were living in the lowest social and economic environments and were almost completely dependent upon supportive individuals who provided the necessary mechanisms of survival in the community.

These illustrative studies suggest several conclusions: (1) Intellectual functioning, as measured by standardized tests of intelligence, is negatively affected by institutionalization. (2) This detrimental effect is amplified by such variables as length of institutionalization and age of residential placement. (3) Verbal ability in particular seems adversely affected by institutionalization. (4) A great percentage of individuals who are discharged from institutions fail to remain in the community because of inadequate skills for coping with societal demands. (5) Those individuals who have been discharged and remain in the community typically exist at the lower end of the social and economic continuum. These conclusions must be qualified because of pervasive methodological problems. However, when one considers the potential impact of institutions on the lives of their residents, the mere suggestion of deleterious effects is sufficient to question the efficacy of predominant patterns of institutional placement.

Nonresidential Intervention Programs

The system generally used by the public schools for identifying children in need of special services is an adaptation of the previously discussed classification schemes. In many school systems programs have typically been designated for the *educable mentally retarded* (EMR) or the *trainable mentally retarded* (TMR) child. The most predominantly used criterion for identifying a child as EMR or TMR is his score on an individual intelligence test. Children who obtain scores in the range between 50 and 80 are classified as educable; those who obtain scores between 30 and 50 are classified as trainable. School systems generally do not provide educational programs for individuals whose scores on an intelligence test are below 25. The general view has been that such children cannot benefit from an educational program.

The educable mentally retarded child has the following characteristics: general intellectual functioning below the average of the general population, predicted or demonstrated inability to cope with the school curriculum designated for others of his chronological age, potential for achieving the third- or fourth-grade level in basic academic skills if provided with the appropriate curriculum, and potential for developing social and occupational skills necessary for independent adult living (Heber, 1963). Many children in EMR classes have difficulties only with the regular school curriculum; these children function "normally" in the home and community (Hurley, 1969; President's Committee on Mental Retardation, 1970).

The trainable mentally retarded child is probably not capable of being totally self-sufficient but has the potential to learn basic self-care skills and vocational skills which could be used in a sheltered setting (Kirk, 1964). Based on these characteristics, educational programs for the trainable child stress self-help, socialization, and oral communication skills.

In a discussion of school-based programs for mentally retarded children, Dunn (1963) points out that IQ is the primary criterion for assignment to a special class. However, children in such classes have usually met the adaptive behavior criteria of the AAMD definition of retardation because they have also failed several grades in regular classes. As Dunn has emphasized, labeling a child *educable* or *trainable mentally retarded* is a very grave event and should not be done unless beneficial special services can be offered on the basis of that label.

Numerous studies have been made to determine whether special class placement results in greater academic achievement and social adaptation for the educable or trainable child (for reviews of such studies see Guskin and Spicker, 1968; Kirk, 1964). In most of the studies of children labeled *educable mentally retarded,* children who scored within the EMR range on an individual intelligence test and remained in the regular class were compared with children who were matched on scores on the same test but attended a special class. In many studies pairs or groups of children were also matched on mental age, chronological age, sex and, in some cases, socioeconomic status. The results of such investigations indicate that the achievement of special class children is either equal to (Ainsworth, 1959; Goldstein, Moss, and Jordan, 1965; Mullen and Itkin, 1961; Thurstone, 1959; Wrightstone and others, 1959) or inferior to (Bennett, 1932; Cassidy and Stanton, 1959) the achievement of children who remain in the regular classes. These studies, however, reveal selection bias or failure to meet the AAMD criteria. For example, in the Mullen and Itkin (1961) study, students who were already in a special class were matched with those on a waiting list for special classes, which constitutes selection bias. In the Goldstein, Moss, and Jordan (1965) investigation, children entering first grade were randomly assigned to special classes or regular classes. This assignment was on the basis of IQ only, and hence the AAMD criterion of impairment in adaptive behavior was not met.

Special educators have argued that even if special class placement has not proved advantageous to academic achievement, it does seem to be efficacious when the social and emotional adjustment of the child is considered. The various studies of personal and social adjustment of children placed in EMR classes, however, contain several methodological problems (as pointed out by Guskin and Spicker, 1968). For example, sociometric status, frequently used as an index of personal and social adjustment, is often based on teacher ratings, and the special class teacher's basis of reference is not the same as that of the regular class teacher, who is comparing the retarded child to normally developing peers. This same criticism holds for peer sociometric ratings as well. Therefore, according to Guskin and Spicker (1968, p. 251), "there is little definitive evidence either that [educable retarded] children are seriously maladjusted outside of special classes or that special classes have a consistently favorable effect on adjustment of the retarded."

In summary, studies of the efficacy of special class placement suggest that the educable retarded child does at least as well academically if allowed to remain in the regular class. The humanitarian's plea that the retarded child's social and personal adjustment will be better if he is placed in a special class without frustrating pressure also has not been empirically validated.

Educational provisions for the *trainable retarded child* within the public schools are a much more recent development than programs for the educable child. As Dunn (1973) has pointed out, special day classes have increased rapidly since 1950, primarily due to the efforts of parents of retarded children. But even though enrollments in special classes increased 260 percent in the years 1953 to 1958 (Mackie and Robbins, 1961), such classes were widely criticized as ineffective (Dunn, 1963; Goldberg and Cruickshank, 1958). Consequently, investigations of the efficacy of school programs were initiated in several states: Minnesota (Reynolds and Kiland, 1953), Illinois (Goldstein, 1956), Michigan (Guenther, 1956), New York (Johnson and Capobianco, 1957), and Tennessee (Hottel, 1958). Results of these studies are difficult to summarize due to variability among them with respect to the population studied and methodological procedures employed. Since intelligence tests such as the WISC were not useful in assessing behavioral changes, unvalidated self-care or social-adjustment scales were frequently used. In addition, due to the small number of TMR children in communities (two out of one thousand individuals), investigations frequently were not conducted with randomly selected groups. Also the heterogeneity of etiology and behavioral characteristics within the population made matched-pair comparisons on the basis of characteristics such as brain injury a questionable procedure. In spite of these methodological problems Dunn (1973, p. 98) concludes: "There is little evidence from these studies to suggest that special day classes are effective as they have been constituted, emphasizing as they have the development of self-care and socialization by informal, total-group instruction for groups of children with IQs over the full range from about 25 to about 50."

Several follow-up studies of the postschool adjustment of trainable mentally retarded individuals have been conducted (Delp and Lorenz, 1953; Jewell, 1941; Saenger, 1957; Tisdall, 1960). The results of these studies indicate that one fourth to two thirds of the graduates of special programs remained at home. Some individuals were still in special classes or had been institutionalized. Very few held jobs, and those who did typically received the job through the intervention of a family member. Generally, individuals without special class training were found to be as effective in later life as those who had attended special classes. No information is available on individuals in this intellectual range who were not labeled *mentally retarded.*

Although definitive conclusions are not possible, the findings of the studies discussed above are suggestive of the direction which future research on educational programs for the individual who is classified TMR might take. If the goal of intervention is the development of independent living skills, more suitable classification and evaluation instruments, which would be sensitive to subtle changes in behavior, are needed. In addition, procedures designed to develop the skills necessary for maximal independent living should be developed and presented in special programs. As Cain and Levine (1963) have indicated, most of the time children spend in community special classes could be classified as noninstructional.

A major trend in the education of the mentally retarded child is the provision of *preschool programs.* Some of these programs are designed specifically for organically involved children (Fouracre, Connor, and Goldberg, 1962; Kirk, 1958); others are for culturally disadvantaged children (Gray and Klaus, 1965; Hodges, McCandless, and Spicker, 1971; Weikart and Lambie, 1970). Some of them are designed for very young children, less than three years old, and have been focused upon language development, preacademic skill development, and social development (D. Bricker and W. Bricker, 1971, 1972, 1973; Heber and Dever, 1970). Numerous reviews have appeared of the available research on preschool programs (Bronfenbrenner, 1973; Gray and Klaus, 1965; Guskin and Spicker, 1968; Kirk, 1964; Miller, 1970; Weikart and Lambie, 1970).

Data on the long-term effects of preschool programs are

available only on those projects which involved intervention with children of three years or older. In general, such interventions have produced statistically reliable gains in IQ scores for experimental children when compared with local and distal control groups (Gray and Klaus, 1965) and at-home control groups (Hodges, McCandless, and Spicker, 1971). Control groups, however, showed gains in the first year of school which were not as great as experimental groups but which were generally statistically reliable. After several years all groups tended to show a decline in IQ. This decline led Gray and Klaus (1965) to issue the caveat that early intervention cannot be considered an inoculation against effects of future deprivation.

Problems encountered in evaluating the effects of early intervention programs include the lack of adequate assessment measures. Stevenson (1973), among others, has criticized standardized intelligence tests as a means of evaluating disadvantaged populations. Similarly, many investigators agree that a measure of general intellectual functioning is not an appropriate evaluation instrument for a program designed to develop appropriate school behavior. While a large number of preschool programs exist, a lack of comparability among them in procedures and evaluation tools makes critical comparisons difficult. In general, however, researchers in this area are optimistic about the possible contribution of programs that identify children according to their level of functioning within a developmental continuum and intervene to promote further development within that framework.

Expectancies, Attitudes, and Self-Concepts

As we have indicated, the use of standardized test scores for determining special class placement has been and continues to be an integral part of the public education system. In many cases the test scores and other reasons for labeling the individual *retarded* have been given to teachers and other persons responsible for providing educational instruction. Such information, as well as special class placement per se, provides a possible mechanism for a priori expectancies of the child labeled *retarded*. These expectancies may have the effect of removing the responsibility for a child's subsequent failure from the teacher.

If it can be demonstrated that a child performs according to the expectancy of his teacher, and that his teacher expects him to fail because of a classificatory label (usually based on standardized test scores), then the value of the label as a convenient shorthand notation is outweighed by the negative effects of unnecessarily poor child performance (Haywood, 1971). The relationship between teachers' expectations and IQ changes among students has been demonstrated by Rosenthal and Jacobson (1966, 1968). Although their work has been criticized (for instance, by Thorndike, 1968) on methodological grounds, several other studies provide rather convincing demonstrations of the potentially pervasive nature of teacher expectancies.

Beez (1968) provided sixty graduate students in education with false information regarding sixty Head Start children and then asked each graduate student to teach a randomly selected child the meaning of a series of symbols. Thirty of these student teachers received reports stressing the children's cultural deprivation and predicting difficulty in school (low ability); the remaining thirty were given information predicting that the children would do well in spite of cultural deprivation (high ability). The teachers who had been given high-ability information attempted to teach significantly more symbols than did those given low-ability information. In addition, the high-ability children learned significantly more symbols than did the low-ability children.

Meichenbaum, Bowers, and Ross (1969) have demonstrated that biased instructions can affect the quality of interaction between teacher and student. Following a six-day baseline period during which teacher-pupil interactions were observed, four teachers were told that a "new test" had indicated that six of fourteen adolescent girls with whom each teacher had daily contact were "late bloomers." After receiving this information, two teachers increased the number of positive interactions with these six students, one decreased negative interactions, and one decreased positive interactions.

Haskett (1969), in an additional test of the expectancy hypothesis, selected thirty-two special education teachers and provided them with information regarding the results of achievement tests of their 267 educable mentally retarded adolescent students. The achievement-test scores given to half of the teachers were adjusted up or down; the other teachers were given accurate reports. The teachers were then asked to predict future academic achievement and social development of their pupils. Videotaped observations of teacher-pupil interaction were taken to determine the relationship between induced expectancy and teacher behavior. A significant correlation was found between teacher expectancy and subsequent pupil achievement. Moreover, teacher classroom behavior correlated with predicted gains in pupil reading skills.

The results obtained by Beez (1968), Meichenbaum, Bowers, and Ross (1969), and Haskett (1969) indicate that a teacher's expectancies may influence his estimates of pupil performance as well as his behavior toward students, which, in turn, may affect actual pupil performance. However, although notions of mental retardation engender many negative stereotypes (Wilson, 1970; Jones, 1972), to what degree these stereotypes result from the labeling process is still an open question.

A number of studies (Dent, 1967; Guskin, 1962; Jaffe, 1966; Mahoney and Pangrac, 1960; Willey, 1967) do suggest that isolated information regarding test results and special class placement can adversely affect the attitudes of others. Jaffe (1966), for instance, has shown that the label *mentally retarded* can influence the perceptions of others concerning the individual to whom the label has been attached. In this study, 240 high school seniors received one of two written descriptions of a fictitious person and then were asked to rate that person on a series of scales (semantic differential, an adjective checklist, and a social-distance scale). One description (retarded) included a statement that the person "had attended classes for the mentally retarded," the other description (nonretarded) was identical except that it did not include any reference to retardation. Some of the subjects who rated the nonretarded sketch were also asked to rate the term *mentally retarded*. The person described in the retarded sketch was rated, on the semantic differential, as significantly "smaller and weaker and more passive and suggestive" than the individual described in the nonretarded sketch. In addition, the label *mentally retarded* was rated more negatively than the retarded person sketch. Subjects who had had previous contact with retarded people rated the retarded sketch more favorably than did those subjects with no previous contact with retarded people. In a later replication (Jaffe, 1967), previous contact was again found to be an important determiner of attitude.

Dent (1967) attempted to determine the relative importance of mental retardation as a component of perceptions of social distance. Terms which described intelligence, ethnicity, dependability, and friendliness were arranged in all possible combinations to describe sixteen fictitious persons. Each of 132 college students was requested to rate, on a five-point scale, his willingness to associate with each of the described persons. Data analyses indicated that 43 percent of the total variance associated with social scores could be accounted for by statements of intellectual level alone. Dent noted that only those subjects who viewed human nature as complex and difficult to understand considered intelligence to be of less importance than such factors as dependability.

Other investigators have attempted to determine what effect labeling and segregation have upon the self-concept. Edgerton (1967), for instance, interviewed 110 mildly retarded former residents of a California institution for retarded persons. All persons interviewed said that their former status had burdened them with a shattering stigma and that they were forced to create elaborate ways of evading recurrent societal ostracism —for instance, by rejecting as false the initial diagnosis and inventing ingenious ways to cover real deficiencies. Similarly, Jones (1970, 1972) studied the effects on self-concept of individuals placed in educable mentally retarded special classes. Out of twenty-three persons interviewed, seventeen said that they lied about their placement; that is, whenever they were asked, they said that they were enrolled in regular classes. Sixteen stated that they disliked their special class placement because they were ridiculed and made to feel different. Eleven students felt that special class placement actually hurt their chances for later job placement.

Although the studies described here often do not meet the methodological standards of the rigorous experimentalist, they clearly suggest the deleterious effects of expectancies, attitudes of nonretarded individuals, and negative self-concepts. The tendency to attribute no significance to these factors, because of inadequate designs, when in fact they may exert a considerable impact upon the life chances of many individuals, should be avoided. The primary goal of diagnosis and classification should be to facilitate the life chances of individuals who, for various reasons, encounter difficulty in acquiring the skills necessary for independent community living. As Throne (1972) has argued, assessment should be directed toward the "production of intelligent behavior." Defensible reasons exist for maintaining presently popular classification systems which rely upon static measures of mutable forms of behavior. However, we cannot include among these defensible reasons direct contribution to the life chances of children who have been classified mildly, moderately, severely, or profoundly retarded. In fact, the adjustment of many individuals, particularly those classified as mildly or moderately retarded, may have been harmed through the apparent insistence upon the applied utility of such measures as IQ for disposition.

Other Approaches to Diagnosis and Classification[1]

In the active modificational approach to mental retardation (Feuerstein, 1970, 1972), intelligence is viewed as modifiable, with changes occurring as a function of the organism-environment interaction. Rather than emphasizing measurement of static mental functions and knowledge (the products of intelligence), this approach emphasizes assessment of each individual's learning potential. Further, it stresses teaching principles and concepts which can be applied to numerous situations.

Feuerstein (1970) has developed a Learning Potential Assessment Device (LPAD) to "assess general learning modifiability, the amount of teaching investment necessary to bring about changes, the probability of transfer of new learning to other areas, and the examinee's preferred cognitive modalities" (p. 362). On the basis of clinical information obtained from the LPAD, he has also developed an "instrumental enrichment program." Instrumental enrichment focuses on ameliorating deficits in intellectual functioning which have been pinpointed by the LPAD as the causal factors of poor intellectual performance. The rationale for this program is based on the assumption that the individual must develop strategies for interacting with his environment rather than merely increasing his variety of experiences.

Another approach to diagnosis and classification stems from the systematic analysis of intelligence made by Hunt (1961), who has reintroduced Piaget's interaction-adaptation

[1]We are grateful to Gisela Chatelanat for her invaluable contribution to this section. The psychometric integrity of the procedures discussed here is still largely undetermined. Additional research must provide information on reliability and validity.

theory as a major contribution to developmental approaches to human behavior. Piaget's theory (Piaget, 1952, 1954, 1970; Piaget and Inhelder, 1969) provides both the logic and the preliminary data necessary to question most of our current approaches to intellectual assessment and the classification of human behavior (see also Chapter Twenty-Three in this book).

In the model of development proposed by Piaget and his colleagues, interaction is considered the fundamental developmental process. The perspective here is much the same as the one used by geneticists. The epigenetic position is particularly well articulated by Dobzhansky (1972, p. 530):

> In flies, as well as in men, the genetic endowment determines the entire range of reactions, realized and unrealized, of the developing organism in all possible environments. A much less happy formulation, often met with in the literature, is that the genotype determines the limits, the upper and the lower extremes, which a character, say a geotactic response, or stature, or IQ, can reach. This would make sense only if we were able to test the reactions of a genotype in all possible environments. Environments are infinitely variable, however, and new ones are constantly invented and added. . . . It would require not a scientific but something like a divine knowledge to predict how much the stature, or IQ, or mathematic ability of any individual or population could be raised by environmental or educational modifications or improvements.

More simply, this position assumes that the full range of biological and behavioral structures and their functions is determined by an inevitable and unceasing interaction between genetic determiners and the full range of environments encountered by the organism.

As an infant interacts with his environment, structural and conceptual organizations of behavior are formed, which will alter the subsequent interactions the child has with future environments. By analyzing the ways in which particular interactions organize a young child's behavior and by determining how specific organizations operate as prerequisites to subsequent forms of behavior, we can diagnose deficits and structure forms and sequences of subsequent interactions which could ameliorate these deficits.

As an example of the interaction position, Sinclair-de-

Zwart (1969) has described the mechanisms by which the Piagetian sensory-motor developments occur during the first years after birth and the means by which they become coordinated as the basis of complex cognitive processes as well as the foundation of language. The sequence of sensory-motor schemes develops out of the reflexive system of the neonate as a consequence of the biological system interacting with the environment. As schemes become elaborated in this way, they move in the direction of providing a preverbal knowledge of events and relationships. The child learns to depress the button to release the jack-in-the-box. His mastery of wind-up cars progresses from manual propulsion to interest in and competence with the key. His grasp of the permanence of objects moves from search for a partially hidden familiar object to systematic search for an object which is no longer where he last saw it. He learns to chain and embed schemes when he coordinates means to achieve an end, such as pulling a platform toward him to grasp what is on it or pulling a chair to a counter in order to get what is on the counter. He relates objects to action and other objects to himself; for instance, he uses a mallet to sound the xylophone, places a doll in bed, feeds a doll with a spoon, drinks milk from a cup, stirs ice cream with a spoon. These and other facets of knowledge pertaining to space and timing of events in turn become coordinated. This basic interaction between those schemes already in the child's repertoire and new environmental experiences or modification of familiar stimuli allows the child to develop new responses. Clearly, each new response is predicated on the child's existing schemes—a point too often neglected in training programs for children.

The developmental model such as that proposed by Piaget has served as the basis for a diagnostic and educational system called *constructive interaction adaptation* (Bricker, 1973). This system begins with the reflexive behavior of an infant, moves progressively to complex adult performance, and can form a basis of the functional analysis of behavior. Even the most profoundly handicapped infant or child exhibits forms of behavior which fall somewhere within this complex continuum.

The first step in formulating the constructive interaction adaptation system according to a functional analysis approach is to map the sequence and relationships among the progressive developmental steps or stages. Much of this can be done through reference to the developmental literature on children and adolescents. The sequence of development in each of the behavioral divisions selected for schematic representation serves as the critical information, not the age at which each development is supposed to occur. Age of occurrence of a particular development clouds the issue because development is then assumed to occur as a result of maturational processes which are determined by biological clocks rather than by the interactions between the child's repertoire and environmental events. Development does take time, but the determiners of change exist within the interaction of the behavioral organization of the child and environmental inputs or demands on the behavior. Consequently, the age of the child can be ignored while his behavioral organization is assessed and a determination made of the types of environmental stimulation that will foster developmental progress. This, in turn, leads to a focus on critical sequences for development rather than critical periods. Given this focus, the developmental descriptions of Gesell and Amatruda (1962), Irwin and Chen (1946), McGraw (1946), and the more recent reviews of Bayley (1970) and Kessen, Haith, and Salapatek (1970), to name only a few, provide an important source of information about developmental sequences in critical areas of human behavior. As indicated by Budde and Menolascino (1971), the organization of these sequences into lattices provides a systematic and convenient schematic representation of the developmental progression.

According to Piaget, infant development can be divided into six major stages. These stages are defined by the complexity and operative characteristics of the schemes occurring at that point in development in each of the five major domains of sensory-motor development: the object permanence concept, physical causality, imitation, the organization of space, and the concept of time. These domains and their developmental sequences are shown in Figure 1, which presents the theoretical framework for training and diagnostic activities during the sensory-motor period of development.

The ascending box structure in Figure 1 is used to represent increasing complexity of behavior that correlates with increasing chronological age. The constructive interaction adaptation approach does not include a concept of maturation or a requirement of normative patterns of development. Consistencies among the sequences of development of children are viewed as the result of approximately equivalent interactive experiences

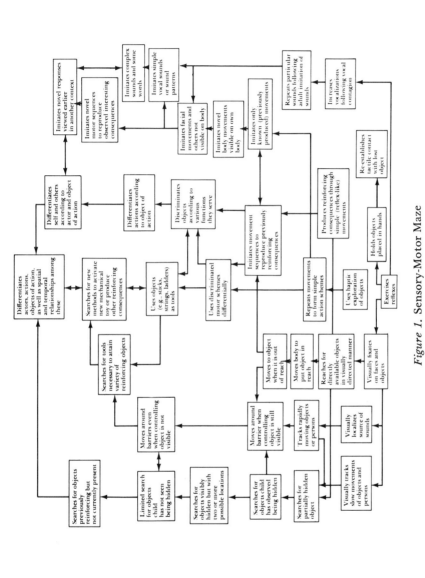

Figure 1. Sensory-Motor Maze

occurring at about the same time as well as logical and empirical requirements of a fixed order of structures or schemes in the developmental process. Thus, starting at the bottom of Figure 1 with the exercising of the reflexes, the order of these schemes is given in a hierarchical manner. This vertical dimension refers to developmental sequences, with schemes the same distance from the baseline coming into existence at approximately the same time. The uppermost boxes in the figure can be viewed as the terminal states in sensory-motor development.

The representation of sensory-motor development presented in Figure 1 is simply an overview of what we have found to be an exciting merger of theory and data at the procedural level. Within the developmental model, procedures must make contact with the abilities of a given child and then specify the range and sequence of instructional events that will provide a stimulating mechanism for moving the child to the next point along the developmental continuum.

An example of how the constructive interaction adaptation system works can be taken from the visual tracking and hand-eye coordination represented at an early level in Figure 1. These forms of behavior have been described developmentally by Bruner (1969) and Burton White (1969), who have indicated the progression of abilities in these areas and the approximate ages at which each phase occurs. In the conventional classification system, the procedures described by Bruner and White could be standardized and then presented to a suitable number of children at various ages to establish more precisely the norms of development. Once this is accomplished, the procedures could then be used to describe the developmental status of a wide range of children (compare the Bayley Scales of Infant Development). With the developmental model, precise norms are not required, since approximations of age of first appearance for each form of behavior could be used to determine whether a child should be tracking a moving object. If assessment indicates that a given child is not tracking in either the vertical or the horizontal directions, then subsequent test items would be irrelevant until this form of behavior could be demonstrated.

One method for training tracking would be to use an object such as a feeding bottle or pacifier that elicits known responses from the child. If the child sucked the pacifier regularly, it could be used directly or it could be dipped in honey if the latter operation produced more active sucking. The pacifier would then be held twelve to sixteen inches from the infant's eyes until the child was judged to make direct visual contact with the pacifier, at which time it would be given to him. This procedure would be repeated a few times until the child fixated on the pacifier almost immediately upon its presentation. Given visual regard of the object, the next step would be to move the pacifier slowly in a horizontal arc for only a few centimeters and then hold it in the new position. If the infant tracked the object, it would then be given to him. If he did not track it, it would be held in the new position until the child made visual contact with the object, which would then be given to him. This cycle could be repeated on a daily basis by the parents, using the pacifier as well as other "interesting" objects in order to stimulate generalized visual tracking in both the vertical and the horizontal planes.

Hand-eye coordination could be established via an over-lapping training routine by moving the pacifier (or other objects) toward the child in a horizontal movement until the object was within reach of the child. His hands could be physically guided to the object and held in the bimanual grasp position as the object was moved by the adult during the early phases to the child's mouth, where he could suck for a few seconds. As the cycle was repeated, the use of physical guidance could be faded until the child was reaching, grasping, and then moving the object to his mouth without assistance. Thus, the parents would not be simply informed that their child's behavior was not at the norm in this area; instead, they would be given a method of instruction that could be used at home. If the child was not severely delayed, then the procedures could be used infrequently and casually, and presented as an interaction game. However, if the child were substantially behind in this skill, the parents could use the procedures daily in a more formal manner. Shaping in the operant sense (using the pacifier as a reinforcer) would be employed in conjunction with a data-based measurement system to detect changes in rate or probability of correct response.

This example of moving directly from testing to instruction demonstrates several important features of the model. *First, the form of behavior being tested is shown to be a fundamental step in developmental progress.* Visual fixation and visual tracking are prerequisite to hand-eye coordination, which

is itself prerequisite to a number of important schemes including that of object permanence. The areas assessed are critical for
development and are not simply forms of behavior that predict
subsequent development. *Second, the test is given sequentially
until the response of the child is not appropriate, at which time
testing stops and instruction begins.* Thus, if the child fails to
demonstrate a prerequisite process, the assumption is made that
he will fail in a more complex area. *Third, the initial forms of
instruction in an area are used to explore the parameters of the
child's repertoire in that area in order to determine the reasons
for his failure.* Once the reasons for failure (for instance, lack of
motivation or the absence of one or more prerequisite processes) have been determined, then the information can be used
to structure the necessary training. When criterion performance
is reached, the assessment procedure is resumed until another
gap or deficiency is detected in the child's repertoire, at which
point training is again initiated.

Essentially, the same approach can be employed in the
establishment of more advanced cognitive, linguistic, preacademic, and academic skills. For example, Figure 2 contains a
language-training lattice that can be used both to identify
behavioral deficits in the area of language and then to provide
the programmatic structure to eliminate the deficits.

The lattice in Figure 2 contains the general areas of the
language model and can be looked at as an upward extension of
sensory-motor development. The boxes above the ascending
diagonal represent the sequence of terminal behavior to be
established as a consequence of the training programs underlying them. In turn, the program boxes under the diagonal contain the hypothesized sequence of training steps. Along the
bottom of the lattice are those programs which are continued
throughout the entire span of language training specified by the
model. The terminal-state boxes represent a sequential arrangement of increasing developmental capability, moving from simple response learning to the production of simple sentences.

The program boxes are placed to represent hierarchical
sequences in both the vertical and horizontal dimensions for the
areas of auditory assessment, receptive vocabulary, verbal imitation of sounds and words, object and event naming, and finally
syntactic comprehension and production. An assessment procedure is used to determine a child's repertoire in each specific
area of this language lattice. The assessment procedure generally

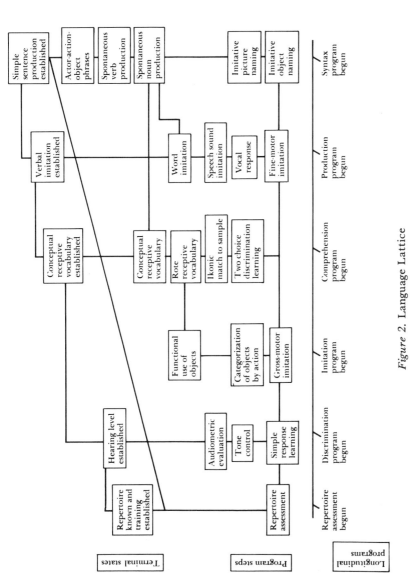

Figure 2. Language Lattice

provides the pretest and posttest data that serve as the target dependent measure. In addition, each assessment procedure is directly linked to the subsequent training strategy, as in the sensory-motor training. Assessment of this nature provides the teacher with information about the responses the child needs to develop to continue to progress upward in the lattice. For example, the child could be given an assessment to determine how many of the twenty-four major English consonants he can imitate. The child's performance might indicate that he is unable to produce the *t, ch, sh, s,* and *z* sounds. This information allows the teacher to begin immediately building a program for training imitation of the five sounds produced in error.

The developmental training models for sensory-motor and language skills presented in Figures 1 and 2 provide the basis for a system of linked assessment and training which is being used in the Infant, Toddler, and Preschool Research and Intervention Project, an early intervention project for young children (D. Bricker and W. Bricker, 1971, 1972, 1973). Although this project includes normally developing children, the target population is preschool children who are demonstrating significant developmental delays or who are at risk for developmental problems such as Down's syndrome or hydrocephalus.

The project, located in the John F. Kennedy Center for Research on Education and Human Development of George Peabody College, is composed of three basic components: classroom, parent training, and research. Educational and social services are provided for approximately seventy-five children and their families. The children, ranging in age from three to seventy months, are assigned to one of five classroom divisions: one crib unit, two toddler units, and two preschool units. All classes but the crib unit contain roughly equal numbers of children who behave within normal limits and children who demonstrate significant developmental delays in critical areas such as language, motor, social, or cognitive processes. Children with no significant deficits are included in order to provide models for the children experiencing developmental problems and to provide data on the acquisition of cognitive and linguistic processes. A parent-training component provides parent counseling and instruction in self-help skills, toileting, language training, motor development, and more general principles of child development. The goal of this training is to assist the parent in becoming the primary change agent in the child's life. The goal of the research component is to answer questions which have direct relevance to the classroom and home setting.

In this project we are attempting to implement the system of linked assessment and training in four major skill areas: language, sensory-motor and preoperational behavior, motor skills, and social development. The basic approach in each area is to assess the specific skills necessary for the development of a generative behavioral repertoire in a specified area. The next step is to build a training program based on the results of the assessment. In the area of language development, for example, functional classification of objects serves as a major link between training in sensory-motor areas and language (W. Bricker and D. Bricker, in press). The use and arrangement of objects according to functional classification appears at the end of the sensory-motor stage and develops throughout the substages of preoperational intelligence, when the child acquires more varied and sophisticated ways of categorizing objects in his environment. Our assessment of the functional classification skills of young children is based on Piaget's concept of classification (Inhelder and Piaget, 1964). We provide the child with a series of common objects and then carefully observe and record how he uses the objects in isolation and/or in tandem with other objects. If, during a pretraining phase, the child indicates that he can use or classify most of the items on the assessment, the teacher or trainer moves to the next step in the program. However, if the child repeatedly demonstrates an inability to use objects appropriately, training is instituted. An object that appears on the assessment and that is particularly relevant to the child is selected for training. The teacher manipulates the object in an appropriate manner while ensuring that the child is observing her. For example, a cup should elicit a drinking response. The teacher demonstrates the drinking movement and then offers the cup to the child. If the child does not spontaneously imitate or model the teacher's response with the cup, the teacher again demonstrates drinking from the cup and immediately prompts the child to drink from it. Over time and as a function of appropriate responses, the physical prompts are gradually faded out. Once the child is spontaneously drinking from the cup, the teacher demonstrates a second appropriate response to be used with the cup, a response such as pouring. A shaping procedure is again used if the child does not spontaneously model the teacher's second demonstration. The teacher proceeds until the child acquires several discrete, appropriate responses to the cup; then a second object is introduced, and the child is trained by the same system. Training is continued across objects until the child demonstrates an ability to classify several objects functionally. The assessment instrument is then readministered and the child's performance compared with his initial responses. If criterion is met, the child is ready to move on in the program. If not, the teacher returns to teaching the use of additional objects.

Once the child is demonstrating an ability to classify functionally many common objects such as spoons, cars, babies, chairs, and apples, training moves into a subsequent program area such as verbal imitation. While the procedures used in the sensory-motor and functional classification areas are again employed, the content is different. The child is asked to produce twenty-four consonants, which are divided into five levels as indicated by an analysis of error-production data of young retarded and nonretarded children (W. Bricker, 1967; W. Bricker and D. Bricker, 1972). Level I of the assessment contains easy-to-produce sounds while Levels II through V contain progressively more difficult sounds. If the child fails to reach criterion at Level I, training is begun with those sounds the child failed to produce correctly. If he produces all Level-I sounds appropriately, he is tested on subsequent levels until error responses are produced, at which point training is begun.

Testing of receptive and expressive processes can occur simultaneously with verbal-imitation assessment and training. Receptive testing and training begins with word-length units and moves gradually to phrase- and sentence-length units. Again, common objects are selected for initial testing. The child is confronted with two or more choices and asked to select a single object from among various items. Training is begun if the child consistently fails to select the named objects. The same procedure is followed with the expressive items except that the child is asked to name specific objects. If the child passes the initial levels of comprehension and expression, assessment is moved to more complex levels of language comprehension and production.

Once the child is producing two-word utterances, assessment and training of his ability to apply syntactical rules is appropriate. Again the child is asked to imitate, comprehend, and produce more and more complex responses as he demonstrates competence at the simpler levels. When the competence breaks down, as before, training is initiated to assist the child in acquiring the set of responses which will lead, eventually, to the generation of novel, grammatically correct, semantically appropriate sentences.

To date, the results of this approach indicate that it is viable, although certainly not the only method that could be employed. As illustrated, this system links assessment directly with intervention. The assessment provides relevant information that assists the teacher and/or parent in structuring the content of the next training step for the child to progress in a developmental sequence.

Conclusions and Recommendations

Current classification systems, heavily dependent upon standardized measures of intelligence, have not contributed directly to the effective and efficient education and training of children diagnosed and classified as mentally retarded. The use of IQ tests can be justified on several grounds: (1) they are legitimate instruments for use in the scientific study of individual differences; (2) they provide a convenient operational definition which enhances communication; (3) they are valid predictors of large-group differences in academic achievement. However, they do not supply information that can be used by a teacher or parent to facilitate the acquisition of essential forms of behavior and therefore should not be used as the sole basis for special class placement (see Neisworth, 1969; Reynolds and Balow, 1972). In discussing the work of Piaget, we have attempted to detail an alternative method of assessment based on the developmental approach to mental retardation. Specifically, we have suggested that the integration of principles derived from the empirical analysis of behavior with a developmental model such as that proposed by Piaget provides a unified approach, termed the *constructive interaction adaptation system,* in which behavior can be classified, not children. Further, the assessment and classification of behavior using a system in which assessment is linked to training leads directly into educational programming for individual children, which presently appears to be the most functional approach to the modification and improvement of retarded development.

The following recommendations are based on the findings presented in this chapter.

1. *Public school systems as a whole must be encouraged to develop programs for all children, even the most severely handicapped, within the domains of regular schools.* Blatt (1972) has pointed out that an incentive system might be useful in accomplishing this goal. If the educational system does not elect to achieve this goal itself, the courts might possibly mandate it. As Ross, DeYoung, and Cohen (1971) have indicated, simply placing handicapped children back in regular programs is not a solution. Emphasis must be placed on developing *quality* programs, not just programs. Regulatory mechanisms, such as time limits for placement in special classes and demonstrated gains by the child, could be used to ensure quality programs. As teachers are trained to fill the roles described in the next recommendation, more and more children will be involved in the mainstream of education. Involvement in regular education does not ensure that retarded children will learn the academic, vocational, and/or social skills they will need for independent community living; however, integration into regular classes will help to prevent the debilitating effects of special class placement on emotional and social adjustment.

2. *Teachers must be trained to deal with categories of behavior, not categories of children, and to view retardation as reversible rather than static.* The special needs of children must be documented for teachers, and at least partial responsibility for the amelioration of difficulties or deficits must be given to teachers. Instead of saying "This child is retarded; therefore, he cannot learn," teachers must be trained to say "This child is not learning; what is wrong with my techniques?" (For specific training models, see Reynolds and Balow, 1972; Melcher, 1972; Cartwright and Cartwright, 1972; Tenorio and Raimist, 1971; Schwartz, 1971.) Retraining of teachers to evaluate and meet the needs of all children will allow children with special problems to become part of the regular education system only if the teacher is provided with additional support systems. The use of parents and teacher aides within the classroom can reduce the adult-child ratio and allow more individual instruction to occur.

3. *Psychologists must be trained to assume responsibility not only for evaluation but also for educational programming.* In order for this recommendation to be implemented, state licensing laws for psychometricians and psychologists must be

evaluated and changed where necessary. Simply having a master's degree in psychology and one course in psychological appraisal should not qualify an individual to serve as the primary determiner of where and how children will be educated, particularly since such evaluations have long-range effects on academic, emotional, and social adjustment. New training programs would have to focus on the needs of children with special problems and provide assessment of their competencies via instruments other than IQ or academic achievement tests. Psychometricians who believe that mental retardation is irreversible, that the retarded child cannot learn, or that the retarded child needs to be protected from the pressures of a regular classroom will need extensive retraining.

Training which focuses not only on developing skills in evaluation but also on prescriptive teaching would do away with the distinction between psychologists and educators. If this system were implemented, individuals responsible for evaluations would have to operate within the classroom framework. The evaluator would serve as a resource person for the teacher and an educational change agent for the child. Such an approach has recently been reported by Tenorio and Raimist (1971), who employed "diagnostic-prescriptive teachers" to evaluate children referred by classroom teachers and to decide, by testing a variety of teaching strategies, the best strategy for the classroom teacher to use with the child.

A further implication of this change in the evaluator's role is that retardation would be removed from the psychologist's domain and placed in the domain of education. Such a change could help focus concern on developing adequate educational programs for retarded children within the mainstream of education.

4. *Public school systems must be encouraged to develop preschool intervention programs for retarded children. Such programs should focus on parent training as well as child training.* Parent-training programs could concentrate upon new developments in education and emphasize the potentiality for development of all children. Such training could bring about increased demands for quality programs and might also help parents become more effective educational change agents with their own children.

In preschool intervention programs for both parents and children, an incentive system might be useful. In this area of preschool intervention, as in functional evaluation, continued research is needed if effective educational programming is to be realized. In addition, research which focuses on the development of early detection procedures for retarded children must receive high funding priority.

5. *Funding priority should be given to proposals aimed at developing functional evaluation procedures which are directly linked to teaching strategies.* As Martin (1971) has pointed out, the ostensible purpose of special education is to serve the individual child. However, the use of labels has generally resulted in unsuccessful attempts at homogeneity within classrooms. The focus within education must be on determining variables which result in children learning, not on categorizing children. Instructional systems which substitute competency areas of teachers for "child category language" need to be developed (Reynolds and Balow, 1972). The retarded child's performance must be examined in important developmental areas, such as academic, social, and language skills, within different environmental contexts. If the results of functional evaluations indicate that a child is performing at a level commensurate with regular classes, for these activities the child should be integrated into regular class programs. In areas where a functional evaluation indicates that a child needs special training, the training sequence must have an exit. The functional evaluation should be directly linked to teaching sequences, and completion of these should lead to return to the regular classroom situation. The contract system proposed by Gallagher (1972) must be carefully evaluated. This system places time limits on how long the educable child can be removed from the regular classroom. Evaluation of such a system should be conducted for all handicapped children, no matter how severe the handicap.

6. *Incentive systems and changes in categorical funding which are designed to enhance the possibility of public school systems working with retarded children must be carefully developed.* As Blatt (1972) has indicated, legislation designed to de-label children can result in decreased support for special services for handicapped children. Removing categorical labels which have been shown to have deleterious effects on children's development should not imply that such children do not need special services. We must develop administrative systems that do not depend on categorical labels, decrease financial support, segregate handicapped persons into totally separate environments, or

encourage labeling of children who could profit from a regular school environment as children with special needs so as to obtain more funds. Placing children with special needs within a regular classroom will not diminish the need for supplementary funding for the education of these children.

References

Adams, J. "Adaptive Behavior and Measured Intelligence in the Classification of Mental Retardation." *American Journal of Mental Deficiency*, 1973, *78*, 77-81.

Ainsworth, S. H. *An Exploratory Study of Educational, Social and Emotional Factors in the Education of Mentally Retarded Children in Georgia Public Schools*. Athens: University of Georgia, 1959.

American Psychiatric Association. *Diagnostic and Statistical Manual of Mental Disorders*. (2nd Ed.) Washington, D.C.: American Psychiatric Association, 1968.

Baumeister, A. A. "The American Residential Institution: Its History and Character." In A. A. Baumeister and E. Butterfield (Eds.), *Residential Facilities for the Mentally Retarded*. Chicago: Aldine, 1970.

Bayley, N. "Development of Mental Abilities." In P. H. Mussen (Ed.), *Carmichael's Manual of Child Psychology*. (3rd Ed.) New York: Wiley, 1970.

Becker, H. S. *Outsiders: Studies in the Sociology of Deviance*. New York: Free Press, 1963.

Beez, W. V. "Influence of Biased Psychological Reports on Teacher Behavior and Pupil Performance." *Proceedings of the 76th Annual Convention of the American Psychological Association*, 1968, *3*, 605-606.

Bennett, A. *A Comparative Study of Subnormal Children in the Elementary Grades*. New York: Teachers College, Columbia University, 1932.

Bijou, S. W. "Theory and Research in Mental (Developmental) Retardation." *Psychological Record*, 1963, *13*, 95-110.

Blatt, B. "Public Policy and the Education of Children with Special Needs." *Exceptional Children*, 1972, *38*, 537-545.

Bricker, D. D., and Bricker, W. A. *Toddler Research and Intervention Project Report: Year I*. Nashville: Institute on Mental Retardation and Intellectual Development, George Peabody College, 1971.

Bricker, D. D., and Bricker, W. A. *Toddler Research and Intervention Project Report: Year II*. Nashville: Institute on Mental Retardation and Intellectual Development, George Peabody College, 1972.

Bricker, D. D., and Bricker, W. A. *Toddler Research and Intervention Project Report: Year III*. Nashville: Institute on Mental Retardation and Intellectual Development, George Peabody College, 1973.

Bricker, W. A. "Errors in the Echoic Behavior of Preschool Children."
    Journal of Speech and Hearing Research, 1967, *10*, 67-76.
Bricker, W. A. "The Constructive Interaction Adaptation System: A New
    Approach to the Education of Young Children." Colloquium pre-
    sented at University of Wisconsin, Madison, Oct. 1973.
Bricker, W. A., and Bricker, D. D. "Assessment and Modification of Verbal
    Imitation with Low-Functioning Children." *Journal of Speech and
    Hearing Research*, 1972, *15*, 690-698.
Bricker, W. A., and Bricker, D. D. "An Early Language Training Strategy."
    In R. Schiefelbush and L. Lloyd (Eds.), *Language Perspectives—
    Acquisition, Retardation and Intervention*. Baltimore: University
    Park Press, in press.
Brison, D. W. "Definition, Diagnosis, and Classification." In A. A. Bau-
    meister (Ed.), *Mental Retardation*. Chicago: Aldine, 1967.
Bronfenbrenner, U. "Is Early Intervention Effective?" Paper presented at
    meeting of Society for Research in Child Development, Philadel-
    phia, March 29-April 1, 1973.
Bruner, J. S. "Eye, Hand, and Mind." In D. Elkind and J. H. Flavell (Eds.),
    Studies in Cognitive Development: Essays in Honor of Jean Piaget.
    New York: Oxford University Press, 1969.
Budde, J. F., and Menolascino, F. G. "Utilization of Systems Technology
    for Vocational Rehabilitation of the Severely Retarded." *Mental
    Retardation*, 1971, *2*, 11-16.
Butterfield, E. C. "The Role of Environmental Factors in the Treatment of
    Institutionalized Mental Retardates." In A. A. Baumeister (Ed.),
    Mental Retardation. Chicago: Aldine, 1967.
Butterfield, E. C. "Basic Facts About Public Residential Facilities for the
    Mentally Retarded." In R. Kugel and W. Wolfensberger (Eds.),
    *Changing Patterns of Residential Services for the Mentally Re-
    tarded*. Washington, D.C.: U.S. Government Printing Office, 1969.
Cain, L. F., and Levine, S. *Effects of Community and Institutional School
    Programs on Trainable Mentally Retarded Children*. Washington,
    D.C.: Council for Exceptional Children, 1963.
Cartwright, G. P., and Cartwright, C. A. "Gilding the Lilly: Comments on
    the Training Based Model." *Exceptional Children*, 1972, *39*,
    231-234.
Cassidy, V. M., and Stanton, J. E. *An Investigation of Factors Involved in
    the Educational Placement of Mentally Retarded Children: A
    Study of Differences Between Children in Special and Regular
    Classes in Ohio*. Columbus: Ohio State University, 1959.
Centerwall, S. A., and Centerwall, W. R. "A Study of Children with Mon-
    golism Reared in the Home Compared to Those Reared away from
    Home." *Pediatrics*, 1960, *25*, 678-685.
Cutts, R. A., and Lane, M. "The Effect of Hospitalization on Wechsler-
    Bellevue Subtest Scores by Mental Defectives." *American Journal
    of Mental Deficiency*, 1947, *51*, 391-393.

Delp, H. A., and Lorenz, M. "Follow-Up of 84 Public School Special Class Pupils with IQ's Below 50." *American Journal of Mental Deficiency*, 1953, *58*, 175-182.

Dent, H. E. "An Investigation of the Influence of Mental Retardation on College Students' Judgments of Social Distance." *Dissertation Abstracts*, 1967, *28*, 1899-1900.

Dobzhansky, T. "Genetics and the Diversity of Behavior." *American Psychologist*, 1972, *27*, 523-530.

Dunn, L. M. *Exceptional Children in the Schools.* New York: Holt, 1963.

Dunn, L. M. "Children with Moderate and Severe General Learning Disabilities." In L. M. Dunn (Ed.), *Exceptional Children in the Schools.* (2nd Ed.) New York: Holt, 1973.

Edgerton, R. B. *The Cloak of Competence: Stigma in the Lives of the Retarded.* Berkeley: University of California Press, 1967.

Farber, B. *Mental Retardation: Its Social Context and Social Consequences.* Boston: Houghton Mifflin, 1968.

Feuerstein, R. "A Dynamic Approach to the Causation, Prevention, and Alleviation of Retarded Performance." In H. C. Haywood (Ed.), *Social-Cultural Aspects of Mental Retardation.* New York: Appleton-Century-Crofts, 1970.

Feuerstein, R. *Studies in Cognitive Modifiability: A Proposal to Study the Effects of IE on the Cognitive Functions of Retarded Early Adolescents.* Jerusalem: Hadassah-Wizo-Canada Research Institute, 1972.

Fouracre, M. H., Connor, F. P., and Goldberg, I. I. *The Effects of a Preschool Program upon Young Educable Mentally Retarded Children.* Vol. 1: *Measurable Growth and Development.* New York: Teachers College, Columbia University, 1962.

Gallagher, J. J. "The Special Education Contract for Mildly Handicapped Children." *Exceptional Children*, 192, *38*, 527-535.

Galton, F. *Inquiries into Human Faculty and Its Development.* London: Macmillan, 1883.

Gelof, M. "Comparisons of Systems of Classifications Relating Degrees of Retardation to Measured Intelligence." *American Journal of Mental Deficiency*, 1963, *68*, 297-317.

Gesell, A., and Amatruda, C. S. *Developmental Diagnosis.* New York: Paul B. Hoeber, 1962.

Goldberg, I. I., and Cruickshank, W. M. "The Trainable But Non-educable: Whose Responsibility?" *National Education Association Journal*, 1958, *47*, 622-623.

Goldstein, H. *Study Projects for Trainable Mentally Handicapped Children.* Springfield: Superintendent of Public Instruction, State of Illinois, 1956.

Goldstein, H., Moss, J. W., and Jordan, L. J. *The Efficacy of Special Class Training on the Development of Mentally Retarded Children.* Urbana, Ill.: Institute for Research on Exceptional Children, 1965.

Gray, S. W., and Klaus, R. A. "An Experimental Preschool Program for Culturally Deprived Children." *Child Development*, 1965, *36*, 885-898.

Grossman, H. J. *Manual on Terminology and Classification in Mental Retardation.* Baltimore: Garamond/Pridemark, 1973.

Guenther, R. J. *Final Report of the Michigan Demonstration Research Project for the Severely Retarded.* Lansing, Mich.: Department of Public Instruction, 1956.

Guskin, S. L. "The Perception of Subnormality in Mentally Defective Children." *American Journal of Mental Deficiency*, 1962, *67*, 53-60.

Guskin, S. L., and Spicker, H. H. "Educational Research in Mental Retardation." In N. R. Ellis (Ed.), *International Review of Research in Mental Retardation.* New York: Academic Press, 1968.

Haskett, M. S. "An Investigation of the Relationship Between Teacher Expectancy and Pupil Achievement in the Special Education Class." *Dissertation Abstracts*, 1969, *29*, 4348-4349.

Haywood, H. C. "Behavioral Research in Mental Retardation: Goals for a New Decade." *Alabama Journal of Medical Sciences*, 1969, *6*, 378-381.

Haywood, H. C. "Labeling: Efficacy, Evils, and Caveats." Paper presented at the Joseph P. Kennedy, Jr., Foundation International Symposium on Human Rights, Retardation, and Research, Washington, D.C., Oct. 1971.

Haywood, H. C. "Intelligence, Distribution of." *Encyclopaedia Britannica*, in press.

Heber, R. F. *A Manual on Terminology and Classification in Mental Retardation. American Journal of Mental Deficiency*, 1959. Monograph supplement.

Heber, R. F. *A Manual on Terminology and Classification in Mental Retardation.* (2nd Ed.) *American Journal of Mental Deficiency*, 1961. Monograph supplement.

Heber, R. F. "The Educable Mentally Retarded." In S. A. Kirk and B. B. Weiner (Eds.), *Behavioral Research on Exceptional Children.* Washington, D.C.: Council for Exceptional Children, National Education Association, 1963.

Heber, R. F., and Dever, R. B. "Research on Education and Habilitation of the Mentally Retarded." In H. C. Haywood (Ed.), *Social-Cultural Aspects of Mental Retardation.* New York: Appleton-Century-Crofts, 1970.

Hodges, W. L., McCandless, B. R., and Spicker, H. H. *Diagnostic Teaching for Preschool Children.* Arlington, Va.: Council for Exceptional Children, 1971.

Hottel, J. V. *An Evaluation of Tennessee's Day Class Program for Severely Mentally Retarded Children.* Nashville: George Peabody College for Teachers, 1958.

Hunt, J. McV. *Intelligence and Experience.* New York: Ronald Press, 1961.

Hurley, O. L. *Poverty and Mental Retardation: A Causal Relationship.*
New York: Random House, 1969.
Inhelder, B., and Piaget, J. *The Early Growth of Logic in the Child.* New
York: Norton, 1964.
Irwin, O. C., and Chen, H. P. "Infant Speech: Vowel and Consonant Fre-
quency." *Journal of Speech Disorders,* 1946, *11,* 123-125.
Jaffe, J. "Attitudes of Adolescents Toward the Mentally Retarded." *Amer-
ican Journal of Mental Deficiency,* 1966, *70,* 907-912.
Jaffe, J. "Attitudes and Interpersonal Contact: Relationships Between
Contact with the Mentally Retarded and Dimensions of Attitude."
Journal of Counseling Psychology, 1967, *14,* 482-484.
Jewell, A. M. "A Follow-Up Study of 190 Mentally Deficient Children
Excluded Because of Low Mentality from the Public Schools of the
District of Columbia." *American Journal of Mental Deficiency,*
1941, *45,* 413-420.
Johnson, G. O., and Capobianco, R. J. *Research Project on Severely Re-
tarded Children.* Albany: New York State Interdepartmental
Health Resources Board, 1957.
Jones, R. L. "New Labels in Old Bags: Research on Labeling Blacks Cul-
turally Disadvantaged, Culturally Deprived, and Mentally Re-
tarded." Paper presented at annual convention of Association of
Black Psychologists, Miami Beach, Sept. 1970.
Jones, R. L. "Labels and Stigma in Special Education." *Exceptional Chil-
dren,* 1972, *38,* 553-564.
Kessen, W., Haith, M. M., and Salapatek, P. H. "Infancy." In P. H. Mussen
(Ed.), *Carmichael's Manual of Child Psychology.* (3rd Ed.) New
York: Wiley, 1970.
Kirk, S. A. *Early Education of the Mentally Retarded.* Urbana: University
of Illinois Press, 1958.
Kirk, S. A. "Research in Education." In H. A. Stevens and R. Heber
(Eds.), *Mental Retardation: A Review of Research.* Chicago: Uni-
versity of Chicago Press, 1964.
Kugel, R. B., and Wolfensberger, W. (Eds.) *Changing Patterns in Residen-
tial Services for the Mentally Retarded.* Washington, D.C.: U.S.
Government Printing Office, 1969.
Lyle, J. G. "The Effect of an Institution Environment upon the Verbal
Development of Imbecile Children." *Journal of Mental Deficiency
Research,* 1960, *4,* 14-23.
Mackie, R. P., and Robbins, P. P. *Exceptional Children and Youth: A
Chart Book of Special Education Enrollments in Public Day
Schools of the United States.* Washington, D.C.: U.S. Government
Printing Office, 1961.
Mahoney, S. C., and Pangrac, I. "Misconceptions of College Students
About Mental Deficiency." *American Journal of Mental Defi-
ciency,* 1960, *64,* 671-678.
Martin, E. W. "Individualism and Behaviorism as Future Trends in Educat-

ing Handicapped Children." *Exceptional Children,* 1972, *38,* 517-525.

McClelland, D. C. "Testing for Competence Rather Than for 'Intelligence.' " *American Psychologist,* 1973, *28,* 1-14.

McGraw, M. B. "Maturation of Behavior." In L. Carmichael (Ed.), *Manual of Child Psychology.* New York: Wiley, 1946.

Meichenbaum, D. H., Bowers, K. S., and Ross, R. R. "A Behavioral Analysis of Teacher Expectancy Effect." *Journal of Personality and Social Psychology,* 1969, *13,* 306-316.

Melcher, J. W. "Labels and Stigma in Special Education." *Exceptional Children,* 1972, *38,* 547-550.

Mercer, J. R. "Social System Perspective and Clinical Perspective: Frames of Reference for Understanding Career Patterns of Persons Labelled as Mentally Retarded." *Social Problems,* 1965, *13,* 18-34.

Mercer, J. R. "Sociological Perspectives on Mild Mental Retardation." In H. C. Haywood (Ed.), *Social-Cultural Aspects of Mental Retardation.* New York: Appleton-Century-Crofts, 1970.

Mercer, J. R. "Sociocultural Factors in Labeling Mental Retardates." *Peabody Journal of Education,* 1971, *48,* 188-204.

Miller, J. O. "Cultural Deprivation and Its Modification: Effects of Intervention." In H. C. Haywood (Ed.), *Social-Cultural Aspects of Mental Retardation.* New York: Appleton-Century-Crofts, 1970.

Miller, M. B., and Bialer, I. "Intellectual Deviancy." In H. C. Haywood (Ed.), *Psychometric Intelligence.* New York: Appleton-Century-Crofts, in press.

Mullen, F. A., and Itkin, W. *Achievement and Adjustment of Educable Mentally Handicapped Children.* Chicago: Board of Education, 1961.

Neisworth, J. T. "The Educational Irrelevance of Intelligence." In R. M. Smith (Ed.), *Teacher Diagnosis of Educational Difficulties.* Columbus, Ohio: Merrill, 1969.

Nihira, K., and others. *Adaptive Behavior Scales.* Washington, D.C.: American Association on Mental Deficiency, 1969.

Piaget, J. *The Origins of Intelligence in Children.* New York: Norton, 1952.

Piaget, J. *The Construction of Reality in the Child.* New York: Ballantine, 1954.

Piaget, J. "Piaget's Theory." In P. H. Mussen (Ed.), *Carmichael's Manual of Child Psychology.* Vol. I. New York: Wiley, 1970.

Piaget, J., and Inhelder, B. *The Psychology of the Child.* New York: Basic Books, 1969.

President's Committee on Mental Retardation. *The Six-Hour Retarded Child.* Washington, D.C.: U.S. Government Printing Office, 1970.

Reynolds, M. C., and Balow, B. "Categories and Variables in Special Education." *Exceptional Children,* 1972, *38,* 357-366.

Reynolds, M. C., and Kiland, J. R. *A Study of Public School Children with*

Severe Mental Retardation. St. Paul: Minnesota State Department of Education, 1953.

Rosenthal, R., and Jacobson, L. "Teacher Expectancies: Determinants of Pupils' I.Q. Gains." *Psychological Reports,* 1966, *19,* 115-118.

Rosenthal, R., and Jacobson, L. *Pygmalion in the Classroom.* New York: Holt, 1968.

Ross, S. L., DeYoung, H. G., and Cohen, J. S. "Confrontation: Special Education Placement and the Law." *Exceptional Children,* 1971, *38,* 5-12.

Saenger, G. *The Adjustment of Severely Retarded Adults in the Community.* Albany: New York State Interdepartmental Health Resources Board, 1957.

Schwartz, L. "A Clinical Teacher Model for Interrelated Areas of Special Education." *Exceptional Children,* 1971, *37,* 565-571.

Sinclair-de-Zwart, H. "Developmental Psycholinguistics." In D. Elkind and J. H. Flavell (Eds.), *Studies in Cognitive Development.* New York: Oxford University Press, 1969.

Skinner, B. F. *Science and Human Behavior.* New York: Macmillan, 1953.

Spitzer, R. L., and Wilson, P. T. "A Guide to the American Psychiatric Association's New Diagnostic Nomenclature." *American Journal of Psychiatry,* 1968a, *124,* 1619-1629.

Spitzer, R. L., and Wilson, P. T. "An Introduction to the American Psychiatric Association's New Diagnostic Nomenclature for New York State Department of Mental Hygiene Personnel." *Psychiatric Quarterly,* 1968b, *42,* 487-503.

Stedman, D. J., and Eichorn, D. H. "A Comparative Study of the Growth and Development Trends of Institutionalized and Noninstitutionalized Mongoloid Children." *American Journal of Mental Deficiency,* 1964, *69,* 391-401.

Stevenson, H. W. "Reaction to: U. Bronfenbrenner, Is Early Intervention Effective?" Paper presented at meeting of Society for Research in Child Development, Philadelphia, March 1973.

Tenorio, S. C., and Raimist, L. I. "A Noncategorical Consortium Program." *Exceptional Children,* 1971, *38,* 325-326.

Thorndike, R. L. "Review of Rosenthal, R., and Jacobson, L., *Pygmalion in the Classroom.*" *American Educational Research Journal,* 1968, *5,* 708-711.

Throne, J. M. "The Assessment of Intelligence." *Mental Retardation,* 1972, *10*(5), 9-11.

Thurstone, T. G. *An Evaluation of Educating Mentally Handicapped Children in Special Classes and in Regular Grades.* Chapel Hill: University of North Carolina, 1959.

Tisdall, W. J. "A Follow-Up Study of Trainable Mentally Handicapped Children in Illinois." *American Journal of Mental Deficiency,* 1960, *65,* 11-16.

U.S. Department of Health, Education, and Welfare. *International Classi-*

fication of Diseases, Adapted for Use in the United States. (8th Ed.) Washington, D.C.: U.S. Government Printing Office, 1967.

Weikart, D. P., and Lambie, D. Z. "Early Enrichment in Infants." In V. H. Denenberg (Ed.), *Education of the Infant and Young Child.* New York: Academic Press, 1970.

White, B. L. "The Initial Coordination of Sensorimotor Schemas in Human Infants—Piaget's Ideas and the Role of Experience." In D. Elkind and J. H. Flavell (Eds.), *Studies in Cognitive Development.* New York: Oxford University Press, 1969.

White, W. D., and Wolfensberger, W. "The Evolution of Dehumanization in Our Institutions." *Mental Retardation,* 1969, *7,* 5-9.

Willey, N. R. "A Study of Social Stereotype and Mentally Retarded Children." *Dissertation Abstracts,* 1967, *27,* 3241-3242.

Wilson, P. T., and Spitzer, R. L. "Major Changes in Psychiatric Nomenclature." *Hospital and Community Psychiatry,* 1968, *19,* 169-174.

Wilson, P. T., and Spitzer, R. L. "A Comparison of Three Current Classification Systems for Mental Retardation." *American Journal of Mental Deficiency,* 1969, *74,* 428-435.

Wilson, W., "Social Psychology and Mental Retardation." In N. R. Ellis (Ed.), *International Review of Research in Special Education.* Vol. 4. New York: Academic Press, 1970.

Windle, C. D. "Prognosis of Mental Subnormals." *American Journal of Mental Deficiency,* 1962, *66,* 1-180.

Wolfensberger, W. "The Origin and Nature of Our Institutional Models." In R. Kugel and W. Wolfensberger (Eds.), *Changing Patterns of Residential Services for the Mentally Retarded.* Washington, D.C.: U.S. Government Printing Office, 1969.

Wolfensberger, W. "Models of Mental Retardation." *New Society,* 1970, *15,* 51-53.

Wolfensberger, W. *The Principle of Normalization in Human Services.* Toronto: National Institute on Mental Retardation, 1972.

World Health Organization. *International Classification of Diseases.* (8th Ed.) Geneva: World Health Organization, 1968.

Wrightstone, J. W., and others. *A Comparison of Educational Outcomes Under Single-Track and Two-Track Plans for Educable Mentally Retarded Children.* New York: New York Board of Education, 1959.

9

PHYSICAL AND SENSORY HANDICAPS

Frances P. Connor, Richard Hoover,
Kathryn Horton, Harry Sands,
Leon Sternfeld, Gloria F. Wolinsky

The need for categories and particularly for labels applied to children has been challenged. However, to assure the necessary special services required by children presently known by terms such as *crippled, health-impaired, neurologically impaired, blind* or *visually handicapped, deaf,* or *hard of hearing,* some kind of classification schema seems imperative. As information emerges

Contributions have been made to this chapter by Russell Love and Daniel Schwartz of the Bill Wilkerson Hearing and Speech Center, Nashville, Tennessee.

on the functioning of these children with a wide range of medical-physical or organic problems, psychological deviations, and
role dysfunctions, highly skilled professionals have expressed
dissatisfaction with discrete labels which disregard the many
operating variants. In each specialty, there is clear dissatisfaction with the apparent assumption that all disabled children in
any one category function in exactly the same way. Calling a
child cerebral palsied or blind provides little information about
his functional levels. Such terms do little more than call attention to the fact that he is subject to some deviation from what
is considered "normal." The extent to which this deviation
interferes with learning or social behavior or whether the child
can respond to therapy, use prostheses, or perform "activities of
daily living" is not reflected in the label. Yet, all too often, it is
the child's diagnostic label that affects educational placement
and the specific qualifications of his teacher.

Current Classification Systems

Almost all descriptive and classification systems applied
to the physically disabled have been closely related to the medical diagnosis or disability of the patient, since the physician is
usually the first professional to whom the child is brought.
Some classification efforts, however, reflect orientation toward
other specific purposes, particularly toward function and performance in particular settings. For almost every disability category (blindness, stroke, cerebral palsy, paralysis, heart disease),
several classification systems exist.

Blindness and visual impairment. The system most frequently used to justify the legal label *blind* had its inception in
1934 during a meeting of the House of Delegates of the American Medical Association. This definition, which still generally
obtains, and which must be respected until a better formula is
prepared, reads: "A person shall be considered blind whose central visual acuity does not exceed 20/200 in the better eye with
correcting lenses or whose visual acuity, if better than 20/200,
has a limit of the central field of vision to such a degree that its
widest diameter subtends an angle of no greater than twenty
degrees." The customary label actually embodies two dictionary
definitions: (1) the blind, who have no sense of vision; and (2)
the cecutients, who have an impaired sense of vision. However,
since the label specifies no levels of disability, it implies that all
"blind" have the same visual needs.

The totally blind are easier to assess and to categorize from the visual standpoint than the cecutients. Services for the totally blind are fairly clear-cut in that such individuals must find other than visual ways of performing. The cecutient, on the other hand, is faced with a myriad of visual problems, and his visual ability or disability is often difficult to evaluate or assess —particularly since, on certain occasions, he does use what sense of vision remains. Certainly a sensory deficit should be served only at the level of the impairment, and the cecutient is not receiving proper services if he is treated as if totally blind. It is every profession's obligation to respect the feelings of those who see poorly but who have some sense of vision.

Although individuals and groups continue to attempt a change in the classification system, many current efforts are not based firmly enough on solid data to offer much hope of improvement. The latest and perhaps the most promising efforts are being made by the International Society for the Prevention of Blindness, which has proposed the adoption of certain agreed-upon terms and definitions. The categories—partial impairment of vision, social blindness, virtual blindness, total blindness, and unspecified or undetermined blindness—are defined by visual acuity in the better eye after correction and by the visual field in the better eye. The society has called for centralized information on the national level, with recognized common denominators to facilitate the development of a multidisciplinary approach to the prevention, treatment, and rehabilitation of blindness. It urges that the main target of public health activities be the preventable and curable causes of blindness, with special reference to developing countries, where preventable eye pathology is mainly caused by infection, malnutrition, and accidents. Similarly, the World Health Organization Study Group on the Prevention of Blindness (1972) offered specific recommendations for the establishment and development of an active program for the prevention of blindness and visual impairment and emphasized the need for a comprehensive program of public health ophthalmology.

For educational purposes, Fonda (1960) suggests four classifications of partial vision: light perception to 1/200 (braille instruction if possible); 2/200 to 4/200 (use of one's eyes if possible); 5/200 to 20/300 (use of one's eyes with the possible aid of low-vision devices and large-print materials); and 20/250 to 20/70 (attendance in regular classes). Esterman (1968)—noting the limitations of the Snellen Scale, which

focuses on central acuity—has developed a grid for the quantitative evaluation of visual fields (the tangent-screen field as well as
the peripheral-acuity field). This grid is a relative-value scale
based entirely upon function; that is, the usefulness of a given
field. It provides a scale for measuring function in different
parts of the visual field and for assessing subtle changes in that
function over time.

Deafness and hearing impairment. Educationally and socially, the deaf are defined as those individuals whose hearing
loss is so severe at birth or during the prelingual period that it
precludes the normal acquisition of language comprehension
and expression. The partially hearing are persons whose hearing
loss, although significant in degree, was either acquired after the
critical period for language acquisition, thus enabling the individual to develop some communicative skills, or does not totally
impair oral language development.

A common method of classifying hearing impairment is
based on the degree of hearing loss in decibels (dB), with accompanying interpretation of the effect of that hearing loss on
the individual's ability to hear and understand speech (McConnell, 1973); the site of the lesion, or the physical origin of the
disorder, also is specified.

The classification of hearing loss requires a multifaceted
assessment of the integrity of the auditory system. The traditional audiological test battery, utilizing pure-tone and speech
audiometry, enables the audiologist to determine the degree of
impairment, the site of lesion resulting in damage to the hearing
mechanism, and the person's ability to hear and comprehend
speech stimuli. Additional special auditory tests are often utilized in an effort to obtain more specific information with
respect to the site of lesion and etiological factors associated
with the anomaly. Based on the results of these tests, the audiologist can make prognoses for medical restoration or alleviation of the disorder, predict educational progress, or suggest
vocational goals. Many of the techniques used for assessing the
hearing acuity of adults are not applicable to very young children. Pure tones, for example, are abstract signals used to measure the sensitivity of the hearing mechanism. They not only
lack meaning to young children, but may result in either a
refusal to cooperate or a measurement that is neither reliable
nor valid.

Problems of multiple pathologies other than reduced

peripheral-hearing sensitivity may contribute significantly to the child's communication disorder (Miller and Polisar, 1964). A complete pediatric evaluation includes the administration of a differential diagnostic test battery that will enable the audiologist to ascertain relevant information concerning the child's level of language, motor, and social functioning, in addition to a measurement of hearing. Audiological evaluation of the young child involves the observation of reflexive and/or localization responses to a variety of stimuli conditions in a sound-field situation. Live-voice presentations of the child's name, tape-recorded samples of music and animal sounds, and pulsed pure tones are administered in a controlled test environment in an effort to determine the degree of hearing loss. Two of the more recent techniques, cortical (EEG) audiometry and acoustic impedance measurements, are providing more specific diagnostic information. When the audiologist is confronted with a more mature or older child, play modifications of the conventional techniques are often utilized for assessing the degree and type of impairment.

The procedures for arriving at a diagnosis of auditory dysfunction, particularly with children, are both time-consuming and complex. Continuing research in the area of auditory phenomena, such as the measurement of the acoustic stapedial reflex, will hopefully result in a more expedient and efficient method for obtaining relevant audiological information. A major goal is the early identification and remediation of hearing loss regardless of the type and degree of involvement.

From the medical and anatomical point of view, there are three distinct, although not mutually exclusive, types of hearing impairment. A conductive-hearing loss implies an obstruction to sound transmission through the sound-conducting apparatus of the ear as a direct result of a lesion to the external- or middle-ear mechanisms. If damage occurs to the nerve endings of the inner ear (cochlea), or to the auditory nerve that permits transmission of sound to the brain, the resulting hearing loss is classified as sensory-neural. The term *central dysacusis* refers to a lesion in the central auditory nervous system and the auditory area of the cortex. Almost all sensory-neural and central auditory disorders require extensive habilitative and educational management. Failure to medically remediate any dysfunction will result in a major communicative disability of speech, language, or hearing.

A final factor with respect to the effects of hearing loss on communication is the age of onset. The Committee on Nomenclature of Executives of American Schools for the Deaf, in its definition of deafness, has noted the importance of age of onset. According to this classification there are two deaf populations: the congenitally deaf (persons born deaf whose sense of hearing is nonfunctional for the ordinary purposes of life) and the adventitiously deaf (those born with normal hearing acuity, but whose sense of hearing becomes nonfunctional later in life through accident or illness) (National Advisory Council, 1969, p. 10).

Although the generic terms *deaf* and *partially hearing* appear to be inadequate, since they fail to recognize the many different types and degrees and consequences of auditory dysfunction, no substitute terminology has emerged. We are therefore faced with the task of providing contemporary management programs while utilizing antiquated terminology (McConnell, 1973). Furthermore, the categories of mild, moderate, severe, and profound hearing impairment are often erroneously interpreted to mean that all individuals within a specified classification will function on a similar level of competence. A person with a moderate impairment, for example, if not managed appropriately or early enough, may present a more significant communicative handicap than a person with a severe hearing loss. The terms *educational, social,* or *occupational deafness* may refer to any individual who has not received proper management, regardless of the type and degree of hearing loss.

Communication disorders. According to Hull and Hull (1973), communication disorders in children in the United States and Canada are classified into two categories: impairment and disability. *Impairment* designates children who are judged to have speech and/or language problems that deviate extremely from a predetermined standard; *disability* refers to children whose speech and/or language deviates from that standard to a greater degree than that of the children in the impairment group. Prevalence figures for delayed speech and language, articulation, voice, and stuttering total 4.14 percent in the impairment category and 2.45 percent in the disability category, yielding a grand total of 6.59 percent in the total population. These estimates are complicated by the fact that certain speech problems, particularly articulation disorders, are influenced strongly by maturational factors. The rate of improvement of articulation disorders is greater during the first two years of school than in the following ten. However, as yet there are no reliable means for predicting which children will outgrow their disorder spontaneously. Therefore, the two-category system of labeling severity of disorder is not of prognostic value.

Children classified as having oral-language disabilities often exhibit deviations in reading and writing and could be classified as having learning disabilities, thereby adding confusion to a classification system which aims at determining prevalence accurately. Another factor confounding designated categories is that children with other disabilities also have a relatively high incidence of speech and language problems. All types of communication disorders tend to increase when the child has a cleft palate or is hearing-impaired, cerebral palsied, or mentally retarded. These overlapping classifications tend to inflate prevalence figures and often result in confusion in educational management.

Of the terms used to describe communication disorders, the one which currently offers the most difficulty is *language disorder* or *language disability* in children. In the past two decades, terms such as *congenital aphasia* and *developmental aphasia* have been employed to describe language-deficient children, but there has been a singular lack of consensus as to what specifies the clinical picture. Moreover, these terms have lacked authority, because the condition is dissimilar to the syndrome of adult aphasia, from which the terminology was derived. Labels such as *language disability* and *language disorder*, however, lack the specificity of implied neurological etiology that was connoted by the term *aphasia* or kindred names. The present term *language disorder* may imply a deficiency in verbal performance whose causes may be neurological deficit or emotional or environmental deprivation (Weiner, 1969). The term has also been employed to characterize those children whose language patterns deviate as a result of cultural or poverty situations (Williams, 1970). Clearly, the label is too broad to convey meaning other than in a very general sense.

There is one striking example of the detrimental effects of labeling in the area of communication disorders. It is clear that overzealous labeling of normal, nonfluent developmental speech performance as *stuttering* can actually produce a disability (Johnson and Moller, 1967). Although some speech specialists have argued that the *stuttering* label should be erased from the language to prevent such misuse, it is unlikely that this will occur because of persistence of the term in popular parlance and the obviousness of this speech disorder.

Physical and neurological handicaps. The classification "crippled and other health impaired," as defined in PL91-230, the Elementary and Secondary Education Act, has been considered by three national study institutes in that field (Connor and others, 1970, 1971, 1973). For educational purposes, the target populations have been seen primarily as the multiply handicapped, considered on three continua: age, stability or outcome of difficulty, and required educational or treatment setting for optimum programing. For the physically handicapped child, the attending physician has the direct responsibility for the initial medical labeling and prescription and for continuing modifications of these as additional relevant information becomes available. It is through this medical detection and referral that most children with physical handicaps come to the attention of educators in hospitals, clinics, and special education centers. However, for educational diagnosis and planning, specialists in the behavioral sciences have a major role.

Physicians have been primarily responsible for developing and refining systems to classify physical impairments. The American Medical Association has produced a series of guides for evaluating permanent mental and physical impairments. The separate guides deal with extremities and back (1958); visual system (1958); cardiovascular system (1960); ear, nose, and throat (1961); central nervous system (1964); peripheral spinal nerves (1964); digestive system (1964); respiratory system (1965); endocrine system (1966); and mental illness (1966). These publications, describing the nature and extent of illness and injury, were designed to enable more precise treatment and to facilitate referral to competent specialists.

Definitions of handicapping conditions have also been developed by private health agencies to specify the pathological-clinical characteristics which admit an individual to their services and support. Each of these agencies—Easter Seals, United Cerebral Palsy Association Inc., Epilepsy Foundation of America, the American Heart Association, and the Muscular Dystrophy Association, for example—was established to serve as advocate for a specified group of disabled children, adolescents, and adults. After early use of such all-encompassing terms as *Little's disease* and *spastic* (as extensively used in Great Britain), efforts have been made to establish subcategories within groups. For example, children with cerebral palsy are generally subclassified according to type (athetoid, spastic, ataxic, rigid, tremor, or a combination of these). Two sets of classifications specify the severity of cardiac involvement. One set is based upon functional capacity, ranging from Group I (no limitation of physical activity) to Group IV (inability to carry on any physical activity without discomfort); the other set of classifications has therapeutic implications, ranging from A (need not be restricted) to E (need complete rest, confinement to bed or chair). Epilepsy diagnoses usually describe the type of seizure—grand mal, petit mal, psychomotor, or other—sustained by the individual. But the seizure, and thus the diagnostic categorization, does not take into account the many factors or variables which are inherent in this disorder.

It is crucial that all the significant variables associated with a physical disability be known and given proper weight. To deal with the neurologically impaired child, for example, as if he or she were limited only by the nature and extent of the physical condition of the disorder is to distort the true nature of the consequent handicap. Neurology addresses itself to the target symptoms of a neurological disorder, such as the seizures in epilepsy or the muscular rigidity and tremors in Parkinson's disease; usually treats these physical symptoms as a single variable; and then defines the resulting handicap in terms of that variable. This focus misses the multivariate nature of most neurological disorders and leads to a limited definition of a handicap. The full extent of the handicap resulting from a neurological disorder can be known only if all the factors arising out of and associated with the physical condition are taken into consideration. This is essential both for an accurate definition of the handicap and for the development of appropriate diagnostic and service programs that will deal realistically not only with the neurological impairment but with all factors involved in producing the handicap.

The discussion here is limited to epilepsy, a common neurological disorder which illustrates the importance of including the multivariate nature of a condition in any classificatory descriptions. It also demonstrates the kinds of variables that need to be taken into account in defining handicaps resulting from other physical disorders. Neurologists, psychologists, social workers, rehabilitation workers, and special educators frequently focus solely on the seizure—the major symptom in epilepsy—and its control. There is no question that this dramatic symptom is important. However, to limit attention to this single factor and not to discover or give the proper weight to the other variables that are associated with the disorder—variables that do not necessarily disappear when the seizures are eliminated—is to define incompletely the handicapping condition of epilepsy. This need for consideration of the multivariate factors also holds true for other neurological disorders.

Some of the variables associated with the handicapping conditions arising out of epilepsy in children, adolescents, and youth and reflected in difficulties in daily living are type of seizures, age at onset of seizures, other physical disabilities, and psychological problems. Overall and for the greatest part, the frequency, duration, and type of seizures, particularly as related to the alteration of consciousness, determine the degree of handicap or disablement experienced by a child with epilepsy. A youngster who has one grand mal seizure per month that lasts for a minute or two, who regains consciousness within several minutes, and who is quickly able to return to the activity that was interrupted by the seizure suffers only a small degree of disablement or handicap. However, a youngster who experiences fifty petit mal attacks or momentary blackouts per day or week without major motor involvement, such as falling to the floor and convulsing, can suffer significant impairment. Because of frequent interruptions of consciousness, he is unable to carry out sustained thinking or learning activities. Fortunately, the antiepileptic drugs used to control the seizures are very effective; they are able to control seizures completely in 50 percent of cases and markedly reduce their number in an additional 30 percent.

The age at which the first seizure occurs (or, for that matter, any major chronic illness) is significant. Any physical or psychological trauma occurring during personality development can adversely affect age-specific needs and tasks (Erikson, 1968), and a major disruptive event like the onset of epilepsy is a trauma. Thirteen percent of persons with epilepsy have their first seizure during late adolescence (age twelve to twenty-one). During this period, according to Wolberg (1965), the normal needs to be met are gradual emancipation from parents, vocational choices, a growing sense of responsibility, courtship, and marriage. Among the tasks to be achieved at this time are resolution of dependency and assumption of a heterosexual role. Accordingly, the onset of seizures during this period can interfere with the normal development of these functions and result in varying degrees of handicap in the form of excessive dependency, devalued self-image, confusion regarding social roles, and sexual inhibition.

The control of the seizure variable, especially as close to onset as possible, will prevent or lessen to some extent the handicapping consequences. However, the factors associated with this time period in personality development must be taken into account in defining the handicap. They also dictate the particular diagnostic and clinical services that need to be available as preventive or effective measures for dealing with this aspect of the handicap. These services should include individual and group counseling and advocacy programs to prevent family and community attitudes from interfering with the normal development of such traits as independence.

In addition to seizures, other physical dysfunctions stemming from this neurological disorder must also be dealt with as possible generators of handicapping conditions. The possible side and toxic effects of anticonvulsants, such as drowsiness and difficulties in coordination, can now often be avoided by the use of gas liquid chromatography, which adjusts drug dosage. Hyperactivity and perceptual and psychomotor deficits that disrupt reading and writing (dyslexia, dysgraphia, other learning disabilities) call for judicious chemical therapies, individual and family counseling, and special education procedures. These can, at the very least, limit the resulting handicap and help the child cope with his functional difficulties; developmental growth and maturation can help the individual to further master or reduce these dysfunctions and handicaps.

Psychological factors play a significant role in causing handicapping conditions. The problem of personality adjustment to seizures is all too often underestimated by the medical rehabilitation team and by the person with epilepsy. The individual's high anxiety and fear of having a seizure can deter him from coping with the demands of daily living; his self-image and his feelings of self-esteem also play a central role in his adjustment. These anxieties are reinforced by parents, whose reactions frequently span the gamut from overprotection to rejection, and by siblings, who harbor resentment at the disproportionate time the child with epilepsy receives from his parents.

Siblings may also feel guilty when asking for any attention from their parents when their parents need to devote so much to their handicapped brother or sister.

The family is not the only factor reinforcing maladjustments and dependency. Community attitudes, too, are major determiners of handicapping conditions. These are embodied in driver's license codes (driving a car plays a significant role in a teenager's development), in admission requirements for camps and colleges, in working papers for summer and after-school employment, in workmen's compensation laws, and particularly in employer resistance to hiring those with epilepsy (even when seizures are completely controlled). All these stressful experiences convey the message that the youth with epilepsy does not enjoy all the rights and privileges which are normal for other young persons.

Services

Although classification does indeed label a child, its purpose is to obtain maximum resources, to explore and advocate systems for children who because of their handicaps are unable to utilize the standard educational provisions in the community. Broadened and alternate service systems came about as health and physical conditions were identified, stabilized, and/or remediated, but probably more directly as a result of social thinking about children and educational opportunities.

Development of services. In the first quarter of the nineteenth century, special schools for the blind and for the deaf were established. In general, these early schools were residential, and children were admitted on the basis of what today would be considered global definitions of specific disability. The beginning of the twentieth century saw the establishment of institutional programs to meet the pragmatic needs of crippled children and those with chronic health problems who were segregated because of the nature of their problems. However, the prevailing social climate demanded that these children be afforded the same (or equal) educational opportunities enjoyed by their peers. Therefore, special classrooms and schools quickly appeared in hospitals for the post-polio, asthmatic, arthritic, or rheumatic child, and in sanitoriums for the tubercular. In large cities children who were potential risks for tuberculosis or who were "delicate" or crippled were assigned to "open-air" or special health classes. Specialized day or residential schools were also established, and schooling at home was provided for those who could not make it to the specialized settings.

As early as 1863 a physician, James Knight, insisted that children in the Hospital for the Ruptured and Crippled in New York City receive academic and religious education. In 1868 Boston opened the first day school for the deaf. In 1900 Chicago opened the first public school class for crippled children in the United States. Classification of children to participate in such educational programs was, and for the most part still is, dependent upon a medical referral. During the period 1917-1920, the service needs of physically handicapped children aroused nationwide concern—mainly because poliomyelitis outbreaks had left a large number of children with various disabilities, some of which were amenable to partial correction through orthopedic surgical procedures. In 1921 the Shepard-Towner Act, which provided grants-in-aid to the states for maternal and child health services, was passed; and some of the states began developing medical services for children disabled by polio. Furthermore, when the Social Security Act was being developed, orthopedic surgeons brought considerable pressure to include provisions for physically handicapped children. As a result, there were included in Title V (at that time) two grants-in-aid to the states for medical and related services, one for "maternal and child health services," and the second for "crippled children's services." As a result of these grants, each state established service programs for mothers and children and for physically handicapped children. The former in all instances were developed in state departments of health. The programs for physically handicapped children, however, were placed in various state agencies: in health departments (in about half of the states), in welfare or education departments, in separate state commissions, and even in the medical school of a state university. Although the Children's Bureau, the federal agency designated to administer these grants, issued standards and guidelines, a considerable diversity of programs developed, particularly in regard to eligibility of children, types and amounts of services, and goals and objectives of the programs.

Inequities in service systems. The fact that many rehabilitation programs were and are called "Crippled Children's Services" has probably adversely affected these programs, since a number of families needing the program services elected not to avail themselves of them. The supposed stigma was intensified where the program was administered by a state welfare department.

Moreover, since many rehabilitation programs were initially administered by orthopedic surgeons, the early programs reflected a marked bias toward children with conditions that could be managed by orthopedic surgical procedures. In many states the eligible diagnostic conditions were essentially orthopedic: congenital conditions such as club foot, dislocated hip, extra digits; birth injuries such as fracture of the clavicle or of one of the extremities or torticolis (wry neck); and acquired conditions such as the osteochondritides, tuberculosis of bones and joints, disabling sequelae of poliomyelitis, or other central nervous system infections.

The limitation of funds resulted in further inequities during the early years of these programs. Numerous eligibility requirements were imposed: geographic location (for example, metropolitan Boston was excluded from the Massachusetts Plan for Services for Crippled Children), economic status (particularly for all services exclusive of strictly diagnostic), age, and diagnostic category. All children labeled *severely, permanently, terminally,* or *multiply handicapped* were usually excluded from medical, special educational, and rehabilitation programs. Moreover, a number of programs serving crippled children required that the child have a measured IQ of 70 or better. As late as the 1960s most physically disabled children with IQs under 70 or 75 were not eligible for attendance in a special public school class under the jurisdiction of a state's Division or Bureau for the Physically Handicapped. If they resided in a state institution for the mentally retarded, they were not eligible for admission to full service in an orthopedic hospital under the same state's auspices.

Many of the early inequities have been corrected. As the years went on, children with physical handicaps other than orthopedic—congenital cardiac conditions amenable to surgery, cleft lip and palate, severe malocclusions, severe convulsive disorders, and cerebral palsy—became eligible for services in many states. Services for emotionally disturbed and mentally retarded children without concurrent physical handicaps also became available—not within the crippled children's programs but in those for mental health and mental retardation. In spite of these improvements, however, the diagnostic label still determines the kind and amount of services a child will receive, and these services may vary markedly from program to program and from state to state. Children who do not have a simple diagnostic label still do not receive needed services, or they experience delays and barriers in obtaining services. A child with the label *cerebral palsy* is a typical illustration. If one considers the entire population of persons with cerebral palsy, about 60 or 65 percent will have some degree of intellectual impairment (although less than 20 percent of this group will have severe retardation); about 35 percent will have convulsive seizures (most of them effectively controlled by medication); about 80 percent will have some degree of speech impediment; about 65 percent will have some sensory handicap (visual, auditory, or both)—all in addition to a mild or severe neuromotor handicap and, frequently, perceptual problems, cognitive difficulties, and emotional disturbances. The label *cerebral palsy* can refer to a child with all of these handicaps; but in many states that label irrevocably blocks a child from getting basic essential services, such as immunizations and routine well-child care, as well as the many specialized services that are needed.

Multipurpose classification systems. One approach to correcting the inequities resulting from univariate labels has been the development of multipurpose classification systems. Several suggested systems are described below.

Essentially for World War II recruitment and induction purposes, the Canadian army (1943) proposed a classification system called PULHEMS. The letters represent body parts and/ or functions: P (physique), U (upper extremities), L (lower extremities), H (hearing and ears), E (vision and eyes), M (mental capacity), and S (stability); ratings ranged from 1 (normal) to 5 (totally unfit). The United States army (1956) employed a similar system (PULHES), in which S involves both M and S of the Canadian classification approach. The United States system was later modified to describe the chronically ill and had extended possibilities for special school placement of children and youth. However, as Barry (1971) concluded, these systems are mainly descriptive and do not suggest means of promoting function, where possible, which might circumvent irremediable disability. Ehrle (1972) suggests that the functional perspective of the individual should replace the usual medical-physical, psychosocial, or educational-vocational viewpoints. Functional disabilities may be (1) instrumental dysfunctions—limited mobility, ineffective communication, problems in "activities of daily living," use of prosthesis, and the resultant learning and economic consequences; (2) psychological dysfunctions, related to the individual's tolerance for frustration and ambiguity, response to limited choice, acceptance of changed status, limited ego strength, personal identity, internal controls over behavior, and learning to defer gratification; and (3) role dysfunction, suggesting failure to learn to carry out behaviors society expects, such as competitive, interpersonal relations in school, family, and community.

A system for describing a disabled individual's ability to perform ordinary "activities of daily living" (ADL)—dressing, eating, mobility, and other skills—was initiated in the 1940s for both adults and children. A recent presentation (Scranton, Fogel, and Erdman, 1970) of this system is now widely used in rehabilitation centers, hospitals, and school settings with interdisciplinary staff. In another system (Sokolow, Taylor, and Rusk, 1970) the physical, emotional, social, and vocational capacities of a disabled person can be indicated on a 79-item checklist.

The National Institute of Neurological Diseases and Stroke (Riviere, 1970) has produced several major classification documents which warrant further study and refinement. These codes were designed to meet the need for a common language to improve communication among the professions as well as between them and the community, to help reorient attitudes toward the disabled person, to improve implementation of service, to enable collection and analysis of quantitative and qualitative data consistent from one program to another, and to facilitate research based upon the data. They provide information about characteristics of the disabled person and his living environment that may affect his response to service. For example, they specify at least five areas in which there might be impairment in visual function: central acuity, visual field, ocular mobility, binocular vision, and color vision. Total impairment is defined as "no light perception in both eyes, properly called 'blindness.'" For communication disorders, the Rehabilitation Codes Classification System includes four major areas: (1) voice disorders (related to pitch, loudness, control, intonation, quality associated with phonation, and quality associated with resonance); (2) hearing-function disorders, including impairment due to reduction of sensitivity to hearing speech (decibels for hearing), speed reduction of intelligibility for speech (percentage of correct responses), estimated reduction of hearing in the speech range (decibels based on thresholds for pure tones in speech-hearing range), estimated reduction of auditory sensitivity based on procedures not otherwise covered or specified, distortion of hearing function, and apparent disturbance of hearing function; (3) speech-function disorders (impairments of articulation, inappropriate disfluencies, inappropriate rate, impairments in patterning, impairments of concomitant audible behavior, and impairments of concomitant visible behavior); (4) disorders of language comprehension and use (limitations of language comprehension, of ability to formulate language, of ability in spontaneous expression, of ability to imitate linguistic patterns, and of ability to imitate nonlinguistic patterns).

Denhoff and Robinault (1960) have long argued for a functional classification for neurologically handicapped children along such lines as neuromotor, intellectual, neurosensory, behavioral, and perceptual functioning. Unless the disabled person is dealt with on a multifactor basis, classifications, programs, and legislation will deal with only one element of the problem. The delivery of services based on unifactor definitions will continue to fall short of ameliorating or eliminating the handicap.

Another multifactorial diagnostic system has been developed by the United Cerebral Palsy Association, which considered current medical classifications of cerebral palsy to be inadequate. Physicians working with children with cerebral palsy customarily designate type (spastic, athetoid, ataxic, mixed), anatomical involvement (monoplegia, diplegia, hemiplegia, quadraplegia), severity (mild, moderate, severe), and associated handicaps. To improve classification practices, especially for the very young child, the United Cerebral Palsy Association publishes a descriptive intake/screening form upon which are recorded gross indications of neurological damage, visual and auditory functions, convulsions, oral-pharyngeal functions, behavior, genetic factors, and congenital deviations, as well as the designation of a specific diagnosis.

Other attempts are being made to develop a classification based on a developmental model within a time-frame parameter. The term *developmental disability* has been formalized into federal law. As defined in the Developmental Disabilities Act (1969), "the term . . . means a disability attributable to mental retardation, cerebral palsy, epilepsy, or another neurological condition of an individual found by the Secretary [of Health, Education, and Welfare] to be closely related to mental retardation or to require treatment similar to that required for mentally retarded individuals, which disability originates before such individual attains age eighteen, which has continued or can be expected to continue indefinitely, and which constitutes a substantial handicap to such individual." The hope is that this term will not just be a euphemism but that it may lead to genuine improvements in classification which will avoid misleading labels and will best serve the interests of children, irrespective of their types of handicaps.

Failures of Classification Systems

The initial push to meet a specialized need often degenerated over the years into unfortunate uses of classification systems. Those who employed classification systems to administer programs were not always sensitive to changing needs and populations. In many instances labels were used to isolate children on the basis of society's perception of illness and disability rather than in terms of the specific needs of children. The misuse of classification systems may be partly understood by Talcott Parsons' (1951) concept of the sick role as institutionalized by society to protect itself from nonproductive members, to legitimate illness as a time for not performing tasks appropriate to age and sex, and to a certain extent to isolate the sick because of differences. Society's perceptions of the deviant sick role have spread to other forms of differentness, like the child with whom it is difficult to cope or to communicate.

While there has been considerable concern about categorization and the harm it does to children, youth, and adults who are classified as disabled, it is clear that classification was primarily designed to help, to assist, and to maintain life. For many children, classification is the only way their problems can be met; it is an attempt to define their pathological-clinical problems in terms of the specific types of treatment and the array of services needed. Classification can rightly be conceived as one of the original approaches to accountability and systems planning. Without it, children who are different are lost, and specific needs cannot be met; without the commitment that comes from expressed recognition of these special needs in an intellectual and social sense, these "exceptional" children can become expendable in the face of the overriding problems of a larger community.

Questioning the way categorization is done and its effect on children is justified, for it has been abused and has often degenerated into "labeling," with its supermarket-packaging aspect. Instead of being part of a process, it has become the end and the ultimate meaning. To a certain extent knowledge has been manipulated and not always to the benefit of children. This abuse, however, is not intrinsic to the categorization system itself. It is what has been done to it and with it.

The Future: Asking the Right Questions

Classification systems in the area of physical disabilities evolved out of specific needs; they resulted from extraordinary advances in various areas of knowledge; they began to interact with various cultural components; and they have sometimes been abused. It is time to capitalize on the achievements and to correct the deficiencies that specific classification systems present.

The question is how. It is not realistic to expect that a classification system which serves its purpose in a prescriptive sense (medical or scientific) and is the system on which many children's lives depend is going to be basically altered except as new knowledge in a field develops. It is also unrealistic to single out systems or categories that were developed out of specific scientific research and practice and to attack them in terms of social-political developments that emerged parallel to the category system. That ultimately classification and social factors interact is not questioned.

The issue of concern, however, is what questions are to be asked about children to best meet their special needs. That is, we should ask not merely "What must be done to control a child's seizures?" but "What must be done to help him cope with the demands of a school situation where problems of children with convulsions may not be understood?" We should ask not only "How can we save this child who is severely burned?" but "What plans must be made for him as he spends the next years of his life in a rehabilitation center undergoing multiple surgical procedures?" Most of the present classification systems are based on observations for the purpose of diagnosis, enlightenment, or treatment. But this "enlightenment" may lock the child and his family into an institutionalized form of deviancy, with all that self-fulfilling hypotheses imply. Apparently descriptive statements have been too easily intermingled with inferential statements, to the concern and dismay of everyone. Questions must differentiate in terms of description, inference, and intervention. These are the real classification concerns, for this nondifferentiation of the specific meanings and use of description, inference, and intervention has been leading us into a cul-de-sac regarding classification.

Not only must differentiated questions be raised, but a concerted effort is required to hasten the development and refinement of various diagnostic techniques to assist with the differentiated questions that are to be asked. At the present there are limited diagnostic techniques, with various levels of sophistication. This limitation poses its own dilemma in that all too often what is used is not appropriate, or it is used with awesome finality to place a child in social situations which are more devastating than the category itself.

Because of the subtleties and complexities, the wisdom of many professions is needed. Small evaluation-diagnostic-intervention teams, based on task-oriented approaches that focus on the needs of the child in his particular situation, could serve as a monitoring and advocacy system to ascertain that the original placement and/or classification system is not being abused. The problem, it would seem, is not in the original classification system but in what follows. There is as yet no efficient system for follow-up, either of the adequacy of the classification or the results of the classification system. In short, those who are most involved with the process and results of categorization need to be concerned with both the practical and philosophical aspects of the results of this system of knowing.

References

American Medical Association. "Guides to the Evaluation of Permanent Mental and Physical Impairments." *Journal of the American Medical Association,* 1958-1966.

Barry, John R. "Behavioral Classification of the Physically Disabled." *Psychological Aspects of Disability,* 1971, *18*(3), 136-142.

Canadian Army. *Physical Standards and Instructions for Medical Examination of Serving Soldiers and Recruits.* Ottawa: Canadian Army, 1943.

Committee on Nomenclature of Executives of American Schools for the

Deaf, 1937. Cited in National Advisory Council on Neurological Diseases and Strokes, *Human Communication and Its Disorders*. Bethesda, Md.: National Institute on Neurological Diseases and Stroke, 1969.

Connor, F. P., and Cohen, M. (Eds.) *Leadership Preparation for Educators of Crippled and Other Health-Impaired Multiply Handicapped Populations*. New York: Teachers College Press, 1973.

Connor, F. P., Rusalem, H., and Baken, J. W. (Eds.) *Professional Preparation of Educators of Crippled Children: Competency-Based Programming*. New York: Teachers College Press, 1971.

Connor, F. P., Wald, J., and Cohen, M. (Eds.) *Professional Preparation for Educators of Crippled Children*. New York: Teachers College Press, 1970.

Denhoff, E., and Robinault, I. P. *Cerebral Palsy and Related Disorders: A Developmental Approach to Dysfunction*. New York: McGraw-Hill, 1960.

Ehrle, R. A. "Diminishing Functional Disability: Complementary Rehabilitation Efforts." *Rehabilitation Psychology*, 1972, *19*(4), 174-179.

Erikson, E. H. *Identity, Youth, and Crisis*. New York: Norton, 1968.

Esterman, B. "Grid for Scoring Visual Fields." *Archives of Ophthalmology*, 1968, *79*, 400-406.

Fonda, G. "Definition and Classification of Blindness with Respect to Ability to Use Residual Vision." In *Blindness, 1960 AAWB Annual*. Washington, D.C.: American Association of Workers for the Blind, 1960.

Hull, F. M., and Hull, M. E. "Children with Oral Communication Disabilities." In L. M. Dunn (Ed.), *Exceptional Children in the Schools*. New York: Holt, 1973.

Hull, F. M., Mielke, P. W., Jr., and others. "The National Speech and Hearing Survey: Preliminary Results." *ASHA* (Journal of the American Speech and Hearing Association), 1971, *13*, 501-509.

Johnson, W., and Moller, D. (Eds.) *Speech Handicapped School Children*. New York: Harper, 1967.

Katz, D., and Kahn, R. L. *The Social Psychology of Organizations*. New York: Wiley, 1966.

Kuhn, H. S. *Industrial Ophthalmology*. St. Louis: Mosby, 1944.

McConnell, F. "Children with Hearing Disabilities." In L. M. Dunn (Ed.), *Exceptional Children in the Schools*. (2nd Ed.) New York: Holt, 1973.

Miller, M. H., and Polisar, I. A. *Audiological Evaluation of the Pediatric Patient*. Springfield, Ill.: Thomas, 1964.

National Advisory Council on Neurological Diseases and Strokes. *Human Communication and Its Disorders*. Bethesda, Md.: National Institute of Neurological Diseases and Stroke, 1969.

New York Heart Association. *Nomenclature and Criteria for Diagnosis of*

Diseases of the Heart and Blood Vessels. (5th Ed.) New York: Heart Association, 1953.

Parsons, T. *The Social System.* New York: Free Press, 1951.

Riviere, M. *Rehabilitation Codes: Proceedings of the Workshop on Nomenclature of Communicative Disorders.* Bethesda, Md.: National Institute of Neurological Diseases and Stroke, 1962.

Riviere, M. *Rehabilitation Codes: Classification of Impairment of Visual Function.* Bethesda, Md.: National Institute of Neurological Diseases and Stroke, 1970.

Rusalem, H. *Coping with the Unseen Environment.* New York: Teachers College Press, 1972.

Scranton, J. A., Fogel, M. L., and Erdman, W. J. "Evaluation of Functional Levels of Patients During and Following Rehabilitation." *Archives of Physical Medicine and Rehabilitation,* 1970, *51,* 1-21.

Silverman, S. R., and Lane, H. S. "Deaf Children." In H. Davis and S. R. Silverman (Eds.), *Hearing and Deafness.* (3rd Ed.) New York: Holt, 1970.

Sloan, L. L. "Measurement of Visual Acuity." *Archives of Ophthalmology,* 1951, *45,* 704.

Sokolow, J., Taylor, E. J., and Rusk, H. A. *Development and Standardization, Validation, and Field Trial of a Method of Clarifying the Physical, Emotional, Social, and Vocational Capacities of the Disabled Individual Function.* Washington, D.C.: U.S. Government Printing Office, 1970.

U.S. Army. "Physical Standards and Physical Profiling for Enlisting and Induction." *U.S. Army Regulations,* 1956, *40,* 503.

U.S. Department of Health, Education, and Welfare. *Social Service Administration: Disability Evaluation Under Social Security.* Vol. 89. Washington, D.C.: U.S. Government Printing Office, 1970.

Weiner, P. S. "The Cognitive Functioning of Language Deficient Children." *Journal of Speech and Hearing Research,* 1969, *12,* 53-64.

Williams, F. (Ed.) *Language and Poverty: Perspectives on a Theme.* Chicago: Markham, 1970.

Wolberg, L. A. (Ed.) *Short-Term Psychotherapy.* New York: Grune and Stratton, 1965.

World Health Organization. *Report of the Study Group on the Prevention of Blindness.* New York: World Health Organization, 1972.

10

~~~~~~~~~~~~~~~~~~~~~~~~~~~~~~~~~~~~~

EMOTIONAL
DISTURBANCE IN
CHILDREN

Dane G. Prugh, Mary Engel, William C. Morse

~~~~~~~~~~~~~~~~~~~~~~~~~~~~~~~~~~~~~

No matter what conceptual framework is employed, classifying a person is an arbitrary process. Much controversy exists today over the usefulness as well as the ethics of classification. It has been pointed out that overt or covert ethnocentrism may have a potentially destructive effect on the lives of those who are classified. Elsewhere in this book much has been said about this; nevertheless, a brief restatement is necessary and serves as a backdrop for what follows.

Strong competitive tendencies do not rule out powerful forces of conformity. In our society, the discernment of deviance often carries with it the assignment of value; "sick" behavior is easily equated with weakness, inadequacy. Social systems do define what are "emotional problems." Mobilizing resources for children who have been classified in various ways often involves political issues. For this reason and also because the general public often misunderstands the professional language of psychiatry and psychology, classification often creates resentment among parents and teachers.

Among mental health professionals there is disagreement about the etiology of many emotional problems. Competing conceptual models increase the intellectual and emotional stresses which surround any discussion of classification. In this chapter the rationale for classification is examined, current approaches are critically reviewed, and a conceptual approach to a useful classification system is offered.

The Purpose of Classification

Much of the confusion underlying the controversy in this area stems from the use of a variety of often imprecise terms to refer to classification by professional workers from fields ranging from clinical mental health through behavioral theory to sociology. *Classification* refers to the act or process of arranging or grouping objects or facts by classes, based on similar attributes or relations; the process may involve the gathering together of similar things in classes or the splitting of general groups into more specific divisions. (The term *taxonomy* is sometimes used as a synonym for classification, referring to that activity of science involved in classification.) At its simplest level, a systematic approach to classification is based upon observation and description, the first steps in the scientific approach to the study of natural phenomena.

As the process of classification proceeds, certain inferences or hypotheses may be tentatively employed regarding the nature of the things to be classified, and various categories are created relating to common attributes or qualities. However, the basic purpose of classification is still to systematize the ordering of data to permit the carrying forth of the scientific process to the point of the induction of testable hypotheses, with, in some instances, the ultimate modification of existing phenomena.

Classifications are of two basic types, *descriptive* and *explanatory,* with often some overlap in the health fields (Newbrough, 1972). Where behavior is highly variable and "the purposes range from understanding the behavior to its control and usage, the situation is much more complex than if the phenomena to be classified do not change or if the purpose is solely descriptive. Scientifically, the approach would be one of differentiation and specificity. This could be expected to lead, at early stages of the process, to differences in approaches and results" (Newbrough, 1969).

Other terms which have sometimes been loosely employed include *nomenclature, nosology, diagnosis,* and *prognosis. Nomenclature* refers to a system of names applied to the subjects of study in any art or science; in a classification, the nomenclature refers to the categories established within the system. With a number of systems of classifications of disturbed behavior available, the resultant variations in nomenclature offer anything but clarification. *Nosology* and the related term *nosonomy,* deriving from the Greek word *nosos* (meaning disease or sickness), refer respectively to the systematic classification and the nomenclature of diseases, in the medical tradition. *Diagnosis* (from the Greek for "knowing between") has been identified with the medical tradition; the term refers to the clinical determination of individual disease pictures, employing categories drawn from a system of classification of diseases, often with etiological implications. A diagnosis is regarded as tentative or provisional until proven. Follow-up may be necessary for the establishment of a diagnosis, and, with behavioral disorders particularly, the diagnosis may not be established until treatment is in process. Thus diagnoses can and should be changed if necessary, and do not represent fixed labels. *Prognosis* involves a prediction, based upon clinical knowledge, of the future course of an illness or disorder in response to treatment or intervention; the term has been used in medicine and in other fields as well.

The term *nosology* should be reserved for discussions dealing with the traditional medical-pathological or "disease-oriented" model, which no longer seems adequate even to many physicians (G. Engel, 1960; Prugh, 1963). The term *diagnosis,* however, has been applied widely by mental health clinicians to the assessment and evaluation of children and adults exhibiting emotionally disturbed behavior. If used in its etymologically correct sense, diagnosis refers only to the act of distinguishing between categories of disturbance within a classificatory system; it does not necessarily carry implications for etiology.

Diagnosis has been also used to refer to the identification of events or forces within a system. Prognosis or "future outlook" also has no necessary tie to medical or etiologic considerations. The term *nomenclature* has an appropriate place in relation to a system of classification, and the term *classification* has a scientific justification, with no inevitably pejorative or other unhealthy significance.

Problems in Classification

There are abiding reasons for the use of a system of classification of disturbed behavior "based on explicit and clearly defined categories which can be employed by clinicians from varying conceptual backgrounds" (Group for Advancement of Psychiatry, 1966). As the Child Psychiatry Committee of the Group for Advancement of Psychiatry (GAP) has indicated, such categories are necessary so that clinicians from differing schools of thought can communicate intelligibly in work and teaching, using some sort of mutually agreed upon "verbal shorthand." In addition, such categories are vital to the scientific collection of comparable clinical data, which can make possible the study of the natural history of psychosocial disorders, the investigation of epidemiologic and other factors, the development of specific treatment approaches or methods of intervention, and the accurate assessment of treatment outcome and prognostic outlook. To argue against any system of classification because of attendant difficulties, as has often been done recently, is to abandon the scientific and the clinical approach. Because the same symptoms do not have the same meaning at varying ages, a separate classification of children's from adult disorders is indicated (GAP, 1966; Rutter and others, 1969).

Having made this brave statement, however, we recognize the problems involved in current classification schemes and the difficulties inherent in the construction of an ideal classification. Engel (1969) has commented cogently on the problems involved in achieving an "epistemology of understanding," even in regard to what may constitute data in this area. As Morse (1973) has indicated, an approach to the classification of the problems of childhood and adolescence must deal with certain fundamental issues: (1) the *child's current status* (clinical picture); (2) *the genesis of the child's problems* (etiology) in relation to a developmental framework, family experiences, and

other factors; and (3) the *implications of intervention,* in regard
to choice of treatment method and prognosis, with some un-
avoidable interlocking among these factors.

Although attempts have been made (reviewed in Group
for Advancement of Psychiatry, 1966; Rutter and others, 1969)
to classify children's disorders on the basis of etiological considerations, considered today by most clinicians to be multiple
(including physical, psychological, and social factors), no basic
agreement exists as yet in this area. As indicated in a recent
review (Prugh, 1969), classifications on the basis of parent-child
relationships, family interactions, and other social interactional
factors are not widespread if only because of the discrepancies
among conceptual approaches. Fish (1969b) has offered a personality typology based on response to drug therapy, but this
has only limited applicability. As the GAP Committee concluded, only the clinical-descriptive aspects of the child's behavior can be dealt with today in a classification which can be
handled statistically and used by people from a variety of
schools of thought. "As of today the other components must
still be left for a diagnostic formulation" (Group for Advancement of Psychiatry, 1966).

In such an approach, the behavioral or phenomenological
approach to the study of symptoms and symptom clusters reviewed by Newbrough (1972) has the advantage of keeping "the
level of inference at a minimum, yielding more reliable data and
verifiable criteria for classification" (Kanfer, 1973). However, as
Kanfer points out, such a system involves the misleading assumption that common etiological factors are involved in different symptoms. In addition, a symptom or a point on a scaled
dimension has meaning only in the context of a total relationship; the function of a clinician cannot be substituted for by
atomistic lists, nor by factor-analytic or other "machine" production of syndromes from symptoms (Morse, 1973). A noncategorical approach thus is potentially dangerous because it
easily becomes oriented toward symptomatic treatment only
and away from diagnosis and classification.

In view of the theoretical problems discussed elsewhere
(Group for Advancement of Psychiatry, 1966; Prugh, 1969;
Rhodes and Tracy, 1972), we feel that the only possible approach to a system of classification of disturbed behavior in
childhood and adolescence today is a typological one which is
primarily descriptive (rather than explanatory) and based on

operational definitions. A dimensional approach can be employed during clinical assessment, diagnostic formulation, and treatment planning, as will be discussed later, but such an approach will not suffice for classificatory purposes. As Kanfer (1973) has pointed out, traditional systems have attempted to devise one classification to provide the information required for individual treatment planning, for epidemiologic purposes for administrative decisions, and for theoretical and research reasons. This is obviously a large order, and no available classification can be said to fulfill all these needs. *Multiple classification* or multiple axes in a single classification undoubtedly are required (Group for Advancement of Psychiatry, 1966; Engel, 1969; Rutter and others, 1969). The distinguished evolutionist and taxonomist George Gaylord Simpson had earlier made the same point (Simpson, 1961).

An additional problem in the classification of behavior has to do with the variation in perception arising from the professional background and limits of tolerance of the observer. Here Newbrough's (1972) creative model of Perceived Behavioral Discrepancy can be of much value in the approach to the study of disturbed behavior and its definition and handling by clinicians, educators, and others; but it does not provide conceptual help in the objective construction of categories for classification.

The limitations and potentially destructive effects upon minority group children of categorizations based on "culture-bound" intelligence or other testing have been thoroughly discussed by Mercer (1972) and others. Because of the history of discrimination and abuses, it is easy to understand why minority-group members are wary of being classified (or treated) by mental health professionals who are not of the same racial or ethnic background. In fact, many parent groups now insist upon racial or ethnic identity with their children on the part of teachers and psychologists. Although some immediate adjustments should be and are being made, the long-term implications of this approach could be rather grotesque. It would essentially lead to fragmenting the social sciences into at least as many subunits as there are subcultural groups in the population, with destructive impact on most fields. Our experience, as well as that of others, leads us to conclude that personality and social class differences often override racial or ethnic differences in testing and treatment.

Although theoretical considerations have not been dealt with in detail in this chapter, one theoretical issue must be discussed at this point. This has to do with the fact that many professionals, with their interest in ecology and ethology, seem to be taking the position that everything in behavior is reactive to external stimuli, and that nothing is internalized within the child. Instead of employing an inside-outside dichotomy of this type, however, it seems wiser for our purposes to place behavior on an environmentally responsive continuum, as Hinde (1966) has suggested in his discussion of animal behavior. Some behaviors are more responsive to environmental factors and therefore to environmental manipulation than others. It is recognized of course that all therapies are environment-external except self-analyzed and self-generated change; the problem is what type of external influence is induced (Morse, 1973). A conceptual model dealing with the external-internal and environmental responsivity issues in relation to clinical classification is offered later in this chapter.

Following a review of available classifications, the chapter will address itself to three basic issues: (a) a useful classification of disorders, including a conceptual framework; (b) clinical diagnostic assessment along dimensions, with qualitative and quantitative criteria; and (c) the needs of children, built around support systems.

Review of Existing Classifications

In the GAP Report (1966) on classification of psychopathological disorders in childhood, twenty-four classification schemes from the United States and Europe were reviewed. These schemes were based on descriptive or phenomenologic points of view, currently popular concepts of etiology (ranging from somatic origins to psychogenesis), total versus partial personality reactions, the degree of treatability, or a combination of such conceptual views. Although each has made some contribution to understanding and systematization, none has proven satisfactory for widespread clinical use.

DSM classification. The classification of psychiatric disorders offered by the 1961 revision of the *Standard Nomenclature of Diseases and Operations* (American Medical Association, 1961) drew upon twentieth-century dynamic psychology as a conceptual framework in the section dealing with diseases of

Issues in the Classification of Children

the psychobiologic unit (formulated by the American Psychiatric Association in its *Diagnostic and Statistical Manual,* 1961—*DSM-I*). It offered descriptive-dynamic definitions for its classificatory categories, but left untouched many of the developmental features of psychopathology of childhood and adolescence.

The current revision of the *Standard Nomenclature* (based on a 1969 revision of the American Psychiatric Association nomenclature, *DSM-II*) has added a category for "Behavioral Disorders of Childhood and Adolescence." This has been sharply criticized by child professionals in the United States (Bemporad and others, 1970; Finch, 1969; Fish, 1969a; and Silver, 1969), as well as by those in Britain (Rutter, 1965), and Australia (Ashburner, 1968). The criticisms have centered around the fact that the terms in this category offer an inadequate range of disorders, involving mainly symptom complexes or partial symptom responses, with some inappropriate and confusing items. Somewhat similar criticisms have been made also of the typology offered by Jenkins and his colleagues, who did much of the factor analytic and other work underlying the symptom complexes in *DSM-II* (Jenkins and Cole, 1964).

Bemporad and his colleagues (1970) employed a symptom list devised from data on presenting symptoms of child patients, collected by Shaw and Lucas (1970); they demonstrated that the symptoms which corresponded to most of the *DSM-II* categories did not show any uniform clustering within any diagnostic category established in their eventual diagnoses on a group of child patients. They saw little if any prognostic value in such symptom complexes and even less indication of the severity of the underlying disorder. Criticisms by the authorities cited above, especially Finch (1969) have been even stronger regarding the inadequacy for the classification of children's disorders of the eighth revision of the *International Classification of Diseases* (ICD) (World Health Organization, 1967), which employed much the same approach as the *DSM-II*.

GAP classification. In 1966, in response to the long recognized need for a separate, more adequate and useful classification dealing with mental and emotional disorders in children, the Committee on Child Psychiatry of the Group for Advancement of Psychiatry (1966) offered a proposed classification. The classification involved a set of operational definitions of clinical categories, based on a conceptual framework with which it was hoped that clinicians from varying backgrounds could agree. This embraced psychosomatic, developmental, and psychosocial points of view, with contributions from psychoanalytic theory as well as the fields of learning theory, neurophysiology, child development, social science, and ethology. As Engel (1969) has indicated, the GAP approach offered "the beginnings of multiple classification"; the scheme provided independent assessment of symptoms, allowed for the diagnosis of "normality" ("healthy responses") and offered a concept of "developmental deviations" appropriate to childhood, in addition to definitions specific to childhood in regard to other categories.

The GAP classification was presented simply as a point of departure for clinicians working with children to use, criticize, and modify since there was no available classification of childhood disorders on which a group of clinicians could agree, in spite of over twenty previous attempts by individuals. A glossary of terms was included. Since its publication, the Report has been widely circulated and has been reviewed in major journals in a number of countries.

As expected, the classification, though received favorably in general, has not found universal approval. Some cogent criticisms are offered of the structure of the classification itself (Ashburner, 1968; Bemporad and others, 1970; Fish, 1969a) and of the conceptual approach upon which it was based (Kessler, 1971; Santostefano, 1971). It does not have the predictive power which Rutter (1965) calls for, although Eisenberg (1967) considers it unrealistic to expect predictive power from a classification. It is criticized (Kessler, 1971) for its theoretical framework, which draws heavily, although not at all exclusively, upon psychoanalytic theory. However, Ashburner (1968) feels that its conceptual approach is coherent, and he believes that it can readily be understood by clinicians from different schools of thought. Criticisms of its failure to employ criteria for disorders in psychosocial functioning which may not correspond with clinical diagnoses have been rightly put forth (Kessler, 1971; Santostefano, 1971). In order to try to meet these criticisms and to permit usage of the GAP classification by other than mental health professionals, the first author of this chapter later offered to the Joint Commission on Mental Health of Children an attempt at a classification based on levels of psychosocial functioning (Prugh, 1969). This involves a developmental framework and correlates with the GAP nomenclature.

Since its publication, the GAP classification has been widely employed by individuals and by children's psychiatric facilities in the United States (Bemporad and others, 1970), in Australia (Ashburner, 1968), and elsewhere. Its study as an alternative to the *Standard Nomenclature* has been recommended by at least two major textbooks (Freedman and Kaplan, 1967; Shaw and Lucas, 1970), and it has been translated into several languages. In the United States, it has been recommended for usage by members of the American Association of Psychiatric Services for Children (Harrison, 1967; Rexford, 1969) and, concomitantly with *DSM-II*, by the new *Standards for Psychiatric Facilities Serving Children and Adolescents*, formulated by a committee of the American Psychiatric Association (1971). Although it deals only to a limited extent with social class factors (McDermott and others, 1970), its appropriateness for employment in an urban child psychiatry service is supported by Bemporad and his colleagues (1970), following usage over a year's time. At least parts of the classification have been found helpful in dealing with the problems of rural children in Appalachia (Loof, 1971). In addition, one clinical description of a group of cases falling into one of its newer subcategories has been published (Jordan and Prugh, 1971). Thus the applicability of the classification in different settings and in different countries has been demonstrated, and it may properly be thought of as at least having international implications.

Bemporad and his colleagues (1970) and Fish (1969a) believe that the inclusion in the GAP classification of childhood variants of some of the adult personality disorders allows the diagnosis of less severe and as yet unsolidified personality pictures. These include the use of *isolated* rather than *schizoid* personality disorder, and *mistrustful* rather than *paranoid.* They also feel that the inclusion of new subcategories of personality disorders, such as *overly dependent, oppositional,* and *overly inhibited,* permit clinicians to describe more specifically the types of personality problems actually encountered in children. They approve the use of *developmental deviations* either as a primary diagnosis or combined with an accompanying personality diagnosis, feeling that this approach highlights the importance of this area for clinicians working with children. The category of developmental deviations accounts for approximately 15 percent of the clinic population reported on by Bemporad and his colleagues (1970).

Bemporad's group approves the use of *healthy responses,* with the three proposed subgroups (*developmental crises, situational crises,* and *other responses,* the latter "embracing individual variations") in the GAP classification, and they found that 9 percent of their clinic population fell into this category (Bemporad and others, 1970). Fish (1969a) is critical of the terms *tension-discharge disorders* and *schizophreniform disorder,* feeling that these do not add clarity of conceptualization, although others (Ashburner, 1968; Bemporad and others, 1970; Harrison, 1967; Rexford, 1969) approve of the use of these terms. A number of workers (Anthony, 1967; Harrison, 1967; M. Engel, 1969; Shaw and Lucas, 1970) have found the GAP Symptom List, related specifically to child and adolescent disorders, to be helpful. Although there is not yet a published study based on the results of systematic concomitant usage of the GAP nomenclature and *DSM-II* in a clinical setting, a method recommended by Bahn (1968), such an approach has been employed (Finzer and Wagonfeld, 1969), with the impression that the GAP classification has greater reliability and is more readily susceptible to statistical treatment. Bemporad and his colleagues (1970) compared the results of their usage of the GAP classification with that of the *DSM-I* in another clinic population, with equivalent impressions.

Several investigators (Ashburner, 1968; Bemporad and others, 1970; Fish, 1969a), have suggested specific ways in which the GAP classification might be modified or adapted to the *DSM-II* and the *ICD* to permit more effective and appropriate classification of children's psychopathological disorders. One approach is based upon the recommendations of Ashburner (1968), regarding ways of integrating the GAP classification into Section 5 of the *ICD*; these have been accepted by the Australian and New Zealand Child Psychiatry Society. Such recommendations are based on the use of the *Glossary of Mental Disorders* of the National Health and Medical Research Council of Australia.

The GAP schema represents a descriptive classification of typological nature, not an explanatory classification, although some inferences about etiology are inevitably implicit in its operational definitions of certain categories. The overall classification is not based on developmental stages, but the conceptual framework involves a developmental approach, and parts of the classification deal with clinical manifestations at different stages

of development. The categories are meant to be clearly deline-
ated and largely mutually exclusive, with the criterion variables
for class membership fairly well spelled out. There is inevitably
some overlap, however, and multiple diagnoses must be employed in certain instances. The relationship between categories
and available methods of intervention is not spelled out, although some inferences regarding treatability and prognostic
outlook are inevitably implicit in some of the operational definitions. In Prugh's (1969) psychosocial classification, however,
appropriate treatment modalities are spelled out for children
with different levels of psychosocial dysfunction, correlated
with the GAP diagnoses. The use of specific treatment modalities depends heavily upon the views of the clinician. A variety
of clinical instruments are of course used by different clinicians
to arrive at a diagnosis leading to classification, and there is
considerable variability in their reliability and validity.

   WHO classification. One other approach to classification
of children's disorders has been recommended by the Third
Seminar on Psychiatric Disorders, Classification, and Statistics
held in 1968 by the World Health Organization (Rutter and
others, 1969). The participants were an "international group of
people of different disciplines, backgrounds, and theoretical
views." This group offered a "triaxial" classification, which includes the "clinical psychiatric syndrome"; the "child's level of
intellectual functioning (regardless of etiology)"; and "any associated or etiological factors" (physical and environmental factors, with environmental factors broken down into "factors of a
social or material nature and factors of an emotional or attitudinal nature"). They have recommended more recently the
coding of such items as age, sex, referral agency, current parental situation, duration of symptoms, level of social adjustment,
follow-up, and amended diagnosis. Although a glossary of diagnostic terms was offered, the group acknowledged that much
work remains to be done on the etiological factors, particularly
the environmental and psychosocial ones, before general agreement is possible.

   The clinical categories suggested by the WHO group bear
considerable similarity to those in the earlier GAP classification
(see Table 1).

   One of the unique features of the WHO seminar was a
"diagnostic exercise" conducted as a preparation for the meeting. Twelve case histories were distributed to the twenty-four

Table 1

Comparable Terms in GAP and WHO Classifications

WHO Term	GAP Term
Normal Variations	Healthy Responses
Adaptation Reactions	Reactive Disorders[a]
Specific Developmental Disorders[b]	Developmental Deviations[b]
Neurotic Disorders	Psychoneurotic Disorders
Personality Disorders	Personality Disorders
Mental Subnormality	Mental Retardation
Psychosomatic Disorders	Psychophysiological Disorders
Psychosis	Psychotic Disorders
Neurological Disorders	Brain Syndromes
Conduct Disorders	Tension-Discharge Disorders[c]
Other Clinical Syndromes	Other Disorders

[a] A term discarded by the WHO group because of possible confusion with the European term *reactive psychosis.*
[b] Refers to disorders in speech and language, cognitive functions, and motor behavior.
[c] Included under the category of personality disorders.

participants and to other persons in different countries. On the basis of basic information on family history, individual history of the child (including early development and schooling), presenting disorder, mental and physical status, and the results of relevant investigations, these individuals were asked to make a diagnosis, using their own terminology, and to code their diagnosis according to a classification of categories drawn up by the preparatory working party for the conference. The eleven categories were similar to those mentioned above, with slight differences in terminology: the use of the category of *disorders directly due to demonstrable acute or chronic brain conditions* to refer to *neurological disorders,* and the employment of the terms *reactive disorders* and *antisocial disorders* to refer respectively to *adaptation reactions* and *conduct disorders.* The individuals participating in the diagnostic exercise were later given information on the child's subsequent progress based on follow-up data and were asked whether they then wished to revise their diagnosis in the light of the additional information. At the seminar, cases of different types of children's disorders were presented by videotaped recordings, together with summaries of case histories.

In general, a high degree of concordance in diagnosis was obtained among this group, largely child and adult psychiatrists working in different countries, on cases of reactive disorder, neurotic disorder, developmental disorder, personality disorder, and psychosis. For three of the twelve cases, however, agreement on personality disorder and psychosis was largely dependent on follow-up information.

The WHO group has made a clinical contribution to the study of the issues of reliability and validity which has heretofore only been approached in research on one or two clinical categories. Although their "high degree of concordance" was not specified and other methodological problems may apply, at least an international group, composed largely of psychiatrists from differing backgrounds, was able to communicate with a high degree of agreement—no mean achievement.

Official status of current classifications. Of all the classifications discussed above, only the *DSM-II* and the *ICD* have any official recognition and this in medical circles only. The *DSM-II* represents the psychiatric portion of the official classification of the American Medical Association (*Standard Nomenclature*), which recognizes also the *International Classification of Diseases* (*ICD*). Psychiatric hospitals and community facilities accredited by the Joint Commission on Accreditation of Hospitals use the *DSM-II*, which is coded to correlate with the *ICD*. Psychiatrists and pediatricians, as well as internists and family practitioners who work in these hospitals, thus have the authority to record diagnoses of disturbed behavior, even though these are not strictly medical diagnoses. The Psychiatric Accreditation Council of the Joint Commission on Accreditation of Hospitals, of which one of the authors of this chapter (Prugh) is a member, representing the American Psychiatric Association, is setting up standards for psychiatric facilities for children and adolescents, based on the recent publication of such standards by the A.P.A. (1971), which were formulated by a committee of child psychiatrists. A number of child psychiatrists and other mental health professionals in this country would like to see the GAP classification for children adopted officially for use in the *Standard Nomenclature,* which would then give it the official recognition of the Joint Commission on Accreditation of Hospitals. Whether the WHO triaxial classification will be adopted officially by the *ICD* in its coming revision in 1975—and thus gain official international psychiatric and medical recognition—remains to be seen.

The official status of the classifications referred to applies of course only to physicians. Other mental health clinicians are

free to use any classification they choose or to use no classification, although many of them work in psychiatric facilities
which report statistics in medical terms. Many states and the
Biometry Branch of the National Institute of Mental Health
collect epidemiologic data using the *DSM-II,* a practice which,
because of the limitations mentioned earlier, results in gross
inaccuracy of incidence-prevalence impressions of disorders
occurring in childhood and adolescence. A classification should
not of course be the property of any one discipline, and truth,
as the clinician sees it, should always take precedence over
bureaucratic rigidity. When a national health insurance system
comes in this country, coverage for mental health services
should not be based on a label or on the professional discipline
of the person who provides such services. Nevertheless, the
efforts of a number of people to bring about change in the
existing system have met with frustrating resistance, and any
recommendations we make for change in classification and
reporting systems must take these considerations into account.

Recommendations

Reference was made earlier to three basic issues: (1) a
clinically useful classification of disordered behavior, (2) the
approach to clinical assessment along different dimensions, and
(3) meeting the needs of children through support systems. It is
our position that the GAP classification offers such a useful
approach to classification by mental health clinicians. When
taken with its conceptual framework, it has no pejorative, professional, or institutional implications, and it can be easily
modified as a result of its clinical usage, which is currently
widespread. It can be integrated into the *ICD* (Ashburner,
1968) and could be unified with the WHO "triaxial" scheme
(Rutter and others, 1969). With the addition of some type of
classification on the basis of psychosocial functioning (for
example, Prugh, 1969, correlated with the GAP categories), it
can be integrated into a system which can be used by other than
mental health clinicians. With a little work, for which there is
currently insufficient time because of our schedule, the definitions of levels of psychosocial functioning could be translated
into a listing of the fundamental needs of children, healthy and
disordered, at different levels of development, such as dependency needs, the need for limits, needs for peer interaction and

for figures for identification, and cognitive needs. These could be correlated with environmental factors which are involved in children's problems, such as parent loss or poverty, as well as with necessary support systems, inside or outside of the home, as has been attempted for mental health services (Prugh, 1969) or as has been done for the educational needs of emotionally disturbed children (Michigan Association for Emotionally Disturbed Children, 1973).

Such an ultimate approach would enable treatment systems to be planned on the basis of need rather than diagnostic label and would respond to a recent call for a noncategorical approach to treatment programs for children and youth (Lourie and Lourie, 1970). Thus, as they have recommended, institutions now defined by category could be replaced by functional institutional arrangements, such as the Re-ED program in Tennessee, with planning also for the child who needs no category but has no home. Categorical terms will still need to be used for clinical and research purposes, but need not dictate treatment patterns, as has often happened in the past in this country. At the same time, the developmental needs and special characteristics of children and adolescents can be highlighted and met.

Clinical Considerations

The remainder of this chapter is devoted to conceptual considerations which underlie clinical assessment and treatment planning, and to the process of assessment itself. For purposes of clarity, the term *psychosocial disorder* will be used, rather than *emotional disturbance, psychiatric problems,* and so on. To avoid further some of the limitations of "medical" terminology, the terms *assessment, planning,* and *levels of intervention* will be employed, wherever possible, as somewhat broader terms than *diagnosis* and *treatment* and ones which can be used by a person from any background. The basic considerations in assessment and planning for intervention are: (1) what does one need to know, (2) what are the recommendations, (3) who does what to intervene, and (4) who decides what is done and who does it? These should be clinical considerations, based on the needs of the child and family and the broader community, as well as on the qualifications and level of sophistication of the people who assess and intervene; they should *not* be based on issues related to financial cost, professional rivalry, theoretical commitment, or political questions. Intervention should be tailored to the needs of the child and family; the child and family should not be fitted to a therapeutic mold, for any reason.

Definitions of *diagnosis* and *classification* were offered earlier. As implied, classification, or the assignment of a person to a group, is a part of the diagnostic process. As Engel (1969) has pointed out, "classification is often confused with diagnosis, and the diagnostic process comes to a standstill at the point at which the child has been 'labeled,' that is, classified. Since the label brings with it neither directives for specific interventions nor explanations of the illness, it is easy to see why those who equate diagnosis with classification soon regard the process as useless from either the educational or psychological point of view."

In an attempt to clarify further the distinction and overlap between classification and diagnosis, Engel distinguishes several levels of diagnosis. At the first level, *the level of discernment of difference,* the assessor engages in a "contrast-and-compare process which is essential and basic to science," comparing the child to a relatively homogeneous group, the comparison resulting in a separation of the child from a group as "different." The next level is *the level of assignment of value.* Here, for example, the child is regarded as "sick" and *not* "bad," with certain action implications in the direction of some sort of intervention; this step involves some inferences and tentative hypotheses. At the third level, *the assignment of a label* (such as *learning problem* or *mentally retarded*), an obvious act of classification takes place. This classification is predicated on the two previous judgments and should lead to intervention by one of the "helping professions." Finally, at the level of *explanation or diagnosis,* an attempt is made to reconstruct the origin or genesis of the disorder and to evaluate the child's strengths in relation to his symptoms (the adaptive modes at his disposal for coping with emotional or physical disability). Involved also is an approach to the examination of the total developmental consequences of the child's symptoms; this should be done not simply in the light of the present, but also of the future. Finally, it is necessary to attempt to connect as fully as possible the relationships of certain personality processes with others, such as the relationship of memory to concentration, or the degree to which the child may be flooded with feelings which outstrip his cognitive, skills and ability to communicate. Inferences of this nature pass beyond classification because they compare the child with himself, not with groups of children. This last and most critical stage, which involves a choice of recommendations based on understanding and explanation, is often not reached in the diagnostic process, so that appropriate action cannot be recommended with confidence, leading to skepticism about the utility of "diagnosis," which may be just "classification disguised by more words."

Engel (1969) points out that the classification problems of research workers are most often dealt with by "operationalizing" the selection of subjects into high and low groups on variables such as anxiety, motility, or verbal behaviors, but that clinicians and educators cannot categorize in this way. She cites problems which arise in legislative approaches, in relation to the definition of "emotionally disturbed" or other groups of children, and calls for a renewed interest in diagnostic work, over and beyond classification, in order to differentiate the effectiveness of varying treatment approaches for children with differing psychological makeups.

Following Engel's thinking we believe that a *diagnostic formulation,* involving clinical, developmental, familial, and other dimensions, is more helpful and valid than the simple selection of a diagnostic category. Some of the considerations in such a diagnostic formulation can be drawn together by the clinician, relying on the history, clinical examination, and observations of other professional personnel, such as the nurse or the teacher. Other aspects may be more obscure, and the help of a child psychiatry consultant, psychological testing, speech or hearing consultation, or other assessments may be necessary in order to arrive at a final formulation which will allow a reasonably accurate prognosis and an appropriate plan for intervention.

In the following outline, adapted from the GAP formulation (1966), various dimensions are included which should be considered in arriving at a diagnostic formulation. Not all are pertinent to the evaluation of any given child in a particular family. The goals of such a formulation, based on a psychosocial assessment, include the determination of the presence, nature, and severity of any disorders in the psychosocial functioning of child and family; the assessment of any possible relationship of these to physical problems if present; and the arrangement for appropriate intervention.

A. Individual Personality Characteristics
1. Child (current status)
  a. Appraisal of intellectual capacity and functioning (based on clinical estimate, psychological tests, school tests or achievement, use of Denver Developmental Screening Test in preschool children, or other sources)
  b. Basic personality picture (overly dependent, oppositional, overly inhibited), if not included in clinical diagnosis
  c. Central areas of conflict, whether external or internal
  d. Characteristics of personality functioning
    (1) Cognitive capacities (attention, concentration, perceptual-motor functions, time sense, self-awareness, fantasy, concept formation, abstraction, memory, judgment)
    (2) Capacity for social relations and functioning
    (3) Nature of self-concept, level of self-esteem, identity
    (4) Predominant defenses (denial, projection)
    (5) Nature of conscience or superego operations
    (6) Level of psychosocial and psychosexual development (fixations, regressions, developmental deviations, unevenness, discrepancies)
    (7) Overall adaptive capacity (coping skills, capacity for mastery, special strengths, handling of competition, frustration tolerance, potential for sublimation, balance of progressive versus regressive forces)
    (8) Psychosocial functioning (capacity for development, play, learning, socialization; whether optimal, vulnerable, incipient dysfunction, moderate dysfunction, severe dysfunction; see Prugh, 1969)
    (9) Perception of family members, relation to reality
  e. Physical health, energy level, neurological status, as well as the relationship of any such factors to psychopathological picture (if not included in clinical diagnosis)
2. Parents
  a. Mother (basic personality structure, intellectual

capacity, conflicts in relation to child, capacity
for social or occupational functioning, physical
health)
b. Father (same as above)
3. Other members of family constellation
a. Siblings (same as above, plus current developmental level)
b. Others, including grandparents (same as above)

B. Interpersonal Situation
1. Marital relationships
a. Husband-wife (mutual reciprocity, cooperation,
communication, unbalanced, interlocking, immature)
b. Interaction as parents (fit, mutuality, cooperation, division of labor, complementarity)
2. Parent-child relationships
a. Mother (capacity for mothering, type of figure
for identification by child of same sex, nature of
interaction with child, nature of response of
child)—supportive, positive communication, con-
flictual, primitive, dominating, symbiotic, over-
indulgent, overprotective
b. Father (same as above)—healthy, appropriate
compliance, overdependent, withdrawn, rebel-
lious, manipulative, perception of child
3. Child-sibling relationships (mutual acceptance, rival-
rous, dominating, dependent, parasitic, interlocking,
sharing of parents)
4. Other family relationships
5. Family functioning
a. Degree of cohesiveness or integration of family
unit (balanced cohesiveness, too closely knit,
noncohesive, disorganized, broken)
b. Significant subgroup operations (healthy align-
ments, triangular—mother and child against father or vice versa, double-bind, scapegoating)
c. Equilibrium-disequilibrium balance (patterns of
leadership, dominance, nature of role complementarity or "fit" among family members)
d. Patterns of communication and expression of
emotions (open, comfortable, mutual, inhibited,
blocked, distorted, displaced)

    e. Integration of family in community (balanced, overcommitted, isolated, nomadic)
    f. Value orientations, belief systems
    g. Degree of family tolerance of child's behavior
  6. Sociocultural setting
    a. Family residence, housekeeping patterns, immediate environment
    b. Socioeconomic (social-class) status and relevant patterns
    c. Ethnic background and relevant patterns
    d. Religious affiliation(s)
    e. Occupational status of family members, income level, obligations, debts
    f. Educational background of family members
    g. Peer-group interactions (neighborhood gang)
    h. Community mores and values; behavior required for making adequate adjustment to the community "set"
    i. Degree of community tolerance of child's behavior

  C. Clinical Diagnosis (degree of severity, acute or chronic, symptomatic manifestations)

  D. Summary of Developmental Etiological Considerations
    1. Precipitating factors (event or events impinging upon psychosocial functioning, developmental stage, conscious or unconscious perceptions or misperceptions)
    2. Predisposing factors (parent-child relationship, family patterns, personality structure, hereditary endowment, biological constitution, integrative capacity, previous events, fixations, chronic physical illness)
    3. Contributory factors (intercurrent or related physical illness, limitations in mental endowment, illness or depression in another family member)
    4. Perpetuating factors (secondary gain, use of child by parent as vicarious object, unhealthy or partial solutions of conflict through symptomatology by child or parents, family patterns)

  E. Prognostic Statement (evaluation of nature, severity, duration of problem; based on consideration of factors emerging during diagnostic study, such as capacity of child and parents to relate constructively to professional staff, their degree of psychological awareness, motivation toward change in significant figures within family unit, effectiveness of family functioning, previous efforts to obtain help)

F. Plan for Intervention
   1. Recommendations for appropriate intervention (counseling, crisis intervention, intensive psychotherapy, remedial education, speech therapy, drug therapy)
   2. Referral to appropriate facility (community facility, placement service, pediatric hospital, psychiatric consultant)
   3. Consideration of other environmental steps (activity groups, homemaker services)
   4. Special cautions or contraindications to any particular approach

G. Interpretation (to parents, school, etc., in appropriate terms)

H. Reassessment of Clinical Diagnosis or Plan for Intervention[1]

In contrast to the qualitative approach illustrated by the foregoing outline, Rabinovitch (1973) and his colleagues have

---

[1]The aforegoing material indicates how the complex process of diagnostic formulation does not lend itself to the approach to computer diagnosis, recently lauded by some. Such an approach, however useful for the diagnosis of rare medical disorders, could produce over-reliance on the computer, similar to over-reliance on laboratory tests, which can underwrite a simplistic approach to a complicated process and diminish the observational acuity of the clinician, so important in the evaluation of the psychosocial aspects of children's problems. This statement regarding observational acuity is not meant to negate the observations made earlier regarding the variations in perception of problems arising from the professional orientation of the observer. There is no person-proof system, and the level of expertise of the clinician eventually has to be taken into account and specified. As Polanyi has indicated, science strives to specify; American science in particular tends to undervalue knowledge that is in an inarticulate stage and cannot easily be measured. This applies to the attributes of the observer—in this case the clinician's level of training (Polanyi, 1958).

developed a semiquantitative approach to the assessment of children's psychosocial disorders along diagnostic dimensions. In this assessment schema, dimensions such as neurological integration, intellectual potential, intellectual functioning, clarity of ego boundaries, capacity for depth relations, acculturation, anxiety (endogenous and exogenous), motivation, and self-esteem are rated on a continuum from *very low* to *very high* (specifically, the various ratings are *very low, low, average, high,* and *very high*).

Theoretical Considerations

The term *psychosocial disorder,* or *disorder in psychosocial functioning,* suggests most clearly the lack of "fit" between the child and his family or environment. Such a term also emphasizes the child's capacity to function. Effective functioning suggests an equilibrium within the individual and in his interaction with this environment; it also suggests "adequate and integrated satisfaction of the person's needs related to his own goals and how he sees himself as achieving them" (Linn and others, 1969). *Dysfunction,* however, suggests "discontent and unhappiness, accompanied by negative self-regarding attitudes . . . handicapping anxiety and other pathological interpersonal functions that reduce flexibility in coping with stressful situations or achieving self-actualization in what is to that person a significant role. . . . Dysfunction is seen as coping with either personal, interpersonal, or geographic environment in a maladaptive manner." This approach is consonant with the unitary theory of health and disease articulated by G. Engel (1960) and the adaptation model summarized by Prugh (1963, 1969) as well as the coping model (Murphy, 1962) and the competence model (White, 1963); all of these can be subsumed under Erikson's (1959) developmental psychosocial model, as may appropriate features of learning theory, social theories, and other relevant systems.

Linn and her colleagues (1969) have developed a Social Dysfunction Rating Scale, which has been demonstrated by their methods to have both high total score reliability and reasonable validity. Other somewhat similar scales have been developed for adults by Spitzer and his colleagues (1967) and by others, but none takes into account the developmental sequence and other differences between children and adults; even the ones available for adults do not produce a classification in the sense used in this chapter. The schema developed by Prugh (1969) offers a combination of both, with a basic conceptual framework, but without either tested reliability or validity, which await future research. As expected in this schema, clinical diagnosis does not always correspond with level of psychosocial function.

In searching for a conceptual model which would embody the relativistic, open-system, transactional, developmental, and multiple etiologic features of theoretical nature referred to by G. Engel (1960), Prugh (1963, 1969), and others, and yet would have clinical relevance, we wish to refer to the "environmentally responsive continuum" mentioned earlier. Figure 1 embodies a tentative model based on that conceptualization.

Such an approach has some implications for etiology, in that the disorders at the more responsive end of the continuum can be conceived of as arising more from environmental experience than from inborn or innate factors. It also has implications for levels of psychosocial functioning, prognosis, and general response to intervention, in that the more "responsive" disorders can generally be considered, unless the environmental context is "psychologically lethal," to be functioning at a more effective psychosocial level and to be more likely respond to intervention by environmental-external influences. It does not have specific implications for different types of intervention, except that the more "responsive" disorders could be expected to respond to briefer, less intensive, and more psychologically and interpersonally oriented types of intervention, generally on an ambulatory basis, with hospitalization, drug therapy, and other more somatic types of interventions reserved more appropriately for the disorders at the less responsive end of the continuum. More specific types of intervention, correlated with levels of psychosocial dysfunction and with the GAP diagnostic categories, are listed in the chart developed by Prugh (1969). A few disturbances at the "nonresponsive" end, such as severe mental retardation, may not respond to any available intervention.

The schema offered also has significant implications for development, that central feature of childhood. The stages listed on the left side of the chart represent the axis of development. This moves "up," from the more sensitive, dependent, and vulnerable phase of infancy and the preschool period, through the school-age period (where ideals and values begin to

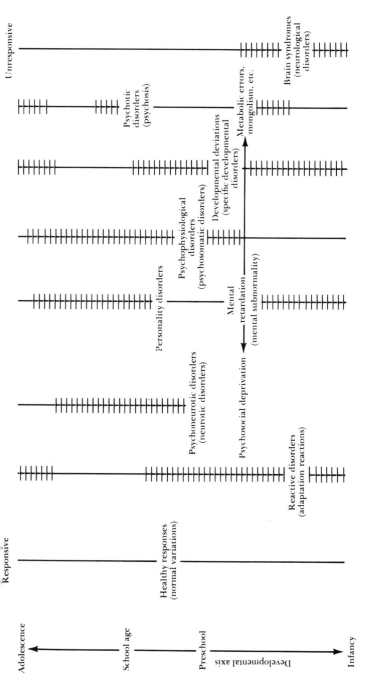

Figure 1. Schematic Representation of Disorders of Psychosocial Functioning. The Clinical categories of the GAP (1966) classification are grouped along a continuum ranging from environmentally responsive to environmentally unresponsive. Where they differ, the terms used by the WHO group (Rutter and others, 1969) are given in parentheses. The placement of the disorders and the lines running above (and in some cases below) the listed disorders can occur or crystallize; the cross-hatches indicate the level of highest incidence for some disorders.

be internalized, feelings are better controlled, and competence and coping devices are more fully developed) to the adolescent phase (where individual identity, self-realization, and independence are crystalized, with relatively less vulnerability). Of course, transactions take place between inborn temperamental qualities, built-in developmental patterns, sexual and physical characteristics, and other innate individual variations, and the attitudes and child-rearing attributes of the parents and other representatives of society, from infancy to adulthood. Even in the more basically physical dimension of personality development, however, autonomic response patterns and other "innate" characteristics of the individual are generally more modifiable in infancy and early childhood. Immunities to certain illnesses are built up as the child grows and develops, in the general direction of less vulnerability to physical and other environmental stimuli by the time adulthood is reached.

In the chart, the region of uncertainty about degree of responsiveness, prognosis, or treatability is not evenly distributed, of course, as would be the case with any such schematic model. In general, uncertainty could be considered to be greatest near the center of the chart. In addition, the methods of assessment of disorders necessarily vary, as do treatment approaches, with the region on the chart; physical and medical diagnostic methods would be used more frequently in the study of disorders nearer the "unresponsive" end of the continuum. Also, the schema has the advantage, in its broad outlines, of being simple enough to be used to communicate with educators, parole officers, parents, and other persons outside the mental health fields; parents, for example, can more easily comprehend how a child with a disorder nearer the unresponsive end of the continuum "can't help it."

Certain special considerations apply to individual categories. Mental retardation, for example, ranges across the chart from the largely "unresponsive" side, where inborn errors of metabolism and neurological disorders (with some overlap with "brain syndromes") belong, toward the "responsive" side, where psychosocial deprivation resulting in mental retardation must be placed. Even in largely "unresponsive" conditions, however (including severe brain syndromes, occurring frequently at birth), there is always an element of responsiveness to the external environment in the course of the child's development; thus no disorder is placed at the far side of the "unresponsive" column, even though minimal response to intervention may be expected in a few conditions. Similarly, since inborn temperamental qualities and other innate factors appear to play at least some part in healthy responses, even that category is not placed at the far side of the "responsive" column. Actually, some cases of disorders placed toward the "unresponsive" end of the continuum may represent milder forms, which can readily respond to intervention; for example, children with diffuse mild brain damage, in whom hyperactivity may be a (nonspecific) feature, may readily respond to stimulant drugs and/or other interventions.

Definitions and Case Examples

Healthy responses. Definitions of the GAP diagnostic terms employed in the chart have been offered in the report proposing their classification (GAP, 1966). The term *healthy responses* refers to developmental and situational crises, in which the child appears to be using appropriately his own coping devices and adaptive mechanisms, as well as the support of key figures in his environment, and refers to individual or "normal" variations in behavior as well. In a situational crisis:

> A three-and-a-half-year-old boy experienced the birth of a female sibling. He had been prepared for the baby's birth and had talked a good deal about his "baby sister" and how he would play with her. When the baby came home from the hospital, however, he seemed only briefly interested, then paid little attention to her. Over the next few days, he repeatedly tried to get his mother's attention when she was with the baby, and exhibited a sharp increase in dependent and fearful behavior, as well as a return to thumbsucking. Although he had been dry at night for six months, he wet the bed regularly for about ten days. On several occasions, he told his father that he wished the baby would "go back where she came from." After two weeks he began to seem less jealous and demanding of attention, especially when the mother arranged to spend some "time alone" with him each day. By three to three and a half weeks, he seemed to have generally returned to his previous level of adjustment. He showed more interest in the baby, although he still occasionally became jealous and demanding, especially when he was tired.

This preschool child exhibited some immediate jealousy and mildly regressive behavior, responses which can be expected in relation to the birth of a sibling. His capacity to cope with the situation was aided by his ability to verbalize his feelings and by his mother's recognition of his needs and the baby's.

An example of a developmental crisis:

> Over the past several months, a twenty-month-old girl, an only child, had become more physically active and exploratory in her behavior, requiring more careful supervision by her parents. Although she still cried and clung tightly to the mother when the parents had to leave her with a sitter, she showed signs of increasing oppositional behavior at other times. She would often vigorously resist attempts to control her behavior and, when asked to do things, regularly replied with a strong "No!" (although she spoke a number of words, she had not yet learned to say "Yes"). Occasionally, the little girl had a brief temper tantrum following any necessary frustration of her wishes. The parents were troubled by her behavior, but were able to avoid pitched battles while maintaining reasonably firm limits in important areas. This behavior continued unabated for about four months, and then gradually, from twenty-four to thirty months, became much more muted. She still tolerated frustration poorly at times, and brief bursts of strongly oppositional behavior continued until around three years.

The behavior shown by this little girl represents a normal push toward "a sense of autonomy" during the toddler phase. The parents were wise enough to understand the developmental significance of her oppositional behavior and "normal negativism." They were able at the same time to meet her conflicting needs for support and limits, thus helping her to resolve the developmental "crisis" in favor of realistic steps toward beginning independence and impulse control.

Reactive disorder. The term *reactive disorder* refers to a type and degree of behavioral response to various environmental stimuli which indicates the child is, temporarily at least, unable to cope adequately. The conflict between the child and his environment is conceived to be an external and largely conscious one, and may remain so. Although reactive disorders may occur at any age, they are seen most frequently in the preschool period.

A four-and-a-half-year-old boy, an only child, had exhibited isolated, withdrawn, and stereotyped behavior, together with bedwetting, nightmares several times a week, and some unclarity of speech, since the age of two and a half. The boy's psychomotor development apparently was within normal limits up to that time, and he was able to speak clearly, using short sentences. When he was two and a half years old, his mother became ill with infectious hepatitis, associated with rather marked depression, and was unable to participate effectively in his care for about six months. During this period, the father cared for the boy, with the help of a series of housekeepers. When the mother went to the hospital for several weeks early in her illness, the boy screamed and clung desperately to her. At first, he seemed depressed and inconsolable in her absence; then he gradually became withdrawn and isolated, reacting little to the mother's return home. He showed sleep disturbances, with marked regressed behavior, including complete loss of speech for a period of several months and temporary loss of bowel control, which he had just attained. From that time to the present, the withdrawn and isolated behavior continued, associated with many rituals around bedtime, frequent nightmares, and unclear speech.

When seen in two play interviews the boy was at first withdrawn and aloof, playing alone in a stereotyped fashion. His speech was infantile in nature, with much difficulty in the pronunciation of consonants in particular. Toward the end of the first interview, he began to include the examiner in his play; in the second interview he was able to relate more comfortably and with increasing warmth, talking more intelligibly about his frightening dreams about monsters "taking her away." Physical examination indicated that he was within normal limits at the time of study, and there was no history of pertinent birth injury or significant illness.

The mother appeared depressed and preoccupied with concerns about her health. She had been herself an only child, very dependent on her mother and rather distant from her father. She became pregnant after six years of marriage, following three miscarriages; she says that she had felt "incomplete" without a baby to care for. Up to the time of her illness, she had been somewhat anxious and overprotective in her handling of the boy, finding it difficult to leave him with sitters, and he had been quite dependent on her. Upon her recovery from the hepatitis, she had still felt depressed. She was disturbed by the boy's with-

drawn behavior and made occasional desperate attempts to
"get through to him," feeling helpless and full of self-blame
when she failed. The father is a driving, dominating person,
who directs his wife's care of the household. He has been
constantly dissatisfied with his son, even from infancy, because of his failure to "take things like a man."

Although there were problems in the parent-child relationships in this family prior to the mother's illness, the boy's
reaction to the temporary loss of his mother appeared to be the
central factor in his rather sudden onset of disturbed behavior.
His previous overdependence upon the mother, in response to
her anxious and overprotective approach as well as the father's
inability to relate warmly to him, represented a predisposing
factor, rendering him especially vulnerable to the loss of the
mother and angry at her for her apparent desertion of him. The
disorder in behavior was of sufficient intensity and duration,
with evidence of failure to cope, to permit its categorization as
a reactive disorder which would not resolve spontaneously. Professional intervention, involving therapy over a number of
months, was necessary to help child and parents resolve their
problems successfully.

Psychoneurotic disorder. In a psychoneurotic disorder, an
originally external conflict is conceived to have become an unre-
solved, unconscious, and internalized one. This process appears
to involve an internal change, related to emotional conflict, in
the way in which the child reacts to events and people, a change
of which he is not aware but which then brings forth reactions
from other people which tend to perpetuate the pattern.
Psychological symptoms, such as phobias or stuttering, appear
and cause the child to suffer. In the GAP conceptual framework, the development of conscience formation and other necessary adaptive mechanisms, involving the handling of guilt in
particular, do not appear until the later preschool and early
school-age period, with the result that the clinical picture does
not ordinarily appear until the early school-age period. This is in
contrast to reactive disorders, which, though they may occur at
any age, are seen most frequently in the preschool period. Why
certain children later show internalization of conflict is not clear.

An eight-year-old girl developed an increasingly severe phobia of "being kidnapped by a strange man." The
phobia had appeared when she was five and a half years old

and was beginning kindergarten. Her mother accompanied
her to school, and the girl was able to adjust to the group
situation only if the mother remained outside the classroom. During first grade and the early part of second grade,
the girl could attend school only if the mother (and not the
father) took her and picked her up. In the classroom she
was very quiet but performed adequately. She would not
play outside at home if the mother were not with her; she
would not go anywhere else away from home for fear of
being kidnapped. When the mother gave birth to a male
infant, she could no longer tolerate the special arrangements made necessary by the girl's increasing phobia, and
professional help was sought.

   During the course of assessment, it was learned that
when the girl was four years old the mother had developed
a mental disorder, related to some marital conflicts, and
was hospitalized for several months. The girl, who had
shown no apparent behavioral disturbance previously, was
cared for by her father, who fed her, bathed her, aided in
her toileting, and supervised her dressing and other activities, thus spending a great deal of time with her. The girl
was somewhat distressed by the mother's absence, but
seemed to enjoy her father's exclusive company. When the
mother returned home, the girl seemed very much concerned about her state of health, spending increasing
amounts of time with her, and gradually withdrawing from
the father. Gradually, over a period of months, the phobia
regarding "strange men" developed.

   At the time of contact, the mother seemed alarmed
at the girl's problem but also somewhat resentful toward
her because of the intensity of the demands on her time as
a result of the girl's symptom. She herself had been fearful
of sexual attack by men in her youth, and her sexual life
with her husband had been distasteful to her. The father
had been delighted with his daughter since her birth and
was puzzled and hurt by her "shutting him out" to an
increasing degree, especially since her phobia appeared. He
felt that his wife was "giving in too much" to their daughter around her symptom and said that he saw very little of
his wife. Later, during the course of psychotherapy with
child and parents, it was learned that the little girl had
thought secretly that her mother had gone to the hospital
because she had wished to be alone with her father.

When wishes accidentally become real, a preschool child,
who is developing a conscience but still employs "prelogical"

cognitive processes, can feel that she has sinned. A traumatic event, the temporary loss of her mother, brought about a change in the role of the father of this girl, with overstimulating implications for her. The resulting guilt unconsciously caused the girl to try to "make it up" to her mother when she returned from the hospital. The developing phobia caused the girl suffering; it kept her close to her mother, however, and away from the father and, indeed, thoughts about all men. Developmental factors also played a role since the little girl was engaged in issues relating to her establishment of a "sense of initiative" as a girl and woman-to-be at the time of the enforced shift in the role of her father. Guilt over leaving her mother and her associated fears also accentuated the normal anxiety over leaving home and entering school on a full-day basis.

Personality disorder. Personality disorders are conceived, like reactive disorders, to have their origins in external conflicts or depriving experiences in early childhood. Internal changes later occur, however, leading to relatively fixed patterns of reaction to events and people (personality patterns or traits). In these disorders, the child ordinarily does not suffer, since—for reasons that are not clear—the compulsive, aggressive, or other traits become embedded in the personality matrix. In seriously aggressive personality disorders, tension is discharged through the behavior, and the external world may suffer, as if in retaliation for depriving or markedly disturbing experiences in very early childhood. Since the crystalization of personality traits does not take place developmentally until the late school-age period, the clinical picture, in its chronic and relatively fixed form, does not appear until that time.

> A sixteen-year-old girl, who had experienced repeated sexual intercourse over a period of several years with a number of older adolescent boys, became pregnant out of wedlock. She had been somewhat headstrong and rather oppositional in her behavior at home since she was a preschool child, with an increase in this behavior at home and in school since she was nine or ten. Although the parents knew that she did not get along well with teachers, resisted pressures to study, and was just "getting by" academically, they had no inkling of her sexual activities. They indicated that they had "raised her strictly" and had not permitted her to have dates with boys, warning her of the dangers of pregnancy.

Assessment revealed that since early childhood the
girl had received little emotional support from her mother,
who was preoccupied with her brother, three and a half
years younger, who had a congenital heart defect. Her father, who had wanted a boy as his first child and was dis-
appointed in his sickly second child, withdrew from the girl
and the mother when the heart defect was diagnosed in his
infant son.

The results of assessment indicated that the girl's genital
contacts were not actually sexual as such. They seemed to represent, on one level, behavior stemming from personality traits
of oppositional nature, which had arisen in response to her
parents' overly strict rearing; these traits became more manifest
during adolescence in reaction to her parents' rigid sexual
mores. On a more basic level, however, her behavior represented
attempts to obtain interest and affection from boys, in order to
make up for her mother's lack of emotional support and her
father's lack of interest in her as a girl and a woman-to-be.

Psychotic disorder. In the GAP framework, the term
psychotic disorder refers to a serious blunting or distortion of
personality development, as the result of an interaction of inborn and experiential factors, to the point where the child is
unable to perceive and relate appropriately to other human beings or to test external reality with any accuracy. Various bizarre behavioral manifestations usually reflect the underlying
disorder in thinking; and the disorder, which may occur in
infancy or at any time later, shows different clinical characteristics related to the stage of development when the adaptive
breakdown began.

Over the past eighteen months, an eight-year-old
black girl has gradually become more isolated and withdrawn. In first grade, she performed well until the latter
part of the year. In second grade, she became increasingly
unresponsive; the teacher who referred her for assessment
said that she "just sits and stares at nothing, as if she is in a
world of her own." The mother described episodes of similar behavior at home, often associated with rocking movements; sometimes when she helped mechanically with the
housework, she seemed to be whispering to herself. Until
she began to attend school, the mother had noted no bizarre behavior, although the girl had been quite dependent
on her grandmother, who cared for her while the mother

worked. The girl was the youngest of four siblings, the older three being adolescent boys. The father had left the family when the girl was an infant. The family was in very limited economic circumstances, living in two rooms in a rat-infested, junkie-inhabited tenement in a ghetto area of a large eastern city.

In interviews the girl seemed aloof and withdrawn at first, but was able to relate intermittently for brief periods of time. Gradually, in whispers at first, she revealed her vivid fantasy world. "Power-baby" and "Super-baby" were its two principal inhabitants. "Power-baby" went to the stars and got into trouble. "Super-baby" followed to rescue her, but for some reason was ineffective in this attempt. There was also a doctor who came to cure, but instead sucked out blood like a vampire. Some of these revelations emerged only after months of psychotherapy, offered twice weekly. The imaginary characters were so real and frightening to the girl that she was in a perpetual state of "meganxiety." Physical examination revealed no significant abnormalities.

It would be easy to attribute a significant component of this girl's psychotic disorder to the environmental deprivation in her family's living situation. Undoubtedly, this played a role at one time. By this time, however, she would undoubtedly have been psychotic under any circumstances. Crisis intervention or other brief forms of therapy could not be expected to be effective with this girl, and she responded only to intensive long-term psychotherapy. During the course of therapy, it was learned that the girl had spent most of the first six months of her life in a hospital, because of recurrent diarrhea. This early psychosocial deprivation and the associated predisposition to possible later difficulties in adaptation apparently had interacted with the presumed biological or constitutional predisposition to psychosis and with the environment to produce a relatively unresponsive disorder. (Actually, *unresponsive* is a relative term as applied to psychotic disorders. The results of intensive psychotherapy, special education, and other measures over years now seem, in the hands of certain therapists at least, to be much more effective therapeutically than was formerly believed, particularly if such measures are undertaken early in the course of the disorder, as with early school-age children or those who develop such disorders in the very early preschool period.)

Other categories. Developmental deviations, involving lags or precocities in motor, sensory, cognitive, social, and other dimensions of development, are conceived to be based on in-born or innate individual characteristics, largely biological in origin, which transcend the boundaries of individual variations in behavior. Transactions between the child and his environ-ment, however, may influence such deviations in such a way as to permit their eventual amelioration or, conversely, their en-hancement through reinforcement or other mechanism. Psycho-physiologic disorder (disturbances in functioning of a particular physiologic system of the body, as in asthma or colitis, in which both biological and psychosocial factors play a role), brain syndromes, and mental retardation carry no broad or specific personality implications in themselves. As such, they can be regarded as "part" diagnoses (as can also certain developmental deviations) and in the GAP system call for an associated "per-sonality diagnosis" if possible, representing a type of multiple classification.

Individual symptoms, such as learning disorder, may rep-resent a developmental deviation or part of a reactive, psycho-neurotic, personality, or psychotic disorder, or may result from mental retardation or a brain syndrome. In the GAP system they would be included as "part" disorders, associated with the basic personality diagnosis, and would be coded with the use of the Symptom List. The GAP classification, like that of the WHO, includes an additional category of "Other Disorders," to be used for any newly described disorders or for use by a clini-cian who has reservations as to how to classify a particular disorder.

Although the GAP terms are used by physicians, their definitions arise from an adaptational and transactional con-ceptual model based on developmental, psychosocial, and psychosomatic propositions. Thus most of the definitions (not the diagnostic terms) do not derive from the traditional "medi-cal" model, and they have been widely used by other mental health professionals.

Summary

In this chapter, an attempt has been made to examine objectively the purposes and problems involved in the scientific process of *classification* of *psychosocial disorders in childhood and adolescence,* with due awareness of the potentially destructive approach to "labeling" which has sometimes been employed. In addition to a definition of terms, a review of existing classifications has been offered. Recommendations have been made regarding the GAP classification, a workable system for mental health clinicians which transcends the traditional "medical" model but which can be integrated into available "official" classification systems at national and international levels. The GAP system has no inherent pejorative, professional, or institutional implications; it can be meshed as well with an existing classification based on levels of psychosocial functioning, for use by other than mental health clinicians, which offers correlations between categories of functioning and appropriate types of intervention and support systems. Discussion of important clinical issues dealing with the relationship between diagnosis, or assessment, along various dimensions, and treatment, or intervention, on different levels, has been offered, and a conceptual model relevant to clinical classification has been put forth.

Ultimately, the definitions of levels of psychosocial functioning should be translated into a listing of the fundamental mental and emotional needs of children, healthy and disordered, at different levels of development. These could be correlated with environmental factors involved in disorders in childhood and adolescence, as a WHO group is currently attempting to do, as well as with necessary support systems, as has been attempted for mental health services and the educational needs of emotionally disturbed children. Such an approach would enable treatment systems to be planned at local, state, and national levels on the basis of need rather than diagnostic label, and it would respond to a recent call for a noncategorical approach to treatment programs for children and youth. Institutions now defined by category could ultimately be replaced by functional institutional arrangements, with planning also for the child who needs no category but has no home.

Categorical terms will still need to be used for clinical, research, and epidemiological purposes, but need not dictate treatment patterns, as has often happened in the past in this country, sometimes with political implications. At the same time, the developmental needs of children and adolescents can be highlighted and met, with a move toward a more appropriate balance between interventions for preventive purposes and those designed to meet treatment needs.

References

American Medical Association. *Standard Nomenclature of Diseases and Operations.* Chicago: American Medical Association, 1961.

American Psychiatric Association. *Diagnostic and Statistical Manual of Mental Disorders.* (1st Ed.; *DSM-I*) Washington, D.C.: American Psychiatric Association, 1961.

American Psychiatric Association. *Diagnostic and Statistical Manual of Mental Disorders.* (2nd Ed.; *DSM-II*) Washington, D.C.: American Psychiatric Association, 1969.

American Psychiatric Association. *Standards for Psychiatric Facilities Serving Children and Adolescents.* Washington, D.C.: American Psychiatric Association, 1971.

Anthony, E. J. "Taxonomy Is Not One Man's Business." *International Journal of Psychiatry,* March 1967, *3,* 173-178.

Ashburner, J. V. "Some Problems of Classification with Particular Reference to Child Psychiatry." *Australian and New Zealand Journal of Psychiatry,* 1968, *2,* 244.

Bahn, A. Personal communication, 1968.

Bemporad, J. R., Pfeiffer, C. M., and Bloom, W. "Twelve Months' Experience with the GAP Classification of Childhood Disorders." *American Journal of Psychiatry,* Nov. 1970, *127,* 658-664.

Eisenberg, L. "The Role of Classification in Child Psychiatry." *International Journal of Psychiatry,* March 1967, *3,* 179-181.

Engel, G. L. "A Unified Concept of Health and Disease." *Perspectives in Biology and Medicine,* Summer 1960, *3,* 459-485.

Engel, M. "Dilemmas of Classification and Diagnosis." *Journal of Special Education,* Fall 1969, *3,* 231-239.

Erikson, E. H. "Identity and the Life Cycle." *Psychological Issues,* 1959, *1*(1).

Finch, S. "Nomenclature for Children's Mental Disorders Needs Improvement." *International Journal of Psychiatry,* June 1969, *7,* 414.

Finzer, W. F., and Wagonfeld, S. Personal Communication, 1969.

Fish, B. "Limitations of the New Nomenclature for Children's Disorders." *International Journal of Psychiatry,* June 1969a, *7,* 393-398.

Fish, B. "Problems of Diagnosis and the Definition of Comparable Groups: A Neglected Issue in Drug Research with Children." *American Journal of Psychiatry,* January 1969b, *125,* 900-908.

Freedman, A. M., and Kaplan, H. I. *Comprehensive Textbook of Psychiatry.* Baltimore: Williams and Wilkins, 1967.

Group for the Advancement of Psychiatry. *Psychopathological Disorders in Childhood: Theoretical Considerations and a Proposed Classification.* New York: Group for the Advancement of Psychiatry, 1966.

Harrison, S. I. "Review of *Psychopathological Disorders in Childhood: Theoretical Considerations and the Proposed Classification,* Formulated by the Committee on Child Psychiatry of the Group for the Advancement of Psychiatry." *AAPCC Newsletter,* Nov. 1967, *14*(4).

Hinde, R. A. *Animal Behavior: A Synthesis of Ethology and Comparative Psychology.* New York: McGraw-Hill, 1966.

Jenkins, R. L., and Cole, J. O., Eds. *Diagnostic Classification in Child Psychiatry.* Washington, D.C.: American Psychiatric Association, 1964.

Jordan, K., and Prugh, D. G. "Schizophreniform Psychosis in Childhood." *American Journal of Psychiatry,* Sept. 1971, *128*, 323-331.

Kanfer, F. H., and others. *Report of Subcommittee on Behavior Disorders, Ad Hoc Task Force on Behavioral Classification, Board of Professional Affairs, American Psychological Association.* Washington, D.C.: American Psychological Association, 1973. Mimeographed.

Kessler, J. W. "Nosology in Child Psychopathology." In H. E. Rie (Ed.), *Perspectives in Child Psychopathology.* Chicago: Aldine and Atherton, 1971.

Linn, M. W., and others. "A Social Dysfunction Rating Scale." *Journal of Psychiatric Research,* May 1969, *6*, 299-306.

Loof, D. H. *Appalachia's Children.* Lexington: University of Kentucky Press, 1971.

Lourie, N. V., and Lourie, B. P. "A Noncategorical Approach to Treatment Programs for Children and Youth." *American Journal of Orthopsychiatry,* July 1970, *40*, 684-693.

McDermott, J. F., and others. "Social Class and Child Psychiatric Practice: The Clinician's Evaluation of the Outcome of Therapy." *American Journal of Psychiatry,* Jan. 1970, *126*, 951-956.

Mercer, J. R. "Discussion of Alternative Value Frames for Classification of Exceptional Children." Working paper prepared for Advisory Committee, Project on Classification of Exceptional Children, Vanderbilt University, 1972.

Michigan Association for Emotionally Disturbed Children (MAEDC). *Educating Emotionally Disturbed Children.* Detroit: MAEDC, 1973.

Morse, W. C. "Working Paper for Task Force on Classification of Emotionally Disturbed Children." Nashville: Project on Classification of Exceptional Children, 1973.

Murphy, L. B. *The Widening World of Childhood: Paths Toward Mastery.* New York: Basic Books, 1962.

Newbrough, J. R. "Concepts of Behavior Disorder." In S. Golann and C. Eisdorfer (Eds.), *Handbook of Community Mental Health.* New York: Appleton-Century-Crofts, 1972.

Polanyi, M. *Personal Knowledge: Towards a Post-Critical Philosophy.* Chicago: University of Chicago Press, 1958.

Prugh, D. G. "Toward an Understanding of Psychosomatic Concepts in Relation to Illness in Children." In A. Solnit and S. Provence (Eds.), *Modern Perspectives in Child Development.* New York: International Universities Press, 1963.

Prugh, D. G. "Psychosocial Disorders in Childhood and Adolescence: Theoretical Considerations and an Attempt at Classification." In Joint Commission on Mental Health of Children, *The Mental Health of Children: Services, Research, and Manpower.* Report of Task Forces IV and V. New York: Harper and Row, 1973. (Originally published in 1969.)

Rabinovitch, R. Personal communication, 1973.

Rexford, E. Personal communication, 1969.

Rhodes, W. C., and Tracy, M. L. *A Study of Child Variance: Conceptual Project in Emotional Disturbance.* Ann Arbor: University of Michigan Press, 1972.

Rutter, M. "Classification and Categorization in Child Psychiatry." *Journal of Child Psychology and Psychiatry,* 1965, *6,* 71-83.

Rutter, M., and others. "A Triaxial Classification of Mental Disorders in Childhood: An International Study." *Journal of Child Psychology and Psychiatry,* Sept. 1969, *10,* 41-61.

Santostefano, S. "Beyond Nosology: Diagnosis from the Viewpoint of Development." In H. E. Rie (Ed.), *Perspectives in Child Psychopathology.* Chicago: Aldine and Atherton, 1971.

Shaw, C. R., and Lucas, A. R. *The Psychiatric Disorders of Childhood.* (2nd Ed.) New York: Appleton-Century-Crofts, 1970.

Silver, L. B. "*DSM-II* and Child and Adolescent Psychopathology." *American Journal of Psychiatry,* March 1969, *125,* 1267-1269.

Simpson, G. G. *Principles of Animal Taxonomy.* New York: Columbia University Press, 1961.

Spitzer, R. L., Endicott, J., and Cohen, G. M. *Psychiatric Status Schedule. Technique for Evaluating Social and Role Functioning and Mental Status.* New York: State Department of Mental Hygiene, Biometrics Research Division, 1967. Mimeographed.

Wallach, S. *Models of Dysfunctional Mental Behavior.* Purdue University, 1972. Mimeographed.

White, R. W. "Ego and Reality in Psychoanalytic Theory." *Psychological Issues,* 1963, *3*(3).

World Health Organization. *International Classification of Diseases.* (8th Ed.) Geneva: World Health Organization, 1969.

11

LEARNING
DISABILITIES

Joseph M. Wepman, William M. Cruickshank,
Cynthia P. Deutsch, Anne Morency,
Charles R. Strother

Many professional disciplines—medical, psychological, and educational—have attempted to identify children with learning disabilities. The medical discipline's early interest in the localization of functions in the brain led to the identification of a wide range of difficulties exhibited by brain-injured adults in speaking, writing, reading, and understanding speech. Physicians working with children then began to report somewhat similar difficulties, which they termed "congenital auditory imperception" and "congenital word blindness" and which they attributed to brain injury. The World War I epidemic of encephalitis directed the attention of physicians to various behavior disorders in children—disorders associated with brain damage resulting from this disease. Studies of cerebral palsy identified a "clumsy child syndrome" and "minor cerebral palsies" and demonstrated that cerebral palsied children might exhibit associated disorders of perception and learning. Epidemiological studies of Pasamanick and Knobloch (1966) and others indicated that minimal brain damage might be much more common than had been supposed. In the medical literature a number of terms have been used to categorize these children—terms such as *minimal brain damage* (Tredgold, 1908), *clumsy child syndrome* (Gubbay and others, 1965), *minimal cerebral dysfunction* (Haring and Miller, 1969), *hyperkinetic syndrome* (Laufer and Denhoff, 1957), *hyperactive child* (Strauss and Lehtinen, 1948), and *hypokinetic behavior disorder* (Wigglesworth, 1963). In American medical circles the term *minimal brain dysfunction* (MBD) has come to be preferred (Haring and Miller, 1969).

A number of nonmedical disciplines have been concerned primarily with the learning problems presented by these children rather than the implied pathological etiology of each condition. Speech pathologists and audiologists have been involved with children who seemed unable to comprehend speech, although they were not deaf, or who were severely retarded in the development of speech. Terms such as *congenital auditory imperception, congenital aphasia,* and *developmental language disability* have been used to designate such children. Educators interested in the teaching of reading (together with some ophthalmologists, optometrists, and child psychiatrists) have identified children with severe reading problems, whom they have designated by such terms as *dyslexia, specific reading disability, primary reading retardation,* or *strephosymbolia* (Haring and Miller, 1969). Following the work of Strauss (see Strauss and Lehtinen, 1948), which demonstrated specific perceptual disabilities, the term *perceptually handicapped child* has gained some currency. In 1962 the general term *learning disabilities* was suggested by Kirk (see Kirk and Bateman, 1962). This term was adopted by the influential Association for Children with Learning Disabilities and by the United States Office of Education and has now come into general use in educational circles. In 1970 the National Advisory Committee on Handicapped Children developed the following definition: "Children with special learning disabilities exhibit a disorder in one or more of the basic psychological processes involved in understanding or using spoken or written languages. These may be manifested in disorders of listening, thinking, talking, reading, writing, spelling, or arithmetic. They include conditions which have been referred to as perceptual handicaps, brain injury, minimal brain dysfunction, dyslexia, developmental aphasia, etc. They do not include learning problems which are due primarily to visual, hearing, or motor handicaps, to mental retardation, emotional disturbance, or to environmental disadvantage."

Unfortunately, there is little agreement either in medicine or in education on criteria for identifying children with minimal brain dysfunction or learning disabilities. Because the disabilities presented by these children are extremely heterogeneous, the search for any commonality in symptoms, pathology, or etiology has so far been fruitless. For example, pediatric neurologists have established sufficiently reliable criteria for identifying as brain-injured those children who show clear-cut signs of central nervous system pathology; disagreement develops, however, in the observation and interpretation of less clear neurological evidence (so-called "soft" signs) and becomes heated if the concept of minimal brain dysfunction is extended to include children who exhibit only behavioral and learning disabilities, with no clinical or historical evidence of brain injury.

Use of the term *minimal brain dysfunction* in this broader sense has had a number of unfortunate consequences. Although this term was originally suggested specifically to avoid any necessary implication of actual brain damage, it has had that implication in the minds of many parents, teachers, and children. Since nothing can be done to repair brain damage, this classification has often implied an unnecessarily pessimistic prognosis. It has had an adverse effect on many parents' level of aspiration for their children as well as on the self-concept of many children. It has led many school districts to require neurological examinations for admission to special education programs, resulting in unnecessary medical expenses and unreasonable demands on already overburdened pediatricians and pediatric neurologists.

Present educational procedures for classification of children with learning disabilities are equally unsatisfactory. There is, for example, great diversity in the terms used in different state statutes, as the following examples indicate: *educational handicap* (California), *specific learning disabilities* (Florida), *extreme learning problems* (Oregon), *communicative and intellectual deviations* (West Virginia), *neurologically handicapped* (or *impaired*) (Connecticut, Nevada, and Oklahoma), *perceptually handicapped* (Colorado, Indiana, New Jersey, and Washington), *brain-damaged* (Pennsylvania), *learning disability* (Delaware). Generally, responsibility for definition of the criteria for admission to special programs for these children is assigned to a state board of education or to a commissioner of education. In practice, criteria are seldom made explicit, and authority for determining whether particular children are eligible for admission to the special programs is usually delegated to local committees that are often unqualified to make such diagnostic classifications. There has been little uniformity from district to district or from state to state in the characteristics of children classified under these various statutory rubrics.

Without explicit criteria, estimates of the prevalence of learning disabilities have ranged as high as 20-30 percent of the total school population. Where school districts are able to obtain additional state or federal funds for each child enrolled in a special class, there has been some tendency to assign almost any child who was having difficulty in school to special classes for children with learning disabilities.

The lack of clear definition of this category of handicap has not only created problems in the control of special education funds; it has also vitiated much unfocused educational, psychological, and medical research. The inconsistent results obtained in much of this research are a consequence of the great heterogeneity of this population and the fact that research samples drawn from an ill-defined population can be expected to differ widely merely by chance.

General terms such as *minimal brain dysfunction* and undefined *learning disabilities* have no consistent meaning and no value as a basis for the development or the application of corrective methods. Efforts must be directed toward more precise and objective definitions of relatively homogeneous subgroups. If order is to be imposed on this confusion, there must first be acceptance of the fact that the population of children involved is heterogeneous. Then criteria must be established whereby the appropriate professional discipline can reach a reasonably mutual understanding as to what a child's problems actually are. Such criteria will ensure appropriate referral to qualified professional personnel and will protect the rights of the child and his parents.

Purposes of Classification

Educational. For the purpose of individualized intervention, some means of classifying children with learning problems is necessary. The school system needs to recognize those children who are not succeeding. It must also be able to recognize the difference between two major groups of children with learning problems. The first, the underachievers with no apparent or determinable problem, may indeed make up a great percentage of those children who have been improperly classified as suffering from a learning disability. These children—children who are slower to learn than others, children who are emotionally disturbed, or children who lack a proper educational background and stimulation for learning—should not be considered as suffering from a learning disability. On the other hand, certain children must be identified by the school system as capable of adequate intellectual activity but unable to acquire a mastery of educational material without special assistance. The identification and intervention proposed for such children needs to be specific to the child and his problem. The school system and its adjuncts must be prepared to provide the special education necessary to assist these children.

Psychological. Continuous failure to achieve as expected is likely to have a continuing, even a progressive, debilitating psychological effect upon a child. Peer relationships often suffer. The children are frequently unable to meet the real or fancied expectations of parents and teachers. The period of early education is especially critical. Starting education "on the wrong foot" may well influence the child's total educational future, not merely his immediate learning. Misclassification, followed then by improper treatment in special programs, may produce more lasting effects than the difficulty in learning. Because of this negative process and because this time in a child's life is so critical for the development of psychological stability, the classifier must exercise extreme caution in labeling children. Where the risk of creating a psychological disturbance in a given child is greater than the potential for assisting him through special educational procedures, the decision should be not to classify. Errors of classification which tend to create increased psychological problems are difficult to remedy, have pervasive and long-lasting effects, and often produce situations which may require the school system to seek highly specialized therapeutic assistance.

Medical. The medical profession has taken an increased interest in learning problems as parents and schools have requested reasons for the behavior of the children. The medical profession not only must identify syndromes of behavior but also must properly classify those children whose learning problems may result from neurological or physiological disability. Most important, the medical profession must not assume a medical reason without establishing acceptable medical criteria for the determination.

An immediate case in point is the growing tendency to prescribe medication for children suspected of having a learning problem, even though no medically verifiable condition has been or can be determined. Aside from the dangers involved in the introduction and use of drugs—since neither side effects nor aftereffects have been verified through sufficient research—the medical practitioner should use such prescriptive treatment cautiously.

Parental. The parent of any child classified as having a learning disability needs to understand the meaning of and reason for the classification and the role of the educator or physician in the diagnosis and handling of the problem. The parents should act in the child's interest if they believe the identification is improper. They also should have recourse to some specific form of appeal, both from the label and from the planned course of training or therapy. Further, wherever possible parents should be part of the special training program. Parental-guidance programs should be established by the schools to maintain continuity and consistency of expectancy and handling of the child at home as well as in the school.

The child. Educational intervention to offset or compensate for a learning problem should be specific to the problems of each child involved. Classification, with its aura of identification of a problem and its proper remediation, must always be considered in terms of the individual. Since the source or etiology of a particular learning problem may vary from specific to generalized areas of learning, the question of type of intervention will be dealt with separately.

Governmental. The state and federal governments need a classification system that permits a consistent evaluation, regardless of where or by whom it is made. Such a system will ensure that the funds made available for the remediation of the problem are accountably allocated. The overall need is great, but the funds available are limited and should be carefully allocated within a demonstrable and practical classification system.

Definition of Specific Learning Disability

Specific learning disability, as defined here, refers to those children of any age who demonstrate a substantial deficiency in a particular aspect of academic achievement because of perceptual or perceptual-motor handicaps, regardless of etiology or other contributing factors. The term *perceptual* as used here relates to those mental (neurological) processes through which the child acquires his basic alphabets of sounds and forms. The term *perceptual handicap* refers to inadequate ability in such areas as the following: recognizing fine differences between auditory and visual discriminating features underlying the sounds used in speech and the orthographic forms used in reading; retaining and recalling those discriminated sounds and forms in both short- and long-term memory; ordering the sounds and forms sequentially, both in sensory and motor acts (Wepman, 1968); distinguishing figure-ground relationships (Frostig, Lefever, and Whittlesey, 1961); recognizing spatial and temporal orientations; obtaining closure (Kirk and Bateman, 1962); integrating intersensory information (Birch and Leford, 1964); relating what is perceived to specific motor functions (Kephart, 1963). Impairment of the processes involved in perception may result from accident, disease, or injury; from lags in development; or from environmental shortcomings. Impairment of perception may distort or disturb the cellular system and/or the normal function of one or more sensory systems.

From this definition it follows that perceptual or perceptual-motor inadequacies produce specific learning disabilities. Learning problems due to emotional, socioeconomic, or peripheral sensory or motor impairment are excluded. Behavior disturbances, severe mental retardation, poverty, lessened educational opportunity, visual impairment, hearing loss, or muscular paralysis all may produce educational problems but do not fall into the classification of specific learning disabilities. For example, a child who is deficient in learning because of an emotional disturbance, but who shows no perceptual or perceptual-motor problem, would not be classified as having a learning disability. On the other hand, a child who is deficient in learning because of a nutritional problem, and who also shows a specific perceptual or perceptual-motor deficiency preceded by a nutritional problem, would properly be classified as having a learning disability. As an additional example, a child with a demonstrable hearing loss as a primary cause of his lack of classroom adjustment or adaptation might also have a visual perceptual deficiency as a secondary but contributing factor to his difficulty in learning in the classroom. He should be classified as a child with a hearing loss and a specific learning disability.

In each instance, then, regardless of other contributing factors or primary etiologies, only when a perceptual or perceptual-motor insufficiency is determined should the term *specific learning disability* be applied. Poor intelligence alone should not be the basis for the classification of specific learning disability—although there will be some degree of correlation between very good intelligence and good perceptual ability, just as there will be some correlation between poor intelligence and poor perceptual ability.

From a purely educational point of view, the etiology of a specific learning disability is relatively inconsequential. The identification of the perceptual problems involved indicates the area of assistance necessary. The direct cause of the perceptual handicap may be maturational or pathological; however, the demonstrable handicap itself is of major importance to the special educator.

Evaluation

Evaluation of children should be based upon a referral from the child's classroom teacher. The referral should indicate the manner in which the teacher believes the child to be deficient. In each educational system the most qualified examiners should be used. These should always be educational personnel. Wherever possible, the examination should be made by a trained psychologist or special educator. If such specialists are unavailable, personnel experienced in testing and evaluating children—personnel such as the school's remedial reading instructor, speech therapist, or teacher-nurse—should be responsible. The examinations can be made by the school's regular classroom teachers if those teachers have had previous experience in testing. However, the evaluation should not be made by the child's present classroom teacher, nor should the classroom teacher make the decision for final classification.

Upon referral the examiner needs to establish two essential factors: (1) the primary cause underlying the educational discrepancy (differential diagnosis); (2) the nature and extent of the perceptual handicap producing the specific learning disability, if it is found to exist.

Differential diagnosis. In order to make a complete and accurate evaluation, the examiner should have an adequate school and social history of the child. Where this is not readily available or is incomplete, such information must be acquired, at least by the time of final determination of the differential diagnosis. Actual direct study of the child can proceed while such information is being collected.

Direct evaluation should proceed with an overall view of the child's intellectual capacity and his present intellectual performance. The examiner should establish the intellectual level through the use of standardized tests of intelligence. The age of the child to be assessed and the qualifications of the examiner should govern the selection of the test instrument to be used.

Parenthetically, the restandardization of many of these instruments, to eliminate what is felt to be an underlying ethnic bias, is under consideration. If new standards for intelligence tests are developed and show adequate reliability and validity, the examiner would be free to substitute such new assessment devices if he feels that a more reliable estimate of intellectual ability can thereby be determined. Until such a new standardization has been achieved, however, it will be necessary for the examiner to interpret the effect of ethnic background, socioeconomic dependency, and bilingualism on the scores obtained.

At this stage the examiner may determine that the child shows a severe, generalized primary mental retardation and recommend such a classification by referral for specialized training or special room placement to the school authorities. Before he makes such a recommendation, however, he should be sure that the child's low intelligence-test attainment is not based on the presence of pervasive perceptual or perceptual-motor problems. Where such conditions suggest themselves by the child's behavior, it is most important that misdiagnosis be avoided. The generally mentally retarded child should not be classified as having a specific learning disability—although he may also have perceptual problems, which can be given attention in his special classrooms.

The next stage of evaluation should follow from clues obtained in the original referral, during the initial interview with the child and the parents, and in the school and social history. When overt behavior or an emotional disorder is suggested as the essential cause of the educational problem, the examiner should explore the emotional stability of the child, his self-concept, and his personality characteristics. The examiner can use any one of a number of widely used projective techniques to aid him in this determination. For younger children, where language development and usage may be a problem, nonverbal projective tests should be used. For older children, the examiner should feel free to use both verbal and nonverbal projective instruments. Since projective tests have not been fully standardized, they should be used subjectively and not form the sole basis for classification. Caution must be exercised in the interpretation of protocols from all projective instruments, since reliability and validity data are most often lacking.

If the initial examiner concludes that the essential problem is a primary emotional condition such as childhood schizophrenia or autism, which has served to block the learning process, confirmation should be sought from other professional sources. The conclusion should not be based on a single examiner's findings, no matter how well trained or experienced he may be. Note, for example, that children with a language problem due to a specific visual or auditory perceptual problem may project unusual and even bizarre-appearing protocols, or their verbal responses may be due to some undiscernible perceptual handicap. If an examiner even suspects that a child may have such a handicap, further exploration of the perceptual processing abilities should be made before any final decision is made to classify the child as a behavior problem or as emotionally disturbed. If no question of perceptual problem exists, however, the child should not be classified as having a specific learning disability. Further, some children's behavior problems may be the result of a perceptual handicap. The perceptual handicap would not be considered secondary to the existing emotional disturbance at the time of the evaluation but will need to be considered in any overall special education program. Where both problems are present, attention must be given to the behavior problem as well as the perceptual problem during any specific intervention.

Finally—during the interview, from the school and social history, and from direct observations during earlier testing—the examiner must take cognizance of any evidence of a primary visual impairment, hearing loss, or muscular paralysis. If such factors appear, the examiner should make appropriate referrals

—usually through the school nurse or school physician—to resolve these possible blocks to educational achievement. Resolution or correction of these problems should precede further evaluation of a potential perceptual problem. When such conditions are confirmed, the child should not be classified as having a specific learning disability, but rather according to his primary handicap. In all instances, after the child's primary problem has been resolved, his perceptual processing ability should be reevaluated.

Identification of perceptual handicap. A wide variety of standardized and nonstandardized assessment instruments have been developed to explore the equally wide variety of conditions labeled *learning disabilities.* At this time, however, no simple diagnostic instrument of adequate reliability and proven validity is available. Some of the existing instruments are in the form of batteries of subtests; others are individual assessment devices for specific functions. Some tap achievement; others were designed to assess developmental processes.

Most such batteries of tests explore both conceptual and perceptual processes. The examiner must use only those instruments or subscales that depict perceptual functions (that is, discrimination, memory, orientation, figure-ground relationships, closure, intersensory integration, and motoric adequacy). While attentional factors may be present, the ability to pay attention to a task is not in and of itself a perceptual problem but may be a counterpart of every perceptual process. The perceptual processes listed are not all-inclusive. They represent those processes which to this point have been identified sufficiently as factors underlying the learning act. As others are isolated and confirmed through research, they should be added to the list.

No attempt will be made here to recommend any of the present approaches being used. Rather, the reader can make use of a number of collections of test instruments. The most extensive source of such material is to be found in the *Seventh Mental Measurement Yearbook* (Buros, 1972). Two recent collections of considerable value are *Principles of Childhood Language Disabilities* (Irwin and Marge, 1972) and *Methods for Learning Disorders* (Myers and Hammill, 1969). These books include instruments for assessing language, intellectual, achievement, and perceptual abilities. The clinician is advised to consider carefully the instruments selected for use in differential diagnosis as well as in defining the perceptual handicap. Any assessment instrument selected for use should meet the criteria listed in the American Psychological Association publication *Standards for Development and Use of Educational and Psychological Tests* (French and Michael, 1966).

Assessment should always be in terms of the individual child. The decision to classify a child should be based not only on the obvious test results but also upon the child's behavior and other observations made by the teacher, the school nurse, and others involved in the evaluation. Where the decision is based on any subjective evidence—teacher's opinion or observations made—it should be so stated.

Exceptions. Exceptions to the arbitrary definition of a specific learning disability as always being represented by a perceptual handicap will occasionally occur. One such exception might well be the older underachieving child who may have had demonstrable perceptual handicaps at an earlier point in his life but no longer demonstrates them. It is suggested that such children be considered as learning disabilities followed by a modifying term in parentheses—for instance, "(dyslexia)." Other exceptions to the rule may occur from time to time as more experience is gained with the specific handicaps. If and when they do occur, any state or local agency should describe the handicapping condition and label the condition as a specific learning disability, with the explanatory modifying term in parentheses. This amount of flexibility will always be needed, since no system that could be devised could cover all the exigencies. The agencies making such a distinction should be cautioned not to use this category without demonstrable proof that the condition is an exception to the general ruling.

Review board. Each school system should establish a review committee, composed of its most qualified faculty (preferably school psychologists, special educators, and remedial instructors). This committee should be responsible for (1) confirming the diagnosis and classification determined, (2) approving recommendations for placement for special training, (3) periodically reviewing the child's performance after placement, (4) declassifying the child when he is prepared to discontinue special education, and (5) functioning as an appeal board for parents who question the classification and/or intervention program (Cruickshank, 1971). The establishment of such a review

312   Issues in the Classification of Children

board would meet the standard expressed by the American Psychological Association's Committee on Ethics in Research with Human Subjects (Cook, 1970).

Qualifications and Training of Special Education Teachers

Very special training is needed by the teacher of the child with a specific learning disability. Experience working with the handicapped of any kind would be of additional value but should not be considered the basic criterion for working with this particular group of handicapped children. The teacher must be trained to recognize the individual aspects of perceptual development and to understand the role of the various perceptual processes in the total learning process. A background in the neurological and psychoneurological characteristics of these children as well as a grounding in developmental theory is essential.

The teacher must be further equipped to provide a general curriculum for the teaching of reading, mathematics, handwriting, and spelling and should have undergone a basic educational program in motor skills and training in prescriptive teaching leading to a proper perceptual-motor match. The teacher's training also should include an understanding of language problems in childhood and the labels commonly attached to them, such labels as *childhood aphasia* and its various kindred disorders, *dyslexia, agnosia,* or *apraxia.* Children with these problems frequently also show specific learning disabilities. Studies have shown, for example, that in aphasic children auditory inadequacies of a perceptual nature are basic to the language handicap (Johnson and Myklebust, 1967).

The teacher should be equipped and trained in remedial educational principles and should appreciate the value of supportive as well as compensatory training. The teacher should be prepared to handle the behavior problems that arise from frustration and failure within the student population; consequently, each teacher must be well grounded in psychological principles of counseling and educational guidance.

Special consideration should be given to the training of a corps of university professors to establish adequate programs wherein teachers of perceptually handicapped children can receive training. Such professors in training centers must know the subject matter that is advised for the teacher. These university professors would need to undertake direct supervision in training of the new teacher corps. A learning-disabilities teacher then would have to be a graduate of an approved learning-disabilities program (Cruickshank, 1972).

Guidelines for Intervention

The goals of intervention "refer to systematic attempts over an extended period of time to make some changes which we hope will be substantial and lasting in the functioning of an immature (impaired) organism" (Gray, 1971). There must be an insistence that the human subject emerge from the experience unharmed and, if possible, with an identifiable gain. Several factors must be considered before a program of intervention designed to reduce or resolve a specific learning disability is established. At this time, only general suggestions can be made. Each such program must in a sense be tailored to the needs of a community and, whenever possible, designed to meet the needs of each child. Certain important features, however, should be recognized and implemented as resources are developed locally.

Each educational community should aim at establishing resources on the basis of the age and number of children involved, the availability of qualified personnel, and the financial support available from local, state, or federal agencies. For example, large urban school systems may have sufficient children to establish individual classrooms for special educational assistance; smaller schools in a large community may find it more feasible to establish a program in a central location, where children can be referred at specified times. Small, isolated schools may need to establish facilities for a learning-disabilities specialist, who, like a visiting nurse, can spend a day or two a week on a preplanned schedule at each of several schools. In such situations children would participate in regular classroom activity and receive tutorial assistance for their handicapping conditions. The classroom teacher would need to follow special instructions provided by the special education teacher at the time of her visit.

Research has demonstrated that a child's perceptual processes are not completely developed until he is at least nine years old (Flavell, 1963; Wepman, 1968). Therefore, for children at the early elementary age level, a direct approach in which the intervention can be specifically related to the perceptual impairment should be established, with as much individual training as is feasible locally. For example, where specific perceptual processes involving auditory, visual, or visual-motor impairments have been isolated, training designed to help the child reduce the effects of his specific disability should be instituted. However, when a child receives some of his education in a regular classroom, the classroom teacher should be asked to emphasize his best-functioning capacities. If all his education is provided by a special class for learning disabilities, training to reduce the impairment as well as teaching to the child's perceptual strength (a dual approach) can be the model. The dual approach should be used, however, only when the child has sufficient intellectual capacity to encompass both assistance and correction without confusion. Younger children often show perceptual handicaps *because* they could not master such dual or multidimensional approaches in the regular classroom. The child who has demonstrated a lifelong language problem with marked perceptual handicaps due to central nervous system dysfunction benefits most from specific perceptual training (Eisenson, 1966). Whatever approach is used, the child must receive the personal satisfaction that comes with success during these crucial years.

For the child above nine years of age, intervention will need to be thought of as mainly compensatory rather than corrective. Where perceptual problems of discrimination, memory, sequencing, closure, or spatial orientation still exist, direct remediation is unlikely to be effective, since basic processing ability is by this age as developed as it ever will be. Guidance and concentrated effort directed at assisting the child to utilize his best skills and substitute them for undeveloped or inadequate skills is essential. For example, if a child at twelve years still shows inadequate auditory perception, the teacher probably should concentrate on helping him use his visual skills.

Where many children, mainly children below nine years of age, present similar handicaps, group approaches may prove most effective, since children frequently learn best from other children and are more easily motivated within groups. A school might, for example, develop class activity in auditory training for a group of children who all show inadequate auditory discrimination to be at the root of their learning problem. Group rather than individual training also has been found beneficial in certain perceptual-motor problems (Frostig and Horne, 1964; Kephart, 1963). For children above nine years of age, the instruction usually must be individualized. It must be directly designed to meet the individual's present needs, even though the problem involved may have originated in an earlier period, when the perceptual handicaps were directly related to learning. The educational demands on older children are such that in almost every instance attempts to reduce the perceptual handicap are likely to produce further failure and to reduce motivation for learning.

Early identification as well as timely intervention is most important, since corrective and compensatory education become more and more difficult with age. Screening children in the very early school years can often help avoid later problems which are more difficult to correct, not only because of the specific perceptual problems involved but also because of the many psychological concomitants that can magnify the problems of the child and his special teachers. Very often these may need to be reduced before successful special education can be undertaken.

Although much research is still needed in the area of intervention, successful techniques have been developed (Goldiamond and Dyrud, 1966), and new knowledge about the problems of the child with a specific learning handicap are being constantly reported in the professional literature.

Public-Policy Issues

Every child classified without the cooperative agreement and understanding of his parents should have all the protection necessary to maintain his rights. A review board should act as a board of appeal and explanation for parents who question the classification.

The state should be responsible for establishing guidelines and criteria for approving both the examiners and the teachers of the learning-disabled. It should monitor the work done. It should distribute to the school systems the monies available for special training on a per capita basis. Supervision and assistance must be provided for any community that seeks to establish a learning-disabilities program.

The federal government, through the state boards of education, should allocate funds for support of the additional intervention essential for the training of teachers and for the special education of the learning-disabled child. It should further be responsible for organized research efforts designed to explore further the validity of this concept of learning disability. A further federal responsibility should be the monitoring of the state programs; to continue to obtain federal funds, the states must show that they are maintaining the quality of work being done. Where research is needed but not presently forthcoming from any research and development area in the field, such research should be contracted to increase the knowledge base which today is lacking.

References

Birch, H. G., and Leford, A. "Two Strategies for Studying Perception in 'Brain-Damaged' Children." In H. G. Birch (Ed.), *Brain Damage in Children*. Baltimore: Williams and Wilkins, 1964.

Buros, O. K. (Ed.) *Seventh Mental Measurement Yearbook*. Highland Park, N.J.: Gryphon Press, 1972.

Cook, S. W. (Chairman) "Ethical Standards in Human Research." Workshop at annual meeting of American Psychological Association, Miami, 1970.

Cruickshank, W. "Special Education: Instrument for Change in Education for the '70's." In D. Walker and D. Howard (Eds.), *Selected Papers from the University of Virginia Lecture Series, 1970-71*. Charlottesville: University of Virginia, 1971.

Cruickshank, W. "Some Issues Facing the Field of Learning Disability." *Journal of Learning Disability*, 1972, *5*(7), 380-388.

Eisenson, J. "Perceptual Disturbances in Children with Central Nervous System Dysfunctions and Implications for Language Development." *British Journal of Disorders of Communication*, 1966, *1*, 23-32.

Flavell, J. H. *The Developmental Psychology of Jean Piaget*. Princeton, N.J.: Van Nostrand, 1963.

French, J., and Michael, W. *Standards for Educational and Psychological Tests and Manuals*. Washington, D.C.: American Psychological Association, 1966.

Frostig, M., and Horne, D. *The Frostig Program for the Development of Visual Perception*. Chicago: Follett, 1964.

Frostig, M., Lefever, D. W., and Whittlesey, R. B. "A Developmental Test of Visual Perception for Evaluating Normal and Neurologically Handicapped Children." *Perceptual Motor Skills*, 1961, *12*, 383-394.

Goldiamond, I., and Dyrud, J. "Reading as Operant Behavior." In J. Money (Ed.), *"The Disabled Reader."* Baltimore: Johns Hopkins Press, 1966.

Gray, S. W. "Ethical Issues in Intervention Research." In *DARCEE Papers and Reports*. Nashville, Tenn.: George Peabody College, 1971.

Gubbay, S. S., and others. "Clumsy Children: A Study of Apraxic and Agnosic Defects in 21 Children." *Brain*, 1965, *88*, 295-312.

Haring, N., and Miller, C. A. (Eds.) *Minimal Brain Dysfunction in Children.* Proceedings of National Project on Learning Disabilities in Children. Washington, D.C.: U.S. Public Health Service, 1969.

Irwin, J., and Marge, M. (Eds.) *Principles of Childhood Language Disabilities.* New York: Appleton-Century-Crofts, 1972.

Johnson, D., and Myklebust, H. R. *Learning Disabilities: Educational Principles and Practices.* New York: Grune and Stratton, 1967.

Kephart, N. C. *The Brain-Injured Child in the Classroom.* Chicago: National Society for Crippled Children and Adults, 1963.

Kirk, S. A., and Bateman, B. "Diagnosis and Remediation of Learning Disabilities." *Exceptional Children*, 1962, *29*(2), 73-78.

Laufer, M. W., and Denhoff, E. "Hyperkinetic Behavior Syndrome in Children." *Journal of Pediatrics*, 1957, *50*, 463-474.

Myers, P., and Hammill, D. *Methods for Learning Disorders.* New York: Wiley, 1969.

Pasamanick, B., and Knobloch, H. "Retrospective Studies on the Epidemiology of Reproductive Casualty: Old and New." *Merrill-Palmer Quarterly*, 1966, *12*(1), 7-26.

Strauss, A. A., and Lehtinen, L. E. *Psychopathology and Education of the Brain-Injured Child*, Vol. I. New York: Grune and Stratton, 1948.

Tredgold, A. F. *Mental Deficiency (Amentia).* New York: William Wood, 1908.

Wepman, J. M. "The Modality Concept—Including a Statement of the Perceptual and Conceptual Levels of Learning." In H. Smith (Ed.), *Perception and Reading.* Newark: University of Delaware Press, 1968.

Wigglesworth, R. "The Importance of Recognizing Minimal Cerebral Dysfunction in Paediatric Practice." In M. Bax and R. MacKeith (Eds.), *Minimal Cerebral Dysfunction.* London: Heineman, 1963.

12

LOW-INCOME AND MINORITY GROUPS

Paul R. Dokecki, Barbara A. Strain,
Joe J. Bernal, Carolyn S. Brown,
Mary Electa Robinson

Poverty is vicious in its effects on families and children. Similarly, a "vicious circle" is "set in motion by a teacher's labeling of a child as *disadvantaged*" (Bronfenbrenner, 1970, p. 153). Both poverty and poverty-oriented labels, then, can be viewed as vicious and destructive. Our analysis of classification and labeling of low-income and minority-group children is concerned primarily with implications for policy and intervention strategies. We maintain that our society requires major changes in its approaches to this area of classification and intervention.

The chapter on mental health and poverty in *Crisis in Child Mental Health: Challenge for the 1970's* begins with this chillingly eloquent testimony from an unidentified parent:

> Listen, it's hell to be poor
> It's nothin' less than nothin' that we got. For me it isn't so bad, it's for the kids I can't stand it. When you can't even feed your own family, you know you're really down.
> We get by, by the hardest. It's beans and coal off the railroad track and hoping the luck will change. But it doesn't. I keep asking—where will it all end for the kids? Boys get big, you know, and they get so's they won't take it any longer.
> I don't know, I just don't know. All my life I work and work—take anything that comes my way. But it just doesn't add up. Can't even send them to school—no shoes, no money for books. And you don't go anywhere without you get education.
> I brought you my baby. You can see for yourself she's dead. The relief killed her: no milk, no doctor, us out in the street in the snow. That no-relief killed her—just like it's killing us all—only slower.
> You sit there in your nice office and your good clothes and say you understand. You *can't* understand. You have never lived with rats running over the babies and biting them at night. You have never told your kid he couldn't go to the movies this week or next week or any week because there isn't any money. You never lived on a street where junkies and tramps pestered your kids. You never tried like I've tried to raise your boys decent, and lost—with John sent upstate and Dick gone, God knows where, and Joan fighting with me and her teachers all the time, I say there's no justice to it—no justice at all. What are you going to do to help? There's been enough sitting and talking.
> We want help. We want it now. And we don't want any more studies. Things have got to change. You don't need a study to find out that being poor is no damn good for anybody except maybe the rich.
> I worry and worry about what's going to happen to us. Sometimes I think I'm going crazy with it all. I can't sleep, I can't rest. It's those questions all the time in my head—how can we get out of this trap? People are against us; they want to get rid of poor people like me and the wife and kids [quoted in Joint Commission on Mental Health of Children, 1969, pp. 181-182].

The Joint Commission on Mental Health of Children (JCMHC), composed of an extensive and distinguished group of professionals and concerned citizens, was comprehensive in its coverage, with mental health defined as psychological and physical growth and development in the broadest sense. Issues regarding low-income and minority-group children and families were central; issues regarding classification and labeling were not. While drawing upon data presented in the JCMHC report, we shall attempt to extend the message of the JCMHC report through detailed consideration of the dynamics and adequacy of the classification process.

Basic Issues

Children are classified for many reasons, but we decided to investigate the adequacy of classification as it relates to intervention programs aimed at helping children develop into healthy, competent, and fully functioning human beings. This development is not construed as automatic or natural but rather as a continuing achievement. That is, as Dokecki and Strain (1973) suggest, human development and parenting are tasks to be mastered—tasks that require personal and environmental resources. *All* families can use some form of societal help in the struggle to master these tasks. Intervention programs, therefore, are social instrumentalities aimed at actualizing the rights of children and families by helping maximize human development. The JCMHC (1969) suggests that these "rights of children" include the rights to be wanted, to be born healthy, to live in healthy environments, to have basic needs satisfied, to have continuous loving care, to develop necessary skills, and to receive treatment and care through relevant institutions.

Regarding strategies of intervention to promote and protect these rights, we emphasize those that are *universalistic* rather than exceptionalistic (Dokecki, Scanlan, and Strain, 1972; Dokecki and Strain, 1973). Ryan (1971, pp. 16-17) has drawn this distinction clearly and succinctly:

> The *exceptionalistic* viewpoint is reflected in arrangements that are private, voluntary, remedial, special, local, and exclusive. Such arrangements imply that problems occur to specially defined categories of persons in an unpredictable manner. The problems are unusual, even

unique, they are exceptions to the rule, they occur as a result of individual defect, accident, or unfortunate circumstances and must be remedied by means that are particular
and, as it were, tailored to the individual case.

The *universalistic* viewpoint, on the other hand, is
reflected in arrangements that are public, legislated, promo-
tive or preventive, general, national, and inclusive. Inherent
in such a viewpoint is the idea that social problems are a
function of the social arrangements of the community or
the society and that, since these social arrangements are
quite imperfect and inequitable, such problems are both
predictable, and, more important, preventable through public action. They are not unique to the individual, and the
fact they encompass individual persons does not imply that
those persons are themselves defective or abnormal.

The JCMHC's (1969) Committee on Children of Minority
Groups adopted a universalistic position when it maintained
that maximal growth and development for all citizens, majority-
and minority-group members alike, is necessary for our nation's
continued survival and well-being: "While the financial cost of
eradicating racism in all walks of national life will obviously be
immense, the result of making it possible for millions of wasted
human beings to contribute to our national production and
creativity, the development of millions of new consumers for
our national product, the improvement of our commercial relations with problems of other nations, and the cut in the present
enormous costs of inadequate welfare programs would seem to
make it a relatively sound investment. The society can truly
find new strength and integrity by an acceptance of all diversity" (JCMHC, 1969, p. 218).

One of our theses, to be elaborated in a subsequent section, is that the classification and labeling of low-income and
minority-group children has been accomplished almost exclusively within an exceptionalistic framework that is counter-
productive to human values and destructive of the rights of children. An exceptionalistic framework promotes a view of the
poor as "strangers, barbarians, savages. This is how the distressed and disinherited are redefined in order to make it possible for us to look at society's problems and to attribute their
causation to the individuals affected" (Ryan, 1971, p. 10).

While the JCMHC has separate chapters on poverty and
minority-group status, its analysis suggests that they are inter-

related and virtually inseparable phenomena. Data reported by
the JCMHC support this assertion. Specifically, in 1967 American Indians earned an average of $1500 per year; Puerto Ricans,
representing less than 10 percent of the 1964 population of
New York City, constituted over half of all the city's poor people; 13 percent of whites, as compared to 4 percent of blacks,
had prosperous incomes (more than $15,000) in 1966—essen-
tially the reverse pattern held for those with critically poor incomes (less than $2000). Another study (Texas Office of Eco-
nomic Opportunity, 1972) found that 45.3 percent of Mexican-
Americans in Texas are poor. The comparable figures for blacks
and Anglos are 44 percent and 12.6 percent, respectively. While
blacks and Chicanos together constitute only 30 percent of the
population of Texas, they account for 60 percent of the poverty group. These and other data support our intent to treat
poverty and minority-group status as a single, albeit multifaceted and complex, phenomenon.

Existing Approaches

In this section we review several approaches to classifying
families and children regarding income/majority-minority-group
status. Rainwater's (1970) scheme for conceptualizing the disinherited is important to our analysis. In a subsequent section we
advance the notion that an underlying moralizing perspective in
Rainwater's sense (that is, an orientation that "poor people are
evil people") has been at the core of America's approach to the
classification of low-income and minority-group families and
children. We discuss some of the history of this core approach,
trace its influence on the prevailing rationale for national intervention efforts, describe some of its effects on the systems constructed to deal with low-income and minority families and children, look at some of the consequences for children within
these systems, and finally propose an alternative classification
scheme and intervention approach based on Rainwater's normalizing and naturalizing perspectives.

Attempts to conceptualize families and children along income and majority-minority-group lines typically do not qualify
as fully developed classification systems with complex schemes
for ordering the diverse elements of a group. Rather, these approaches generally assert a core theoretical notion that is used
to distinguish the low-income or minority group, as a whole,

from the rest of society. Therefore, we are actually reviewing broad theories or paradigms rather than technical classification systems.

The plight of the "other America"—a segment of this society relatively low in income, status, power, and basic resources, with disproportionate representation by persons of minority ethnic origins—was forcefully brought to the attention of professionals and the public in the early 1960s (Harrington, 1962). Numerous behavioral and social scientists rallied to the poverty cause—perhaps for the first time participating broadly and influentially in many aspects (theory, research, and policy formation) of a major social problem (Guttentag, 1970). A range of conceptualizations was used to identify and label the populations which would be targets of subsequent large-scale data-collection and intervention efforts. *Culturally* or *educationally deprived, socially* or *culturally disadvantaged, underprivileged, multiproblem families, slum culture, hard-core, lower-lower class* were only a few of the terms bandied about. No single taxonomic system has reached any general level of professional or political acceptance; the basic definitional issue of who should be considered among the "poor" and "disadvantaged" is continually being reworked and is influenced by ever changing political, economic, and social forces.

Two sets of criteria, which make independent and distinctly divergent contributions to the classification of persons at the lower end of the economic continuum, can be identified. First are those schemes which employ class criteria; that is, socioeconomic ranking. Second are those behavioral and social science approaches in which the primary data are life-style or performance variables; the culture-of-poverty concept is a prototype of this approach. These two systems are often interrelated in the research literature and are individually and jointly confounded with a third previously mentioned factor, race-ethnicity.

Social and behavioral scientists often take a position similar to the following: "A category of people homogeneous on the economic index of poverty consists on other indices of an extremely heterogeneous lot. . . . Having one characteristic in common—lack of financial resources—does not necessarily imply the common possession of other characteristics (psychological traits)" (Allen, 1970b, pp. 367-368). But although researchers do recognize this heterogeneity, the predominant research design used with low-income individuals has been a "two-groups" design, with reliance on global racial or socioeconomic-status variables to define the groups (Campbell, 1961; Cole and Bruner, 1971; Mercer, 1972). Little attention is paid to the multifaceted environmental realities of low-income groups (LaVeck, 1968).

Economic criteria, moreover, are not unidimensional and undifferentiated but can be used to describe family variations and dynamics as to level, source, and stability of income. Illustrative is the work of Klein (1972). He reports that one definition of poverty widely accepted and used for policy purposes relates total family income to three times the cost of a minimally adequate diet, with adjustments made for family size and composition. In a longitudinal design, Klein studied the dynamic economic behavior of representative panels of families. He identified distinct subgroups by partitioning individuals according to mobility, stability, and level of income: the upwardly mobile, the downwardly mobile, the chronically poor, the stable poor, the stable nonpoor, and the unstable occasional poor. Klein reported detailed compositions and histories of these subgroups. He observed, for example, that the nonwhite representation among the upwardly mobile is almost twice the predicted representation, evidence of the partial success of recent programs; that among the chronically poor almost half of the families are headed by females, two thirds of whom are over age fifty-four; that the downwardly mobile family heads are not acquiring more education, are steadily dropping out of the labor force, and are receiving almost no income contribution from a wife's employment; and that only among the stable nonpoor are nonwhites *underrepresented.* Several other classification systems in use by social scientists combine level of income with parental education, occupation, or stability variables (Hollingshead and Redlich, 1958; S. Miller, 1965), although none approach the sensitive and informative observations reported by Klein.

premise that "the direct distribution of money or
e availability of community facilities cannot make
the life of the poor" (Minuchin and others, 1967,
cts with the policy suggestions of direct economic
and public employment. Resolution of this con-
an increase in adequately researched descriptive
Klein's (1972) and field-experimental studies of

labor-force and economic behavior (see, for instance, Goodwin, 1972; Wright, 1972) to provide accurate predictions about the utility and effects of economic interventions.

Rainwater (1970) outlines a paradigm for examination of social science and common-sense understandings of individuals in poverty—a paradigm that can serve as a general conceptual framework here. According to Rainwater, individuals within the system, both the common man and the professional, develop perspectives to explain the existence of disinherited individuals, individuals who are not a part of mainstream society. Rainwater's analysis of these perspectives is presented in Table 1; the perspectives imply labels, etiologies, and diagnostic or policy implications. Rainwater emphasizes (1) that each perspective has an irrational core, which can distort an accurate understanding if pursued in isolation, (2) that each perspective (excluding the "biological determinism" version of the naturalizing perspective) can contribute toward an adequate conceptualization of the nature of poverty, and (3) that each perspective can generate both ideologically left-wing and right-wing versions of therapy or policy choices. It is important to keep these three assertions in mind to guard against an oversimplified application of Rainwater's analysis.

In the *moralizing* perspective the disinherited are perceived as evil and potent and are labeled "sinners." Historically the oldest perspective, a moralizing approach identifies a moral flaw in the labeled individual or in some aspect of his environment as the etiology of his condition. Therapy implications of this perspective involve punishment and control, redemption and salvation, policies exemplified in adamant support for law and order or in fundamentalist or evangelistic religions imposed upon or arising from within disinherited segments of society.

The *medicalizing* perspective perceives disinherited individuals or their environments as distorted by pathological forces. When the "sickness" is in the person, distorted child-rearing practices, absence of certain critical experiences, and so forth, are said to cause the pathology. Psychotherapy, compensatory education, and individual and clinical diagnoses are the emphasized policy alternatives. When the "pathology" primarily affects the environment, the etiology is identified as the association of the weak individual with a disorganized community with deviant goals. The derivative policies include efforts to build new community systems or, at the other extreme, to remove

Table 1
Perspectives for Explaining the Existence of Disinherited Individuals[a]

Perspective	Diagnosis	Etiology	Therapy
1. Moralizing (oldest approach)	"Sinner"—evil and potent	Moral flaw in person or environment	Punish-control/Redeem-save (e.g., fundamentalist churches, Black Muslims)
2. Medicalizing (replaces sin with sickness)	"Sick"—evil and weak	*Pathology in person:* apathetic orientation, disturbed child rearing, trained incapacities, absence of certain experiences	Psychotherapy, compensatory education, clinical approaches and individual diagnosis
		Pathology in environment: disorganized community with deviant goals	Build new community systems, community involvement, remove children from disorganized environment
3. Apotheosizing	"Natural Man" "Heroic Culture"—virtuous and potent	Special capacities; life of beauty and virtue (as compared to sterile suburbs)	Natural man and heroic culture adopted as symbols (in dress, slang, etc.); attack rest of society and join disinherited for new power base
4. Normalizing	"Ordinary People" (although mistreated and poor)—virtuous and weak	Conditions of disinheritance have only superficial effects on personalities	Debunk other perspectives and their policy implications; emphasize "opportunity" rather than radical alterations in the system (e.g., training, counseling, better coordinated services)
5. Naturalizing (value-free perspective)	a. Biological Determinism	Inferior internal structures	Benign totalitarianism, eugenics
	b. Cultural Relativism	Valid, functional way of life; different but with inner coherence	Cultural pluralism (liberal policy)
			Do-nothing (conservative policy)

[a]Based on Rainwater (1970).

children of the disinherited from their "diseased" environment.

From the *apotheosizing* perspective the disinherited individuals are perceived as virtuous and potent, "natural men" within a "heroic culture." The disinherited possess special competencies and live a more valid, less alienated life as a result of their forced adversities. Derivative policies include adoption of certain symbols of the apotheosized group or emigration to join with the disinherited to create a new social power structure.

In the *normalizing* perspective the poor are perceived as "ordinary people," virtuous and weak. The discrimination that they experience from the larger social system creates only a superficial impact on their personal existence. The major effect of the normalizing perspective is to underemphasize the fundamental personal deprivation and destructive experiences of disinherited individuals.

Finally, in the *naturalizing* perspective an attempt is made to rise above the weak-potent, evil-virtuous dimensions and to study the disinherited within a natural science, nonevaluative context. Rainwater discusses two versions of this perspective: biological determinism, in which inferior structures or genetics are responsible for the condition of the disinherited; and cultural relativism, in which the disinherited are said to live a different yet valid and functional life. Biological determinism fosters policies of benign totalitarianism or eugenics. Cultural relativism can give rise to policies which preserve the status quo. On the other hand, it can lead to an emphasis on cultural pluralism, in which the larger society imputes integrity rather than stigma to minority groups and, while recognizing their need for additional resources, does not demand compliance with the priorities of the majority culture.

Each of the behavioral science models to be discussed subsequently, as well as the perspective on low-income, minority families that we develop in the last section of this paper, fits into Rainwater's paradigm with varying degrees of correspondence and amalgamation.

Culture-of-poverty and deficit approaches. The concept of a culture or subculture of poverty has gained prominence through the writings of social anthropologists (for example, Gladwin, 1961; Lewis, 1966; W. Miller, 1958). Culture-of-poverty theorists maintain that the poor, or a subsection of the poor, have a distinct way of life or design for living that is handed down across generations. Consequently, the poor are not integrated into major societal institutions and replace the value systems of the larger society with a deviant set of values: "By the time children are six or seven they have usually absorbed the basic attitudes and values of their subculture. Thereafter they are psychologically unready to take full advantage of changing conditions or improving opportunities that may develop in their lifetime" (Lewis, 1966, p. 21).

Since its promulgation the culture-of-poverty concept has been widely criticized (see, for example, Allen, 1970b; Kreisberg, 1970; Ryan, 1971; Valentine, 1968) on conceptual, methodological, and interpretational bases. First, the concept has been attacked as being tautological; that is, the values inferred from the behavior of the poor are in turn used to explain the same behaviors. Second, the methods used by the proponents of this concept have been criticized. The degree of homogeneity and consensus attributed to communities of individuals in poverty, critics contend, is an issue to be determined through empirical investigation, by methods other than intensive historical studies of several families or participant observation (Allen, 1970b). A third criticism states that the structural characteristics common to the poor and ethnic minorities are not necessarily traits internal to the culture but can be reasonably attributed to sources external to the group (Ryan, 1971; Valentine, 1968). Finally, empirical studies have demonstrated that the value system attributed to the poor is much broader and more flexible than the culture-of-poverty theorists allow (Rodman, 1963) and that the "inherited personality of poverty" (Minuchin and others, 1967, p. 23) is based on "very unstable empirical foundations" (Allen, 1970a, p. 259). Over and above these logical and empirical arguments, the subculture concept is criticized because it gives rise to negative stereotypes and maintains inequality in American life (Gladwin, 1967; Ryan, 1971).

Closely allied to the culture-of-poverty concept is the approach of the so-called deficit theorists (for instance, Deutsch, 1967; Hess and Shipman, 1965; Pavenstedt, 1967). These theorists assume—erroneously, their critics believe—that the condition of poverty implies "a disorganized community, and this disorganization expresses itself in various forms of deficit" (Cole and Bruner, 1971, p. 867). Thus, the poor and ethnic-minority "subject" is deficient in certain areas because of a corresponding deficiency of certain environmental elements.

Culture-of-poverty and deficit models are salient examples of Rainwater's medicalizing perspective, with varying emphasis given to pathology in the *person* or pathology in the *environment*. The rationale and conclusions of these models have generated clinical, individual, exceptionalistic intervention strategies; for children these have been translated into early cultural "injection" approaches incorporated into many early Head Start programs, where little attention was given to the possibly more basic factors of parental occupation and stability of family income.

Cultural-deprivation approaches. A second insufficiency model, cultural deprivation, is closely related to the culture-of-poverty and deficit models. *Deprivation* as a label evolved from the studies of stimulus deprivation of isolated laboratory animals and from studies of the homogeneous and sparse settings of many orphanages and child institutions. In the mid-1960s, however, as Gewirtz (1971) has pointed out, the term was generalized to apply to the life conditions and experiences of entire subgroups of individuals.

Empirical studies of the environments of the "culturally deprived" (see, for example, Labov, 1970; Wachs, Uzgiris, and Hunt, 1971) have not substantiated the hypothesized stimulus deprivation. Moreover, the cultural-deprivation metaphor, by emphasizing unspecified and absent conditions, has diverted attention from those human and physical stimulus conditions *actually present* in the home and neighborhood environments which may relate functionally to development. Gewirtz (1971) contends that the behavior patterns of the "culturally deprived" child are defined as inadequate primarily because they deviate from modal behavior required for general (usually educational) success. The label carries no information about the adaptiveness of the behavior in other contexts or about its deviation from a model of optimal child development. This is an illogical conceptual leap from the original intent of the stimulus- and maternal-deprivation paradigms.

Intervention policies arising from application of the cultural-deprivation approach are like the culture-of-poverty and deficit approaches in emphasizing early compensatory experiences. Moreover, since the "culturally deprived" child has most often been identified by his performance in school or on standardized tests, the label diverts attention from very real defects in these schooling and testing settings to supposed defects in the child (Farber and Lewis, 1972; Labov, 1970); consequently, the label contributes to "the perpetuation of inferior education for lower-status children, whether their lower status is socioeconomic or racial" (Clark, 1965, p. 125). Most seriously, the alleged failure of these strategies to reduce "cultural deprivation" has on occasion generated support for a genetic-inferiority interpretation, a hypothesis that this position was originally designed to avoid (Dokecki, Scanlan, and Strain, 1972; Labov, 1970).

Difference approaches. According to the cultural-difference model, variations in performances between different groups (groups classified separately because of economic, ethnic, or linguistic differences) are accounted for by the different situations and contexts in which the competencies are learned and expressed. This model derives from two theoretical sources, anthropology and sociolinguistics. According to Cole and Bruner (1971, p. 868), the anthropological tradition basically asserts that "different conclusions about the world are the result of arbitrary and different, but equally logical, ways of cutting up the world of experience." The second source, sociolinguistics, emphasizes that languages do not differ in their degree of development or involvement of complex cognitive processes and that individuals diagnosed as "culturally deprived" have basic logic and competencies in their thought, language, and other behaviors which are not adequately assessed in standardized testing contexts (Baratz, 1970; Labov, 1970). The issue is the question of the representativeness of the settings in which the individual is expected to demonstrate and apply his abilities. Both anthropological and sociolinguistic arguments raise the serious question of the logic and adequacy of current comparative research methodologies used by behavioral scientists and emphasize the need for assessing the motivational and ecological significance of experimental stimulus arrangements. As Cole and Bruner (1971, p. 869) stress, "Formal experimental equivalence of operations does not insure de facto equivalence of experimental treatments."

The difference model, then, corresponds to elements of the naturalizing perspective in Rainwater's paradigm. It explains the cycle of poverty in a manner quite different from the cultural-deficit and cultural-deprivation perspectives. "From the deficit point of view, populations stay in the cycle because of lack of capability to escape, whereas from the difference point of view populations stay in the cycle because the majority society keeps them there. . . . The deficit position would have the equalization of economic opportunity gained by intervening in the sociocultural development and education of the poverty child so as to make him a candidate for the majority society. . . . The difference proponents would change society more than the individual, the goal being to equalize economic opportunity while maintaining sociocultural differences" (Williams, 1970, p. 8). According to proponents of the difference model, our society denies certain "different" individuals access to economic opportunity. If one believes in the *right to be different* (specifically, the right to express one's culture), then certain adjustments have to be made in societal response to these differences. Of course, the "different ones" may also have to adapt in certain respects in order that a society of some fashion may be possible.

Current Commitments to the Poor

The JCMHC has challenged the United States of America to actualize the American dream:

> This nation, the richest of all world powers, has no unified national commitment to its children and youth. The claim that we are a child-centered society, that we look to our young as tomorrow's leaders, is a myth. Our words are made meaningless by our actions—by our lack of national, community, and personal investment in maintaining the healthy development of our young, by the miniscule amount of economic resources spent in developing our young, by our tendency to rely on a proliferation of simple, one-factor, short-term, and inexpensive remedies and services. As a tragic consequence, we have in our midst millions of ill-fed, ill-housed, ill-educated, and discontented youngsters. . . . This nation, which looks to the family to nurture its young, gives no real help with child rearing until a child is badly disturbed or disruptive to the community [an exceptionalistic approach]. The discontent, apathy, and violence today are a warning that society has not assumed its responsibilities to *ensure an environment which will provide optimum care for its children* [a universalistic approach]. The family cannot be allowed to withstand alone the enormous pressures of an increasingly technological world. *Within the community some mechanism must be created which will assume the responsibility for ensuring the neces-*

sary supports for the child and family [Joint Commission
on Mental Health of Children, 1969, p. 2, italics added].

This analysis is in line with an observation made by Robinson and Robinson (1972), writing as members of the eleven-
nation International Study Group for Early Child Care. Speaking about national orientations to welfare, they distinguish between "future-oriented" and "emergency-induced" approaches.
The former, often associated with socialist economies, have as
their aim the prevention of problems concerning children and
families; the latter, often associated with free-enterprise economies, have as their aim the treatment of already existing problems. In the future-oriented countries developmental services
are thought of as the right of each child and family. In the
emergency-induced countries "It is assumed that most families
will manage without such assistance, and that, except in extreme cases endangering the child, the family must take the
initiative to seek out the public services it needs for which it can
prove its eligibility" (Robinson and Robinson, 1972, pp.
294-295). This cross-national analysis relates to the JCMHC
challenge to the United States to be more future-oriented in its
approach. This challenge may be extended by urging the nation
to negotiate the delicate and sensitive issue of blending socialist
and free-enterprise philosophies in the operation of the American society toward human development ends.

How has the lack of a United States commitment to children and families—a lack that is harmful especially, but not
exclusively, to those in low-income and minority-group situations—come about? In our opinion (see also Wright, 1972;
Goodwin, 1972), it has come about largely because rank-and-
file Americans, including most policy makers, tend to "blame
the victim" (Ryan, 1971), to assume that the plight of the poor
is indeed the fault of the poor. "A majority of Americans, in
1969, held poor people themselves responsible for poverty and
were correspondingly reluctant to support new programs aimed
at eradicating poverty" (Feagin, 1972, p. 101). Those classified
as poor, therefore, are held responsible, are to be blamed, and,
presumably, should be punished. A look at history helps us
understand some of what is behind these harsh judgments.

[In the early nineteenth century] the middle class
could no longer bear the pressure of the multitude or the

contact of the lower class. It seceded: it withdrew from the vast polymorphous society to organize itself separately in a homogeneous environment, among its families, in homes designed for privacy, in new districts kept free from all lower-class contamination. The juxtaposition of inequalities, hitherto something perfectly natural, became intolerable to it: the revulsion of the rich preceded the shame of the poor. The quest for privacy and the new desires for comfort which it aroused (for there is a close connection between comfort and privacy) emphasized even further the contrast between the material ways of life of the lower and middle classes. The old society concentrated the maximum number of ways of life into the minimum of space and accepted, if it did not impose, the bizarre juxtaposition of the most widely different classes. The new society, on the contrary, provided each way of life with a confined space in which it was understood that the dominant features should be respected, and that each person had to resemble a conventional model, an ideal type, and never depart from it. . . . *The concept of the family, the concept of class, and perhaps elsewhere the concept of race appear as manifestations of the same intolerance toward variety, the same insistence on uniformity* [Aries, 1962, pp. 414-415, italics added].

In Aries' historical analysis we see the roots of some of the ramifications in modern Western cultures of classifying families on the bases of economics and social class: the moral overtones of being poor, the comfort that the more affluent take in living in homogeneous environments, issues regarding the sacredness of one's home and the importance of privacy, and the use of classification to preserve privileged self-interest.

Piven and Cloward (1971) have analyzed the functions of public welfare in the United States, in part by tracing the development of the giving of relief in Europe over the last four hundred years. In late eighteenth- and early nineteenth-century England, they report, "the English countryside was periodically besieged by turbulent masses of the displaced rural poor and the towns were racked by Luddism, radicalism, trade unionism, and Chartism. . . . It was at this time that the poor relief system—first created in the sixteenth century to control the earlier disturbances caused by population growth and the commercialization of agriculture—became a major institution. . . . The relief system, in short, was expanded in order to absorb and regulate the masses of discontented people uprooted from agriculture but not yet incorporated into industry" (Piven and Cloward, 1971, pp. 20-21). Throughout history, then, relief arrangements have expanded and contracted to serve the dual purposes of (1) quelling actual or impending turmoil on the part of the poor and (2) enforcing a work ethic and work norms. Relief "also goes far toward defining and enforcing the terms on which different classes of men are made to do different kinds of work; relief arrangements, in other words, have a great deal to do with maintaining social and economic inequities" (Piven and Cloward, 1971, p. xvii). In other words, society's prime intervention approach for dealing with those classified as poor, the relief system, can be seen as preserving, rather than overcoming, the negative consequences associated with poverty classification.

Of similar relevance is the New England Puritans' treatment of those classified as deviant. "The deviant is a person whose activities have moved outside the margins of the group, and when the community calls him to account for that vagrancy it is making a statement about the nature and placement of its boundaries. It is declaring how much variability and diversity can be tolerated within the group before it begins to lose its identity. . . . Deviant forms of behavior, by marking the outer edges of group life, give the inner structure its special character and thus supply the framework within which the people of the group develop an orderly sense of their own cultural identity" (Erikson, 1966, pp. 11, 13). The Puritans' harsh and brutal treatment of deviants grew from moral and religious concerns, specifically from the belief in predestination and the doctrine of the Elect (see also Chapters Five and Seven in this book). "Persons who had felt grace would be so touched by the experience that they would develop a new sense of responsibility toward the community and slowly move into positions of leadership; persons who remained in doubt would stay in the middle ranks of the community and pursue their honest callings until they learned more of their fate; persons who had reason to fear the worst would drift sullenly into the lower echelons of society, highly susceptible to deviant forms of behavior. Thus, the social structure of the Kingdom of God closely resembled that of the English nation, and it was obvious to the dullest saint that confirmed deviants belonged in the lowest of these ranks" (Erikson, 1966, p. 189). Thus, we see a tie between the economically related class structure and an underlying moralizing perspective in Rainwater's (1970) sense. (See Weber, 1958, for a historical view of the relationship between Puritanism and economic principles.)

The moralizing perspective as applied to deviants, and to the poor and minority-group members, is seemingly still with us. "The theological views which sustained . . . the ways of dealing with deviants . . . have largely disappeared from the religious life of the society, but the attitudes toward deviation which were implied in the pattern are still retained in many of the institutions we have built to process and confine deviant offenders. We are still apt to visualize deviant behavior as the product of a deep-seated characterological strain in the person who enacts it, rather than as the product of the situation in which it took place, and we are still apt to treat that person as if his whole being was somehow implicated" (Erikson, 1966, p. 198).

Consonant with Erikson's (1966) analysis of deviance, we suggest that low-income and minority-group families and children are viewed by American society as "modern wayward Puritans," as individuals who are morally lacking, responsible for their own plight, and therefore deserving of harsh treatment. These modern wayward Puritans, however, fulfill important functions in our society in helping the more affluent majority group define its boundaries (Aries, 1962; Erikson, 1966) and operate its economy efficiently and in an orderly fashion (Farber, 1968; Piven and Cloward, 1971).

It is as if our society operates according to the principle of *Social Darwinism with a conscience.* (See Hofstadter, 1944, for an account of the role of Social Darwinism in American history.) Social Darwinism, reinforced by Puritanical attitudes, leads us to view those who do not make it in our society as unfit, unworthy, and immoral. This is our predominant view of low-income and minority-group individuals. Blacks in our society were granted their legal "personhood," and then with some reluctance, only within the last one hundred years; and blacks, Chicanos, American Indians, Puerto Ricans, and Appalachian whites often talk about the majority culture's attempts to dehumanize them, to imply that they are nonpersons. We speak, however, of Social Darwinism *with a conscience.* While probably motivated in part by the need to regulate the poor (Piven and Cloward, 1971) and to guarantee their controlled and limited participation in the labor force (Farber, 1968), the modern

American conscience rejects open and blatant brutal treatment of the poor. We do *talk* about national efforts to eradicate poverty and racism, and we have mounted certain programs ostensibly aimed at meeting the human-development needs of low-income and minority groups. But has our conscience overcome our Puritanically tinged, economically oriented, Darwinistic attitudes? The persistent fear we seem to have of the poor and minority-group members, the virtually permanent stigma of being classified and labeled on income/minority grounds, the reluctance to mount truly national programs, and the current rash of particularly negative attitudes toward the poor suggest that our conscience has not won the day.

Issues concerning the regulation of the poor and the enforcement of the work ethic suggest the existence of an adversary or enemy relationship, fueled by the moralizing perspective, between the system and the poor. A "brittle relationship . . . exists between many welfare workers and the poor. The cumulative abrasive effects of the low levels of assistance, the complicated eligibility requirements, the continuing efforts required by regulations to verify eligibility—often by means that constitute flagrant invasions of privacy—have often brought about an adversary relationship between the case worker and the recipient family" (National Advisory Commission on Civil Disorders, 1968, p. 460). According to the Advisory Council on Public Welfare, these insufficiencies in social-service policies "are themselves a major source of such social evils as crime and juvenile delinquency, mental illness, illegitimacy, multigenerational dependency, slum environments, and the widely deplored climate of unrest, alienation, and discouragement among many groups in the population" (quoted in National Advisory Commission on Civil Disorders, 1968, p. 460).

Let us look now at the general educational system as it affects low-income and minority-group children. Many analysts (Ryan, 1971; Rhodes, 1972; Farber and Lewis, 1972; Levy, 1970) attribute the failure of education for the poor to concerns about economic self-interest.

> The middle-class liberal is committed to viewing ghetto education as a failure to implement his liberalism and nothing more. One alternative he fails to consider is that [the ghetto school] operates in the service not of his morality but of his social and economic interests. He can-

not afford to see that, in an important sense, [the ghetto school] has not failed.

[The ghetto school's] inability to move its children toward the middle class stems from a larger political reality, which transcends the abstract morality of these suburbanites, professors, professionals, and corporate liberals who lend financial and ideological support to ghetto education. When [the ghetto school] is seen not as an instrument of liberal ideology but of political reality, it becomes clear that the school's task is the exact opposite of its publicly stated purpose. In a time when American society is unprepared to absorb its lower-class youth into the middle class, [the ghetto school] successfully serves the purpose of not training its children for middle-class life [Levy, 1970, p. 173].

Children in ghetto schools receive the message that "they are unworthy of entrance into middle-class society. They are told and shown that because of their 'stupidity' and 'disruptiveness' they are not going anywhere" (Levy, 1970, p. 173).

Consistent with Levy, Bowles (1969) emphasizes the importance of the *socialization function* of education; that is, its preparation of children for living in a society and dealing with its economic system. Illich (1970) has made a similar point. Bowles (1971, p. 479) also emphasizes a related notion, the *correspondence principle*: As the social structures of the schools in a given society "reproduce the social relations of production in each age group, the class structure is also reproduced from generation to generation, [producing a] correspondence between education and the economy." We come back again, therefore, to the complex interrelationship of (1) poverty (minority labels and their negative moral overtones), (2) the structure and purpose of human-development-intervention institutions, (3) preservation and promotion of class interests, and (4) a society's economic system.

The JCMHC (1969) has outlined some of the problems facing the large number of the nation's children who come from poverty families: (1) As compared to children from more affluent families, low-income children have higher rates of early school dropout, unemployment, dealings with the juvenile courts, and problems with drugs. (2) Low-income and minority-group mothers receive inadequate prenatal and obstetrical care. (3) Low-income children are overrepresented in the ranks of those labeled *mentally retarded* (see also Mercer, 1972). (4) Low-income children have high rates of tuberculosis, blindness, chronic conditions, and other physical disabilities. (5) Low-income families often suffer from malnutrition, with its retarding effect on children's development. Clearly, then, America's institutions have failed to actualize the rights of children and families and perhaps have even actively contributed to the denial of these rights, especially for those classified on income/minority grounds—the modern wayward Puritans and their children.

Recommendations for Improvement

One of the clearest and strongest findings in all of developmental psychology is that a warm, predictable relationship within which there is an increasingly complex series of reciprocal and contingent interactions is associated with excellence of early childhood development (Bronfenbrenner, 1972). This type of relationship is best provided within the family (not only the nuclear family but any intergenerational group with close personal relationships). Throughout the course of child development, beyond the early years, parents continue to have a significant impact on children. The importance of the family for healthy development and for prevention of problems in development seems obvious but periodically needs to be reemphasized. Significant policy implications flow from this acknowledgment of the family as society's key system for enhancing child development, especially in a society committed to human-development ends. "If our society is committed to maximizing the psychological development of its children, then it must engage in *ecological intervention*—the provision to all families of resources that are required for them to operate as child-development-enhancing systems. This type of intervention has broad political, economic, and social implications, since it involves medical care, adequate income levels, conditions of housing, employment patterns, nutrition, and many other issues. It obviously involves the government at all levels and requires cooperation of the professional guilds, labor unions, schools, and various community groups" (Dokecki and Strain, 1973, pp. 178-179).

Bronfenbrenner recommends activities in at least four areas: (1) In the world of *work* there is need for part-time jobs, flexible work schedules, and other arrangements, including adequate salaries, to fit the particular and diverse circumstances of American families. (2) Parents need to be meaningfully involved in the *education* of their children, and older children should become involved in the education of younger children. (3) *Neighborhoods* should have family centers, parent-child groups, and the like, where parents can develop their skills as educational and behavioral change agents for their children (see also Gray, 1971; Sandler and others, 1973) and where the community at large can become more involved in the lives of its children. (4) The family in the *home setting* should be given information on nutrition and parenting; access to medical care; and a variety of services, including social services, homemaker service, and television teaching. These program elements, implemented very broadly, would go a long way toward establishing a universalistic intervention approach for dealing with the problem of families in general and low-income/minority-group families in particular.

Farber (1968) has suggested a similar but even more extensive approach to the problem of mental retardation. His recommendations can be applied more generally to the human-development needs of all families across the nation. Specifically, he recommends the effective use of resources to enhance the competence of individual children and to help the immediate family become an effective system for enhancing human development; some rearrangement of society's institutions, so that the surplus population is permitted to escape from a nonperson status and more fully participate in America's social institutions; attempts to shift America's value system toward more concern with the importance of human growth and development. "This program would be a comprehensive strategy to incorporate the surplus population into the major institutions and public cultural patterns in the society; to be effective, it requires a profound modification of the social structure. . . . Naturally, the value-modification solution with regard to surplus populations is the most difficult to accomplish. The program most immediate and most amenable to manipulation is, however, the least successful. Just how serious we are in wanting to solve social problems relating to surplus populations . . . will determine exactly how much effort and sacrifice we are willing to undergo in order to revise modern society" (Farber, 1968, pp. 269-270).

As mentioned earlier, the cornerstone of our position on a desirable intervention approach to those in the low-income/minority classification, and for society at large, is the delivery of services through families. By this we mean the provision of adequate resources to all American families, so that they may competently negotiate the many transactions between the families and society's service, legal, and economic institutions. We suggest a wide-ranging policy similar to Farber's (1968) scheme. The policy involves at core income distribution and a revised national employment situation. The ideal execution of this policy would not involve classification in the usual sense; rather, assessments of the general and functional needs of families would be carried out, with consequent provision of sufficient and appropriate resources to meet those needs. Resources, therefore, are construed in terms of income, employment opportunities, and services to families. At the national level, one current pilot research and development effort, the Parent-Child Development Center program, spearheaded by Mary Robinson, was planned and is being implemented according to the principle of delivery of services through families as we have elaborated it.

The JCMHC (1969, p. 46) also "strongly endorses the concept of a guaranteed minimum income . . . accompanied by a national commitment to a system which provides guaranteed employment for all who can work and desire to work." Similarly, Bazelon (1973, pp. 11-12) emphasizes that "we *must* . . . take the first step toward breaking the cycle which leads so many of our youths into juvenile courts—a step toward *preventing* trouble, rather than waiting for it and hoping to cure it. That step is to guarantee to every family an income sufficient to enable parents to provide the kind of home environment they want for their children. . . . Commission after commission on crime, race, violence, or children has recommended some form of income redistribution as the only way to begin to solve our toughest social problems. . . . It may be that an adequate family income won't guarantee a stable family life, won't eradicate the effects of bigotry or stop crime cold or solve all the problems of growing up in Sodom and Gomorrah. *But I am convinced that nothing else can begin to work without it.*" Beyond income distribution, Bazelon (1973, p. 15) suggests that we should "reconstruct the economy to provide a competitive job market at the lower end of the pay scale; honor our commitment to excellence, and integration, in education from nursery school upward; subsidize dramatic shifts in housing patterns." Thus, an eminently respected judge joins the ranks of so-called "radicals" to propose a dramatic reordering of national priorities. (See also Moynihan, 1973.)

Beyond income and employment the JCMHC (1969, p. 57) recommends "programs designed to strengthen family life and foster the normal and mental health of our children. . . . Even if our financial investments in the present systems were multiplied several times over, inefficiency and suffering would continue on a massive scale. The system is in need of drastic restructuring. There is need to redesign the technologies for providing services and the organizational methods of delivery. There is need for a more humane approach. Our services need to enlist consumers and parents as planners and coworkers in children's services." (For the feelings of parents on these issues, see Chapter Twenty in this book.)

Returning to Rainwater's (1970) paradigm, our view of the low-income and minority-group families and children is that they are essentially "ordinary people" who have been grossly mistreated by our system. This suggests the normalizing perspective. The system as it typically operates mistreats the weak, whether they be children, women, blacks, Chicanos, American Indians, Puerto Ricans, Appalachian whites, or poor people. In line with the normalizing perspective, Goodwin carefully researched the orientation toward employment of a poverty-level sample and concluded: "The plight of the poor cannot be blamed on their having deviant goals or a deviant psychology. The ways in which the poor do differ from the affluent can reasonably be attributed to their different experiences of success and failure in the world. There is ample evidence to suggest that children who are born poor face discriminatory barriers to advancement in the educational and occupational worlds, which thrust them into failure much more consistently than their middle-class counterparts" (Goodwin, 1972, p. 118). Goodwin argues convincingly that "mothers who are unable to support themselves and their families can be supported at a decent level by public funds without fear of damage to their work ethic or that of their sons" (Goodwin, 1972, p. 115).

Goodwin's support for the normalizing perspective and the policy implications growing from it is encouraging. Related to this perspective, however, is the issue of the valid and functional features of the particular life styles of low-income and minority groups, and the corresponding importance of cultural pluralism and Rainwater's (1970) naturalizing perspective. A combination of normalizing and naturalizing perspectives flies in the face of exceptional, clinical, deficit, moralizing, and medicalizing models. This approach asserts the essential *human similarity* of us all and asks for tolerance of the nonessentials. While political philosophers are likely to *demand* that certain concessions must be made on the part of the citizenry in order to have a lawful and orderly society, the major issue involves the negotiability of the demand.

A useful model for conceptualizing societal and individual survival, growth, and development is to assert that certain conditions are absolutely necessary or *nonnegotiable,* while others are *negotiable* to varying degrees. In order to preserve individual freedom and dignity with respect to public policy and intervention efforts, *the range of nonnegotiable demands should be kept to a minimum.* A convincing case can be made that American society has artificially broadened the nonnegotiable area to the point where the weak, the surplus, the low-income/minority groups, the modern wayward Puritans have been denied their rights. It is as if our society is so (needlessly) insecure that it must enforce a rigid uniformity in order to maintain its self-image and self-esteem. While it may be true, as Erikson (1966) seems to suggest, that there will always be wayward Puritans in order for a society to survive, it is almost certainly the case that America has overextended its use of this boundary-defining mechanism and has, therefore, done grave injustice to many, especially those classified as low-income and minority-group members.

Who, then, is to be the arbiter concerning the negotiation of demands? If we talk about delivery of services through families, do we mean that parents should be forced by society to receive the services? If parents agree to receive the services, should children be forced to receive them? There are clearly many instances of rights in conflict, and a legal advocacy function will be necessary to arbitrate the conflicting rights of children, parents, and society at large. The JCMHC (1969) proposes a network of neighborhood child-development councils, city- or county-wide development authorities, state child-development agencies, and a president's advisory council on children. Through a complex interaction of these agencies, with the essential ingredient of *extensive citizen involvement at the neighborhood level,* perhaps the legal advocacy function could be actualized. The utilization of a human-service-contract mechanism, wherein service providers and service receivers agree in advance on the nature and extent of their transactions, is also indicated (see Pratt and Tooley, 1966; Johnson, Dokecki, and Mowrer, 1972).

> The basic socializing functions that our major institutions have served are being reexamined and the forms that these functions have taken are undergoing critical renovation. The social-welfare system, the legal correctional system, the educational system, the religious system, the family system are all in the midst of accelerated and provoked change. The social codes and cultural legends that they served are being challenged and criticized. In a sense, the culture itself is under siege. . . . This new wave washing over the lives of men seems to be uncontrolled or perhaps uncontrollable, except by some internal rhythm of historical movements, which, once set into motion, sweeps through every facet and territory of human existence. The dreamer, the man of action, and the great mass of people to whom it is happening are *all* being swept along in its force. The very nature and condition of human existence is being changed in such a revolution [Rhodes, 1972, pp. 139-140; see also Chapter Five in this book].

Our country debates crises concerning energy, ecology, threats to the dollar, inflation, movement from a wartime to a peacetime economy, and many less apparent issues. No more important complex of issues faces us, however, than dealing with our distorted value system, which classifies the poor and minority-group members as modern wayward Puritans and unjustly levies against them harsh judgment and punishment.

As a summary and recapitulation, we present the following general recommendations for intervention policies and strategies with families in general and low-income and minority-group families in particular.

The following orientations must replace the existing bases of classification and intervention policies:

1. The area of classification and service delivery to low-income and minority-group families must be approached as a complex set of historically interrelated issues involving prevailing economic structures, differential assignment of moral

statuses to "deviant" groups, and preservation of socioeco-nomic-class self-interests through institutions such as welfare-relief and public education.

2. To promote and protect the rights of all children, in-tervention policies must be conceptualized as universalistic (for all families) and not exceptionalistic (for exceptional categories of citizens with emergency, remedial, and often punitive ar-rangements).

3. The process by which children develop into healthy, competent, fully functioning human beings involves a con-tinuing series of tasks to be mastered by parents and children. This requires for all families a core of personal and environ-mental resources.

4. Optimal survival and development of the society and the individual citizen requires a differentiation between the minimum necessary or nonnegotiable demands upon citizens and the negotiable demands. This latter set must be dealt with to allow individual and subcultural differences a valid and val-ued place in this society.

The following knowledge-base information must be ac-quired:

1. Behavioral and social science research concerning vari-ous socioeconomic/racial/ethnic groups must move away from short-term, two-group comparative strategies based on deficit and pathology models to those which recognize the multifac-eted environmental realities of these groups with in-depth, lon-gitudinal designs.

2. The descriptive and field-experimental work that has been conducted supports a normalizing perspective, recognizing that the majority of those in poverty desire and value employ-ment at regular, adequate wages. More information concerning economic and labor-force behavior is needed in planning for direct economic interventions with families.

The following general implementation directions are rec-ommended:

1. The family, as the source of most impact on the devel-opment of children, must be redefined as the key system for humanizing children and enhancing child development. Services and resources to all children and parents should be delivered through the individual family unit, so that parents are informed and enabled to contract and transact successfully with societal institutions.

2. An ecological intervention policy is proposed to ensure for all families the significant environmental resources necessary to promote safe, healthy, happy, and competent children. Execution of this policy would involve (a) a general and functional needs assessment of individual families, with consequent provision of sufficient and appropriate resources to meet the needs of individual families; (b) income distribution to family units; (c) revised national employment opportunities, with provisions made for flexible work schedules, part-time positions, and adequate salaries.

3. A legal advocacy system will be required from neighborhood to national levels to arbitrate ecological service-delivery issues and potential conflicts among the rights of children, parents, and society. A human-service-contract approach is also indicated. (For a discussion of the human-service contract in education, see Chapter Twenty-Four in this book.)

4. Since ecological intervention is an instrument to meet individual requirements of families, the meaningful involvement and input of parents as planners and consumers in all areas of service to children must be expanded. The critical socialization function of the public school system must be recognized, with movement toward the integration of parents and older children in the education of younger children.

References

Allen, V. L. "Personality Correlates of Poverty." In V. L. Allen (Ed.), *Psychological Factors in Poverty*. Chicago: Markham, 1970a.

Allen, V. L. "The Psychology of Poverty: Problems and Prospects." In V. L. Allen (Ed.), *Psychological Factors in Poverty*. Chicago: Markham, 1970b.

Aries, P. *Centuries of Childhood: A Social History of Family Life.* New York: Vintage Books, 1962.

Baratz, J. C. "Teaching Reading in an Urban Negro School System." In F. Williams (Ed.), *Language and Poverty*. Chicago: Markham, 1970.

Bazelon, D. L. "Juvenile Justice: A Love-Hate Story." Paper presented at a meeting of New York University School of Law, March 1973.

Bowles, S. *Planning Educational Systems for Economic Growth.* Cambridge, Mass.: Harvard University Press, 1969.

Bowles, S. "Cuban Education and the Revolutionary Ideology." *Harvard Educational Review*, 1971, *41*, 472-500.

Bronfenbrenner, U. *Two Worlds of Childhood.* New York: Russell Sage Foundation, 1970.

Bronfenbrenner, U. *Is Early Intervention Effective?* Washington, D.C.: U.S. Government Printing Office, 1972.

Campbell, D. T. "The Mutual Methodological Relevance of Anthropology and Psychology." In F. L. K. Hsu (Ed.), *Psychological Anthropology.* Homewood, Ill.: Dorsey Press, 1961.

Cole, M., and Bruner, J. S. "Cultural Differences and Inferences About Psychological Processes." *American Psychologist*, 1971, *26*, 867-875.

Clark, K. B. *Dark Ghetto: Dilemmas of Social Power.* New York: Harper, 1965.

Deutsch, M. *The Disadvantaged Child.* New York: Basic Books, 1967.

Dokecki, P. R., Scanlan, P., and Strain, B. A. "In Search of a Transactional Model for Educational Intervention: Reactions to Farber and Lewis." *Peabody Journal of Education*, 1972, *49*, 182-187.

Dokecki, P. R., and Strain, B. A. "Early Childhood Intervention 2001: Transactional and Developmental Perspectives." *Peabody Journal of Education*, 1973, *50*, 175-183.

Erikson, K. T. *Wayward Puritans: A Study in the Sociology of Deviance.* New York: Wiley, 1966.

Farber, B. *Mental Retardation: Its Social Context and Social Consequences.* Boston: Houghton Mifflin, 1968.

Farber, B., and Lewis, M. "Compensatory Education and Social Justice." *Peabody Journal of Education*, 1972, *49*, 85-95.

Feagin, J. R. "God Helps Those Who Help Themselves." *Psychology Today*, 1972, *6*(6), 101-110, 129.

Gewirtz, J. L. "Deficiency Conditions of Stimulation and the Reversal of Their Effects via Enrichment." Paper presented at First Symposium of International Society for the Study of Behavioral Development, University of Nijmegen, July 1971.

Gladwin, T. "The Anthropologist's View of Poverty." In *The Social Welfare Forum.* New York: Columbia University Press, 1961.

Gladwin, T. *Poverty U.S.A.* Boston: Little, Brown, 1967.

Goodwin, L. *Do the Poor Want to Work? A Social-Psychological Study of Work Orientations.* Washington, D.C.: Brookings Institution, 1972.

Gray, S. W. "The Child's First Teacher." *Childhood Education*, 1971, *48*, 127-129.

Guttentag, M. "Introduction." *Journal of Social Issues*, 1970, *26*(2), 1-13.

Harrington, M. *The Other America: Poverty in the United States.* New York: Macmillan, 1962.

Hess, R. D., and Shipman, V. "Early Experience and Socialization of Cognitive Modes in Children." *Child Development*, 1965, *36*, 869-886.

Hofstadter, R. *Social Darwinism in American Thought.* Boston: Beacon Press, 1944.

Hollingshead, A. B., and Redlich, F. C. *Social Class and Mental Illness.* New York: Wiley, 1958.

Illich, I. *Deschooling Society.* New York: Harper, 1970.

Johnson, R. C., Dokecki, P. R., and Mowrer, O. H. *Conscience, Contract, and Social Reality: Theory and Research in Behavioral Science.* New York: Holt, 1972.

Joint Commission on Mental Health of Children. *Crisis in Child Mental Health: Challenge for the 1970's.* New York: Harper, 1969.

Klein, L. "A Partitioning Algorithm for Studying Income Dynamics." Unpublished working paper. Washington, D.C.: Policy Research Division, Office of Economic Opportunity, 1972.

Kreisberg, L. *Mothers in Poverty.* Chicago: Aldine, 1970.

Labov, W. "The Logic of Nonstandard English." In F. Williams (Ed.), *Language and Poverty.* Chicago: Markham, 1970.

LaVeck, G. D. (Ed.) *Perspectives on Human Deprivation: Biological, Psychological, and Sociological.* Washington, D.C.: U.S. Government Printing Office, 1968.

Levy, G. E. *Ghetto School: Class Warfare in an Elementary School.* New York: Pegasus, 1970.

Lewis, O. "The Culture of Poverty." *Scientific American,* 1966, *215*(4), 19-25.

Mercer, J. R. "Discussion of Alternative Value Frames for Classification of Exceptional Children." Working paper prepared for Project on Classification of Exceptional Children, 1972.

Miller, S. M. "The American Lower Classes: A Typological Approach." In A. B. Shastak and W. Gomberg (Eds.), *New Perspectives on Poverty.* Englewood Cliffs, N.J.: Prentice-Hall, 1965.

Miller, W. B. "Lower Class Culture as a Generating Milieu of Gang Delinquency." *Journal of Social Issues,* 1958, *14*(3), 5-19.

Minuchin, S., and others. *Families of the Slums: An Exploration of Their Structure and Treatment.* New York: Basic Books, 1967.

Moynihan, D. P. *The Politics of a Guaranteed Income.* New York: Random House, 1973.

National Advisory Commission on Civil Disorders. *Report of the National Advisory Commission on Civil Disorders.* New York: Bantam, 1968.

Pavenstedt, E. (Ed.) *The Drifters: Children of Disorganized Lower-Class Families.* Boston: Little, Brown, 1967.

Piven, F. F., and Cloward, R. A. *Regulating the Poor: The Functions of Public Welfare.* New York: Pantheon Books, 1971.

Pratt, S., and Tooley, J. "Human Actualization Teams." *Ames Journal of Orthopsychiatry,* 1966, *36*, 881-895.

Rainwater, L. "Neutralizing the Disinherited: Some Psychological Aspects of Understanding the Poor." In V. L. Allen (Ed.), *Psychological Factors in Poverty.* Chicago: Markham, 1970.

Rhodes, W. C. *Behavioral Threat and Community Response.* New York: Behavioral Publications, 1972.

Robinson, N. M., and Robinson, H. B. "A Cross-Cultural View of Early Education." In I. Gordon (Ed.), *Early Childhood Education: The*

Seventy-First Yearbook of the National Society for the Study of Education. Part II. Chicago: University of Chicago Press, 1972.

Rodman, H. "The Lower Class Value Stretch." *Social Forces,* 1963, *42,* 205-215.

Ryan, W. *Blaming the Victim.* New York: Random House, 1971.

Sandler, H. M., and others. "The Evaluation of a Home-Based Educational Intervention for Preschoolers and Their Mothers." *Journal of Community Psychology,* 1973, *1,* 372-374.

Texas Office of Economic Opportunity. *Poverty in Texas.* Austin: Texas Department of Community Affairs, 1972.

Valentine, C. A. *Culture and Poverty.* Chicago: University of Chicago Press, 1968.

Wachs, T. D., Uzgiris, I. C., and Hunt, J. McV. "Cognitive Development in Infants of Different Age Levels and from Different Environmental Backgrounds: An Explanatory Investigation." *Merrill-Palmer Quarterly,* 1971, *17,* 283-317.

Weber, M. *The Protestant Ethic and the Rise of Capitalism.* Trans. T. Parsons. New York: Scribner's, 1958.

Williams, F. "Some Preliminaries and Prospects." In F. Williams (Ed.), *Language and Poverty.* Chicago: Markham, 1970.

Wright, S. R. "Social Psychological Effects of Labor Supply in the New Jersey-Pennsylvania Experiment." Paper presented at annual meeting of American Sociological Association, New Orleans, Aug. 1972.

13

THE JUVENILE COURT

Frank A. Orlando, Jerry P. Black

The classification of juveniles for antisocial conduct is an embodiment of the concept that juveniles, like adults, are accountable at law for violations of the law. The problem is to reconcile the interests of society in being safe and secure in life and property with the interests of society in having a child become a productive citizen. Juvenile courts have traditionally been thought of as vehicles to accommodate these interests and as a means of securing aid and rehabilitation for deviant children. Included under the umbrella of juvenile court jurisdiction are acts ranging from murder and armed robbery to curfew violations and running away from home. Studies reveal that 90 percent of all youths have engaged in activities which could have led to involvement with the juvenile court (President's Commission on Law Enforcement, 1967a, p. 55).

349

This chapter examines the classifications employed by juvenile courts and the impact of these classifications upon the lives of children, especially the reality of that impact when contrasted with the theory of the juvenile justice system. The object of the system has been to reform, to uplift, to develop, and to make the child a worthy citizen (Mack, 1909). Yet "studies conducted by the [President's Commission on Law Enforcement], legislative inquiries in various states, and reports by informed observers compel the conclusion that the great hopes originally held for the juvenile courts have not been fulfilled. [The juvenile court] has not succeeded significantly in rehabilitating delinquent youth, in reducing or even stemming the tide of delinquency, or in bringing justice and compassion to the child offender" (President's Commission on Law Enforcement, 1967a, p. 80).

Juvenile courts are confronted with the fact that youths are responsible for a substantial portion of the nation's serious criminal activity. It is not simply a case of youths acting out or "boys being boys." In 1965, 30 percent of all persons arrested were under twenty-one years of age, and 20 percent were under eighteen; moreover, 50 percent of all persons arrested for serious property crimes were youths eleven through seventeen (President's Commission on Law Enforcement, 1967a, pp. 55-56). Only when one recognizes the multiplicity and complexity of the causes of youth crime can one appreciate the difficult task confronting the court in attempting to modify effectively the behavior of children.

A report by the House Committee on Crime, Juvenile Justice, and Corrections (U.S. Congress, House of Representatives, 1971) has suggested the complexity of the problem:

> Crime and delinquency are multicausal phenomena with roots in the political, social, and economic inequalities which exist in a large, heterogeneous society. An individual's norms, values, and code of conduct are shaped by his life experiences, which, in great measure, are dictated by the physical and moral environment of his youth. Among the forces, conditions, and circumstances most often singled out as "breeders" of crime and delinquency are (a) the undesirable and pervasive condition associated with poverty; (b) the weakening of the traditional institutions (family, school, religion) as agents of socialization and social control; (c) the failure of the educational system to meet

the academic and vocational needs of today's youth; (d) the prolongation of childhood as a period of nonresponsibility; (e) the failure of society to provide meaningful work opportunities and vocational training for those lacking the ability or desire for higher (academic) education; (f) the lack of youth and community involvement in policy making and decision making in matters which directly affect them; (g) the failure of society to provide adequate and relevant services (medical, dental, social, psychological, psychiatric) to large segments of the population; (h) the inability of our judicial and correctional systems to provide adequate and effective rehabilitation programs for those already enmeshed in the delinquent, deviant, and criminal subcultures.

While recent studies (see, for instance, Haney and Gold, 1973) are calling into question the stereotyped juvenile delinquent, it is clear that those children who are caught in the system demand more than a man with a gavel; they need a fairy godmother with a magic wand.

Development of Juvenile Court

In common law, juveniles beyond the age of fourteen who committed antisocial acts were treated in most respects as adults. Children under seven years of age were considered incapable of possessing criminal intent. Children seven through fourteen were presumed incapable of possessing the necessary *mens rea,* but the state was permitted to rebut that presumption. Those children tried as adults were entitled to all the rights accorded adults, but they were similarly subject to the same penalties—imprisonment, capital punishment, and so on.

The reformers of the 1850s were concerned about the brutalization of youth by the criminal justice process and sought to change the notion that children are criminals who deserve the moral condemnation of the community. Instead, these reformers contended, children are to be cared for, educated, and protected. Consequently, in their view, juvenile courts are supposed to examine the relations of the child to his parents, to other adults, and to the state and society, adjusting these relationships according to scientific findings about the child and his environment (Lou, 1927, p. 2). These basic purposes are embodied today in state legislation describing the purposes of the juvenile court: "(1) to provide for the care, protection, and wholesome moral, mental, and physical development of children coming within its provisions; (2) consistent with the protection of the public interest to remove the taint of criminality and the consequences of criminal behavior and to substitute therefor a program of treatment, training and rehabilitation" (Uniform Juvenile Court Act, 1973). The lofty ideals first set out by the reformers and later incorporated into the juvenile court acts recognize that the child is a product of his environment and reflect the belief that a child in his formative years can benefit from treatment.

The Illinois Juvenile Court Act of 1899 represented the initial shift in law where the state no longer engaged in punishing antisocial behavior but instead sought to assist wayward children. In so doing, juvenile court legislation interjected a new party into the basic relationship of parent and child. It was still the primary right of the parent to have custody and control of the child and the primary responsibility for successfully rearing the child. As stated in the ruling on *In re Johnson* (1961), "If every juvenile misdemeanor is to result in the state taking charge, few parents are secure in the custody of their children. It has been said that the right of parents to the society and custody of their children is inherent. . . . [The legitimate object of the Juvenile Court Act] should not be held to extend to cases where there is no substantial ground for interference to protect the child."

Under the new juvenile court legislation, however, the state could intervene, not as a punitive force but as a protector of the child. When the state did intervene, it did so as a substitute parent and was viewed as only "demanding and enforcing obedience to both the natural duties and obligations of the parent or guardian as well as the legal duties and obligations demanded by society and the public welfare" (*Ex parte Sharp*, 1908). In this new setup, the child was not a legal entity but an "object" entitled to care and protection—either by the parent or, where the actions of the child indicated an inability on the part of the parent to provide the needed care and supervision, by the state.

Under the original juvenile court acts, the sole function of the system was to identify those children who required the special intervention of the "state parent": "The problem for determination by the judge is not has this boy or girl committed a specific wrong, but what is he, how has he become what he is, and what had best be done in his interest and in the interest of the state to save him from a downward career" (Mack, 1909, pp. 119-120). Due process did not play a role, since the child was entitled to care and custody—not freedom. "The natural parent needs no process to temporarily deprive his child of liberty by confining it in his home, to save it and to shield it from the consequences of persistence in a career of waywardness; nor is the state, when compelled, as *parens patriae,* to take the place of the father for the same purpose, required to adopt any process as a means of placing its hands upon the child to lead it into one of its courts. . . . [The court] determines [the child's] salvation and not its punishment" (*Commonwealth v. Fisher,* 1905). The fatherly judge sought to select those children who needed his care and guidance.

The reformers and the early juvenile court legislation made no distinction between neglected and delinquent children. By *parens patriae,* "they were articulating the duty of the government to intervene in the lives of all children who might become a community crime problem" (S. Fox, 1972, p. 19). The thrust of the whole process centered first on identifying deviant children and second on providing the child with a better place to live when he was in state custody. Although due process was not thought to play a role in the classification process, any basic notion of fairness would dictate that a child deprived of his former family relationship under the guise of giving him a better life should receive treatment and help, not punishment. Little was done, however, to accomplish this goal of treatment. Under the provisions of the Illinois Act of 1899, the first Juvenile Court Act, "institutional conditions were barely changed. Nothing was done about the children in the poorhouse; a provision to remove them was deleted from the final bill. Local jails remained as they were. The only change was the provision that forbade placing children under twelve in a jail or police station. They were to be confined in a 'suitable place,' although no money was provided to lease, build, or otherwise find such a place. A provision to pay for such special detention was deleted by the legislature" (S. Fox, 1970, p. 1224). The new institutions which were built were heavily punitive. The maltreatment of children continued and exists today in most states (Rector, 1970, p. 96; James, 1970). Thus, the state was failing, just as the child's parents had failed, to deliver the care, custody, and education promised the child.

The Supreme Court in *Kent v. United States* (1966) stated that "there may be grounds for concern that the child receives the worst of both worlds: that he gets neither the protection accorded to adults nor the solicitous care and regenerative treatment postulated for children." Thus, the warning was sounded that to identify someone for treatment without providing that treatment poses grave constitutional problems. Finally, in the *Gault* case (*In re Gault*, 1967), the Supreme Court expressly rejected the idea that the juvenile is entitled to custody and care in place of liberty. As in *Kent* the court did not quarrel with the laudable purposes of juvenile courts. But in view of the failure of the system to deliver treatment and rehabilitation, the court altered the primary role of the juvenile court from informally identifying wayward youth to emphasizing due process in the classification scheme of the court. The court-based social work is now subservient to legal due process, and the court is charged with the responsibility of forcing the state to prove its right to intervene in the life of the child. In so doing, the Supreme Court interjected yet another party into the proceedings—the child, who has the right to have his side heard and the right to be assisted by counsel in putting the other side to the task of proving the allegations which give the state the right to intervene with treatment.

What has evolved in juvenile court, then, is a legitimate concern on the part of society that the arbitrary age limitations existing in the common-law treatment of children exhibiting antisocial conduct be supplanted with a more humane approach. At the same time, fundamental fairness dictates that the state legitimately establish jurisdiction over the child before intervening in his behalf. The use of the court classification system with its resultant consequences should, at a minimum, be limited to those instances where the state has demonstrated its right to intervene. The following sections attempt to set out the bases for state intervention where the child has engaged in antisocial behavior and to assess critically the propriety of using the juvenile court as the mechanism of intervention.

Classification System

The term *juvenile court* refers to those courts that constitute a distinct division of a trial court and hear nothing but juvenile cases, and also to those courts that have judicial matters in addition to juvenile cases—often the probate or county court. For purposes of discussion the procedures employed by either of the above systems should be the same, although the latter courts are not likely to provide the same opportunities for development of specialized skills on the part of the court. (See Figure 1 for an abbreviated flow chart of the juvenile court system.)

Juvenile courts are involved with children who commit acts which violate criminal laws, children who commit acts which violate laws applicable to children alone (running away from home), children who are habitually ungovernable by their natural guardians, and children who are neglected or abused by their guardians. Juvenile court legislation forms the basis for the distinctions between the delinquent, the child in need of supervision, and the neglected and dependent child. The classifications *delinquent* and *child in need of supervision* involve proceedings initiated as a result of some act by the child himself. On the other hand, neglect and dependency proceedings are essentially actions against the parents or guardians and are initiated because of some act of misfeasance, malfeasance or nonfeasance on the part of the parent with respect to the welfare of the child. Since the category of neglected and dependent children generally does not involve children who commit antisocial acts, it will not be covered here.

The classifications *juvenile delinquent* and *child in need of supervision* are nonscientific classifications representing legislative attempts to delimit the boundaries between conduct which warrants state intervention and conduct which does not. Consistent with the original formulation of the juvenile court, the concept *delinquency* includes conduct injurious to the community, such as property crimes, and conduct basically injurious to the child himself, such as running away from home. Sussman and Baum (1968, p. 12) list the following acts as subsumed under delinquency definitions: violations of any law or ordinance; habitual truancy; knowingly associating with thieves or with vicious or immoral persons; incorrigibility (being beyond control of parent or guardian); growing up in idleness or crime; deporting self so as to injure self or others; absenting self without just cause or without consent; immoral or indecent conduct; habitual use of vile, obscene, or vulgar language in a public place; jumping trains or entering cars or engine without authority; patronizing public poolroom or bucket shop; im-

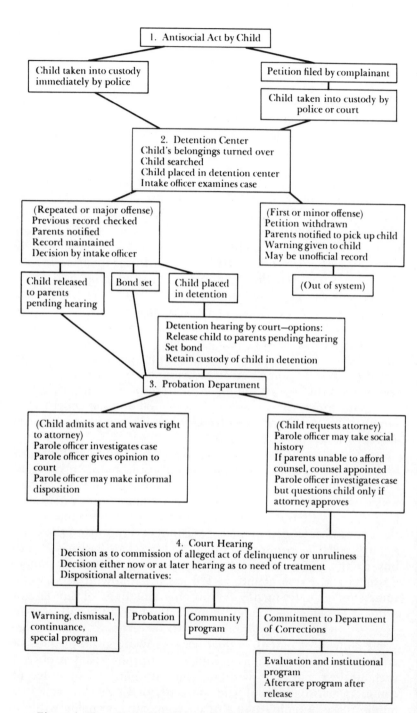

Figure 1. Flow Chart: Juvenile Court System for a Delinquent Child
or Child in Need of Supervision

moral conduct around school; engaging in illegal occupation; engaging in occupation or situation dangerous or injurious to self or others; smoking cigarettes or using tobacco in any form; frequenting places whose existence violates the law; being found in a place for permitting which an adult may be punished; being addicted to drugs; being disorderly; begging; using intoxicating liquor; making an indecent proposal; loitering; sleeping in alleys; vagrancy; running away from state or charity institution; attempting to marry without consent in violation of law; being given to sexual irregularities. Under such definitions of delinquency, the state in its role of *parens patriae* was unchecked. It could intervene in the life of a child and find him delinquent at little more than the drop of a hat. Natural parents were expected to be concerned with the whole gambit of undesirable behavior, from criminal activity to smoking cigarettes; and the statutes were drawn to permit state intervention in these instances as well.

Recently in many jurisdictions the classification *juvenile delinquency* has been refined to include only conduct which if committed by an adult would be a violation of the criminal law. Those persons who are habitually truant, who persistently refuse to obey the reasonable commands of their guardians, or who violate laws applicable only to children are classified as *children in need of supervision, persons in need of supervision, incorrigibles,* or *unruly children.* Two main reasons exist for the development of these new categories. First, the 1967 *Gault* decision required procedural safeguards for children and necessitated more precise notice of charges than that provided in the loose language of many of the juvenile court definitions of delinquency. Second, legislatures became concerned with the stigma attached to the label *delinquent* and sought to limit that label to violations of the criminal law. Many legislatures now prohibit placement of children classified as *in need of supervision* in the same institutions as delinquents. Under many state laws (for instance, in California and Tennessee) children classified as *in need of supervision* cannot be directly committed to the state department of corrections; however, a noncriminal minor may be so committed in a supplemental petition where he can be shown to be not amenable to treatment as prescribed in the original disposition. At present, twenty-two states have created a separate legal status for children charged as runaway, truant, incorrigible, or wayward.

In order for a child to be classified *delinquent* or *in need of supervision,* two essential elements must be present. First, if the child is to be found delinquent, he must have committed an act which constitutes a crime if committed by an adult; if he is to be found in need of supervision, he must have engaged in a pattern of conduct which makes him unruly. Second, the child must also be found to be in need of treatment or rehabilitation (Uniform Juvenile Court Act, 1973). Thus, to determine that a child committed an act without determining a need for treatment should be insufficient to support a finding of delinquency and lead to no action by the court.

The juvenile court classification process cannot begin unless the child allegedly commits some act which brings him within the jurisdiction of the court. The first step is the apprehension and investigation of the child believed to be an offender. The initial decision to institute proceedings lies with the would-be petitioner. This person has three alternatives: involving the court by either turning the youth over to the court or by filing a petition in the court; releasing the child but filing some report with the court; or releasing the juvenile outright, with or without some warning (see "Juvenile Delinquents," 1966). Obviously the decision is governed to a large degree by the biases of the individual petitioner, and little can be done in an official way to ensure uniform treatment of the children involved except where police or other public officials are the would-be complainants. In these latter cases, the court can attempt to develop standards for official court involvement and thus strive to protect the community without unnecessarily thrusting a child into a traumatic court involvement.

When the petitioner opts for formal court involvement, he files with the court a petition setting out the alleged misconduct and expressing a belief that the youth is in need of treatment. The intake unit receives the petition and is charged with the responsibility of determining whether the alleged facts constitute a prima facie case and, if they do, whether the interests of the community and the child warrant further court action (Ferster, Courtless, and Snethen, 1970).

This initial screening phase provides the opportunity for dispensing justice and treatment to the alleged juvenile offender. The intake department has four primary options: (1) to file a formal petition, (2) to engage in informal supervision by the probation staff, (3) to refer the child to another agency for treatment, and (4) to dismiss the case (National Juvenile Law Center, 1971). Factors which appear to be given the heaviest weight in evaluating the particular case include the seriousness of the act, the child's prior record, and the attitude of the child and his parents (Ferster, Courtless, and Snethen, 1970, p. 873).

Most state statutes require some sort of preliminary investigation, but specific guidelines or criteria for conducting the preliminary investigations are almost nonexistent. While this flexibility permits the courts to avoid stigmatizing the juvenile by adjudicating him a delinquent, it also provides an opportunity for abuse by the intake staff. To prevent such abuse, "written guides and standards should be formulated and imparted in the course of in-service training. Reliance on word of mouth creates the risk of misunderstanding and conveys the impression that pre-judicial dispositions are neither desirable nor common. Explicit written criteria would also facilitate achieving greater consistency in decision making" (President's Commission on Law Enforcement, 1967b, p. 21).

Cases which proceed beyond the intake stage for formal court action are referred to a probation officer, who is charged with investigation of the case. Often juvenile court acts permit the probation officers to dispose of the case informally in much the same manner as the intake department would.

After the *Gault* decision, juveniles alleged to be delinquent have been guaranteed certain constitutional rights. In general, these same rights should be afforded children alleged to be in need of supervision. These rights attach with the decision of the court staff to proceed formally with the case against the child. Children are guaranteed procedural rights because the state can intervene in the child's life only when certain behavioral facts exist (for instance, the fact that the child deliberately robbed a store). These procedural rights help ensure reliable fact finding.

The child and his parents have a right to timely written notice, specifying the factual basis for the allegation against the child. This notice must specify in detail the nature of the facts alleged to give the court jurisdiction and must be given to parent and child sufficiently in advance of the date of trial so as to permit adequate preparation.

Since the child may be deprived of his freedom as a result of the finding of delinquency, he has a right to the assistance of counsel. Both the child and his parents must be notified of this right; they must also be informed that counsel will be provided at state expense if they cannot afford counsel.

The hearing before the judge is adversarial in nature when the child disputes the factual allegations which would give the court jurisdiction over him. At the hearing the state will present its witnesses in an attempt to establish the necessary act on the part of the child. The state may not introduce any hearsay evidence, over objection, into the proceeding, for this would violate the child's right to cross-examine the witness against him. After the conclusion of the state's evidence, if it is sufficient to establish a *prima facie* case against the child, the child then has the right to introduce evidence and otherwise be heard in his own behalf. The child cannot be compelled to be a witness against himself, although he may testify if he deems it in his best interest.

After hearing all the testimony, the judge decides whether the child committed the alleged act. The child is presumed innocent, and the judge must be convinced beyond a reasonable doubt that he committed the act in question (*In re Winship*, 1970). If the judge finds that the state failed to prove its case, the case is dismissed and the proceeding ends. On the other hand, if the court finds the child to have committed the act, it then proceeds to the dispositional phase of the hearing—that is, deciding whether the child needs treatment and, if so, what treatment.

At the dispositional hearing, the court considers the child, his family, and his environment. Ideally the court has had psychological testing administered to the child, has developed a social history of the child, and has assessed the child's needs in light of the state resources. Unfortunately, many courts do not have the resources available to assess the child's needs adequately. As a result, they end up committing children to training schools because they do not know what else to do with them. Even where the court appears to know what the child needs, woefully inadequate resources preclude effective implementation of good plans of treatment. What *Gault* accomplished was an orderliness in the proceedings. In the matter of intervention, however, much is left to be done if society is to fulfill its promise of care, custody and guidance (Ketcham, 1962).

Assessment of the System

The juvenile court, to be sure, has a number of beneficial aspects which make it preferable to its adult counterpart, the criminal court. Judges in juvenile court normally view their role differently from that of the criminal court judge. The emphasis in juvenile court is primarily on helping the child, so that diagnostic and rehabilitation services (although frequently inadequate) are provided. Moreover, the end result of a finding of delinquency is significantly different from that of a criminal proceeding; most notably, a finding of delinquency does not result in civil disabilities such as loss of the right to vote or to hold public office or to be employed under the civil service system. Finally, the system allows for wide discretion in the intake procedure, and there is certainly more flexibility at the dispositional phase of the proceedings.

The juvenile court system, however, has major shortcomings as well as strengths. There are serious flaws in the classification scheme employed by the court. Difficulties are encountered when the interests of society and those of the child do not coincide. The labels *delinquent* and *child in need of supervision* often have unintended consequences in stigmatizing the children so labeled. Also, since many statutes concerning children in need of supervision attempt to reach children guilty of no specific antisocial conduct, constitutional problems arise.

Conflicts between interests of child and community. As was indicated earlier, juvenile courts are required to make two findings: (1) that the child committed the alleged antisocial act and (2) that he is in need of treatment. The first finding involves the procedural safeguards of *Gault*. The second finding centers on helping children rather than punishing them. It is based upon the premise that the best interests of the child and the community are identical; thus, according to this premise, if a child does not need help, the interests of the community are fully served when he is released. However, when a child has committed an act, particularly a substantial antisocial act such as malicious destruction of property, many judges have difficulty in adjudging him not delinquent even if he has no need for treatment. Undoubtedly part of the difficulty lies with the fact that the community feels a very real need to be protected, to make an example out of this wrongdoer, and to punish him for his indiscretion. Even in cases where treatment is needed, often the court is called upon to correct conditions which are beyond its capabilities, with the result that the inadequate "treatment" prescribed is more like punishment.

The failure to assess accurately the role that the court plays in protecting the community has several unintended consequences which are detrimental to the child. Society has al-

lowed laxness and unfairness in the use of the juvenile court
process because of the assumption that the court is simply looking out for the welfare of the child, when it is clear that what
the court is being called upon to do is to protect the community. Furthermore, the emphasis upon the therapeutic efforts of
the court creates the danger of unrealistic expectations; that is,
the court is called upon to right situations which can be better
handled by other agencies in the community. Finally, this unrealistic picture of the role of the court has led society to escape
critical evaluation of the system and to overburden the system to
such an extent that it is unlikely to be effective even in those areas
where it could operate successfully (see Allen, 1964, p. 457).

   Stigma. Many recent studies have emphasized the consequences of juvenile court adjudications. In analyzing these materials, we must recognize at the outset that the official label of
delinquency is not necessarily synonymous with the public's
concept of delinquency (Williams and Gold, 1972, p. 210). The
public fails to make distinctions between the delinquent child
who commits a criminal act and the child in need of supervision
who commits an act of truancy or curfew violation. Rather, it
considers any juvenile to be "delinquent" if he has been subjected to juvenile court intervention; stigma thus attaches when
the public conceives the child to be delinquent, and it operates
as an additional means of sanction for the child other than the
specific statutory consequences of a finding of delinquency (see
Paulsen, 1962, pp. 45-46, 73; President's Commission on Law
Enforcement, 1967b, p. 28; Gough, 1966, p. 174; Handler,
1965, p. 13; Lerman, 1970, p. 5; Williams and Gold, 1972, p.
210; Shoham, 1970, p. 13; Wheeler, Cottrell, and Romasco,
1967, pp. 417-418).

   The traditional stance of the courts was that adjudication
of delinquency is not criminal in nature and that no adverse
consequences attach to the adjudication (see, for instance, *Pee
v. United States,* 1959; *United States v. Borders,* 1957; *In re
Holmes,* 1954). Although consistent with the goals set out in
the statutes, this assumption ignored reality. The Supreme
Court expressly rejected it in *Gault,* maintaining that classification as a delinquent involves "only slightly less stigma than the
term *criminal.*" The court has since reaffirmed that position in
the Winship case (*In re Winship,* 1970; see also *McKeiver v.
Pennsylvania,* 1971). Similarly, as early as 1946, in *Jones v.
Commonwealth,* the Virginia Supreme Court had noted: "The

judgment against a youth that he is delinquent is a serious re-
flection upon his character and habits. The stain against him is
not removed merely because the statute says no judgment in
this particular proceeding shall be deemed a conviction for
crime or so considered. The stigma of conviction will reflect
upon him for life. It hurts his self-respect. It may, at some
inopportune, unfortunate moment, rear its ugly head to destroy
his opportunity for advancement, and blast his ambition to
build up a character and reputation entitling him to esteem and
respect of his fellow man."

Similar awareness was expressed by other courts in the
following years (*In re Contreras*, 1952). Note especially the
colorful language of Justice Musmanno (*In re Holmes*, 1954):
"A most disturbing fallacy abides in the notion that a juvenile
court record does its owner no harm. The grim truth is that a
juvenile court record is a lengthening chain that its riveted pos-
sessor will drag after him through childhood, youthhood, adulthood, and middle age. Even when the ill-starred child becomes
an old man the record will be there to haunt, plague, and tor-
ment him. It will be an ominous shadow following his tottering
steps, it will stand by his bed at night, and it will hover over him
when he dozes fitfully in the dusk of his remaining day."

Judge Orman Ketcham (1962, p. 27) of the District of
Columbia listed as one of the unfulfilled promises of the juvenile court the fact that the findings resulted in a stigma much
akin to a criminal court connotation. There has also been judicial recognition of the inherent dangers involved in the exposi-
tion of juvenile records (see, for instance, *Henry v. Looney*,
1971; *In re Smith*, 1970; *Menard v. Mitchell*, 1970; *Gregory v.
Litton Systems, Inc.*, 1970). Recent legislation and proposals
for legislation have attempted to mitigate the effects of stigma
(see Fox and Spencer, 1972; National Council on Crime and
Delinquency, 1972; "Juvenile Delinquents," 1966).

Recent sociopsychological research (for instance, Becker,
1964; Lemert, 1951; Merton, 1957; Schur, 1971) suggests that
official response to delinquent behavior may often act to push
the juvenile further into deviant conduct. The thrust of the
concept (which is analogous to the "dramatization of evil," first
suggested by Tannenbaum, 1938) is that being identified as a
juvenile delinquent results in a "spoiled" public identity. The
label results in a degree of public liability, through exclusion
from participation in groups and events, which would not occur

without the prior attachment of the label. The social liability has the further effect of reinforcing the deviance (Foster, Dinitz, and Reckless, 1972, p. 202).

> The assumption is that the public responds to a person informally and in an unorganized way unless that person has been defined as falling into a clear category. The official labeling of a misbehaving youth as *delinquent* has the effect of placing him in such a category. This official stamp may help to organize responses different from those that would have arisen without the official action. The result is that the label has an important effect upon how the individual is regarded by others. If official processing results in an individual's being segregated with others so labeled, an additional push toward deviant behavior may result. . . . The individual begins to think of himself as delinquent, and he organizes his behavior accordingly (Wheeler, Cottrell, and Romasco, 1967, p. 417).

Under this theory the societal reaction is initially critical. Society, of course, first determines what behavior is to be considered deviant (see Schur, 1965, 1968). Stigma results when the deviant behavior and the offender are exposed (see Schur, 1969). At this point the delinquent's self-concept becomes crucial. The social rejections caused by the stigma can reinforce a negative self-image and persuade the juvenile that he cannot make it in normal society (Lemert, 1967, p. 93). The result is continued delinquency. That is, in line with the "self-fulfilling prophecy" (Merton, 1948), a person treated like a criminal is likely to become one. "Under the impact of negative social reactions the individual may, then, be propelled from isolated acts of criminality into more complete involvement in criminal ways of life (heightened 'commitment' to criminal roles), and he may come increasingly to view himself as an enemy of society (since society seems so determined to consider him one)" (Schur, 1969, p. 117).

Several writers regard delinquency as cyclical in nature. One recent study (Empey and Lubeck, 1970) advances the hypothesis that when juveniles are confronted with poor institutional relationships—family, school, social contacts, employment situations—strain and tension result. Often the more intense the resulting strain becomes, the worse the institutional ties become. Peer pressures may add to the tension. Finally, the strain results in a deviant act. However, the tension is not necessarily broken, since society's reaction to the delinquency often heightens the strain. The societal reaction is expressed through stigma. As the strain worsens again, so do the institutional ties; and when delinquency recurs, it is most likely of a more serious nature, with the resulting stigma more severe and the pattern starting anew. Thus, the cycle has two "feedback loops"–strain worsening institutional ties, and stigma intensifying strain.

According to the noted criminologist Shoham (1970), stigma is used as a "generic tool of social control," demanding conformity to established norms while threatening individualism. It often leaves the offender facing almost total "apartness" from regular society, the only alternative being association with others having the same handicap, delinquency. Thus, stigma can have the effect of creating deviant subcultures.

Empirical research attempts to support the labeling hypothesis have been inconclusive. However, significant work has been done by Martin Gold and Jay Williams at the University of Michigan. In one of their studies, the researchers assembled thirty-five matched pairs, in which one member of the match had escaped apprehension for essentially the same delinquent act that had resulted in apprehension for his "twin." (Variables were matched as evenly as possible between the members of each pair.) The subsequent records of the two youths were then compared. The survey concluded that "apprehension itself encourages rather than discourages delinquency" (Gold and Williams, 1969, p. 3). The rate of recidivism was higher when there was any type of official intervention, from apprehension to incarceration, than when nothing at all had been done. The same conclusions were reached by Gold (1970) in an independent research project using similar methods. According to Gold and Williams (1969, p. 10), "It is unlikely that two separate studies would both yield statistically significant similarities in continuing delinquent behavior between apprehended and unapprehended juveniles merely by chance. [We] believe that these data indicate that apprehension itself contributes to further delinquency." In response to these findings, Juvenile Court Judge John Steketee maintained that the study certainly lends credence to the theory that there is a self-fulfilling prophecy at work.

The effects of court adjudication on a juvenile's school performance have also received empirical study. A 1966 study concluded that "the school itself inadvertently contributes to alienation, rejection, misbehavior, and delinquency—in its very attempt to do the opposite" (Schafer and Polk, 1967, p. 251). An alienating cycle was detected, and the labeling process was held responsible.

On the other side of the coin, there are recent studies (see, for instance, Fisher, 1972) which conclude that an adverse reaction does not necessarily arise as a serious obstacle to school achievement for those labeled deviant. That is, the negative association between public status as a delinquent and school performance existed before the identification of the juvenile as deviant, as well as after. The label may, however, exacerbate the already ongoing process.

Recent studies also raise questions about the validity of the labeling hypothesis. One study found extremely minute differences between those classified delinquent and those not so classified but who committed delinquent acts; as a result of this finding, the investigator concluded that "a delinquent record does not appear to be particularly stigmatic by itself" (Jensen, 1972, p. 97). Another study focused upon the extent to which delinquent boys perceived themselves as having incurred any social liability as a consequence of public intervention. The investigators took cases in an urban community from both the police department and the juvenile court, and interviewed all the chosen subjects within a week to ten days after disposition of their cases. Recognizing that stigma may result in subtle and diffuse ways, the researchers are planning follow-up studies, but their early research supports the following conclusions: (1) only a relatively small proportion of youths perceive any significant change in interpersonal relationships with friends or family; (2) only a relatively small proportion anticipate any difficulties in completing school as a direct consequence of the public intervention; (3) slightly more than half of the youths expect increased police surveillance as a consequence of public intervention; (4) slightly less than half of the youths perceive that they may have endangered their chances of obtaining desired employment (Foster, Dinitz, and Reckless, 1972, p. 207). The authors list three possible explanations for the result: (1) The boys were unable to project a stigmatized status into the future. (2) Awareness of stigma grows with passage of time. (3) The group of predominantly lower-class boys may have already neutralized the unfavorable consequences which result from stigma.

(For evidence contrary to the findings of this study, see Gough, 1966, pp. 153-155.)

Economic consequences to the juvenile classified as delinquent arise despite statutes in every state requiring the confidentiality of juvenile court records. (For a listing of each of these statutes, see Gough, 1966, pp. 168-169). The statutes fail for a number of reasons. First, they apply only to court records, thus leaving police departments free to form their own policies concerning their records of juvenile arrests (*In re Gault,* 1967; Ketcham, 1962, p. 29). The loopholes in the statutes are significant, and information is regularly supplied to the FBI, the military, government agencies, and even private employers ("Juvenile Delinquents," 1966, pp. 784-785, 800; *State v. Arbeiter,* 1966; President's Commission on Law Enforcement, 1967a, pp. 87-88). In addition, employers can obtain the information simply by asking for it on the application forms or in interviews (President's Commission on Law Enforcement, 1967b, p. 54). Employers and agencies can also demand waivers of confidentiality from applicants (*In re Smith,* 1970; Coffee, 1972, pp. 591-592).

The classical study on the economic problems was performed by Schwartz and Skolnick (1962). They sent identical employment information on one hundred employees in application for the same type of unskilled-labor job. The only variable was that twenty-five of the dossiers admitted an arrest and a conviction for assault; twenty-five showed an arrest but no conviction, twenty-five included a letter from the judge affirming the applicant's innocence of the charges, while the remaining twenty-five made no mention of any arrest. Nine employers gave positive responses to the "no record" folder, six accepted the applicant with the letter from the judge, only three offered employment to the arrestee without the letter, and only one would accept the convicted applicant. Subsequent studies (for instance, Rubin, 1970; President's Commission on Law Enforcement, 1967b, pp. 54, 591; Gough, 1966, pp. 153-154) have demonstrated that a juvenile record can be almost as damaging as an adult record.

Employment opportunities are affected in more subtle ways. Obtaining bonds required for many jobs becomes extremely difficult, and there may be substantial obstacles to procuring automobile liability coverage, thus making impossible any employment that would require driving a vehicle (Gough,

1966, p. 158). "The delinquency label may preclude membership in labor unions or participation in apprenticeship training"
(President's Commission on Law Enforcement, 1967b, p. 54).
Occupational licensing practices may also prevent those with a
record of juvenile delinquency from engaging in certain careers
(President's Commission on Law Enforcement, 1967b, p. 54;
see also Rubin, 1971).

When an individual's avenues for financial stability are
closed off, he has little choice but to resort to crime for needed
funds and status (see U.S. Congress, Senate, 1972; Neier, 1973;
Rubin, 1971). Some courts have recognized that a juvenile record "may stigmatize and impede its victim throughout his lifetime" and have accordingly ordered expungement of his records
in certain circumstances (*Henry v. Looney,* 1971; see also *In re
Smith,* 1970; Coffee, 1972, pp. 602-611; Gough, 1966, pp.
170-173). However, expungement is not the total answer, since
employers can still demand the information from the individual.

Child in need of supervision. With the growing awareness
of the stigma attaching to the classification of *delinquent* and in
response to *Gault,* legislatures developed the category *child in
need of supervision.* These children are "guilty" of committing
what can only be called status offenses. That is, their antisocial
act is one of being a truant or a runaway. In addition to defining certain conduct as being impermissible for children alone,
many of the statutes have omnibus clauses which attempt to
identify and reach children who are "likely to engage in criminal activity at some future date." Unfortunately, these omnibus
clauses are incapable of precise definition. Under the omnibus
clauses children are alleged to be "morally depraved" or "in
danger of becoming morally depraved" or "leading a life of
idleness" or "in danger of leading an idle, dissolute, lewd, or
immoral life" (see New York Judiciary Code, 1971; for a general listing of state laws in this area, see "Juvenile Court Jurisdiction," 1972, p. 568). One does not need to be a logician to
comprehend that such language lends itself to arbitrary implementation, since it does not make clear specifically what conduct is prohibited.

In its zeal to "help" children, society all too often ne-
glects the warning of the New York Court of Appeals in 1927:
"The concept that in juvenile court the state acts as *parens
patriae* is being somewhat overdone. Even if the state assumes
the parental role, this assumption does not prove that, by divine

omniscience, it cannot be other than just. It is not impossible for a father, or even a mother, to be unreasonable with offspring. What a child charged with crime is entitled to is *justice,* not a *parens patriae* which in time may become a little calloused, partially cynical, and somewhat overcondescending" (*People v. Fitzgerald,* 1927).

Two recent federal court decisions confronted the problem of the child's right to fairness versus the state's asserted need to reach children before they engage in specific antisocial conduct. In *Gesicki v. Oswald* (1971) the court ruled that the terms *morally depraved* and *in danger of becoming morally depraved* are impermissibly vague. Although the state attempted to classify its statute as noncriminal, juveniles who violated the statute were susceptible to confinement in adult correctional programs and facilities. Thus, the court applied the vagueness standard applicable to criminal laws and held that the terms *morally depraved* and *in danger of becoming morally depraved* violate due process of law. In *Gonzalez v. Mallard* (1971) a similar California law—which, unlike New York's, did have the redeeming feature of limiting dispositional placement to separate camps or homelike institutions—was declared unconstitutional. The court found that a child charged under the California law could not formulate a defense, since the basis for the allegation included "the entire moral dimension of one's life."

These cases reject the arguments that *parens patriae* virtually grants to the states a free hand in defining prohibited conduct. The holdings require the states to define proscribed conduct with a degree of specificity, so that the statute is not "so vague that men of common intelligence must necessarily guess at its meaning and differ as to its application." These rulings require a fair warning, reduce the opportunities for arbitrary application of the juvenile code, and minimize encroachment by overzealous court personnel upon constitutionally protected areas of behavior (see "Parens Patriae," 1973).

Status offenses represent a significant proportion of the cases handled by the juvenile court. The U.S. Department of Health, Education, and Welfare has estimated that 40 percent of the cases disposed of by the juvenile courts involve unruly behavior (National Advisory Commission, 1973, p. 35). The experience gained in the attempts to separate criminal from noncriminal behavior is not extensive, but recent indications lead one to surmise that the attempt is a failure. The President's

Commission on Law Enforcement and the Administration of Justice recommended as early as 1967 that noncriminal conduct be removed from juvenile court jurisdiction. It reached this position after concluding "that even the most earnest efforts to narrow broad jurisdictional bases in language or practice will not remove the possibility of overextension" (President's Commission on Law Enforcement, 1967b, p. 27). "The new nomenclature makes no difference whatsoever. . . . The only noticeable trend . . . is to retain jurisdiction over nonviolators, and, in fact, to deal correctionally with delinquents and misbehavors in the same institution. Thus, the ostensible trend toward separation of criminal from noncriminal jurisdictional bases for dealing with children is a hoax" (Glen and Weber, 1971, p. 7). The net result of these status offenses is that children in need of supervision are swept up into the juvenile court system just as are the delinquent children.

Of course, there is a danger in limiting juvenile court jurisdiction to criminal law violations. One can certainly argue that a child who exhibits a pattern or course of conduct which is "antisocial" in nature may be more in need of treatment than a child who commits but a single violation of the criminal law. However, the answer for the latter child appears to be judicious judicial recognition of the definition of delinquency; to wit, that the child not only committed the criminal act but also is in need of treatment. As for the "antisocial child": he is likely to be experiencing problems in his home, school, or community and can best be dealt with outside the court setting. Family counseling, improved educational opportunities, improved living conditions, and in general an improved existence for the child seem much more positive than the present classification of status offenses. As Milton Luger, Commissioner of the New York Division of Youth, observed in the *Gesicki* case (quoting from Samuels, 1971, p. 146): "With the exception of a relatively few youths, it would probably be better for all concerned if young delinquents were not detected, apprehended, or institutionalized. Too many of them get worse in our care."

Conclusion: The Neglected Child

Juvenile courts have operated under the assumption that if the natural parent does not provide the necessary guidance and help, the state parent can and will. Yet the reality for the child of the state parent is that his plight is strikingly similar to that of a neglected or abused child. The state has woefully underfunded its juvenile courts, so that services for children are more of an accident than a planned program for assistance. Probation staffs are undermanned. As a result, inadequate investigation occurs, making ecological approaches to understanding a child at best incomplete and all too often nonexistent. Even when one grasps the crux of a child's problem, inadequate resources mean that help is rarely in the offing. The net result is that the state undernourishes the children charged to its care just as the poor parent may undernourish his baby. In the latter case, it is easy to recognize that the result may be stunted growth, even brain damage. Unfortunately, realistic appraisals of the former have not been forthcoming until recently, and the nation has not realized that children are being starved by the state parent. That is, children of the state parent (*parens patriae*) realize limited opportunities in later life.

The first task facing a responsible state parent is to define carefully the role of the juvenile court as community protector and as child protector. It is relatively easy to understand the role of the court as community watchdog—for it is much like the role of the criminal court. In these instances, we recommend that all *procedural due-process safeguards be strictly adhered to.*

It is not as easy to understand the role of the court as a helping parent. Clearly, classifying the child as delinquent or in need of supervision does little, if anything, to meet the responsibility placed upon the court. If the juvenile court is to function properly, its first task is to understand fully the jurisdictional limits upon it. This means that the court should engage in two steps in a hearing. First, it should determine, in accordance with the mandates of *Gault* and *Winship,* whether the child committed the act which allegedly gives the court jurisdiction over the child. If the court so determines, it then proceeds to the issue of whether the child needs treatment and, if so, what treatment. Thus, we recommend *two separate proceedings: first, a hearing to determine whether the child committed the act; second, a hearing to determine whether and what treatment is needed.*

Gault and *Winship* have forced states to deal more fairly with children concerning the question of commission of the specific act. However, having decided that the child committed the act, many courts are woefully lax in assessing need for treatment, in designing appropriate treatment, and in seeing that treatment is received. To comprehend why this child went wrong, the state must fully understand the child's environment. To do this, juvenile courts must have access to social and psychological services. Although departments of corrections presently may be relegated the duty of designing treatment programs, that responsibility should be administered by the court, since it is charged with the duty of determining whether this child is in need of treatment. If the court makes an erroneous determination, the department of corrections often cannot devise a satisfactory plan. Thus, we recommend that *courts have access to social and psychological services* and that *juvenile courts be required to make a finding for the need of a specific treatment* in their attempt to prevent further acts of delinquency. It is not sufficient simply to establish diagnostic centers at the level of the department of corrections, for the judge has already made (1) a determination of the need for treatment and (2) a preliminary decision, at least, as to the type of treatment required—for example, removal from the community. Diagnosis, to be maximally effective, is required prior to the dispositional hearing by the court.

If we are going to give credence to a separate judicial system for children which is protective in nature, it should provide that adjudications against the child cannot be used against him in later life. To that end, we recommend *enactment of laws which require expungement of all juvenile court records of a child when he reaches the jurisdictional age limit.* While the juvenile is within the jurisdictional age limits of the court, we recommend that *access to records be limited to court personnel and to other persons or agencies who require the information in their efforts to treat or assist the child.* To ensure that employers do not evade the spirit of the law, we recommend that employers be forbidden to inquire whether a person has had a juvenile court record.

The child in need of supervision is one experiencing problems with his home, school, or community. The solution to his problem does not appear to be effectively lodged with the juvenile court. The clear alternative is to adopt the recommendation of the President's Commission on Law Enforcement and Administration of Justice and to eliminate status offenses from juvenile court jurisdiction. The cycle of recidivism would be grounds alone for elimination of the category. Accordingly, we recommend that the *definition of delinquency be limited to the commission of an act by a child which, if committed by an adult, would constitute a crime; that the status offense statutes be eliminated from the court's jurisdiction.*

References

Allen, F. A. *Borderland of Criminal Justice.* Chicago: University of Chicago Press, 1964.

Becker, H. *Outsiders: Studies in the Sociology of Deviance.* New York: Free Press, 1964.

Coffee, J. C. "Privacy Versus Parens Patriae: The Role of Police Records in the Sentencing and Surveillance of Juveniles." *Cornell Law Review,* 1972, *57*(4), 571-620.

Commonwealth v. Fisher, 213 Pa. 48, 62 Atl. 198, 200 (1905).

Empey, L. M., and Lubeck, S. G. *Delinquency Prevention Strategies.* Washington, D.C.: U.S. Government Printing Office, 1970.

Ex parte Sharp, 15 Idaho 126, 96 P. 563, 565 (1908).

Ferster, E., Courtless, T., and Snethen, E. "Separating Official and Unofficial Delinquents: Juvenile Court Intake." *Iowa Law Review,* 1970, *55*(4), 864-893.

Fisher, S. "Stigma and Deviant Careers in School." *Social Problems,* Summer 1972, *20,* 78-83.

Foster, J., Dinitz, S., and Reckless, W. C. "Perceptions of Stigma Following Public Intervention for Delinquent Behavior." *Social Problems,* Fall 1972, *20,* 202-209.

Fox, R. G., and Spencer, M. J. "The Young Offenders Bill: Destigmatizing Juvenile Delinquency?" *Criminal Law Quarterly,* 1972, *14*(2), 172-219.

Fox, S. J. "Juvenile Justice Reform: An Historical Perspective." *Stanford Law Review,* June 1970, *22,* 1187-1239.

Fox, S. J. *Cases and Materials on Modern Juvenile Justice.* St. Paul: West, 1972.

Gesicki v. Oswald, 336 F. Supp. 371 (S.D.N.Y. 1971), aff'd mem. 406 U.S. 913 (1972).

Glen, J. E., and Weber, J. R. *The Juvenile Court: A Status Report.* Washington, D.C.: U.S. Government Printing Office, 1971.

Gold, M. *Delinquent Behavior in an American City.* Belmont, Calif.: Brooks/Cole, 1970.

Gold, M., and Williams, J. "National Study of the Aftermath of Apprehension." *Prospectus,* 1969, *3*(1), 3-12.

Gonzalez v. Mallard, No. 50424 (N.D. Cal. 1971), *appeal docketed,* 39 U.S. L.W. 3500 (U.S. Apr. 9, 1971) (No. 1565, 1970-71 Term, *renumbered* No. 70-120, 1971-72 Term).

Gough, A. R. "The Expungement of Adjudication Records of Juvenile and Adult Offenders: A Problem of Status." *Washington University Law Quarterly*, 1966, *1966*(2), 147-190.

Gregory v. Litton Systems, Inc., 316 F. Supp. 401 (C.D. Cal. 1970), modified No. 26,669 (9th Cir. Dec. 7, 1972).

Handler, J. F. "The Juvenile Court and the Adversary System: Problems of Function and Form." *Wisconsin Law Review*, Winter 1965, pp. 7-51.

Haney, B., and Gold, M. "The Juvenile Delinquent Nobody Knows." *Psychology Today*, Sept. 1973, pp. 49-55.

Henry v. Looney, 65 Misc. 2d 759, 317 N.Y.S. 2d 848 (Sup. Ct. 1971).

In re Contreras, 109 Col. App. 2d 787, 241 P. 2d 631, 633 (1952).

In re Gault, 387 U.S. 1 (1967).

In re Holmes, 379 Pa. 599, 109 A. 2d 523 (1954).

In re Johnson, 30 Ill. App. 2d 439, 174 N.E. 2d 907 (1961).

In re Smith, 63 Misc. 2d, 198, 310 N.Y.S. 2d 617 (N.Y. City Fam. Ct. 1970).

In re Winship, 397 U.S. 358 (1970).

James, H. *Children in Trouble*. New York: McKay, 1970.

Jensen, G. F. "Delinquency and Adolescent Self-Conceptions: A Study of the Personal Relevance of Infraction." *Social Problems*, Summer 1972, *20*, 84-102.

Jones v. Commonwealth, 185 Va. 335, 38 S.E. 2d 444, 447 (1946).

"Juvenile Court Jurisdiction over 'Immoral' Youth in California." *Stanford Law Review*, February 1972, *24*, 568-586.

"Juvenile Delinquents: The Police, State Courts and Individualized Justice." *Harvard Law Review*, 1966, *79*(4), 775-810.

Kent v. United States, 383 U.S. 541, 556 (1966).

Ketcham, O. "The Unfulfilled Promise of the American Juvenile Court." In M. K. Rosenheim (Ed.), *Justice for the Child: The Juvenile Court in Transition*. New York: Free Press, 1962.

Ketcham, O., and Paulsen, M. *Cases and Materials Relating to Juvenile Courts*. Brooklyn: Foundation Press, 1967.

Lemert, E. *Social Pathology*. New York: McGraw-Hill, 1951.

Lemert, E. "The Juvenile Court—Quest and Realities." In President's Commission on Law Enforcement and Administration of Justice, *Task Force Report: The Challenge of Crime in a Free Society*. Washington, D.C.: U.S. Government Printing Office, 1967.

Lerman, P. *Delinquency and Social Policy*. New York: Praeger, 1970.

Lou, H. *Juvenile Courts in the United States*. Chapel Hill: University of North Carolina Press, 1927.

Mack, J. "The Juvenile Court." *Harvard Law Review*, 1909, *23*(2), 104-122.

McKeiver v. Pennsylvania, 403 U.S. 528, 544-45 n. 5 (1971).

Menard v. Mitchell, 430 F. 2d 486 (D.C. Cir. 1970).

Merton, R. "The Self-Fulfilling Prophecy." *Antioch Review*, 1948, *8*, 193-210.

Merton, R. *Social Theory and Social Structure*. New York: Free Press, 1957.

National Advisory Commission on Criminal Justice Standards and Goals. Working Papers for National Conference on Criminal Justice, January 23-26, 1973.

National Council on Crime and Delinquency, Council of Judges. "New Concepts in Juvenile Court Laws." Rough draft proposal. New York: National Council on Crime and Delinquency, 1972.

National Juvenile Law Center. *Law and Tactics in Juvenile Cases*. St. Louis: National Juvenile Law Center, 1971.

Neier, A. "Marked for Life." *New York Times Magazine*, April 15, 1973, pp. 16-17ff.

New York Judiciary Code, 712 (McKinney Supp. 1971).

"Parens Patriae and Statutory Vagueness in the Juvenile Court." *Yale Law Journal*, 1973, *82*(4), 745-771.

Paulsen, M. G. "The Delinquency, Neglect, and Dependency Jurisdiction of the Juvenile Court." In M. K. Rosenheim (Ed.), *Justice for the Child: The Juvenile Court in Transition*. New York: Free Press, 1962.

Pee v. United States, 107 U.S. App. D.C. 47, 274 F. 2d 566 (1959).

People v. Fitzgerald, 244 N.Y. 307, 316, 155 N.E., 584, 588 (1927).

President's Commission on Law Enforcement and Administration of Justice. *The Challenge of Crime in a Free Society*. Washington, D.C.: U.S. Government Printing Office, 1967a.

President's Commission on Law Enforcement and Administration of Justice. *Task Force Report: Juvenile Delinquency and Youth Crime*. Washington, D.C.: U.S. Government Printing Office, 1967b.

Rector, M. G. "Statement Before U.S. Senate Subcommittee to Investigate Juvenile Delinquency." *Crime and Delinquency*, 1970, *16*(1), 93-99.

Rubin, S. *Crime and Juvenile Delinquency*. (3rd Ed.) Dobbs Ferry, N.Y.: Oceana Publications, 1970.

Rubin, S. "The Man with a Record: A Civil Rights Problem." *Federal Probation*, 1971, *35*(3), 3-7.

Samuels, G. "When Children Collide with the Law." *New York Times Magazine*, Dec. 5, 1971, pp. 44-45, 138-146.

Schafer, W. E., and Polk, K. "Delinquency and the Schools." In President's Commission on Law Enforcement and Administration of Justice, *Task Force Report: Juvenile Delinquency and Youth Crime*. Washington, D.C.: U.S. Government Printing Office, 1967.

Schur, E. *Crimes Without Victims*. Englewood Cliffs, N.J.: Prentice-Hall, 1965.

Schur, E. *Law and Society*. New York: Random House, 1968.

Schur, E. *Our Criminal Society*. Englewood Cliffs, N.J.: Prentice-Hall, 1969.

Schur, E. *Labeling Deviant Behavior*. New York: Harper, 1971.

Schwartz, R. O., and Skolnick, J. K. "Two Studies of Legal Stigma." *Social Problems*, Fall 1962, *10*, 133-142.

Shoham, S. *The Mark of Cain.* Dobbs Ferry, N.Y.: Oceana Publications, 1970.

State v. Arbeiter, 408 S.W. 2d 26 (Mo. 1966).

Sussman, S., and Baum, F. *Law of Juvenile Delinquency.* (3rd Ed.) Dobbs Ferry, N.Y.: Oceana Publications, 1968.

Tannenbaum, F. *Crime and the Community.* Boston: Ginn, 1938.

Uniform Juvenile Court Act. In *Uniform Laws Annotated: Matrimonial Family and Health Laws.* Vol. 9. St. Paul: West, 1973.

U.S. Congress, House of Representatives, Select Committee on Crime, Juvenile Justice, and Corrections. *There but by the Grace of God Go I.* House Report No. 91-1906, 91st Congress, 2d sess. (Jan. 2, 1971).

U.S. Congress, Senate, Judiciary Committee, Subcommittee on National Penitentiaries. Statement of Aryeh Neier on S. 2732, March 15, 1972.

United States v. Borders, 154 F. Supp. 214 (N.D. Ala. 1957), aff'd, 256 F. 2d 458 (5th Cir. 1958).

Wheeler, S., Cottrell, L. S., and Romasco, A. "Juvenile Delinquency: Its Prevention and Control." In President's Commission on Law Enforcement and Administration of Justice, *Task Force Report: Juvenile Delinquency and Youth Crime.* Washington, D.C.: U.S. Government Printing Office, 1967.

Williams, J. R., and Gold, M. "From Delinquent Behavior to Official Delinquency." *Social Problems,* Fall 1972, *20,* 209-229.

14

CLASSIFICATION IN THE TREATMENT OF DELINQUENCY AND ANTISOCIAL BEHAVIOR

Herbert C. Quay

Subgroup classification in the field of juvenile corrections has arisen out of the recognition that the label of *delinquent* is a legal one and as such does not imply psychological or sociologi-

I am indebted to Alfred R. Bennett, Roy E. Gerard, Robert L. Smith, and Marguerite Q. Warren for many valuable comments on an early draft of the chapter. Responsibility for the content, however, remains mine.

cal homogeneity. Thus, beginning with the pioneering work of
Hewitt and Jenkins (1946), behavioral scientists and correctional administrators charged with the responsibility for prevention and treatment have sought ways of classifying heterogeneous populations of delinquents into more treatment-relevant
subgroups. Methods of generating the subgroups vary considerably among investigators but usually involve clinical observation, theoretical derivation, or the use of multivariate statistical
techniques. An exhaustive treatment of all these approaches is
beyond the scope of this paper. A publication of the National
Institute of Mental Health (Rubenfeld, 1967) provides a reasonably comprehensive overview of many of these approaches,
as does a more recent review by Warren (1971).

Despite the many systems of subgroup classification proposed, only two have been seriously utilized in attempts to
provide differential treatment to any large numbers of delinquents. These are the California I-level typology developed by
Marguerite Warren and her associates (see Warren, 1969) and
the behavioral classification techniques developed by Quay and
his coworkers (see Quay and Parsons, 1971).

Interpersonal Maturity and Delinquent Subtypes

The theory upon which the Warren system is based (Sullivan, Grant, and Grant, 1957) postulates a series of stages of
normal personality development. Each stage is defined by a
characteristic perceptual style in regard to self and others. It is
theorized that most delinquents are fixated at the second, third,
and fourth stages (I_2, I_3, and I_4). Within these stages of personality integration the system has clinically identified nine
delinquent subtypes. Brief descriptions of the three maturity
levels as well as the nine subtypes are provided by Warren
(1969, pp. 53-54) as follows:

> *Maturity Level 2* (I_2): The individual whose inter-
> personal understanding and behavior are integrated at this
> level is primarily involved with demands that the world take
> care of him. He sees others primarily as "givers" or "with-
> holders" and has no conception of interpersonal refinement
> beyond this. He has poor capacity to explain, understand,
> or predict the behavior or reactions of others. He is not
> interested in things outside himself except as a source of

supply. He behaves impulsively, unaware of anything except the grossest effects of his behavior on others.

Subtypes: (1) *Asocial, Aggressive* (Aa) responds with active demands and open hostility when frustrated. (2) *Asocial, Passive* (Ap) responds with whining, complaining, and withdrawal when frustrated.

Maturity Level 3 (I_3): The individual who is functioning at this level, although somewhat more differentiated than the I_2, still has social-perceptual deficiencies which lead to an underestimation of the differences among others and between himself and others. More than the I_2, he does understand that his own behavior has something to do with whether or not he gets what he wants. He makes an effort to manipulate his environment to bring about "giving" rather than "denying" response. He does not operate from an internalized value system but rather seeks external structure in terms of rules and formulas for operation. His understanding of formulas is indiscriminate and oversimplified. He perceives the world and his part in it on a power dimension. Although he can learn to play a few stereotyped roles, he cannot understand many of the needs, feelings, and motives of another person who is different from himself. He is unmotivated to achieve in a long-range sense, or to plan for the future. Many of these features contribute to his inability to predict accurately the response of others to him.

Subtypes: (3) *Immature Conformist* (Cfm) responds with immediate compliance to whoever seems to have the power at the moment. (4) *Cultural Conformist* (Cfc) responds with conformity to specific reference group, delinquent peers. (5) *Manipulator* (Mp) operates by attempting to undermine the power of authority figures and/or usurp the power role for himself.

Maturity Level 4 (I_4): An individual whose understanding and behavior are integrated at this level has internalized a set of standards by which he judges his and others' behavior. He can perceive a level of interpersonal interaction in which individuals have expectations of each other and can influence each other. He shows some ability to understand reasons for behavior, some ability to relate to people emotionally and on a long-term basis. He is concerned about status and respect and is strongly influenced by people he admires.

Subtypes: (6) *Neurotic, Acting Out* (Na) responds to underlying guilt with attempts to "outrun" or avoid conscious anxiety and condemnation of self. (7) *Neurotic,*

Anxious (Nx) responds with symptoms of emotional disturbance to conflict produced by feelings of inadequacy and guilt. (8) *Situational Emotional Reaction* (Se) responds to immediate family or personal crisis by acting-out. (9) *Cultural Identifier* (Ci) responds to identification with a deviant value system by living out his delinquent beliefs.

According to data provided by Warren (1969) and Jesness (1971), the two neurotic subtypes (acting out and anxious), the immature conformist, the cultural conformist, and the manipulator are the most frequently found subtypes and account for about 85 percent of the delinquent population. The other four subtypes are each infrequent, and none accounts for as much as 10 percent of the total.

In the process of I-level classification, the primary diagnostic procedures are a sentence-completion test and a semistructured interview (one to one and a half hours in length), which is tape-recorded for later rating (see Warren and Community Treatment Project Staff, 1966). The end product is a determination of the I-level, followed by classification into one of the associated subtypes. Although Warren suggests that formal training is needed for effective classification, Jesness (1971) reports attempts to simplify and objectify the procedures.

Reliability. Palmer (1968, p. 33) reports reliabilities between the intake interview and the first follow-up interview (computed by means of a formula devised for the Community Treatment Project, p. 33), ranging from .69 to .74 for the I-levels taken together and .62 to .83 for the subtypes. Reliabilities between the intake interviewer and a different rater using the same materials ranged from .63 to .84 for the I-levels and .46 to .76 for the subtypes. In a study of differential treatment in an institution, Jesness (1971, p. 42) reports varying degrees of agreement between different approaches to arriving at the subtype classification: "Overall, the interviewer's impression agreed with the final staff diagnosis in 56 percent of the cases, the sentence-completion-test diagnosis agreed in 35 percent of the cases, and the classification based on the inventory in 49 percent of the cases. Agreement among independent interviews occurred in 55 percent of the cases, and agreement in diagnosis between independent staff teams was 60 percent."

It is difficult to draw definitive conclusions about the reliability of the process of I-level classification because dif-

Delinquency and Antisocial Behavior

381

ferent types of estimates have been used. However, as Beker and
Heyman (1972) maintain, reliability is perhaps not fully satisfactory but it does appear higher in most instances than is usually reported for clinical psychiatric diagnoses.

Construct validity. One of the criteria for the evaluation
of the meaningfulness of a set of psychological or behavioral
categories is the nature of relationships of these categories to
other relevant personal and social characteristics. The establishment of such relationships is necessary to get beyond the rather
narrow confines of the originally postulated set of categories or
subtypes. Thus, it becomes important to be able to describe
more fully and to discriminate from one another the delinquent
subtypes in the I-level systems in terms other than those used to
describe the groups in the first place.

Zaidel (1970) found that I-level groups differed in the
size of their vocabulary for describing other people, in their
natural set to attend to affect cues, and in their ability to judge
affect from facial expressions. Increasing I-level was associated
with larger vocabulary, greater attention to affect, and better
ability to judge nonverbal affect communications. However,
intelligence accounted for a substantial portion of I-level differences in the measures of affect awareness.

Werner (1972, p. 43) found correspondence between empirically derived clusters on the California Psychological Inventory (CPI) and I-level: "Differences in typological cluster-score
configurations were in part explainable in terms of I-level variation, a result consistent with the considerable emphasis given in
I-level theory to the relationship between maturity and each of
the following variables: internalization of cultural and subcultural values, interpersonal sensitivity and perceptual abilities,
empathy, abstractness of cognitive and learning processes, and
self-differentiation and development within interpersonal contexts."

Cross and Tracy (1971) found I-level to vary positively,
within their total sample of male delinquents, with age, intelligence, social class, and locus of control or perceived locus of
responsibility for self. Furthermore, in their study correlates of
I-level seemed to be a function of the racial group considered:
future time perspective, locus of control, and global rating of
guilt all played a more significant role in predicting I-level for
blacks than for whites.

As Beker and Heyman (1972) have pointed out, the limited evidence for construct validity is a basic weakness of the I-level approach to classification. Clearly, there is need for additional research to provide more evidence that the members of the various I-levels and delinquent subtypes described are discriminably different from one another in relevant social and behavioral characteristics beyond those used in the original clinical formulations of the subtypes themselves.

Treatment research. Of greatest concern, however, is the extent to which the delinquent subtypes can form a basis for more rational and effective treatment. The I-level approach to classification has been utilized and evaluated in two major projects: the Community Treatment Project (Warren, 1969; Palmer, 1971) and the Preston Typology Study (Jesness, 1971).

The Community Treatment Project, a long-term research and demonstration project, uses the I-level system to classify and differentially treat delinquents who are on probation or parole. The treatments, the treatment settings, and the agents of treatment are conceptualized to meet the needs of the delinquent subtypes described in the system. A detailed description of this laudable effort in advancing the practice of corrections is beyond the scope of this paper. In addition to publications of the California Youth Authority describing the project (see Warren, 1969; Palmer, 1971), the project has been the subject of critical review by Lerman (1968), Gibbons (1970), and Beker and Heyman (1972). Each of these reviews, using parole revocation as the criterion, questions whether the experimental group profited more than the control group from differential classification and treatment. However, as Warren (1969) points out, certain subtypes do seem to profit more from institutionalization, while others benefit to a greater extent from a community program. Such a finding is crucial to the whole notion of differential treatment.

Since parole may be revoked for many reasons other than the behavior of the parolee, perhaps this criterion simply cannot be used to evaluate the possible benefit of the system as a basis for treatment. Perhaps the real criterion for the success of a treatment program is reliably measured change in behavior *during* the course of the treatment (see Quay, 1973). Abstinence from postrelease delinquent activity is certainly desirable, but perhaps no technology of behavior change is currently capable of insulating anyone from the subsequent effects of the personal and social environment outside the treatment setting. Perhaps all that can be asked of a treatment strategy is that it be effective and efficient in changing the behavior that it purports to change.

The second major study (Jesness, 1971) utilized the I-level system as a basis for classification and differential treatment in an institutional setting. According to this study, living units consisting of boys grouped homogeneously on the basis of delinquent subtypes reported fewer management problems than units not so grouped. Changes on psychological measures, both self-report and behavior ratings, favored the experimental subjects in some of the groups. Parole data, however, revealed no difference between the experimentals and controls in later violations. Both groups had a failure rate of about 65 percent. Neither were there differences among the subtypes within either the experimental or the control groups. As a pioneering research effort, the Preston Typology Study has demonstrated that a correctional institution can, in fact, undertake a rather complex classification and treatment program. According to Jesness (1971, p. 48), the program had a major impact in improving staff attitudes and morale and in increasing professionalism. That fact that something other than blanket programming can be done—and that this effort is coupled with increases in staff morale, apparent decreases in management problems, and at least the suggestion of more positive psychological changes among inmates—is encouraging. However, the extent to which the utilization of the I-level classification system itself was responsible for the positive effects is not at all clear. "The integration-level theory itself did not seem to play an important role in the establishment of treatment goals. . . . In the classification decisions, the theory of developmental levels sometimes appeared to be a help and at other times a hindrance" (Jesness, 1971, p. 50).

Differential Behavioral Classification

The second major approach to classification has been developed through the use of multivariate statistical techniques in the search for statistically homogeneous clusters of characteristics in samples of delinquent children and adolescents. The data analyzed have been derived from direct ratings of behavior (Quay, 1964a, 1966), from responses to questionnaire items (Peterson, Quay, and Cameron, 1959; Peterson, Quay, and Tiffany, 1961), and from ratings of life-history variables (Quay, 1964b, 1966).

The factorial analysis of data from all the sources has been remarkably consistent in revealing the presence of four principal clusters: (1) Unsocialized-Psychopathic (unbridled aggression, hostility, defiance, interpersonal alienation, lack of regard for others, impulsivity, sensation seeking); (2) Neurotic-Disturbed (anxiety, social withdrawal, subjective distress, guilt, escape behaviors, worrying); (3) Socialized-Subcultural (peer-oriented, group delinquent activities, defiance of adult authority, interpersonal closeness, delinquent value orientation); (4) Inadequate-Immature (passivity, dependence, tendency to day-dreaming). Similar factors emerge when samples other than the legally delinquent—for instance, child-guidance-clinic cases and behavior-problem children in the public schools—are studied. Thus, it appears that the four constellations are the principal dimensions of deviant behavior from early childhood through adolescence (see Quay, 1972).

Reliability. Along with the analyses that have produced the behavioral clusters, three instruments have been developed to measure the dimensions. Each of the three instruments makes various types of reliability estimates for the four subscales. The Behavior Problem Checklist rates three of the dimensions. Two-rater reliabilities have ranged from close to .90 to as low as .25, depending upon raters and circumstances (see Quay, 1972, p. 16). Internal-consistency reliabilities for the three dimensions on a sample of over one thousand male delinquents were obtained from ratings of correctional workers; the estimates were .89 for Unsocialized-Psychopathic, .83 for Neurotic-Disturbed, and .68 for Inadequate-Immature (see Quay and Parsons, 1971, p. 18). The Personal Opinion Study, a true-false questionnaire (consisting of one hundred items), measures three of the dimensions. Internal-consistency reliabilities of .92, .87, and .62 for the three scales were obtained from the sample of one thousand noted above. Test-retest correlations over a three-month interval of .76, .75, and .61 were obtained from a small sample of delinquents (see Quay, 1972, p. 16). The Checklist for the Analysis of Life History Records provides scales to measure all four of the dimensions. Only internal-consistency reliabilities have been obtained; these have ranged from a low of .23 for Inadequate-Immature to a high of .77 for Unsocialized-Psychopathic. No reliability data are available for the use of the instruments jointly to arrive at a subgroup classification. However, a method has been developed for combining scores on the four dimensions, in additive fashion, to arrive at a categorical or typological score (for use as an aid in treatment in the correctional setting). The procedure is based on norms obtained for over one thousand youthful offenders in federal institutions and is described in detail by Quay and Parsons (1971). One of the features of the process is that it permits a confidence estimate to be attached to each classification, so that the likelihood of an error can be estimated.

Construct validity. A number of investigators have used the instruments, either singly or in combination, to select subjects for further study. The purpose of these investigators has generally been to examine subgroup differences that can be predicted on the basis of a theoretical conception of the subgroups. That is, the writers first predict how subgroups should differ and then test these predictions experimentally. Space permits only a brief review of these studies; more details can be found in the original publications and in Quay (1972).

Skrzypek (1969) contrasted groups of institutionalized psychopathic and neurotic delinquents (chosen on the basis of the Behavior Problem Checklist) on a number of tasks selected to test hypotheses as to how the groups should differ on the basis of a theory of psychopathic behavior (Quay, 1965). Results generally conformed to expectations and provide evidence of the validity of using the ratings to select the two groups. The psychopathic delinquents preferred complex rather than simple stimuli and novel rather than familiar pictures and were less anxious than the neurotic delinquents. Preference for complexity and novelty in the psychopathic subgroup was also increased by a brief period of perceptual isolation.

Borkovec (1970) contrasted institutionalized psychopathic, neurotic, and subcultural groups on GSR (galvanic skin response) and heart-rate responses to auditory stimuli. The psychopathic group gave significantly lower GSR response to the initial stimuli and showed lower (although not statistically significant) heart-rate changes and pre-post-stimuli basal skin conductance increases. Results generally confirmed the theoretical predictions and provide additional evidence of differences among groups selected on the basis of the Behavior Problem Checklist.

A number of studies have utilized the Personal Opinion

Study as a selection device. Orris (1969) compared groups of psychopathic, neurotic, and subcultural delinquents on a task requiring continuous attention. As was predicted, the psychopathic group performed consistently poorer than the other two groups. Hetherington, Souwie, and Ridberg (1971) found extensive differences in the family backgrounds of psychopathic, neurotic, and subcultural boys and girls identified by means of a forced-choice form of the Personal Opinion Study.

The instruments have also been utilized in combination to identify subgroups. A major longitudinal study of institutional adjustment (Quay and Levinson, 1967) demonstrated a wide variety of differences among inmates in the four behavioral categories in their response to various aspects of a correctional program. Differences were most marked between the neurotic and psychopathic groups on such variables as number of disciplinary offenses, institutional "grades," and success in a work-release program.

In a subsequent study (Ingram and others, 1970), an attempt was made to develop an experimental treatment program for a psychopathic group within an institution. When compared with an institutionalized group not receiving the special program, the experimental group showed improvement in institutional adjustment.

Hedlund (1970) compared subjects in the four behavioral categories on the factors of Cattell's 16 PF test. Her results indicated meaningful differences among the groups on some of the dimensions of normal personality measured by the 16 PF.

In another study in a correctional setting, Smyth and Ingram (1970) compared the four groups in terms of reasons for sick call. In general, the sick calls of the neurotic group were for emotional reasons, whereas the sick calls of the psychopaths very frequently involved malingering.

Three groups of incarcerated youthful offenders (neurotics, psychopaths, and subculturals) were verbally conditioned to dependency and aggressive verbs by Stewart (1972). Both aggressive and dependent verbs were reinforced. The neurotics increased their use of dependent verbs; the subculturals increased their use of aggressive verbs; the psychopaths decreased their use of both classes of reinforced verbs.

While we are far from a full understanding of the genesis, or even the characteristics, of individuals representative of the four behavioral categories, it is highly encouraging that meaningful differences on a variety of psychologically relevant variables can be demonstrated among the groups. We can be confident that individuals separated into groups by one or more of the instruments can, in fact, be shown to be different from one another by experimental and correlational research.

Treatment research. Two of the studies briefly discussed above (Quay and Levinson, 1967; Ingram and others, 1970) support the contention that the four dimensions of delinquent behavior predict differential responsiveness to an undifferentiated institutional program and form a rational basis for a differentiated program for at least one subtype (Unsocialized-Psychopathic). The results of these two studies provided the basis for an experimental program in differential classification and treatment at an open youth institution operated by the Federal Bureau of Prisons. Gerard (1970) gives a detailed description of this program. In brief, the program provided for homogeneous living units, some degree of matching staff, and the use of different modalities (for example, group counseling, individual counseling, reality therapy, behavior modification) to bring about behavior changes.

A variety of different approaches have been taken to evaluation. Results suggest that disciplinary problems, particularly of an assaultive nature, have been reduced and that both staff and inmates perceive the social climate of the institution as therapeutic.

A follow-up comparison of releases from the experimental institution and two other federal institutions is currently in progress. Preliminary analyses of an incomplete sample do not suggest any advantage for the differential treatment program, although parole-violation rates for all three institutions (about 30 percent one year after release) are lower than would be expected, based on data from other published studies with roughly comparable samples. As noted, parole-violation rates are not ideal measures of the success of an institutional program when postrelease experience is in no way controlled.

Common Features of the Two Approaches

Both systems offer an aid in the conceptualization and implementation of treatment strategies—although, to be sure, conceptualization and implementation are not nearly so well developed as is the classification process itself. It is not a simple matter to go from an analysis of the subgroups themselves to an appropriate differential treatment, but it is an absolute necessity to try.

In neither system are the labels considered fixed and immutable. The I-level system is hierarchical in nature. Through treatment the individual is moved from lower stages to higher stages and, within stages, from a delinquent orientation to a nondelinquent one. In the behavioral system, progression is along a continuum from deviant to less deviant; one does not move from unsocialized to neurotic, but rather from the less socialized end of the dimension to the more socialized.

In both approaches the subtype labels themselves may be said to be "socially undesirable." It is hard to see how such connotations can be escaped, since the behavior subsumed by all these labels is generally conceded to be antithetical to effective personal and social functioning in most societies. At the same time, there is no evidence that the self-fulfilling-prophecy phenomenon occurs when these labels are used in correctional settings. In fact, a test of the self-fulfilling-prophecy notion has recently been undertaken at the Robert F. Kennedy Youth Center (V. S. Johnson, personal communication, 1973). Since residents are grouped in living units by the classification arrived at during a two-week stay in an orientation center, the self-fulfilling-prophecy hypothesis would require that they become more representative of their classification with the passage of time. However, when the original scores on the classification instruments were compared with scores obtained later, results showed that the subjects had become less representative of their label. Such a decrease, in fact, would be predicted as a desired effect of the differential treatment program on the principal category of deviant behavior being treated. Clearly, then, effective treatment provides the antithesis of the self-fulfilling prophecy.

It is also clear that both systems have considerable appeal to those charged with the responsibility for the rehabilitation of delinquent and antisocial children and youth. A reasonably valid and reliable classification system provides a focus for the utilization of treatment resources, a guide for staff observation and understanding of behavior, and a philosophical focus for what the mission of the correctional process should be. A crucial point, however, is that the decision to utilize any system of classification in the correctional setting is in the hands of the correctional administrator. It is he who must be aware of the need to fulfill the requirements of the system in terms of the methods by which classification is made. More important, it is he who must marshal the resources necessary to provide treatment approaches relevant to the classification. Without commitment to adequate treatment, the classification process is of little value except for further research into the nature of the subgroups themselves. Furthermore, classification may be used by the unknowing, or unscrupulous, administrator as "window dressing." If such be the case, the system has been misused—a danger inherent in any test, classification system, drug, or other human invention.

Finally, although neither approach, in its current form, is either perfectly reliable or directly linked to surefire treatment strategies, the current alternatives for correctional treatment are not at all attractive. The first alternative is continued application of some single-treatment modality in blanket fashion to all delinquents. Such an approach will very likely lead to continued failure by almost any criterion, with a resultant decrease in professional and public confidence in correctional treatment. A second alternative is the application of differential treatment to groups who are either self-selected or selected on the basis of some impressionistic process *without* labeling. This alternative may avoid formal assessment and consequent labeling, but it actually will result in treatment decisions about children and youth made on the basis of less, rather than more, evidence. As Cronbach and his associates (1972, p. 383) have pointed out, "One can make tests taboo if they embarrass one's doctrine by continually making unwelcome differences evident; but to do so is only to force decisions of employers, teachers, physicians, and policy makers back onto biased, inaccurate impressions."

References

Beker, J., and Heyman, D. S. "A Critical Appraisal of the California Differential Treatment Typology of Adolescent Offenders." *Criminology*, May 1972, pp. 1-59.

Borkovec, T. D. "Autonomic Reactivity to Sensory Stimulation in Psychopathic, Neurotic and Normal Juvenile Delinquents." *Journal of Consulting and Clinical Psychology*, 1970, *35*(2), 217-222.

Cronbach, L. J., Gleser, C. C., Nanda, H., and Rajaratnam, N. *The Dependability of Behavioral Measurements: Theory of Generalizability for Scores and Profiles.* New York: Wiley, 1972.

Cross, H. J., and Tracy, J. J. "Personality Factors in Delinquent Boys: Differences Between Blacks and Whites." *Journal of Research in Crime and Delinquency*, 191, *8*, 10-22.

Gerard, PR. E. "Institutional Innovations in Youth Corrections." *Federal Probation*, 1970, *39*, 37-44.

Gibbons, D. C. "Differential Treatment of Delinquents and Interpersonal Maturity Levels Theory: A Critique." *Social Service Review*, 1970, *44*, 22-33.

Hedlund, C. S. "A Validational Study of a Program Utilizing a Differential Treatment Approach for the Treatment of Juvenile Delinquency." Unpublished master's thesis, West Virginia University, 1970.

Hetherington, E. M., Stouwie, R. J., and Ridberg, E. H. "Patterns of Family Interaction and Child-Rearing Attitudes Related to Three Dimensions of Juvenile Delinquency." *Journal of Abnormal Psychology*, 1971, *78*, 160-171.

Hewitt, L. E., and Jenkins, R. L. *Fundamental Patterns of Maladjustment: The Dynamics of Their Origin.* Springfield: State of Illinois, 1946.

Ingram, G. L., Gerard, R. E., Quay, H. C., and Levinson, R. B. "Looking in the Correctional Wastebasket: An Experimental Program for Psychopathic Delinquents." *Journal of Research in Crime and Delinquency*, Jan. 1970, *7*, 24-30.

Jesness, C. F. "The Preston Typology Study: An Experiment with Differential Treatment in an Institution." *Journal of Research in Crime and Delinquency*, 1971, *8*, 38-52.

Lerman, P. "Evaluative Studies of Institutions for Delinquents: Implications for Research and Social Policy." *Social Work*, July 1968, *13*, 55-64.

Orris, J. B. "Visual Monitoring Performance in Three Subgroups of Male Delinquents." *Journal of Abnormal Psychology*, 1969, *74*, 227-229.

Palmer, T. B. *Recent Research Findings and Long-Range Developments at the Community Treatment Project.* CTP Research Report 9, Part 2. Sacramento: California Youth Authority, 1968.

Palmer, T. B. "California's Community Treatment Program for Delinquent Adolescents." *Journal of Research in Crime and Delinquency*, 1971, *8*, 74-92.

Peterson, D. R., Quay, H. C., and Cameron, G. R. "Personality and Background Factors in Juvenile Delinquency as Inferred from Questionnaire Responses." *Journal of Consulting Psychology*, 1959, *23*, 392-399.

Peterson, D. R., Quay, H. C., and Tiffany, T. C. "Personality Factors Related to Juvenile Delinquency." *Child Development*, 1961, *32*, 355-372.

Quay, H. C. "Personality Dimensions in Delinquent Males as Inferred from the Factor Analysis of Behavior Ratings." *Journal of Research in Crime and Delinquency*, 1964a, *1*, 33-37.

Quay, H. C. "Dimensions of Personality in Delinquent Boys as Inferred from the Factor Analysis of Case History Data." *Child Development*, 1964b, *35*, 479-484.

Quay, H. C. "Psychopathic Personality as Pathological Stimulation-Seeking." *American Journal of Psychiatry*, 1965, *122*, 180-183.

Quay, H. C. "Personality Patterns in Preadolescent Delinquent Boys." *Educational and Psychological Measurement*, 1966, *26*, 99-110.

Quay, H. C. "Patterns of Aggression, Withdrawal, and Immaturity." In H. C. Quay and J. S. Werry (Eds.), *Psychopathological Disorders of Childhood*. New York: Wiley, 1972.

Quay, H. C. "What Corrections Can Correct and How." *Federal Probation*, 1973, *37*, 3-5.

Quay, H. C., and Levinson, R. B. "The Prediction of the Institutional Adjustment of Four Subgroups of Delinquent Boys." Unpublished manuscript, 1967.

Quay, H. C., and Parsons, L. B. *The Differential Behavioral Classification of the Juvenile Offender*. Washington, D.C.: Bureau of Prisons, U.S. Department of Justice, 1971.

Rubenfeld, S. *Typological Approaches and Delinquency Control*. Washington, D.C.: U.S. Department of Health, Education, and Welfare, 1967.

Smyth, R. A., and Ingram, G. "Relationship Between Type of Offender and Reasons for Seeking Medical Care in a Correctional Setting." *Nursing Research*, 1970, *9*, 456-458.

Skrzypek, G. J. "Effect of Perceptual Isolation and Arousal on Anxiety, Complexity Preference, and Novelty Preference in Psychopathic and Neurotic Delinquents." *Journal of Abnormal Psychology*, 1969, *74*, 321-329.

Stewart, D. J. "Effects of Social Reinforcement on Dependency and Aggressive Responses of Psychopathic, Neurotic, and Subcultural Delinquents." *Journal of Abnormal Psychology*, 1972, *79*(1), 76-83.

Sullivan, C., Grant, M. Q., and Grant, J. D. "The Development of Interpersonal Maturity Applications to Delinquency." *Psychiatry*, 1957, *20*, 373-385.

Warren, M. Q. "The Case for Differential Treatment of Delinquents." *Annals of the American Academy of Political and Social Science*, 1969, *381*, 47-59.

Warren, M. Q. "Classification of Offenders as an Aid to Efficient Management and Effective Treatment." *Journal of Criminal Law, Criminology, and Police Science*, 1971, *62*, 239-259.

Warren, M. Q., and Community Treatment Project Staff. *Interpersonal Maturity Level Classification: Juvenile Diagnosis and Treatment of Low, Middle, and High Maturity Delinquents*. Sacramento: California Youth Authority, 1966.

Werner, E. *Relationships Among Interpersonal Maturity Personality Configurations, Intelligence, and Ethnic Status.* Sacramento: California Youth Authority, 1972.
Zaidel, S. *Affect Awareness, Intelligence, and the Interpersonal Maturity Level Classification.* University of California, Los Angeles, 190.

15

DRUG-TAKING BEHAVIOR

Oakley S. Ray, John T. Wilson

Whether one has worked for a considerable period in the field of drug use, misuse, and abuse or is entering the field for the first time, the old story about the airline pilot seems true: "Ladies and gentlemen, this is your pilot. I have some good news and some bad news. First, the bad news—we're lost. The good news is that we're moving at a record speed." There are few areas in which so much social concern and money have been expended with so little knowledge of the situation or evidence of meaningful change as in the presenting problems of drug use.

A great scientist once said that finding answers is relatively simple—once the right question is asked. Knowing what to ask and how to ask it are the hardest tasks. Perhaps one of the difficulties in dealing with drug use, misuse, and abuse in young people is that we have been asking the wrong questions.

393

From a survey of the literature it seems to us that the professionals in the area are trying to run before they have demonstrated that they can walk. To attempt an "ultimate cause" analysis of drug use or to design lasting treatment or rehabilitation programs for specific drug using individuals seems naïve when much more work is still needed to develop the right questions.

The concepts developed here are based on the belief, stemming from a review of the literature and our own study of the problem, that today the understanding of drug use and drug users is at about the same point where understanding intelligence was when Binet first developed the intelligence test. Binet was successful in his assigned task because he focused on doing the job that needed to be done. He did not concern himself initially with the determinants of intelligence or differences in the nervous system between bright and dull people. All those quite legitimate concerns have since become meaningful questions. But if Binet had first tried to identify all the causes of variability in school performance, he could never have solved the immediate problem of predicting which students could benefit from regular schooling.

Our primary conviction, then, is that certain immediate problems must be attacked. Further, though, we believe that this attack must contain a basis for collecting and analyzing data. These data should result in better handling of the immediate problems and also should provide the information needed for developing a more rational approach to the prevention and treatment of drug use, misuse, and abuse.

It is easy to be caught up in the immediate situation and to decide that the way things are "right now" is the way they always have been and will continue to be. In any psychosocial situation this is clearly not so. The drug scene has been a particularly fluid area in the American culture of the last thirty or forty years. The best response to a changing problem is to avoid absolutes and to develop approaches that contain multiple guidelines and options for action.

An illustration of the changing scene is what has happened in the area of narcotic use (Ray, 1972, chap. 12). The illegal narcotic user of the 1930s was typically a white, over-thirty adult who was a relatively skilled criminal. In the 1950s the prototype narcotic user was black, less than thirty, a ghetto inhabitant, and an unskilled criminal. Through the 1960s and into the early 1970s the average age of narcotic users decreased and other economically deprived groups (especially Puerto Ricans) became more common. In this same period narcotic use also expanded into the white middle-class suburbs. To base a program or a long-range plan on the narcotic use of any of these populations would be a mistake. Changes have also occurred in other areas. In fact, all aspects of the drug situation are still actively changing—the users, the drugs, society's response to drug use.

In May of 1973 the director of the White House Special Action Office for Drug Abuse Prevention (SAODAP) told a House of Representatives subcommittee that federal policy in the area of drug abuse is to "reduce the social cost of drug abuse" (Jaffe, 1973, p. 10). We concur in that aim but believe that both the short-term goals and the long-range policy must also be directed toward reducing the *personal cost* of drug abuse. These two endpoints are not necessarily congruent. The overriding issue is an ethical one: the extent to which an individual's behavior can be monitored and controlled when there is no clear evidence that the individual is directly harming other people or society at large. The classification system outlined below specifically separates social and personal goals.

Etiology of Drug Use

Throughout this chapter the emphasis is on behavior—what the individual is doing with drugs and what behaviors result from drug use. Although we do discuss some psychosocial factors related to drug use, we accept the fact that the etiology of most drug taking is unknown. "The motivations for drug consumption differ from society to society (and even within subcultural groups), and little is presently known, especially from a historical perspective, about how societies perceive the problem or, for that matter, about what measures of an educational, social, or legal nature have been taken to combat the drug-abuse problem" (UNESCO, 1972a, p. 2). Recognizing and lamenting this lack of information, the United States delegation to the UNESCO general conference on drug-abuse prevention and education has made the following recommendations:

> 1. UNESCO should place a high priority on the defi-
> nition and analysis of drug abuse in its broadest perspective.

What, in fact, are the cultural, social, and educational, as
well as psychological, antecedents of drug abuse? To what
extent is the drug problem essentially part of more general
social and personal problems?
    2. Research is also needed to gain greater under-
standing, from group to group, of differing motivations for
use, of different modes of perceiving what is or is not a
drug-use problem, and of historical attempts, both successful and unsuccessful, to deal with drug-use problems by
way of educational, legal, social, medical, or other measures
[UNESCO, 1972b, p. 7].

In spite of the generally admitted absence of good predictors of drug misuse, many investigators have tried to deal
with the problem of etiology. Some of their conclusions are
almost truisms or do not pretend to be based on hard data. Salk
(1973, pp. 80, 84), for example, suggests that "certain personality factors and early childhood experiences" make some people "more prone to drug abuse. . . . People who abuse drugs are
usually unable to channel their anxiety into constructive use. If
a person cannot gain a sense of self-esteem through achievement, accomplishment, and putting off immediate gratification,
he may discover that many drugs offer an immediate sense of
well-being or self-esteem 'internally.'" Densen-Gerber and her
associates provide a somewhat different explanation: "The
young adolescent accepts drugs because he has not fully learned
to discriminate between constructive and destructive alternatives in the growing-up process. He does not realize that drugs
are a dangerous means of working through his own omnipotent
fantasies regarding life and death, and his need to find his identity separate from the adult world" (Densen-Gerber, Murphy,
and Record, 1971, p. 10).
    Some etiological studies have compared well-defined
adolescent groups of drug abusers, clients treated for nondrug
reasons at a mental health center, and normals (people who are
neither drug abusers nor in treatment for a mental health problem). Herl (1972), for example, compared three such groups
and found no significant differences on measures of *alienation,
dogmatism*, and *internal-external control*. He concluded, therefore, "that strong commonalities in attitudinal and belief orientations (cognitive orientations) existed among the three adolescent comparative groups" (Herl, 1972, p. 411). On one measure, *sensation seeking,* he did find that drug abusers scored

significantly higher than nonabusers (those being treated for mental problems not related to drug use); the scores of drug abusers and normals, however, were not significantly different.

Somewhat similarly, Rohrs and Densen-Gerber (1971, p. 3) emphasize the similarities between adolescent drug abusers and other adolescents: "It is difficult to consider adolescent drug abuse in terms of deviant behavior on the part of an individual. There seems to be nothing that sets him apart from his peers physically, mentally, or emotionally, nor does he appear to be different from his counterparts of previous generations in these respects. Rather, he appears to be a normal adolescent that is relating in a normal manner to a group that exhibits deviant behavior. This is exactly the opposite of the position of the adult addict, who operates outside of the commonly accepted behavior patterns of his peer group. This, then, is properly a problem of group pathology, and an adequate treatment modality must concentrate on the group in order to help the individual."

In general, investigators insist that drug abusers must not be classified by the particular drugs they use. "In the handling of individual adolescents who are taking drugs, one is not particularly concerned about the type of drug or its pharmacological action. One is more concerned with the specific psychodynamic factors in the youngsters which make them so vulnerable that they resort to drugs. A number of them would have caused concern even if no drugs had been available" (Evans, 1971, p. 371). "It is important that we do not try to classify patients according to the type of drug they use. There is very little difference, if any, between the barbiturate user, the amphetamine user, the opiate user, and the hallucinogen user. He will abuse whatever is available—basic to the adolescent problem is a multidrug pattern" (Rohrs and Densen-Gerber, 1971, p. 4).

In spite of the repeated admonition not to classify users by the drug they use, Braucht and his associates (1973) have reviewed the literature of the past twenty years and have grouped studies, and users, into three main classes: alcohol, narcotics, and psychedelics. They have attempted to separate the sociocultural and personality variables linked to those individuals who characteristically misuse and abuse each of the three groups of drugs. The following paragraphs summarize their main findings.

Most studies of alcohol consumption have been completed at the college level, and there is no way of knowing whether the general results noted here are true of younger individuals. The authors point to three sociocultural factors which correlate well with adolescent problem drinking: parental models, peer models and sanctions, and religious affiliation. More students with Jewish, and perhaps Catholic, upbringings drink than do those with Mormon or Protestant backgrounds. Because of the absence of religious and cultural standards for alcohol consumption, however, those Protestants and Mormons who do drink are more likely to be problem drinkers. At least one of the parents of the adolescent problem drinker probably is also a problem drinker; in fact, the best single predictor of drinking behavior in adolescents is the parents' pattern of drinking. However, although parental models and religious affiliation strongly predispose the adolescent to certain drinking patterns, the maintenance of drinking habits resides primarily with the individual's peer group. Regarding the personality structure of adolescent problem drinkers, investigators largely agree that "adolescent problem drinkers are individuals lacking in personal controls, as evidenced by relatively high aggressiveness and impulsiveness. At the same time, ... some evidence ... indicates that adolescent problem drinkers have some basic neurotic tendencies which form a coherent cluster of traits: relatively low self-esteem, high anxiety, depression, and a general lack of success in the attainment of life goals" (Braucht and others, 1973, p. 95).

The well-established background correlates of today's narcotic user are threefold—membership in an ethnic minority, often from an impoverished urban environment and from a broken home; availability of narcotics; peer-group deviance—although, clearly, not all adolescent narcotic users fit this mold. The parents of narcotic users frequently present a poor model to the adolescent. Personality characteristics of the narcotic user are still largely undetermined, although there is agreement that most are immature, insecure, irresponsible, and egocentric. It is not clear whether these personality characteristics antedate or are uniquely predictive of the use of narcotics.

Perhaps in part because of the shorter time period, there are few comprehensive or convincing studies about the psychosocial factors involved in psychedelic drug use. The conflicting data may indicate only that the population of users is changing rapidly. On only one generalization do most studies agree: Psychedelic users come primarily from the middle and upper socioeconomic classes. Unfortunately, the absence of agreement is even greater when personality characteristics have been studied. There are many conflicting reports, so that the personality of the psychedelic user still cannot be adequately described.

In spite of the impressive work done by Braucht and his associates, any attempt at classification by specific drugs must take into account one important trend since the late 1960s: the rapid increase in multiple drug use (Dodson and others, 1971; Thompson, 1972). The fact that more and more individuals are using a number of different drugs suggests that there is little value to classifying users by the drug used. If there are not enough studies to make it possible to identify populations at high risk for drug use, and if the specific drug being used is more a matter of chance than of choice, then the only basis for classifying drug users seems to be on the effects which stem from drug use. The system outlined in the following section is based on these considerations.

Classification of Psychoactive Drug Takers

What guidelines can be established to limit the population of individuals who take psychoactive drugs—those chemicals that have as their primary effect some alteration of consciousness or feeling? What groups of individuals are specifically not included in the classification? For what purposes is the population being classified? The total population of psychoactive drug takers can be distributed on three axes: use-abuse, legal-illegal, medical-recreational. These represent *presently* important dimensions along which many in society classify drug takers. As such, these dimensions represent possible bases for intervention in our society. Keep in mind, however, that in a constantly changing situation even these broad dimensions may soon prove inadequate. For now, it must be clear that these three dimensions are independent of one another. Crucial to an understanding of our classification system is continued awareness of this independence.

The use-misuse-abuse dimension refers to the personal and social consequences of the use of a drug. An individual can use a legal or an illegal psychoactive drug for medical or recreational reasons with various degrees of disruption of his personal life or impact on society. If the frequency, mode, or amount of drug taking causes a serious and continuing disruption of the relationship between the individual and others, or of his own self-image, then the drug taking is labeled *drug abuse*. If there is little or no impact on the course of the individual's life or on his relationship to the rest of society, the drug taking is categorized as *drug use*. This use-abuse dimension, then, varies along a continuum of *degree of disruption to the individual's personal life and/or to society*.

The legal-illegal dimension is not really a dichotomy, since some illegal drugs are *more illegal* than others (in the sense that more severe penalties are meted out for their possession and sale) and there is a continuum of enforcement policies. Rarely if ever do police monitor sales of cigarettes to individuals —even though it is frequently illegal for individuals under eighteen to purchase them. Some business establishments, and some police forces, regularly check the age of individuals who attempt to purchase alcoholic beverages; others do not. Under some limited conditions even widespread public use of a categorically illegal drug such as marijuana is ignored by enforcement agencies. *This dimension refers to the extent to which society attempts to control through civil or criminal injunctions the availability of a psychoactive drug.*

The medical-recreational dimension describes the reason for which a drug is taken. There is considerable uncertainty in this dimension. For example, central nervous system stimulants, such as the amphetamines, are frequently prescribed by physicians for the medical reason of weight control. Many individuals continue to have the prescriptions reissued and refilled because the drug makes them feel happier; that is, for recreational reasons (U.S. Congress, 1970, p. 44). Interestingly, a drug may be prescribed for medical reasons (a legal use) but be taken for other reasons. When the same drug in the same dose and the same frequency of use is used admittedly for recreational purposes, then the use is illegal. In general, *if the primary motivation for taking a drug is to alter a state of consciousness and the drug has not been medically prescribed for that purpose, then the drug use is termed recreational.* Because there is no clear way to separate medical and recreational use when a drug is obtained medically, this dimension will not be used in the classification scheme. It is included here both for completeness and to point up the difficulty in trying to classify drug users on the basis of the motivation underlying their drug use.

These three dimensions seem important to us because

they represent different categories of drug taking but are frequently confused. When the forms and effects of drug use are
not clearly identified and separated, then proposals for prevention, treatment, and rehabilitation cannot be specified. Too frequently an occasional marijuana smoker or a seventeen year old
who drinks alcoholic beverages in moderation is labeled a drug
abuser. Actually each of them should be classed as illegal drug
users. Similarly, the adult alcoholic is not usually classified as a
legal drug abuser, but that is what he is. When these dimensions
are confused, they result in bad laws and ineffective behavioral-
change programs. When they are kept separate, they can form
part of the basis for a classification system. If a classification
system is to be more than descriptive or statistical (for example,
percent of students who use amphetamines), it must be an integral part of a behavioral-change philosophy.

What groups are specifically excluded from the populations classified? Individuals whose primary involvement in the
drug scene is based on profit are not included. Although phar-
maceutical companies and their contact men, as well as distribu-
tors of illegal drugs, are very much involved in drugs and drug
use, they do not, as sellers, fit into the population considered
here. Most illegal drug misusers and abusers also sell drugs, but
the sale of these drugs is irrelevant to the proposals to be mentioned. The confusion between selling and using—with both
activities labeled as abuse—has resulted in much poor program
planning and in many ill-conceived laws.

The final question to be answered is perhaps the hardest:
For what groups and individuals is the classification schema
proposed? For whose use are the concepts presented? Perhaps
no system can be all things to all people, but the plan presented
here attempts to be just that. That is, in place of the various
informal classification systems that meet the needs of specialized groups, we hope that the concepts and proposals developed
here will be adopted by helping agencies and schools; by medical, law-enforcement, and governmental groups; and, most especially, by the man in the street.

The classification system is based on the behavior of the
individual and the interaction of his behavior with society. *Drug
taking is self-selected behavior, which may or may not produce
negative personal or social consequences.* A similar situation
exists with respect to sexual activity. In the areas of drug taking
and sexual activity, there is considerable debate over the line

between personal rights and the constraints which may right-fully be established by society. The question of the personal right to engage in drug use which has no clear deleterious effects on society is still being discussed in the courts and in legislative houses. As the laws change, so will certain aspects of the operation of the classification system.

In developing the classification scheme to be presented, we asked the question—What are the present grounds on which society can intervene in an individual's drug taking behavior? And further, once society has decided to intervene, what types of intervention are acceptable socially, legally, and ethically? It is our belief that society should deal only with the basis for the intervention. It should not force the individual to alter his life style (behavior) in any way other than is necessary to remove society's basis for intervention.

Specifically, we see four major bases on which society has the right and the obligation to interfere with an individual's drug-taking behavior. Society may intervene because the individual asks it to—the individual requests society to help him change his drug-taking behavior because it is causing him personal problems. Second, society may intervene because the individual's drug-taking behavior is illegal and is identified as illegal. Third, the individual's drug taking may give rise to medical problems. Sometimes the individual will request help with his drug-based medical problems; in other instances he may not be aware of the relationship. Finally, an individual's drug taking may cause problems for other individuals or for society in general.

These four channels, or reasons, for intervention should be kept separate and the intervention aimed at removing the basis for the present intervention. It is not deemed reasonable or ethical to carry the behavioral-change program beyond the basis for intervention. The channel through which a drug user becomes identified—personal, legal, medical, societal—thus becomes the basis for the program.

This classification system and the philosophy it rests on does not carry any connotation that drug taking will necessarily decrease because of the intervention. Successful intervention will be evidenced by the individual's not being identified again through the same channels. The only purpose in identifying and classifying an individual in this system is to make clear what behavioral-change program should be initiated, so that there is no longer a need to identify the individual as a drug taker.

There is no suggestion in this system that the individual is "sick" or immoral. As such, he does not need to be "cured" or punished. Certain new behaviors must be learned so that he does not again become identified.

Identified Drug Users

Quite simply, before a drug user can be dealt with, he must be identified. He becomes identified either because he identifies himself or because the behavior resulting from drug use is such that society (through legal, medical, or societal channels) decides to intervene in his life. There are many drug users who never are identified. The primary function of intervention should be to move the individual from the class of identified drug users back into the large group of unidentified users.

The initial intervention—the identification of drug-taking individuals—can be called stage 1. Once the individual has been identified as a drug user, certain of his characteristics need to be known in order to select an effective behavioral-change program. The specification of these characteristics is stage 2 of the classification system. We cannot deal here with the many programs that exist or may develop as a result of the stage-2 classification. The programs, though, are intrinsically tied to the classification. Information obtained in stage-2 classification should be limited to that necessary for specifying a behavioral-change program.

Legal channel. To be identified through the legal channel, an individual must engage in illegal drug use—and get caught. In our view, any intervention program should attempt either to decrease his illegal drug use or to decrease the probability of his being caught in illegal drug use. To determine which of these options is more likely to succeed, we must ask certain questions about the user. First, how long has he been using drugs? The longer a drug has been used with satisfaction, the less likely it is that it will be given up. Does the user's peer group also use drugs? The more the individual is surrounded by drug-using peers, the less likely it is that he will stop using drugs. Does the drug use satisfy some psychological needs that are not met in any other way? If so, it is unlikely that drug use will stop. Is his being caught a hostile act toward parents or other authority figures? In that case, it is unlikely that the individual will try to conceal his drug use and avoid arrest. Is his being caught a plea for help in other areas of life? Then the individual will persist in getting caught until the other problems are resolved.

If the answers to such questions indicate that the individual is highly unlikely to decrease his drug use, the intervention program should be aimed in part at decreasing the probability of his being arrested again. The individual must be classified on those characteristics which were important in his being identified, and the program must be aimed at modifying those characteristics. If the answers to the questions indicate that the individual wants to be caught and therefore will not conceal his drug use, then continual reappearance in the law-enforcement system is to be expected until the underlying motivations are dealt with.

Medical channel. Another acceptable basis for intervention in our society is medical. When a drug user develops medical problems associated with drug use, *and the problems are identified as such,* the user becomes an identified drug user. Medical intervention usually comes about as a result of an individual's appearing at an emergency room or clinic for treatment (for example, see Goldberg, 1972). To deal adequately with a drug-related emergency, it is essential to determine the types of drugs used: addicting (narcotic, nonnarcotic) or nonaddicting (stimulant, hallucinogenic, solvent); specific drugs used; mode of administration (oral, intravenous, subcutaneous, sniffing); frequency of use; amount used each administration; how procured; and presenting medical complaint. This information is also needed when any detoxification program is to be carried out in conjunction with other interventions that the individual requests or society mandates. Moreover, since most drug users today (other than many who use only marijuana) are multidrug users, the medical problems that occur are not the result of several independent drug crises but frequently result from the interactions of two or more drugs. Thus, for medical-channel treatment all forms and frequency of drug use must be identified, no matter what the specific presenting complaint.

Societal channel. For intervention via the societal channel, the behavior identified must have resulted from, or be intrinsically tied to, drug use. For example, not every runaway who uses marijuana should be labeled as an illegal drug user. If conflict with the parents over marijuana use led to the running away, the individual should be so classified and a behavioral-change program initiated. All too frequently the appearance of socially maladaptive or disruptive behavior in a drug user results in the incorrect assumption that the drug use caused the behavior. It is of crucial importance that there be clearly established some causal or intrinsic link between the disruptive behavior and the drug use before the individual is labeled as a drug user via the societal channel.

If an individual is arrested for nondrug-related criminal behavior and is concomitantly identified as someone who uses drugs for personal use, he should be classified as being identified via the legal channel. If the criminal behavior appears to be based in drug use—for instance, burglary to obtain money to maintain an expensive drug habit, or aggression related to the use of a drug—the individual should be classed in the societal category of identified drug users.

Many instances of drug-based socially disruptive behavior do not involve criminal acts: the alcoholic who loses a job or wrecks his car; the husband who abandons his family because of increasing involvement with drugs. In these situations the user should be classified in the societal group (unless he first presents himself for help; then he is classed in the personal category). Behavioral change in these individuals is particularly difficult. Since there is an integral relationship between the drug use and the behavior, there are few possibilities of decreasing the socially disruptive behavior without also changing the pattern of drug use.

Personal channel. The personal basis for intervention is relevant only for those individuals who go to some agency or professional, identify themselves as drug users, and present a problem based on their use of a drug or drugs. Usually, one of three things has occurred: the drugs no longer give the desired effect, but they still give more of it than any alternative the individual sees open to him; personal and social disruptions due to drug use have begun to appear, but they are subthreshold to society; the drugs are still delivering what the individual wants without any observable disruption in his life, but other factors suggest to him that this cannot continue indefinitely.

Whatever the basis for the individual's request for help, the prognosis seems better here for successful changes and removal from the identified-drug-user population than with individuals identified via the societal channel. The belief is that those labeled via the societal channel have already moved beyond the position of those classified via the personal channel.

Stage 2 and behavioral-change programs for individuals identified via either of these channels should probably be the same,
although successful outcomes may differ.

Ethical Issues

The prevailing philosophy underlying most if not all
treatment programs is to move the individual to the population
of individuals who use drugs only for legal medical purposes.
That is, most programs today attempt to transform the individual and eliminate illegal drug use and prevent the abuse of
legal drugs. Another option, however, is to consider in what
way—through which channel—the individual became identified
as a drug user and to work with him so that he will not again be
labeled as a drug user *for the same reason.* For example, if, as
noted, an agency decides that a drug user who has been identified because of legal intervention is unlikely to eliminate illegal drug use, then his behavioral-change program would focus
on ways for him to conceal his drug use. To repeat what was
earlier said, this approach aims not at reducing drug use but at
reducing the visibility and bad effects which form the basis for
society's intervention. A drug user identified via the medical
channel might be taught how to evaluate the purity and po-
tency of street drugs and how to sterilize or clean his parapher-
nalia. These and other aspects of an individual's program would
aim at reducing the probability that society will have to intervene again in his drug-taking behavior because of medical problems.

To the above possible intervention programs there might
be raised the objection that their purpose seems to be to make
it easier or at least safer for identified drug users to continue
their drug habits. This is probably true. This form of intervention, however, would decrease both the personal and the social
cost of illegal or medically stupid drug use.

In addition, objections might be raised against helping
identified drug users avoid the legal or medical consequences of
illegal drug use, because drug use is related to crime. That is, by
aiding identified drug users in their efforts to become and remain nonidentified drug users, this classification and behavioral-
change program actually contributes to an increase in crime and
thus increases the social cost of drug use. The hypothesized
relationship between crime and drug use probably forms the

basis for many of society's present beliefs about how drug users should be handled. Because of this we will present a brief discussion of what is known in this area.

The relationship between crime and illegal drug use or abuse is complex and not nearly as close as many people believe. In 1925 Kolb wrote about a belief that still exists: "There is probably no more absurd fallacy extant than the notion that murders are committed and daylight robberies and holdups are carried out by men stimulated by large doses of heroin or cocaine, which have temporarily distorted them into self-imagined heroes incapable of fear." Not only does the fallacy persist but political action is taken and laws enacted on the belief that the relationship is real. In April of 1974 the Fellows of the Drug Abuse Council commented on this issue: "Former Governor Nelson Rockefeller, for example, in using theft statistics to justify harsher criminal penalties for drug users, cited data collected by the New York State Narcotic Addiction Control Commission which claimed that 'drug addiction costs New York State about $6,500,000,000 a year in thefts.' Such inflated figures, we believe, should be examined carefully. In New York City (where over 80 percent of the state's heroin addicts are reported to reside), the amount of stolen property reported to the police in 1972 totaled $238,000,000. It is unlikely, we believe, that addicts steal over twenty-five times the amount of all property reported stolen."

What, then, is the relationship between criminal activity and drug use? The data are quite sparse, and only recently have studies appeared which speak meaningfully to this question. Tinklenberg (1972), after reviewing the literature on this subject in a report prepared for the National Commission on Marijuana and Drug Abuse, concluded: "A large number of studies indicate that alcohol, the most widely used drug in the world, is clearly linked with violent crime. . . . The users of either amphetamines or barbiturates were more likely to be arrested for criminal homicide, forcible rape, or aggravated assault than were users of heroin, morphine, cocaine, marijuana, hashish, tranquilizers, psychedelics, methadone, and special substances. *However, amphetamine and barbiturate users were no more likely to be charged with violent crimes than were individuals who were identified as non-drug users*" (pp. 75, 76, italics added).

In another recent study Tinklenberg and his associates (in press) reported on the relationship between violent crime and

drug use in two matched groups of incarcerated California juvenile offenders. One group was incarcerated for assaultive and
the other for nonassaultive offenses. These investigators concluded: "Subjects who had never been charged with any assaultive or sexual offense generally reported that they used a greater
variety of drugs more frequently than individuals who committed serious assaultive crimes. . . . However, when serious
assaultive crimes were committed, the youths involved more
frequently described themselves under the influence of one or
more drugs than in a nondrug state. . . . In concordance with
studies focusing primarily on adults, alcohol was the drug most
often linked with violence in this study of adolescents. Seco-
barbital was the drug that was next most often associated with
serious crime."

A final definitive statement cannot be made at this time
about the relationship between criminal activity and drug use.
The most comprehensive study yet done was published in De-
cember 1971 by the U.S. Department of Justice. The authors
studied criminal records and interviewed and tested drug-using
and nondrug-using arrestees in six large metropolitan areas of
the United States. The authors admit that the means of selecting individuals to be studied made it more likely that a relationship would appear between criminal activity and drug use.
There is much of value in their report, but only two issues can
be mentioned here. One refers to the general question of whether *any* generalizations can be made about drug use and criminal
behavior. The second question is whether individuals who use
drugs show an increase in convictions following the initiation of
drug use. The first question is best answered by saying that
there are two generalizations:

> For all drug substances considered (heroin, cocaine,
> morphine, methadone, marijuana, hashish, amphetamines,
> barbiturates, tranquilizers, psychedelics, and special sub-
> stances such as glue, ether, etc.), the distributions of arrest
> charges for "users" of these substances versus "nonusers"
> are either essentially the same (no significant differences) or
> significantly different in that "drug users" are *less often
> involved* in crimes of violence, including homicide, rape,
> kidnapping, and aggravated assault. [However,] there is
> strong evidence that robberies account for a large propor-
> tion of arrest charges among "current drug users" (18.3
> percent), a considerably higher proportion than among ar-

restees for which there is no evidence of drug usage at any
time (11.3 percent) [U.S. Department of Justice, 1971].

The second question is not so easily answered. The data
presented suggest that for those individuals who began drug use
in the 1960-63 period there was a significant increase in convictions after the onset of drug use. For those who started drug use
in the 1964-67 period there was an increase in convictions, but
the increase was no greater than for the nondrug group. The
increase here may reflect changes in society or changes in the
way that serious crimes are reported.

As can be seen from the above data, there is mixed information on the crime-drug relationship. At the least, there is no
vindication for establishing programs on the assumption that
drug use results in criminal activity.

Some might object to providing the drug user with information that he can use to decrease the medical consequences of
drug use. If drug use is made safer, they might argue, the probability of drug use will increase. There are data to support this
argument. Most drug-education programs, along with pointing
out the medical dangers of certain forms of drug use, provide
information about how to ensure safe drug use. There is no
evidence that drug-education programs reduce drug use; there is,
in fact, some evidence that such programs may increase drug use
(Ray, 1973; New York Times, 1972). Beyond these programs,
however, many socially approved activities—community-spon-
sored RAP houses, crisis-intervention centers, and crash pads as
well as community support for nonprofit laboratory analyses of
street drugs—are already probably increasing drug use by making it safer.

The major question raised about this classification system
and the behavioral changes necessarily associated with it could
be one of social philosophy. Some may feel that drug taking is
wrong and should be abolished no matter what the cost. Whether drug taking in any form is acceptable or not is a matter of the
assumptions made about man and society. We personally believe
that the use of certain drugs is antithetical to the mainstream
philosophy in our culture (see Ray, 1972, pp. 271-272). We
strongly support better and additional educational programs to
provide alternatives to drug use or to make improbable certain
forms of drug use in individuals who are not yet illegal drug

users or drug abusers. These programs will not, however, reduce the practical and immediate problem of the personal and social cost of drug use today. The concepts and the implications outlined here are relevant only for the classification and type of intervention required by drug users. There is little in the system that speaks to the problem of preventing or reducing drug use per se. The emphasis is on reducing the personal and social cost of present drug use.

In brief, we believe that a classification system should serve both society and the individual by indicating a behavioral-change program which would remove the need for the classified individual to continue as an identified drug user. Classification has value in this field only when it is tied to a program that will result in declassification.

There are two intertwined problems: What are effective change programs for identified drug users, and what user characteristics are related to successful outcomes following different behavioral-change programs? There is considerable debate over whether any program can successfully modify an individual's life style (Stuart, 1970). Change programs aimed specifically at decreasing the probability of a drug user's becoming identified through the legal or medical channels have not been developed; however, they would probably be generally more effective than therapies directed at making changes in life styles.

Stage-2 information collecting must serve two purposes. First, data relating to any successful treatment are needed for the classification system. The following statement, although it refers to narcotic addicts, seems to apply to all identified drug users: "We have come to believe that those addicts that are relatively more committed to our more widely accepted psychological and social standards, such as 'stable' object relationships or 'good' work records, respond more favorably to various forms of treatment" (Coppolillo, 1972, p. 373). Second, since most of the treatment programs are still experimental, much information is needed to study the relationship between characteristics of identified drug users and program outcome. To this end, in stage 2 as much psychosocial data as possible must be obtained from each identified drug user. These data should not now be used for classification purposes, since they do not reliably predict success or failure in existing treatment programs. If certain characteristics do prove to have predictive value, then they should be incorporated into the classification process (Ein-

stein, 1969). This information collection—both within and outside the classification system—may also prove valuable in developing effective drug-use prevention programs.

References

Braucht, G. N., and others. "Sociocultural and Personality Factors Related
    to Drug Misuse." *Psychological Bulletin*, 1973, *79*(2), 92-106.
Copolillo, P. "The Age of Aquarius." *Journal of Occupational Medicine*,
    1972, *14*(5), 373-376.
Densen-Gerber, J., Murphy, J. P., and Record, W. J. "The Changing Ado-
    lescent Addiction: A Changing Pattern." Paper presented at annual
    meeting of American Psychological Association, 1971.
Dodson, W. E., and others. "Pattern of Multiple Drug Abuse Among Ado-
    lescents Referred by a Juvenile Court." *Pediatrics*, 1971, *47*, 1033-
    1036.
Einstein, S. "The Addiction Dilemma: Gaps in Knowledge, Information-
    Dissemination, Service, and Training." *International Journal of the
    Addictions*, 1969, *4*(1), 25-44.
Evans, J. "Drug-Taking in Adolescents." *Scottish Medical Journal*, 1971,
    16, 369-375.
Fellows of the Drug Abuse Council. "Disabusing Drug Abuse." *Social
    Policy*, 1974, *4*(5), 43-45.
Goldberg, E. "Extent of the Drug Abuse Problem." *Maryland State Medi-
    cal Journal*, 1972, *21*(4), 73-76.
Herl, D. "A Study of Select Cognitive Orientations Among a Drug-Abuse,
    Nonabuse, and Normal Adolescent Population." *Arizona Medicine*,
    1972, *29*(5), 408-412.
Jaffe, J. "Jaffe Finally Defines Federal Drug Policy." *U.S. Medicine*, May
    15, 1973, p. 10.
Kolb, L. "Drug Addiction in Its Relation to Crime." *Mental Hygiene*,
    1925, *9*(1), 74-89.
New York Times, Dec. 3, 1972, Section I, p. 165.
Ray, O. S. *Drugs, Society, and Human Behavior*. St. Louis: Mosby, 1972.
Ray, O. S. Unpublished manuscript, 1973.
Rohrs, C. C., and Densen-Gerber, J. "Adolescent Drug Abuse: An Evalua-
    tion of 800 Inpatients in the Odyssey House Program." Paper pre-
    sented at scientific program of American Psychiatric Association
    annual meeting, Washington, D.C., May 3-7, 1971.
Salk, L. "Emotional Factors in Pediatric Practice: Adolescent Drug
    Abuse." *Pediatric Annals*, Feb. 1973, pp. 80-86.
Stuart, R. B. *Trick or Treatment*. Champaign, Ill.: Research Press, 1970.
Thompson, R. E. "Letter to the Editor." *Pediatrics*, 1972, *49*(1), 152-153.
Tinklenberg, J. "Drugs and Crime." Consultant's report prepared in 1972.
    Cited in *Drug Use in America: Problem in Perspective*. Washington,

D.C.: National Commission on Marijuana and Drug Abuse, 1973.

Tinklenberg, J. R., and others. "Drug Involvement in Criminal Assaults by Adolescents." *Archives of General Psychiatry,* 1974, *30*(5), 685-689.

UNESCO. *Report of Working Group of Government Representatives on UNESCO Drug Abuse and Education Program.* New York: UNESCO, 1972a.

UNESCO. *United States Intervention at 17th Session of UNESCO General Conference on Drug Abuse Prevention and Education.* New York: UNESCO, 1972b.

U.S. Congress, House of Representatives. *Crime in America—Why Eight Billion Amphetamines?* Hearings before the Select Committee on Crime, House of Representatives, Ninety-First Congress, First Session. Washington, D.C.: U.S. Government Printing Office, 1970.

U.S. Department of Justice, Bureau of Narcotics and Dangerous Drugs. *Drug Usage and Arrest Charges.* Washington, D.C.: U.S. Government Printing Office, 1971.

NAME INDEX

SUBJECT INDEX

430

Northeast Airlines v. C.A.B., II: 416
Norwalk CORE v. Norwalk Board of Education, II: 311

Organizations and change, II: 141-145, 319-382
Otis-Lennon Mental Ability Test, II: 248-249, 252, 257-258

Pacific State Hospital, I: 131; II: 65-68
Parent and voluntary organizations, II: 179, 186-188, 468, 480, 482, 485-487, 491-492. *See also* specific organizations
Parent-Child Development Center, I: 340
Parental Role Questionnaire, II: 522
Parents: counseling and training of, I: 224, 229, 305; II: 156-159, 162-167, 183-188, 281-282, 529; and labeling, II: 154-188; and placement decisions, II: 21-22, 37, 49-51, 162-164, 397-399, 421-423, 479-480; and professionals, II: 156-164, 183-184. *See also* Ecological system of child; Families
Partlow (Alabama) State Home and School for the Retarded, II: 295, 298-301, 303-304, 306, 308, 312. *See also Wyatt v. Stickney*
Pathological model of exceptionality. *See* Medical model of exceptionality
Peabody Picture Vocabulary Test (PPVT), II: 252, 254, 493
Pediatric Multiphasic Program, II: 503, 509
Pee v. United States, I: 362, 375
Pennsylvania Association for Retarded Children, II: 324-347
Pennsylvania Association for Retarded Children v. Commonwealth of Pennsylvania, II: 37, 278, 292, 293-300, 302-303, 305, 314, 317, 320-347, 386-387, 389, 395-396, 398-400, 402-410, 413-417, 424-427
People v. Fitzgerald, I: 369, 375

People v. Norwood, II: 554, 564
Perceptual handicap, I: 301-303, 306-315. *See also* Learning disabilities
Permanente Medical Group, II: 523-524
Perry v. Sindermann, II: 388
Personal data system. *See* Records
Personal Opinion Study, I: 384-386
Personality disorders. *See* Emotional disturbance
Physical and sensory handicaps, I: 239-258; II: 11-27, 481-482, 502-511. *See also* Hearing impairment; Neurological impairment; Visual impairment
Physicians, I: 240-246, 251-252; II: 91-93, 103-104, 156-167. *See also* Medical model of exceptionality
Piagetian theories of cognitive development, I: 215-227; II: 251-263
Pinehills project (Provo, Utah), II: 129, 134-135, 138, 140-141
Pittsburgh Child Guidance Center, II: 110
Placement decisions: in juvenile justice system, I: 360-362, 382-383, 387; II: 132-135; in special education, I: 109-112, 186-187, 207-211, 307-312; II: 20-22, 26, 30-35, 49-51, 167-182, 274-279, 294, 296-297, 316-317, 319-382, 386-431, 484
Pointer v. Texas, II: 388
Poor families. *See* Low-income families
Poverty, classifications and definitions of, I: 322-331
Prejudice against deviance by community, I: 35-37, 101-127, 250, 334-335, 361-362, II: 143-144, 463-494. *See also* Segregation of handicapped
Preschool-age children: early screening of, II: 497-536; and mental health system, II: 91-98
Preschool Attainment Record, II: 521-522

Preschool programs, I: 210-211, 224-227; II: 93-98. *See also* Head Start Program

President's Commission on Law Enforcement and Administration of Justice, I: 349-350, 359, 362, 367-368, 370, 372, 375; II: 134, 148

President's Committee on Mental Retardation, I: 207, 236; II: 33, 52, 60, 339, 440, 504, 528, 541

President's Panel on Mental Retardation, II: 554, 564

Preston Typology Study, I: 382-383

Privacy and confidentiality, II: 114-116, 545-546, 553, 560-562. *See also* Records

Professionals: and parents, II: 183-184; and placement decisions, I: 89-97, 123-127, 307-310; II: 132-135, 183, 403-407, 419-421. *See also* Lawyers; Physicians; Psychologists; Teachers

Profile of child's assets and liabilities, II: 109-111

Progress Assessment Chart, II: 524

Project Follow Through, II: 225, 235

Protestant ethic, I: 112-113, 334-336. *See also* Communities

Psychiatric disorders. *See* Emotional disturbance

Psychiatric services. *See* Mental health services

Psychological Corporation, I: 153

Psychological testing. *See* Intelligence tests

Psychologists, role of in school placement decisions, I: 228-229, 307-311; II: 33, 328-330, 371-373, 403-407, 419-421, 484-485

Psychomotor deficits. *See* Learning disabilities

Psychopathology. *See* Emotional disturbance

Racism: and education of minority groups, I: 130-156, 336-337; II: 33-34, 220-242, 263, 293-318, 488-494; and labels, I: 121-127, 130, 133-134, 140-156, 198, 266, II: 33-34, 47-49, 113, 130, 220-231; and mental health of minority-group children, II: 214-220, 222-227; in schools, I: 336-337; II: 220-242

Rapid Developmental Screening Checklist, II: 524-525

Raven's Progressive Matrices, II: 249

Records, II: 544-563; access to data in, I: 367; II: 456, 548-553, 560-563; and rights of parents to information, II: 163, 174, 548-553, 562-563

Records policy boards, II: 552, 563

Re-ED program, I: 276

Reed v. Reed, II: 309

Referrals between agencies of "difficult" cases, II: 159-160, 179-181, 273

Rehabilitation Services Administration, II: 433-434

Religious institutions, I: 112-113

Residential institutions: alternatives to (*see* Deinstitutionalization; Foster homes; Normalization); and community, II: 75-78, 128-129, 138-141; conditions in, II: 67, 106-107, 133-134, 164-167, 298-304; for delinquent and antisocial youth, I: 377-389; II: 124, 129-146; differences between, II: 71-75, 130-131, 133-139; for emotionally disturbed, I: 115-121; II: 106-107; history of, I: 114-118, 203-204; II: 473-474, 476-478, 481-482; for mentally retarded, I: 203-207; II: 62-80, 298-304, 473-474, 476-478; for physically or sensorially handicapped, I: 250-251; II: 481-482; residents of, I: 204-207; II: 67-76, 106-107, 124, 140-141, 208, 307

Retardation. *See* Mental retardation

Revels v. Brian, II: 363

Review panel for special education placements, II: 412-416
Rights of handicapped. See Legal rights
Rimland Diagnostic Checklist, II: 520
Riverside (California) epidemiological study, I: 131-139
Robert F. Kennedy Youth Center, I: 388, II: 133
Role. See Self-concept
Roth v. Board of Regents, II: 409
Rouse v. Cameron, II: 299
Russell Sage Foundation, II: 549, 564

St. Louis Association of Black Psychologists, II: 214
San Antonio Independent School District v. Rodriguez, II: 294-295, 297-298, 302-303
San Francisco Unified School District Board, I: 149, 158; II: 236, 238, 492-493
Schizophrenia, I: 10, 29, 75-77
Scholastic Aptitude Test (SAT), II: 232, 234
School phobia, II: 99-100
School-age children, II: 4-56, 98-111, 167-182, 523-524. *See also* Schools
Schools: classification and labeling in, I: 108-112, 132-134, 138, 143-145, 207-211; II: 4-56, 103-105, 167-182, 189-209, 218-243, 294-296, 386-431, 454-461; exclusion of children from, II: 5, 12-13, 22-23, 29-30, 179-182, 271-274, 293-298, 321-361; minority-group children in, I: 108-112, 132-145; II: 218-243, 263, 294, 308-309, 311-318, 321, 488-494; personnel in (*see* Psychologists; Teachers); records in, II: 25-26, 37, 284, 553-554. *See also* Special education
Screening: comprehensive, II: 522-528; early, I: 154-155; II: 497-536; health, I: 154-155, II: 19, 497-536

S.E.C. v. Chenery Corp., I: 416
Segregation of handicapped, I: 105, 108-111, 115-118, 203-204, 256; II: 36-38, 46-47, 51, 156, 293-318, 447-450. *See also* Stigma
Self-concept, I: 97-98, 211-215, 364; II: 189-191, 193-196, 197-199, 225-226, 237-238; and competence, I: 215-227, 257-258; II: 98-99. *See also* Self-fulfilling prophecy
Self-fulfilling prophecy, I: 20, 46-47, 257-258, 364; II: 189-190, 229, 235
Serial Task (ST), II: 253-261
Services: for delinquency and antisocial behavior, I: 382-383, 387-389; and diagnostic categories, I: 43-47; educational, II: 17-24, 271-292, 421; health, I: 64-66, 250-253, 339, 341; II: 529; for learning disabilities, I: 304-305; and parents, II: 154-156, 160, 167-170, 179-182; for physical and sensory handicaps, I: 250-253; use of statistics to evaluate, I: 65-66. *See also* Community-based services; Fragmentation of services; Funding of services; Mental health services; Social welfare services
Sexes and differential liability to labeling, I: 179; II: 111-118, 369
Shepard-Towner Act, I: 251
Silverlake (California), II: 129, 135-136, 138, 140-141
Smuck v. Hobson, II: 347
Snellen Scale, I: 241-242; II: 19
Social control, I: 89-92, 101-127; II: 214-227, 463-494
Social Darwinism, I: 108, 111, 114, 174-175, 335-336. *See also* Eugenics movement
Social Security Administration, I: 82, 251
Social systems perspective on deviance, I: 132-134, 198; II: 470-471. *See also* Labeling perspective